COMPASSION-JUSTICE CONFLICTS
AND CHRISTIAN ETHICS

We seek to be both loving and just. However, what do we do when love and justice present us with incompatible obligations? Can one be excessively just? Should one bend rules or even break the law for the sake of compassion? Alternatively, should one simply follow rules? Unjust beneficence or uncaring justice – which is the less problematic moral choice? Moral dilemmas arise when a person can satisfy a moral obligation only by violating another moral duty. These quandaries are also called moral tragedies because, despite their good intentions and best efforts, people still end up being blameworthy. Conflicting demands of compassion and justice are among the most vexing problems of social philosophy, moral theology, and public policy. They often have life-and-death consequences for millions. In this book, Albino Barrera examines how and why compassion-justice conflicts arise to begin with and what we can do to reconcile their competing claims.

ALBINO BARRERA is Professor of Theology and Economics at Providence College, Rhode Island. The author of *Catholic Missionaries and Their Work with the Poor* (2019) and *Biblical Economic Ethics* (2013), he is the lead editor of the forthcoming *Oxford Handbook of Religion and Economic Ethics*.

NEW STUDIES IN CHRISTIAN ETHICS

General Editor
ROBIN GILL

Editorial Board
STEPHEN R. L. CLARK, STANLEY HAUERWAS,
ROBIN W. LOVIN

Christian ethics has increasingly assumed a central place within academic theology. At the same time the growing power and ambiguity of modern science and the rising dissatisfaction within the social sciences about claims to value neutrality have prompted renewed interest in ethics within the secular academic world. There is, therefore, a need for studies in Christian ethics which, as well as being concerned with the relevance of Christian ethics to the present-day secular debate, are well informed about parallel discussions in recent philosophy, science, or social science. New Studies in Christian Ethics aims to provide books that do this at the highest intellectual level and demonstrate that Christian ethics can make a distinctive contribution to this debate – either in moral substance or in terms of underlying moral justifications.

TITLES PUBLISHED IN THE SERIES:

(continued after the index)

COMPASSION-JUSTICE CONFLICTS AND CHRISTIAN ETHICS

ALBINO BARRERA

Providence College, Rhode Island

CAMBRIDGE
UNIVERSITY PRESS

Shaftesbury Road, Cambridge CB2 8EA, United Kingdom

One Liberty Plaza, 20th Floor, New York, NY 10006, USA

477 Williamstown Road, Port Melbourne, VIC 3207, Australia

314–321, 3rd Floor, Plot 3, Splendor Forum, Jasola District Centre,
New Delhi – 110025, India

103 Penang Road, #05–06/07, Visioncrest Commercial, Singapore 238467

Cambridge University Press is part of Cambridge University Press & Assessment,
a department of the University of Cambridge.

We share the University's mission to contribute to society through the pursuit of
education, learning and research at the highest international levels of excellence.

www.cambridge.org
Information on this title: www.cambridge.org/9781009384674

DOI: 10.1017/9781009384667

First published 2024

A catalogue record for this publication is available from the British Library

A Cataloging-in-Publication data record for this book is available from the Library of Congress

ISBN 978-1-009-38467-4 Hardback

*For the children of Del Pan, deprived of their childhood
by destitution, hunger, and rag-picking.*

*May God wipe away your tears, make up for my generation's
failures, and restore the joys you have been denied, and more.*

Contents

Tables

General Editor's Preface

Professor Albino Barrera has already contributed two outstanding monographs to New Studies in Christian Ethics: *Economic Compulsion and Christian Ethics* (2005) and *Market Complicity and Christian Ethics* (2011), which together set a new academic standard for Christian ethicists who focus upon the complex world of economics – a world that affects everyone but is still poorly understood by most people. The first was a top-down book, identifying the way in which markets can create economic hardships for some individuals and communities, whereas the second was more bottom-up, examining the various ways in which we are all complicit in the harmful effects of our market choices. Both books informed Stephen Duckett's expert contribution to the series, *Healthcare Funding and Christian Ethics* (2023).

In this new monograph, Barrera has done it again. He now engages with a classic, but unresolved, mid-twentieth-century debate within Christian ethics, between Anders Nygren and Reinhold Niebuhr, about what, from a Christian perspective, might be an acceptable or realistic balance between *agape* (compassion) and justice within personal and social contexts where they conflict. In the process, Barrera demonstrates how this debate might be resolved using insights from both economic theory and theology. He particularly focuses upon agape-justice conflicts, arguing both that justice is foundational if any community is to exist at all and that, since justice is ultimately dependent upon external enforcement and coercive power, it ought to be tempered by agape or compassion. For him, while the societal presumption is to accord priority to the demands of justice when there is agape-justice conflict, acceding to agape's claims may in fact be an even more promising path to significant growth in both personal and collective virtue.

This new and original book is a major and exciting achievement, adding substantial depth and nuance to a long-standing debate. Anyone who writes on this topic in future would be very foolish indeed not to read

Barrera carefully before doing so. He admirably accords with the two central and abiding aims of New Studies in Christian Ethics, namely:

(1)   To promote monographs in Christian ethics which engage centrally with the present secular moral debate at the highest possible intellectual level.
(2)   To encourage contributors to demonstrate that Christian ethics can make a distinctive contribution to this debate – either in moral substance or in terms of underlying moral justifications.

Robin Gill

Preface

Most people strive to be the best of who they can be. We want to be virtuous and lead a good life. We seek to be both loving and just. However, what do we do when agape and justice present us with contradictory duties? What do we do when agape and justice clash in their claims?

The classic case of agape-justice conflicts is the parable of the vineyard owner in Matthew 20:1–16. Recall how the vineyard owner paid laborers who came late in the day and worked only an hour the same wages as those who had been toiling since early morning. The vineyard owner was beneficent. Not only did he regularly patrol the marketplace to ensure that no one was left unemployed, but he also made sure at the end of the day that everyone had enough to meet basic daily needs regardless of the hours worked. Consequently, he paid the last hires more per hour of work. Nevertheless, the earlier hires also had a point in their protestations. They felt aggrieved because of the wage compression caused by the vineyard owner's largesse. After all, whether in an ancient agrarian setting or in the modern industrial economy, people expect due proportion in how they are paid – equal pay for equal work.

Fairness is embedded in people's moral sensibilities of what is right or wrong. Even young children expect due proportion in what they get vis-à-vis their siblings or other children. It is a demand of distributive justice. The vineyard owner was benevolent but deemed unjust by his earlier hires. He could have been just in paying only what was due, but his conscience would not let him be indifferent to the plight of the late hires not having enough for their needs for the day. What should he have done? Which should he have prioritized, the demands of agape or the demands of distributive justice? The vineyard owner faced an unpalatable choice – he could be beneficent but be deemed unjust, or he could be just but be uncaring. He cannot be both loving and just at the same time. Is the parable of the vineyard owner a case of unjust beneficence or of compassionate justice?

Such a predicament happens much more frequently than people realize across a wide range of social issues. We are often confounded with agape-justice conflicts beyond the world of biblical parables. For example, during Covid-19's most deadly early phase in 2020, the United States banned the export of N95 masks, Covid vaccines, and all the key raw materials for the manufacture of vaccines. It scrambled to vaccinate its own citizens first and funnel nearly all domestically produced N95 masks to its frontline workers (per its legal and moral dues), despite the desperate pleas of the World Health Organization (WHO) and other countries for a humanitarian sharing of the limited supplies of lifesaving vaccines and N95 masks with the rest of the world (demand of agape). The EU also imposed restrictions on the export of vaccines during this early stage of the pandemic when it could not get enough supplies for its own needs. India, the largest vaccine supplier in the world, suspended its exports to other poor countries as the Delta variant ravaged its own countryside and cities. It prioritized its domestic needs (to satisfy its legal and moral dues) despite being the main source for COVAX, the principal provider of vaccines to poor countries worldwide (demand of agape).

The UK decreased its foreign aid from 0.7 to 0.5 percent of its gross national income (GNI) during the Covid pandemic, arguing that it was only temporary and necessary since the government was already borrowing for its day-to-day operations. This reduction of £4.6 billion came at a time when poor countries were suffering even worse and already reeling from a twin health and economic emergency. All these cases have the same calculus – meeting the needs of their citizens first to whom they are bound by legal and moral duties over the humanitarian appeals from overseas.

Can one be excessively just? Should one bend rules for the sake of compassion? If so, how far do we go in bending rules? Is this a slippery slope? Can we go as far as to break the law for the sake of compassion? Alternatively, should one simply be inflexible in following established rules? Unjust beneficence or uncaring justice – which is the less problematic moral choice? Why?

Take the case of the National Health Service (NHS) of the UK. It is deemed much more compassionate in its provision of universal healthcare access compared to the market-driven US approach, which inadvertently deprives millions of proper medical care. Nevertheless, it is a hard-nosed compassion. The NHS is responsible for providing medical care within the limited means of the UK, and it routinely denies paying for drugs or treatments because of either medical ineffectiveness or cost (Samuels 2019). On the one hand, justice demands that the nation's scarce medical resources be used in the most equitable and efficacious manner for the good of the whole community. On the other hand, sick patients who have been denied drugs or treatments appeal for compassion because these are their last recourse.

We see a similar clash in the demands of justice versus agape in the case of NHS trusts in England, which are mandated to collect upfront payment from people ineligible for free healthcare, such as failed asylum seekers and visitors overstaying their visas. Many affected by this rule do not have the means to make such payments, and some have died for lack of needed medical treatment (Jayanetti 2018). Being the gatekeeper to these drugs or medical treatments is an unenviable task. Yet such rationing is important for the NHS's long-term fiscal sustainability.

Anti-immigration groups demand that the EU and the United States take care of the well-being of their domestic taxpayers and citizens first (legal due) before adding further strain on local social services in welcoming economic migrants and refugees at their borders (demand of agape). Instead of spending huge sums to accommodate unaccompanied minors showing up at its southern borders (demand of agape), critics bitterly complain that the Federal government should funnel these taxpayer funds instead to the millions of children still in poverty in the United States (legal and moral due). Similarly, there have been repeated attempts in the last few decades in some southern US states to bar undocumented migrant children from enrolling in public schools. Advocates of such action are resentful and believe that it is unfair to use their taxes to pay for the education of these children (*Economist* 2022a).

Recent US presidents and legislators have been caught in the middle between those who appeal for compassion in giving Dreamers[1] a path to citizenship (demand of agape) and those who are adamant that lawbreakers should not be rewarded (demand of justice). Less well known are the cases of children who have lived legally in the United States but who age out of their parents' visas when they turn 21 and will have to leave the country. For those who came as young children, the United States is the only country they have known (Kavi 2022). This is yet another case where the claims of compassion clash with the claims of justice in adhering to the stipulations of the law.

There is leeway in the interpretation of rules, and immigration judges and border officers face a daily choice of being lenient (demand of agape) or strict in implementing regulations to the letter of the law (demand of

---

[1] These young adults were the children brought to the United States by their undocumented parents.

justice) vis-à-vis migrants and asylum seekers showing up at the borders. The legislatures of advanced nations differ in their approaches to legal immigration. Australia, Canada, and the UK employ skilled-based immigration to bolster their economies (demand of justice), while the United States largely bases legal immigration on family reunification (demand of agape).

Leaders of developed countries are urged by their local constituents to help their domestic poor first (legal and moral dues) before sending foreign aid to underdeveloped nations (demand of agape). By opening their economies to even more international trade, advanced nations could greatly assist poor countries out of poverty (demand of agape), but at the expense of their domestic manufacturing workers, who will lose their jobs to cheap imports or outsourcing (legal and moral dues). The Russian invasion of Ukraine in 2022 severely disrupted global supplies of food. In response, Indonesia, Vietnam, and India imposed export controls on vital agricultural commodities such as grain, cooking oil, and fertilizers to ensure domestic supplies and stable prices for their own citizens (legal due), but at the expense of aggravating shortages and price spikes in many poor countries that are in even greater need (demand of agape).

The original owners of Ben and Jerry's would have wanted to pass on their successful ice cream operations to another social enterprise that would have continued their humanitarian work (demand of agape), but they were compelled to sell instead to Unilever, a traditional for-profit firm, to satisfy the statutory requirement of maximizing shareholder value (legal due).

Desperately ill patients plead for the compassionate use of drugs still under development (demand of agape), but pharmaceutical firms deny many of these appeals because of the added risk of adverse results jeopardizing the drugs' subsequent approval, to the detriment of many other patients for whom the drugs are more appropriate and effective (demand of justice).

Indeed, chief executives, judges, legislators, and bureaucrats adjudicate agape-justice conflicts all the time, making exceptions or even stretching the demands of law and justice for the sake of compassion.[2] Even ordinary citizens have had to make hard choices between doing an act of kindness (agape) and observing the law (justice). Courts and law enforcement

---

[2] Not even the classroom has been spared from the clashing claims of agape and justice. Professors often receive requests for extra credit work from students who want to make up belatedly for class work and exams they had blown off early in the semester. Compassion in such cases runs up against the need to be consistent and to be fair to the other students who had done their work diligently and duly earned their grades in a timely manner.

have prosecuted, fined, jailed, or sentenced to probation ordinary citizens and nongovernmental organization (NGO) workers for giving food to the homeless, saving endangered migrants from drowning in the Mediterranean and bringing them to shore, or putting water stations along the deadly desert routes where many migrants have died of dehydration sneaking into the United States.

The clashing claims of agape and justice go beyond the biblical parables of the vineyard owner (Mt 20:1–16) or of the prodigal son (Lk 15:11–32). They are real and consequential for untold millions worldwide, many with life-and-death implications. It is a choice between unjust beneficence and uncaring justice.

On those occasions when agape and justice come into conflict, settling their clashing claims is among the most vexing problems in moral theology, social philosophy, and public policy. Moral dilemmas arise when a person can satisfy a moral obligation but only by violating another moral obligation. These quandaries are also called moral tragedies because despite their good intentions and best efforts, people end up still derelict in living up to their moral duties. They will be blameworthy whichever way they turn. In the above cases, the moral dilemma is made even more significant because it involves the clash of agape and justice – two of the most vital human virtues.

Justice and agape are among the most important values of human life. Justice makes it possible for human communities to exist. People with differing political and philosophical commitments are nevertheless still able to live in harmony with one another because they give one another what is their due. Justice prevents human communities from descending into a Hobbesian state of nature in which every person is at war with everybody else and where might is right. For its part, agape enables people to rise above the chance and contingencies of life and to experience unimaginable joy through their mutual empathy, solicitude, and generosity. Agape provides not only meaning and purpose in life but also hope amid life's burdens and tragedies. Indeed, without justice or agape, human communities would not be possible at all. However, what do we do when agape[3] and justice present us with incompatible duties? Can we be too just to excess (Eccles 7:16)? Can we be too beneficent to excess?

---

[3] As we will see in the next chapter, there are different types of love. Agape is the kind of love that most often comes in conflict with the claims of justice because of its broad outreach – unconditional solicitude for all, including the stranger, the distant, the undeserving, and even the enemy. There are various kinds of agape as well, and we will make the necessary distinctions as the need arises during this study.

We immediately face practical questions. How do we resolve their competing claims? Which do we prioritize – the duties of agape or the duties of justice? Why? We also face important philosophical and theological questions. In particular, how can agape and justice present incompatible claims in what is supposed to be a perfect world of divine governance?

Practical Questions

Philosophers and theologians have long grappled with such moral predicaments. Anders Nygren (1953) prioritizes the claims of agape because it is the foremost virtue flowing from the human's experience of God's unwavering mercy and love. Richard Niebuhr (1957) disagrees and calls for satisfying the claims of justice first because of the more urgent need to address the underlying unjust structures of society. Nicholas Wolterstorff (2011) does not see a clash at all because agape and justice are inseparable.

This is not a peculiarly twentieth-century issue. Enlightenment philosophers grappled with this question and could not arrive at a consensus either. Adam Smith, John Stuart Mill, Hugo Grotius, Samuel von Pufendorf, Lord Kames, and others privilege justice because it is what makes living together as a community viable. Justice is foundational. In contrast, agape is "ornamental," an accessory that merely enhances the quality of life together. Others disagree and note that while justice is indeed a necessary condition for society, it is not a sufficient condition. David Hume strongly argues that there is a concurrent duty of humanity. Immanuel Kant proposes an essential duty of benevolence. There is no consensus on how to resolve the clashing claims of agape and justice.

Philosophical and Theological Questions

The literature also addresses deeper philosophical and theological questions raised by these clashes. Why do such moral dilemmas arise at all in what is supposed to be a well-designed world of perfect divine providence? Did God create a world in which justice and agape clash in their claims, thereby leaving humans in a moral bind? If so, why would God embed such incompatible obligations in the divine order of creation? Is divine will incoherent? Indeed, there is a jarring incongruity between the existence of such moral tragedies, on the one hand, and Christian belief in an all-knowing, almighty, and perfect Divine Creator-Provider, on the other hand.

For Thomas Aquinas, there can be no genuine moral dilemma because of God's perfect governance of the world. It would otherwise be an imperfection in divine providence and divine will. Edmund Santurri (1987) adopts this position and claims that moral perplexities arise only because humans fail to see what their true obligations are and how to triage them. In other words, moral dilemmas are epistemological in nature, that is, they are due to limitations in human knowing, rather than ontological, that is, ingrained in the very structure of the world.

This Study's Task

Despite the scholarly thought devoted to this issue, there is nonetheless one glaring lacuna in the literature, namely, the failure to address how and why these contradictory duties from agape and justice arise to begin with. This is a significant oversight because to triage the competing obligations from agape and justice, we need to understand first their provenance, nature, and dynamics. The history and context of these conflicting responsibilities are relevant information. Indeed, we cannot overstate the importance of finding out what gives rise to these clashing duties.

This study addresses what it sees as the central questions: How and why do these agape-justice conflicts arise to begin with? Answers to these shed light on the earlier two sets of practical and philosophical-theological questions:

- As a practical matter, how do we resolve such competing claims? Whose demands take priority, agape or justice? Why?
- As a matter of academic interest, are such conflicts due to human limitations in knowing (epistemological) or are they part of the cosmic order itself (ontological), or both? After all, it is a world that is supposed to be governed by a perfect divine providence and a coherent divine will.

To my knowledge, the literature has yet to address how and why these agape-justice clashes arise in the first place. This is the main task of this book.

Methodological Choices

This study uses the various sources of Christian moral discernment in examining the moral dilemmas precipitated by agape-justice conflicts. It relies on Sacred Scripture, reason, tradition, and experience. Two methodological choices are important to point out. First, most agape-justice conflicts have significant economic dimensions to them given their competing material demands. Their clashing claims are most evident in socioeconomic life, as we see in the previously mentioned cases. Thus, this study also draws conceptual tools and insights from economic theory, history, and empirical evidence. This interdisciplinary scholarship is an example of how theology and the human sciences can mutually enrich each other's work. Theology cannot weigh social issues all by itself. It needs conversation partners. We see this particularly in agape-justice conflicts.

Second, some will argue that many of the preceding cases (e.g., trade openness as foreign aid, sharing vaccines, welcoming migrants) are in fact demands of justice rather than demands of agape. Thus, they will say that they are not a clash between the demands of beneficence and the demands of justice but a clash between competing criteria of justice. Indeed, many of these claims can arguably be justified on the grounds of justice rather than agape. However, even if these humanitarian claims are indeed presented as demands of justice, when all else fails and their claims based on justice are rejected, their fallback argument is to appeal to compassion. At the very least, these humanitarian claims can be argued based on the demands of agape and our shared humanity. If that is the case, then, we might as well bypass the possible arguments from justice as these require separate studies of their own. Moreover, intra-justice debates are often interminable given fundamental disagreements on who gets to determine what justice is and what it requires in specific cases.

It is much better to present these cases from their weakest position, in which we assume, for the sake of argument, that they lack any legal or moral claims from justice but for an appeal to benevolence. This is a much more compelling win than if we were to argue the above contending claims as differing accounts of what justice requires. Paradoxically, the real strength of a claim is revealed by winning the argument based on its weakest position. Thus, this study presents them and the other cases to follow as agape-justice conflicts rather than as intra-justice clashes. We might as well begin from their fallback position – relying on the moral claims of agape alone. How well do the claims of agape stand up against the claims of justice?

Value of This Study

The books in this series on Christian ethics make the case for a wide variety of moral obligations across all levels, from the personal all the way to the global. For example, we are bound by moral demands stemming from dependent care relations (Sullivan-Dunbar 2017), healthcare (Gill 2006; Duckett 2023), self-love (Weaver 2002), altruism (Grant 2000), and the

common good (Hollenbach 2002), among many other facets of human
life examined in this series. It would be wonderful if we could satisfy in an
easy, straightforward manner the moral duties that these books present.
However, that is not how it is in real life. We do not live in hermetically
sealed compartments that give us the luxury of dealing with each issue
singly at our leisure. We live life in all its dimensions simultaneously. The
issues identified by the works in this series come at us at the same time.
Human life is as rich as it is complex. Many moral obligations presented
in this series will clash with one another because satisfying them requires
our time and material resources, both of which are finite.

This new contribution enriches many of the earlier works in this series
by locating their respective moral claims within a much wider spectrum of
moral obligations bookended by agape, on the one hand, and by justice,
on the other hand. In so doing, we get to see how the manifold moral
obligations presented in this series are related to each other. Putting moral
duties in the context of other competing moral obligations adds a new
dimension to the findings of many of the studies in this series. Consider
the following three examples.

First, this study finds that the strength of the claims of moral obligations often change when juxtaposed with other moral duties with similarly
strong demands. In other words, the obligatoriness of moral duties is a
function of the claims of other competing moral dues. Take the case of
Garth Hallett's (1998) *Priorities and Christian Ethics*. He gives precedence
to the demands of our nearest and dearest vis-à-vis those of the neediest.
This study pushes Hallett's findings further to show that the issue is ultimately not one of priorities but of superfluity. The case for prioritizing our
natural loves is strong, but only up to a certain point because we must also
attend to the needs of the distant and the stranger given love's diffusive
nature. We examine this at length in Chapter 6.

In our second example, we see that putting moral obligations in the
context of one another's claims brings out their complementarity and
reinforces their individual claims. For example, Darlene Fozard Weaver's
(2002) *Self Love and Christian Ethics* and Colin Grant's (2000) *Altruism
and Christian Ethics* separately present competing moral requirements that
need to be satisfied. This study finds that both are in fact necessary conditions for each other. Moreover, it strengthens the conclusions and the
moral obligations put forth in both works by showing that our natural
loves, including self-love, find their perfection in agape, including altruism. It is a matter of sequencing one after the other and putting them
within the larger context of each other's claims.

In a third example, note how this study provides a larger moral backdrop to many of the obligations presented by the works in this series. Take the case of Stephen John Duckett's (2023) *Healthcare Funding and Christian Ethics*. He argues for greater collective responsibility in meeting healthcare as a universal human need. My proposed continuum of moral obligations traces US healthcare insurance from being a perk and supererogatory at the end of World War II to becoming the law of the land seventy years later in what has popularly been called Obamacare Health Insurance. As we will see shortly in Chapters 1, 3, and 4, the boundaries between supererogation, moral duties, and legal dues shift over time. Agape-justice conflicts augur many of these shifts in this continuum of obligations. Duckett's call for greater public funding of healthcare is a vivid illustration of the changing terrain on the issue of healthcare between justice's call for greater personal responsibility, on the one hand, and agape's appeal for greater mutual compassion, on the other hand. It is an example of how moral obligations evolve in the strength of their claims because of a shifting public ethos.

In sum, this study provides a conceptual framework in weighing moral obligations relative to each other, especially on those occasions when they clash with one another. In understanding how and why agape-justice conflicts arise, we are better able to appreciate both the limits and the opportunities afforded by many of the moral obligations put forth by the various studies in this series.

Besides adding to the academic literature, this study also has pragmatic contributions. In the first place, its findings assist public policy. As mentioned earlier, judges, chief executives, legislatures, and public officials routinely choose between the competing demands of agape and justice. How well they decide these is a relevant concern. By advancing our shared understanding of the nature and dynamics of agape-justice conflicts, this study's findings can further the ability of decision makers in arriving at well-informed and wise choices in settling these clashing claims. What makes the stakes even higher is that these agape-justice conflicts often have life-changing consequences. Public officials regularly arbitrate clashing claims from agape and justice, and their decisions affect untold numbers whose destitute lives could be made better or whole, but for a helping hand. We see this in the case of Covid vaccine sharing, immigration, and export restrictions on food and vital agricultural fertilizers, among many other social issues.

Second, this study's findings could potentially narrow down perennial divisions within communities, minimize the animosity of internal discord, and perhaps even get opponents to work together. As we have seen from our sample of issues, agape-justice conflicts are among the most divisive. They are often visceral, and, consequently, the disputes are fierce.

For example, Angela Merkel had to deal with the backlash for her compassion in opening Germany to over a million Syrian war refugees in 2015. She lost her chancellorship not long thereafter. Immigration is a contentious issue in many nations, pitting those who want to be compassionate against local citizens who feel threatened and are protective of the status quo. There is always debate on taxes, income transfers, and the redistribution of burdens and benefits within any community. Legislators disagree with one another on whether to stress the duties of mutual beneficence or the duties of justice that call for greater personal responsibility. That the "America First" policy of the 45th president of the United States has found resonance among the US electorate reflects just how deep and far-reaching these agape-justice conflicts can be. It reveals a deep divide between those who want to reach out empathetically to the distant and the stranger, on the one hand, and those who are resolute in staying within their own circle of kin, associates, and fellow citizens, on the other hand.

Indeed, agape-justice conflicts are often nation-dividing issues. No matter how these conflicts are resolved, there will be aggrieved parties who either feel victimized by a gross injustice or feel abandoned by callous indifference, or both. However, by understanding how and why agape-justice conflicts arise, contending sides might yet tamp down their resentment and even dispel it altogether. They might even reach a mutual accommodation through some compromise.

For all the quandaries they create, agape-justice conflicts can end up, paradoxically, strengthening our common bonds with one another. They bring along unique opportunities. This study finds that agape-justice conflicts turn out to be:

- Diagnostic signals alerting us that public policy and ethos are misaligned with the community's evolving needs (Chapter 4).
- Timely nudges to attend to overlooked past wrongs before they snowball into even bigger problems (Chapter 5).
- Propitious occasions to perfect and complete people's natural loves by expanding their circle of love and responsibility to include the distant and the stranger (Chapter 6).
- The chance to love as Christ loves (Chapter 7).
- Catalysts for building community and growing in collective virtue through a shared sacrificial giving (Chapter 8).

In appreciating these unique opportunities accompanying agape-justice conflicts, contending parties might yet bridge their differences and work together toward a solution. And, indeed, noteworthy examples in Chapter 5 demonstrate that grappling with agape-justice conflicts can improve the way we live and the way we love. In so doing, we might yet collectively extend a helping hand to those who can benefit from some compassion and empathy amidst life's chance and contingencies. It is with this modest hope that I offer this study.

I am deeply grateful to Beatrice Rehl, Robin Gill, Chris Hudson, the editorial and production staff of Cambridge University Press, and the anonymous referees for their unfailing support and assistance in bringing this project to fruition. I am indebted to Sarah Norman for her invaluable copyediting and to Thirumangai Thamizhmani for shepherding the manuscript through final publication. My thanks to Steve Ryan for his counsel on my biblical questions and for his encouragement.

Profoundly thankful for the grace at work in our lives and through one another, I pray that this book might make life a little easier for everyone, especially the poor and the distressed. May we live in a world that is both loving and just.

PART I

Nature of the Conflict

CHAPTER I

Rank Ordering of Claims

Agape and justice clash in domestic public policy debates on spending priorities, international trade, tied-in aid programs, corporate governance, worker compensation, and migration, just to name a few social issues. These conflicts arise frequently and spawn profound consequences. In fact, they are unavoidable and are often central to socioeconomic life. This introductory section examines the nature of these conflicts and their fault lines.

Constitutive Elements of Justice

Justice is about "the conservation of organized society, with rendering to every man his due, and with the faithful discharge of obligations assumed" (Cicero 1913, *De Officiis*, I, V [15]). The duty to be just stems from natural law. Humans, by their nature, are social and need to interact with others. However, for such a social life to be possible, people will have to be just to one another. Thus, to be just (and give people their due) is a first principle of practical reason. "Good is to be done and evil avoided." Part of doing good is to be just. A similar argument can be made for love as part of the good (Rhonheimer 2002, 289).

The term "justice" has been used in the literature to refer to the following:

- Commutative justice (equality in exchange)
- Distributive justice (proportionality in the allocation of shared resources, burdens, and benefits)
- Retributive justice (punishment for wrongdoing)
- Restorative/corrective/reparative justice (liability for damages inflicted)
- Social justice (rectification of institutional ills)
- Legal/general justice (promotion of the common good)

These are not mutually exclusive. In fact, they are complementary and mutually reinforce each other. One could simplify this list. Retributive, restorative, and social justice could arguably be described as subspecies of distributive justice. After all, their functions are well within the task of distributive justice.

Commutative and distributive justice, including the latter's subspecies, are undergirded by a web of formal and informal laws that provide the criteria for determining what is due to people. Informal laws include longstanding customs and practices or whatever other conduct the public expects of its community members. Justice enforces both codified and uncodified societal rules. Moreover, there is a time- and place-utility to justice, that is, claims must be satisfied at particular times and places and among the right parties and in the right manner. Thus, the adage "justice delayed is justice denied" in punitive justice applies just as well to the other types of justice. Justice is time- and place-sensitive.

Legal justice is a general virtue that orients every virtue or human act toward the promotion of the good of the community. After all, anything that affects parts of a whole necessarily ripples through or is reflected on the whole as well. For this reason, St. Thomas also refers to legal justice as general justice (II-II, 58.5, reply) and distinguishes it from particular justice, that is, commutative and distributive justice (II-II, 61.1).[1] General-legal justice puts virtues and human actions at the service of the common good.

General-legal justice is not legally enforceable, nor is it involved in the actual enforcement of laws. No formal laws undergird it. It is aspirational in nature. Nevertheless, general-legal justice presents its own claims – that people contribute to the promotion of the common good in the measure they can according to their capabilities and powers. Obviously, it imposes a moral rather than a legal obligation.[2]

Constitutive Elements of Love

Love comes in different forms. For the purposes of our study, note the following types of love:

- *Philautia* (love of self)
- *Philia* (profound friendship)
- *Storge* (familial love)
- *Eros* (sexual passion)

---

[1] These references pertain to the *Summa Theologiæ* (Aquinas 1920).
[2] I am using "legal" in this instance to refer to the demands of codified law in contrast to St. Thomas' general-legal justice.

- *Pragma* (longstanding love that compromises to make relationships work)
- *Agape* (universal love)

Agape

Agape varies in the stringency of its claims. For the purposes of this study, we distinguish three types of agape. The first is the most basic one. It is an undiscriminating, unconditional concern and empathy for all, including the distant, the stranger, and the undeserving. It calls for solicitude for our fellow humans out of our shared humanity. Included in this are Cicero's (1913) duty of beneficence, Immanuel Kant's (1991) duty of benevolence, David Hume's (1896, 1902) duty of humanity, Gene Outka's (1972) agape as equal regard, and Peter Singer's (1972) duty of easy rescues, among others. One could think of the Golden Rule or Kant's categorical imperative as justification for such care for others' well-being. The obligatory force of this agape's claims stems from our common humanity.

Second, we have the agape that comes from the Hebrew Scriptures with the command to love one's neighbor as oneself (Lev 19:18).[3] We see this reflected in the Mosaic economic laws, whereby the Chosen People were to ensure that there were no poor among them (Dt 15:4). Among these laws were lending without interest, debt forgiveness after six years, mandatory lending, the return of land to their original ancestral owners on the Jubilee year, poor tithing, a sabbatical year, almsgiving, and many other norms. These laws were designed to ensure that they took care of the most vulnerable among them – the widows, aliens, orphans, the poor, and those who had fallen on hard times. Also worth noting in these laws are the motive clauses that have been appended to many of them. For example, in the manumission of slaves, the Mosaic Law is emphatic on the need to be generous.

> [W]hen you send a male slave out from you a free person, you shall not send him out empty-handed. Provide liberally out of your flock, your threshing floor, and your wine press, thus giving to him some of the bounty with which the Lord your God has blessed you. *Remember that you were a slave in the land of Egypt, and the Lord your God redeemed you; for this reason I lay this command upon you today.* (Dt 5:13–15, emphasis added)

---

[3] Biblical quotes for this study are from the New Revised Standard Version (NRSV) drawn from biblegateway.com.

God could ask difficult acts of mutual kindness from the Israelites because God was merely asking them to extend to others the same favors that they themselves had received in their own moment of need. The God who had saved them expects like behavior from them.

The third and most demanding type of agape is biblical as well – Christified agape. The bar set by the two greatest commandments is raised even further – to love as Christ has loved (John 15:12). This is a self-sacrificial agape. It walks the extra mile, turns the other cheek, forgives without end, lends freely and without expecting to be repaid, serves as a slave to all, seeks to be the last rather than the first, and even dies wholeheartedly for the undeserving. Again, there is an element of reciprocity vis-à-vis God in this case because Christ did all these for humanity. God loved us first, and so we in our own turn can love as well (1 John 4:19). Consequently, God's invitation for us to practice Christified agape can be deemed a demand for justice (what we owe to God). However, when it comes to our fellow humans, Christified agape is a completely supererogatory act considering its enormous cost to the giver. We are not obligated to pour out our lives for each other because of any claims we owe one another.

For Anders Nygren (1953), God's love for humans is the paradigm of agapic love. Divine love is spontaneous and unconditional, without reference to whether humans deserve it. An example is God's forgiveness of human sinfulness. So should it be for humans. Human agape must also be spontaneous and unmeasured. The worthiness of the object of one's love is irrelevant. Thus, for Nygren, agape is oblivious to justice. Even if agapic love inadvertently spawns injustice, agapic love simply trumps justice (Wolterstorff 2011, 41–49). There can be no real clash between such radical agapic love and justice.

Christified agape corresponds to St. Thomas' charity (*caritas*), which is an infused agape. This is a pure gift of grace. *Caritas* is distinctive as the general virtue that directs all virtues and human actions to their Final End (*telos*) of friendship and union with God. Chapter 7 examines *caritas* further.

Christian scriptures and theology go beyond the most common understanding of agape as universal love to propose the infused virtue of charity (*caritas*). Unless otherwise mentioned, in what follows, the term "agape" refers to its most common usage of love for all – that is, Cicero's duty of beneficence, Hume's duty of humanity, Kant's duty of benevolence, and Outka's agape as equal regard for all based on our common humanity. One could also refer to these as acquired agape to distinguish them from infused agape (St. Thomas' *caritas*).

Other Loves

The terms "benevolence" and "beneficence" are often used interchangeably in ordinary conversation. However, for this study, we follow St. Ambrose and Kant's distinction between the goodwill and the good deed. Benevolence is the goodwill that one accords to others, while beneficence is the tangible expression of such goodwill.[4]

> Now we can go on to speak of kindness, which breaks up into two parts, goodwill and liberality. Kindness to exist in perfection must consist of these two qualities. It is not enough just to wish well; we must also do well. Nor, again, is it enough to do well, unless this springs from a good source even from a good will. (Ambrose 1952, *De Officiis*, I, 30, 143)

The perfection of kindness requires both benevolence (goodwill) and beneficence (good deed) to work in tandem. Both are two sides of the same coin if kindness is to be perfect. St. Ambrose cites St. Paul's instructions to the Corinthians as an illustration of the need for both good intent and actual deed (2 Cor 8:10–15). Beneficence alone is insufficient. After all, one can be generous but for selfish reasons, as in the case of Greco-Roman patron-client relationships. Patrons spent lavishly on public games and the distribution of bread, but only to the degree that it gave them more power and prestige.

Immanuel Kant differentiates benevolence from beneficence in a similar manner. For him, love is not a feeling or delight vis-à-vis others. Rather, it is a practical love. Thus, note the different terms he uses: "practical love," "active love," "active benevolence," and "maxim of actions." Benevolence is practical love, which is expressed in beneficence. Benevolence is about wishing people well, and doing something about it is beneficence.[5] "Benevolence is satisfaction in the happiness (well-being) of others; but beneficence is the maxim of making others' happiness one's end" (#29).

The various types of love are necessary conditions for flourishing in life. Not all loves are equal in importance. Some are building blocks, while others are perfective. In particular, acquired agape is built up slowly over time. Chapter 6 argues that *philautia*, *pragma*, *philia*, and *storge* are its building blocks. Acquired agape is their crown and perfection in the realm of natural excellence. (Infused agape will supersede it in the realm of supernatural excellence.)

---

[4] Wolterstorff (2011, 23) defines benevolence as the promotion of others' well-being for their own sake, provided this act is not done because justice requires it.
[5] Kant 1991, *Metaphysics, Doctrine of Virtue*, Part II, Ch I, Sect I, #25, 26, 28, 29.

Furthermore, just like justice, there is a time dimension (time-utility) to these loves because some of them correspond to different stages of life. A child learns and experiences love for the first time through *storge* and then later through *pragma*. Simultaneously, a child learns about healthy *philautia*. Married life is prime terrain for living out *storge, eros, pragma,* and *philautia*.

There is a learning process in these loves because they require balance. There can be too little or too much of them. They can also be misused, abused, or morph into unhealthy variants, as in the case of narcissistic love (unhealthy *philautia*). There are other types of aberrant love. Hence, part of the growth in these loves is that of learning and acquiring the right balance. This is a process of learning by doing. Experience is important.

Each of these loves has its rightful claims. For example, children and parents expect each other's affection without having to be commanded (*storge*). Similarly, friends delight in each other and are spontaneous in their concern for one another (*philia*). People watch out for and take care of their own well-being (*philautia*). Each of these loves entails expectations from the various parties involved. They require giving loved ones "their due" affection and care. These are obligations owed to family and friends stemming from human nature itself. Thus, these can be called natural loves and natural obligations. As we will see in Chapter 6, there is an order of charity that must be observed (Aquinas 1920, II–II 44.8; 25.12; 26.1 & 2). It is an injustice to violate this order of charity (Porter 1989, 209).

Since justice is about giving people their due, the claims of natural loves properly fall within the workings of justice. Justice protects and works toward the satisfaction of these natural claims. Justice's role in this regard takes on even greater importance since love's claims must be fulfilled at particular times and places and among specific peoples. Chapter 6 will show that many agape-justice conflicts are in fact competing claims between kin-particularistic love (natural loves) and universal love (agape). Thus, it is wrong to pose the subject of our study as a conflict between love and justice because the claims of some types of love properly fall within the duties of justice. It is more accurate to pose our issue as a clash between the claims of agape and justice.

Clashing Claims

Justice and agape clash in their claims because each has a constitutive economic dimension. Human life is lived and maintained in a material world. Humans are corporeal and need material goods for their survival and growth. They need food, clothing, shelter, and medical care, at a minimum. Humans also have an immaterial dimension to them, and it turns out that this is even more intensive in its use of material goods. For example, nurturing the mind and the soul requires substantial expenditure, as in the case of education.

All these will have to be satisfied within two major constraints. First, the goods of the earth are finite, even as human needs and wants are boundless. Economic resources are shared, scarce,[6] and exhaustible. There will be competing claims over their use. Second, human capabilities are also finite. We are limited in what we can know and what we can do. We only have twenty-four hours in a day and can only be in one place at any single time. We need to allocate the attention that we devote to others. There will be a clash in prioritizing the demands made of us. Life is fraught with opportunity costs because choice entails foregoing many other viable and valuable selections.

St. Thomas notes that even as we should have equal affection for all, when it comes to the material expression of such agape, we must allocate because our resources are finite (II-II, 25.8). Furthermore, economic resources are generally subject to rival consumption – that is, not everybody can enjoy them at the same time.

Since both agape and justice have constitutive material dimensions to them, satisfying their respective demands generally entails the use of scarce economic resources (temporal and material) that are often sizable in their requirements. Thus, regardless of whether there are genuine conflicts between agape and justice by the nature of the divine order of creation, they will be most evident in socioeconomic life. Not surprisingly, economics is at the root of the agape-justice conflicts in the parables of the vineyard owner (Mt 20:1–16), the prodigal son and his older brother's complaint (Lk 15:11–32), and the shepherd looking for a lost sheep while putting the ninety-nine other sheep unguarded and at risk (Mt 18:12–14). Socioeconomic life brings out these conflicts between agape and justice and underscores the hard choices that will have to be made between two legitimate sets of conflicting claims. There will be many clashes in the claims of several types of justice or love relative to each other (intra-justice and intra-love conflicts), but there will also be

---

[6] I am using the term "scarcity" in an economic sense of incurring opportunity costs. I am not using this term to mean insufficiency, that is, a Malthusian scarcity of want due to a stingy earth or divine provider.

Table 1.1 *Competing claims of justice and agape*

Demands of justice	Demands of agape
Commutative justice	
Distributive justice including:	
• Reparative justice	Agape (equal regard for all, including the
• Retributive justice	distant, the stranger, and the undeserving)
• Social justice	
Philautia	
Philia	
Storge	

numerous competing demands between justice and agape.[7] It is the latter that we examine in this study.

Justice, by its nature, is about giving people their due. That is the object of justice. Agape is about impartial care for all, including the distant, the stranger, and the undeserving. Kant notes that our benevolence can be unlimited, but doing good (beneficence) is much more difficult because it entails sacrificing our own welfare.[8] Equal concern (Outka's agape; benevolence) does not necessarily translate to equal action (beneficence) because we take need and circumstances into account (Herman 2001, 253). In other words, agape and its duty of beneficence present their own set of material claims.

Table 1.1 presents the clashing claims that are the subject of this book. General-legal justice is not included in this listing because it does not directly clash with agape. After all, agape's universal love also redounds to the promotion of the common good.

In examining the competing claims of justice and agape, it helps to identify which of the constitutive elements of justice and love are involved. Recall that natural loves and their claims properly fall under the demands of justice. Agape-justice conflicts will involve competing claims from these elements.

Obligatory and Nonobligatory Action

We distinguish between obligatory and nonobligatory actions. These form a continuum of obligatoriness. However, for ease of exposition and facility

---

[7] Some argue that all duties to aid the needy stem from justice alone. If so, there is no conflict between justice and agape. Hume disagrees with this position (Shaver 1992, 546).

[8] Kant 1991, *Metaphysics, Elements of Ethics*, VIII, 2 a, #393.

in distinguishing them from one another, this study divides them into four discrete categories, namely (1) legal dues, (2) relational moral debts, (3) general moral debts, and (4) supererogation.[9]

Legal Duties and Obligations

The first type of obligatory action pertains to the legal duties that stem from the statutes of a community. Legal duties and obligations are the most stringent of all because they are codified in formal law, and they are enforceable. Penalties can be imposed for noncompliance. The coercive powers of the state or of the community are in full force because what is at stake is maintaining order and the rule of law in the community. Human collaborative groupings vary from the simple and basic (e.g., nuclear family) all the way to the biggest and most complex, such as nations and multilateral institutions (e.g., the United Nations, the World Trade Organization). The larger and the more labyrinthine the groups, the greater is the need for formal rules that spell out procedures, the division of responsibilities and benefits, and penalties, among others. This is essential for the smooth and optimal functioning of such groups. Thus, nations draw up constitutions and set up a legal infrastructure that includes courts, law enforcement, and other institutions. Charters guide professional groups and corporations. Local communities put down in writing the governing ordinances within their jurisdictions. The formal defining characteristics of such legal duties and obligations are their codification in law and their external, coercive enforcement.

Some of the more well-known and common-day examples are the payment of taxes, traffic rules and regulations, commercial rules in running a business, zoning restrictions, the payment of minimum wages, and tort liabilities, among others. Included in these are the punitive laws that dissuade people from harming one another. Acts that do not conform to these laws are deemed illegal. The law, depending on the seriousness of the matter at hand, specifies various sanctions. These laws and statutes must always be observed. They are considered essential for the operation of the community, so much so that they are formally enacted into law. The coercive powers of the community or its designated representatives are brought to bear to ensure a high degree of compliance.

---

[9] We can have an even finer division beyond merely four categories, but I limit these to the barest minimum to facilitate this presentation.

Legal dues provide the framework for the existence of the community: how people ought to treat one another, what they may expect from each other, and what they are supposed to contribute to the commonweal. Community procedures and the sharing of burdens and benefits are spelled out with precision, to the extent possible. E. Clinton Gardner (1957, 221) observes that legal dues provide the "ad hoc" structures for coping with the messiness of earthly life by giving people their due. They build a juridic order that allows for living together amicably in community. We are neighbors sharing a finite earth. Thus, justice is an important guardrail if there is to be any community at all – a community of neighbors who share a common earth. Justice is concerned with ensuring order in the natural realm.

These legal duties and obligations are perfect duties because they are "narrow" and precise in specifying what is required, including when, where, how, for whom, from whom, and other matters related to the execution of these statutes. These are determinate and exact in what they require.

Relational Moral Obligations

A second type of obligatory actions comprises uncodified but expected duties and obligations stemming from community praxis and the public ethos. These are aptly called *particular moral duties* because they are owed to the particular communities to which people belong, from which they draw benefits, and to which they ought to contribute. These duties and obligations are often unspoken but clearly understood informal "laws" that groups and communities expect of their membership.

Individuals do not interact directly with some general, abstract "humanity." Instead, people interact with other humans through particular intermediate natural or contractual bodies and groupings. Humans are born into a nuclear family, an extended family-clan-tribe, and a nation. They work and interact with one another through specific groups, as in the case of belonging to a neighborhood, a school, a workplace, a professional group, and a faith group, among others. In other words, individuals draw benefits from and contribute back to "humanity" through their participation in various particular intermediate groups of varying functions and sizes.

Each of these intermediate "communities" has its set of expectations, such as norms of acceptable conduct and requisite contributions. These particular communities impose their respective duties on their membership. Most of these are uncodified, and even if they were codified, many often do not have the coercive power to impose severe penalties for non-compliance. David Owens (2012, 200) calls these *relational obligations* in contrast to general obligations. Relational obligations are owed by virtue of our special ties to particular persons. They have also been called *sui generis* obligations. In contrast, general obligations are what we owe to everybody by virtue of our common humanity.[10] Barbara Herman (2001, 229–232) calls these *primary obligations* in contrast to secondary obligations. Primary obligations are those that we owe to our relations and those for whom we are responsible. In contrast, secondary obligations are those that we owe to everybody else out of our shared humanity.

Take the case of Biblical Israel and its daunting array of expectations for mutual aid, such as lending without interest, debt forgiveness, land return, slave manumission, and gleaning, among many others. Israelites were expected to redeem their kin who have had to be sold into slavery (Lev 25: 47–55). They were also expected to redeem any of the clan's ancestral land that might have had to be sold by their relations (Lev 25:23–34). Israelites were expected to be each other's *go'el* (redeemer). These expectations and duties turn out to be a rational strategy of mutual assistance for mutual survival. In an ancient economy of precarious existence and communal vulnerability, the extended family and the community are key to a person's chances of survival. Not surprisingly, mutual aid was a community expectation, even if uncodified. In fact, these norms are believed to have originated from their nomadic practices, which were then adopted as part of Mosaic laws and set as community custom when they finally shifted to settled agriculture (von Waldow 1970). Note how almsgiving is a tenet for adherents of the Abrahamic faiths to this day. In effect, individuals take upon themselves additional duties and obligations toward fellow members of the particular communities to which they belong.

Recall the parable of the unforgiving servant (Mt 18:21–35). Having been forgiven by his master of his huge debt, the community expected the servant to extend similar kindness to a fellow servant who owed him a much smaller amount. Consequently, his fellow servants reported him to the king, who then punished him accordingly for his harsh treatment of his fellow indebted servant. This parable is a good illustration of the power and importance of community expectations as early as the ancient world, even if these are not codified in formal law.

---

[10] We examine the difference between relational and general moral obligations in Chapter 6 when we discuss the issue of priorities.

These duties and expectations are embedded in the memberships' ethos and praxis. These are informal rather than formal rules that are often unspoken but implicitly accepted as the community norm. The group simply trusts its members to live up to what it expects of them. Enforcement is left up to the individual's conscience. In other words, these duties are largely self-enforced, and there are no legal sanctions or penalties for non-compliance. Nevertheless, the community steps in to name and shame egregious violators.

For example, note the public opprobrium heaped on price gougers, as when the disgraced chief executive of Turing Pharmaceutical raised the price of the life-saving anti-parasitic drug *Daraprim* fifty-six-fold overnight.[11] Recall the early days of Covid-19 when speculators cornered the market for hand sanitizers, face masks, and protective personal equipment (PPEs). The public reaction was swift, forcing some price-gougers to beat a hasty retreat and donate their supplies to charity.[12] There are unspoken, uncodified standards that communities expect from their membership.

Other contemporary examples of such duties that stem from community expectations include tipping (in the United States), doing volunteer work, and paying forward acts of kindness. Corporations are expected to be good citizens and to give back to their local host communities. Many pharmaceutical companies have drug assistance programs whereby ill patients who cannot afford their medications are nonetheless still able to access them. Colleges and universities expect their faculty to continue working assiduously on publications even after they get their tenure. Nations mutually expect each other not to be currency manipulators or mercantilists in their trade policies. Various cultures have their own ethos regarding the threshold of intolerable levels of inequality. For example, CEO pay in the United States averages anywhere from 300 to even as much 1,000 times that of the rank-and-file workers, depending on the study's sample size. The EU tolerates a much lower multiple, while the Japanese have an even narrower acceptable range of inequality.

Friends take upon themselves duties and obligations vis-à-vis each other's well-being (the duties of *philia*). Similarly, family members watch out for one another. Parents bend over backward to lay as promising a future for their children, while the children in their own turn show filial

---

[11] The disgraced chief executive was eventually convicted on unrelated charges. See Lupkin (2019).

[12] See, for example, the Tennessee man who had hoarded 17,700 bottles of hand sanitizers and was shamed into donating them a mere 24 hours after the *New York Times* published an article about him and his stash of hand sanitizers (Nicas 2020). Social media platforms were quick to remove such vendors from their sites.

piety, respect, and love for their parents, especially in their old age (duties of *storge*). Communities assume that their members will take personal responsibility for providing for themselves and their dependents and not be an undue burden on others (duties of *philautia*).

As we will see shortly, a third type of obligatory action is the duty that we owe each other as fellow human beings (general moral duties). Communities expect their members to be even more assiduous in according these to one another. Thus, they presume that their members will prevent harm from befalling their neighbors if they could do so at little cost to themselves (Cicero's costless beneficence). Similarly, we have Peter Singer's (1972) duty of easy rescues. The public presupposes, as a matter of regular community practice, that people will lend a hand to disabled people, help the elderly cross the street, rescue a drowning person, or attend to a lost child. Recall the Old Testament expectation that one takes care of a neighbor's, or even an enemy's, farm animal that has wandered off or is injured (Ex 23:4–5; Dt 22:1–4).

These fall within the scope of justice because they are owed to the community, even if they are not formally codified or legally enforced. Thus, note the efforts of corporations, especially those with name brands to protect, in vetting their sub-contractors for unacceptable employment practices. Since people and corporations draw benefits from the community, they are merely requiting the beneficence that they themselves had received from the community that had nurtured them.

Noncompliance with particular moral duties does not trigger legal sanctions or penalties, but it does reveal a serious character flaw. Enforcement depends on moral suasion and the desire to protect one's standing among one's neighbors. As mentioned earlier, community naming and shaming is the most effective coercive means of enforcement. These duties and obligations are moral in nature, in contrast to the legal duties of codified law. Nevertheless, they fall under the umbrella of justice. After all, these duties and obligations arise from people's membership in particular communities from which they draw benefits and to which they are supposed to contribute. These duties and obligations properly fall under distributive justice. Moreover, they are reliant on the spirit of the law rather than the letter of the law.

As mentioned earlier, this category of moral obligations – *particular moral obligations* – can also be aptly called *relational, primary, or sui generis moral obligations*. They are a mix of both perfect and imperfect duties depending on the size of the particular group or community generating such moral obligations. For example, in a nuclear family, the mutual obligations of family members are perfect duties – there is no ambiguity on what we owe to whom, when, and where. Our familial duties are determinate. They generate correlative rights just like legal duties. Thus, our filial duty gives our parents the right to expect support and consolation from us in their old age. We will explicitly see this in one of our later examples in China and Singapore on the moral and the legal duty of filial support.

As the group or the community generating the obligation gets larger, the duties become more indeterminate, and there may be wider latitude permitted depending on how demanding the requirements of the moral obligations are. Moreover, they tend to become imperfect duties the wider the scope of the people to whom we owe such obligations. In contrast to legal duties, many obligations in larger groupings are imperfect duties because they do not generate correlative rights. For example, my informal duty to pay forward an act of kindness done to me does not give you a right to my kindness because I can pay forward such a favor to somebody else in the community. In other words, there is relatively greater latitude in the performance of many of these duties compared to legal duties or strict primary, relational obligations.

The driving force behind living up to these imperfect duties is our own conscience and our own moral sensibilities. We feel bad if we fail to do the good that we could have easily done. And we have reason to feel bad because such easy rescues and costless beneficence are the decent things to do for fellow community members. It is a community expectation. Thus, note the public outcry and the community angst over the 1964 killing of Kitty Genovese in New York when neighbors failed to intervene, not even to call the police (New York Times 1964). Or, note the national soul-searching in the wake of a Chinese woman run over repeatedly on the road because none of the numerous bystanders came to assist her when she was first hit by a taxi (Shih 2017). Note the outpouring of blood donors in the wake of a major disaster. Both legal and moral duties are ultimately under-girded by the philosophical commitments and values of the community. The community's practices and expectations from its membership reflect and instantiate such a public ethos.

General Moral Duties

General moral duties, the third category, are also moral debts. Our duties and obligations are not limited only to our fellow members in the par-ticular communities to which we belong (e.g., family members, fellow citizens). They extend beyond our kin and close associates to include our fellow humans, whoever or wherever they may be. Furthermore, people voluntarily embrace duties and obligations beyond those stipulated by their particular communities. These duties and obligations arise by virtue of our humanity. After all, this is the most basic group membership that we have – the human family. Thus, these can be called general duties, in contrast to relational or particular duties. They have also been called secondary duties to differentiate them from primary duties (Herman 2001).

These duties derive from the claims of people's common humanity, from their role as fellow humans, as members of the human race. An example is people's grasp of the first principles of moral action, an inborn knowledge of the most basic principles in our interaction with fellow humans, such as the Golden Rule or the norm to do no harm and avoid evil.[13] Others go so far as to say that there is a duty to prevent harm and a duty of beneficence. People are expected to return a lost wallet. They are not to shirk the work for which they are paid. Doctors, nurses, plumbers, teachers, ministers, and others who provide credence goods and services are expected to give their best despite the public's inability to monitor the quality of their work or their efforts. People bind themselves to these duties out of their basic sense of decency and self-respect.

Cicero's Duty of Beneficence as a Duty of Justice

Despite his proposed order of generosity that prioritizes country, kin, and close associates, Cicero is nevertheless open to a much wider circle of people whom we ought to assist. Cicero directly and indirectly touches on beneficence twice in his exposition on the principles that govern moral goodness from which duty is drawn. Recall that justice as a cardinal virtue is about giving people their due, fulfilling obligations, and, in the process, maintaining societal order. Justice as a cardinal virtue has two constitutive elements, namely (1) *iustitia* – justice proper itself[14] and (2) *beneficentia* – beneficence (I, vii [20]). In other words:

Justice as a cardinal virtue = *iustitia* (justice proper) + *beneficentia* (beneficence)

For beneficence, Cicero explicitly notes that charity, kindness, and generosity are "akin to justice." Together, they comprise the second constitutive

---

[13] See St. Thomas on *synderesis* in ST I, 79.12.
[14] It is unfortunate that we do not have separate terms for justice as a cardinal virtue and *iustitia* – justice proper itself, thereby opening the door to some confusion. In what follows, we distinguish between the broader category justice as a cardinal virtue and its subset justice proper (*iustitia*).

element of justice as a cardinal virtue. Beneficence contributes to moral goodness in a direct fashion. Just like justice proper itself (*iustitia*), kindness, charity, and generosity have their unique contribution to preserving and strengthening the "common bonds" that form society. Beneficence does its share in strengthening human society. Indeed, more than that, it is essential. Cicero is emphatic on the rationale and importance of such mutual charity.

> But since, as Plato has admirably expressed it, we are not born for ourselves alone, but our country claims a share of our being, and our friends a share; and since, as the Stoics hold, everything that the earth produces is created for man's use; *and as men, too, are born for the sake of men, that they may be able to mutually help one another; in this direction we ought to follow Nature as our guide, to contribute to the general good by an interchange of acts of kindness, by giving and receiving, and thus by our skill, our industry, and our talents to cement human society more closely together, man to man.* (I, vii [22], emphasis added)

Cicero views beneficence as part of natural law itself since people naturally come to each other's assistance. Such mutual solicitude and acts of kindness and generosity form the very bonds of the human community. Later, in his exposition on justice and generosity, Cicero once again reiterates that humans are closely bound to one another because, of all the creatures, they are the only ones who share reason and speech. Furthermore, they share among themselves the bounty that nature has provided. Thus, he repeats the Greek adage, "Amongst friends all things in common." Cicero concludes by noting that generosity should be extended even to strangers what costs the giver nothing (I, xvi [51]).

Furthermore, Cicero notes that the interests of society and the individual are identical if community is to survive at all. The same law of nature binds all. Thus, individuals willingly promote the well-being of others simply because they are fellow humans. Moreover, Cicero points out the absurdity of refraining from mistreating those who are related or are close to us but not those who are distant or outside the circle of our natural loves. We are bound even to nonrelations and strangers by "mutual obligations, social ties [and] common interests" [III, vi [28]]. People share a common nature and a common humanity. This is what society is all about. One expects mutual respect and solicitude at the very least.

Cicero's justice proper (*iustitia*) entails two duties, namely, (1) to do no harm and (2) to use common property to promote common interests and to use private property for one's own interest, that is, to conserve our common interests (I, vii [20]; I, ix [30]).[15] Given his understanding of the nature of the human community, Cicero expands on these two duties of justice proper by proposing two types of injustice: active and passive injustice. Active injustice occurs when people hurt others. Passive injustice arises when people fail to fulfill their duty to prevent harm that they could so easily accomplish at little to no cost to themselves. This latter duty flows naturally from humans' social nature and their shared lives, as seen in the above quote.

Cicero accords so much importance to the duty to prevent harm to the point of describing nonfulfillment as a grave moral failure: "he who does not prevent or oppose wrong, if he can, is just as guilty of wrong as if he deserted his parents or his friends or his country" (I, vii [23]). He observes that people fail to live up to their duty to prevent harm because of their fear of making enemies, the expense involved, indolence, incompetence, indifference, or self-absorption (I, ix [28]). So reprehensible does Cicero find the failure to live up to the duty to prevent harm that he censures them in strong language: "they are traitors to social life, for they contribute to it none of their interest, none of their effort, none of their means" (I, ix [29]). Evidently, for Cicero, the strong positive duty to prevent harm is constitutive of justice as a cardinal virtue. After all, it is about conserving the common interest, the second duty of justice proper (I, ix [30]).

Note that the duty to prevent harm opens the door to beneficence since kindness, charity, and generosity are the very means by which one prevents harm. Cicero himself acknowledges the costs, effort, risks, and great inconvenience that preventing harm entails. Overcoming these requires generosity, goodwill, and kindness at the very least.

For Cicero, passive injustice arises if one fails to prevent harm at no cost to oneself (I, vii [23]). He censures those who fail to be beneficent to others at no cost to themselves, such as by providing counsel or direction (I, xvi [51]). Cicero's duty of beneficence and, by extension, his duty to prevent harm apply only if they are costless. This is too restrictive if taken literally. Preventing harm and most acts of beneficence entail costs in terms of treasure or time (Nussbaum 2000). Cicero's beneficence would be very slim indeed if we take him literally.

Plainly, the cost of beneficence or the cost of preventing harm is an important benchmark for Cicero regarding the obligatoriness of these duties. Thus, we could provide a gradation in Cicero's duty to prevent

---

[15] St. Thomas similarly notes that the two basic duties of justice are nonmaleficence and living up to our special obligations (I-II, 100.5). Humans get to know these two duties through reason (I-II, 100.3).

harm and duty of beneficence according to the cost they entail. A more generous reading and an extension of Cicero's thought is to acknowledge varying degrees of beneficence, namely:

- Low-cost beneficence – minimal cost (not costless) to the giver
- Costly but affordable beneficence – substantial cost, but within the giver's means
- Self-sacrificial beneficence – exceedingly costly to the point of diminishing the welfare of the giver or putting the giver's own agency at risk, or both.

It is reasonable to claim that the *epikeia* of Cicero's duty of beneficence would accept low-cost beneficence rather than the original standard of being costless. Using Cicero's thought, only low-cost beneficence is a duty.[16] The other two types of beneficence are not strictly obligatory by Cicero's standards.

In sum, beneficence enters Cicero's discussion of justice as a cardinal virtue twice. First, in a direct fashion, is as the second constitutive element of justice as a cardinal virtue. Then, a second time and indirectly, through justice proper's (*iustitia*) duty to prevent harm. For Cicero, beneficence is an essential building block of moral goodness. Beneficence is a duty as part of the even larger duty of justice as a cardinal virtue.

Kant's Duty of Benevolence and Beneficence

For Kant, humans have two obligatory ends. The first is the duty to work toward their own perfection by developing, to the extent possible, their crude natural predispositions and their moral capacities to their fullest so that they might pursue their other ends.[17] The second is the duty to work toward others' happiness. This is the duty of beneficence.

> Since our self-love cannot be separated from our need to be loved (helped in case of need) by others as well, we therefore make ourselves an end for others; and the only way this maxim can be binding is through its qualification as a universal law, hence through our will to make others our ends as well. The happiness of others is therefore an end that is also a duty. (Kant 1991, *Metaphysics, Doctrine of Virtue*, VIII, 2, a, 393)

---

[16] Cost of the beneficence is an important determinant in determining the threshold of such a duty. For Tom Beauchamp (2013), there is a moral duty of benevolence if: (i) Without such action, the beneficiary will incur significant loss; (ii) The subject's action is necessary to prevent such harm (a necessary action); (iii) The subject's action will most likely prevent such harm; and (iv) The subject's action will not impose costs on the subject that will be far greater than the benefits reaped by the beneficiary.

[17] Kant 1991, *Metaphysics, Doctrine of Virtue*, VIII, 1, a, 391–392.

An implication of Kant's second obligatory end is that we cannot confine ourselves only to the circle of our kin, friends, and associates. There is a need to expand our concerns and efforts beyond the circle of our natural loves (Stohr 2011).

As mentioned earlier, Kant differentiates benevolence from beneficence. The former pertains to the goodwill we have for all, while the latter refers to such goodwill put into action. Despite his realistic acknowledgment of the finitude of our resources and capacities, Kant nevertheless submits that there is both a duty of benevolence and a duty of beneficence. Referring to the precept on loving our neighbor, Kant notes:

> [W]hat is meant here is not merely benevolence in wishes, which is, strictly speaking, only taking delight in the well-being of every other and does not require me to contribute to it (every man for himself, God for us all); what is meant is, rather, *active, practical benevolence (beneficence), making the well-being and happiness of others my end.* (Kant 1991, *Metaphysics, Doctrine of Virtue*, Part II, Ch I, Sect I, #28, emphasis added)

On two other occasions in his brief exposition on the duty of benevolence, Kant makes clear that love is about wishing for and actively promoting the well-being of my neighbors. "The duty of love for one's neighbor can, accordingly, also be expressed as the duty to make others' *ends* my own (#25, emphasis original). Later, he reiterates, "beneficence is the maxim of making others' happiness one's end" (#29).

Kant (#24) contrasts the principle (duty) of mutual love with the principle of mutual respect. In the principle of mutual love, people are drawn closer to one another. In contrast, the principle or the duty of according respect to others is about keeping our distance from one another with an eye toward not intruding into each other's sphere. This is the duty of mutual respect. The duty of love is a *wide* duty (#25). It is about finding satisfaction in the well-being of others (#26).

Benevolence and beneficence are universal maxims based on Kant's categorical imperative. Humans naturally desire that others wish them well (benevolence) and would come to their aid in their need (beneficence). The duty to love is a universal law because if I expect others to be benevolent toward me, I myself must be so toward others. The maxims of benevolence and beneficence are duties we all owe to one another, although beneficence is admittedly a duty that can be satisfied only in varying degrees, considering our own needs and staying within our means (#28, 29).

Singer's Duty of Easy Rescues

In what would turn out to be an influential article, Peter Singer's 1972 essay "Famine, Affluence, and Morality" addressed the question of what affluent people's obligations were toward the populace of East Bengal who were starving at that time. He likened that obligation to pulling a drowning child from a shallow pond at little expense to us but with a ruined pair of shoes and trousers and a delay in getting to where we were supposed to be. To ignore the drowning child is to earn censure not only from others but also from our very selves. Our own moral sensibilities will make us feel guilty, and rightly so.

Singer proposes that there is a duty to prevent harm if it will not require us to sacrifice anything of comparable moral importance. Note that this does not entail a duty to promote the good. All it involves is heading off harm from befalling others, which is within our power and resources to accomplish (p. 231). This is an innate duty embedded within people's own self-understanding of what it is to be a human person. It is a minimal duty in the sense that it does not impose an undue burden. Nevertheless, some take issue with Singer's duty of easy rescues, even as others deem collective charity to be a public good itself.[18]

One Body of Christ

Christian philosophy and theology also arrive at the same point regarding the duty of universal benevolence. From the admonition to love one's neighbor as oneself, to the parable of the sheep and the goats (Mt 25: 31–46), to the parable of the Good Samaritan (Lk 10:25–37), to St. Paul's letter on the One Body of Christ (1 Cor 12), humans are one another's keeper by virtue of their common membership in the one family of God. In Christian social philosophy, part two of the principle of subsidiarity affirms that it is a moral obligation (and not merely an option) for individuals, higher bodies, or institutions to aid lower bodies or people who are no longer able to function for the common good (Pius XI 1931, #79). In Christian metaphysics, there is a twofold order of the universe in which individual creatures (including humans) contribute to the attainment of the good of the whole according to the mode of their being and operation (Wright 1957).

In sum, people voluntarily embrace their general moral duties and obligations because of their singular commitment to their fellow human beings. The beneficiaries or obligees of such beneficence extend well beyond their kin, close associates, or fellow citizens to include the distant and the stranger. People simply live up to these duties out of their sense of decency and self-respect.

---

[18] For skeptical views on Singer's duty of easy rescues, see Buchanan (1987, p. 560, fn 9). For those who deem collective charity to be a public good, see Buchanan (1987, p. 564, fn 15). See also Weinrib (1980).

Supererogation

The fourth category is that of supererogation. There are varying degrees of supererogation, from acts that surpass common practice and community expectations, to the exceedingly generous benefactions, all the way to the heroic and the saintly deeds. For simplicity of exposition, we lump all of these under a single category of supererogatory, self-sacrificial, nonobligatory beneficence.[19]

For example, some consumers voluntarily buy fair trade for their apparel, coffee, chocolate, and whatever items offer such an option despite their higher cost. Others buy voluntary carbon offsets for their use of fossil fuels when driving or taking a plane ride. People give to crowdfunding appeals of strangers even from halfway across the globe.

Many teachers buy school supplies, at their own expense, that local school districts should have provided to begin with but have not. During the pandemic lockdown, some teachers went over and above their duties to serve their students. They brought food to poor students who were reliant on the school lunch programs for their meals during the regular school year (Hernandez 2021). A Texas teacher turned her garage into a lending library for her students trapped at home, with the nearest public library 15 miles away (Chalifoux 2020). A Boston teacher turned her car into a traveling lending library for her second graders (Homan 2020).

The 2022 Russian invasion and devastation of Ukraine provide innumerable examples of such beneficence that exceeds the requirements of the law, public ethos, or customary local practice. Early in the invasion, complete strangers booked lodgings in Ukraine via Airbnb as a quick way of sending cash aid to the hapless victims of the invasion (Otis 2022). Volunteers came from all over the world to help the refugees and even fight.

Moderna pledged not to profit from the sales of its mRNA Covid vaccine to poor developing countries for the duration of the pandemic. The original Ben & Jerry's ice cream, Greystone Bakery, and other social enterprises pursued a stakeholder business model rather than the more common shareholder approach long before the recent push toward corporate social responsibility. Pharmaceutical firm Merck pledged in 1987 to give its drug Mectizan free and for as long as needed to eradicate the scourge of river blindness. Thus far, over four billion treatments have been given, with 300 million people benefitting annually from Merck's Mectizan Donation

[19] See Beauchamp (2013) for the varying degrees of supererogation. Young (2013) shows how supererogation sheds light on divine goodness.

Program (New York Times 1987). Early in the Covid-19 pandemic, before it was ravaged by the Delta variant, India pledged to distribute its vaccine production on a 50-50 split for its own use and for other poor countries.

In the Bible, we find many examples of such conduct, as in the case of the Good Samaritan (Lk 10:25–37), the vineyard owner (Mt 20:1–16), and the father of the prodigal son (Lk 15:11–32) – actions that were over and above the usual local practice and expectation. Other well-known examples are kidney donors, Warren Buffet's pledge to give the bulk of his wealth to philanthropy, and Aaron Feuerstein's treatment of his workers when Malden Mills burned down.

At the furthest end of this category are the self-sacrificial benefi-cence distinct for their exceeding generosity. This type of beneficence is extremely lavish to the point of diminishing the agency or the welfare of the benefactor or putting his/her own life goals at risk. This liberality is well beyond the means of the benefactor. It entails sacrifice and self-giving. We have examples in Raoul Gustaf Wallenberg and his use of Swedish visas to save countless Jewish lives from the Nazis' genocide. We have mis-sionaries' self-sacrifice, as in the case of St. Damian of Molokai. Recall St. Maximilian Maria Kolbe, who volunteered to take the place of a fellow prisoner selected for death in Auschwitz. Congressional Medal of Honor US Army Captain Chaplain Father Emil Kapaun, who refused to be evac-uated but chose instead to be captured to be able to minister to wounded US soldiers during the Korean War, also exemplifies heroic, saintly super-erogation. These are all driven by a supererogatory agape – well beyond what is normally seen or expected in the natural order.

Continuum of Obligatoriness

We can juxtapose justice and agape's claims side by side to identify the fault lines where they clash with one another. However, what criteria do we use in lining up these claims and doing a triage? Possible benchmarks include their obligatoriness, immediacy, strength of claims, sources, cost, or other norms of interest. As we will see in the next chapter, the most common criterion used is the distinction between perfect and imperfect duties. Perfect duties are unambiguous in specifying who owes what to whom and when. In contrast, imperfect duties are not determinate in their requirements because people have discretion in deciding when, where, and to whom to discharge these obligations as their circumstances permit.

Table 1.2 follows this common standard and lines up duties from the specific and particular to the general, that is, from perfect duties to

Table 1.2 *Continuum of obligatoriness across justice and agape*

	Justice		Agape	
			Agape as precept (As a duty)	Agape as counsel (As a moral ideal)
	Legal due	**Particular Moral Duties**	**General Moral Duties**	**Supererogation**
	Codified in law	Relational duties from bonds, ties, public ethos & common praxis	Basic duties from shared humanity & divine precept	Deep commitment; Well beyond public ethos & praxis
	External enforcement: coercive fiat	Internal enforcement; moral suasion; public naming & shaming	Internal enforcement; moral suasion	Not required, yet given with alacrity & spontaneity
	Examples	Examples	Examples	Examples
	Paying taxes	*Philautia, storge, philia*	Hume's, Kant's, & Cicero's duty of benevolence	Teachers buying school supplies for their students
	Zoning restrictions	Family child/elderly care	Duty to prevent harm	Maximilian Kolbe's self-sacrifice
	Work safety laws	Jewish *kosher* & Islamic *halal* and *zakat* norms	Care for the needy	Vineyard owner (Mt 20:1-16)
	Military draft	Good corporate citizenship	Truthfulness	
	Non-compliance: illegal act	Non-compliance: grave moral defect, serious character flaw	Non-compliance: moral deficiency	Compliance: virtuous person, praiseworthy

imperfect duties. Based on the common thinking that perfect duties are deemed to have priority over imperfect duties, Table 1.2, in effect, lines up these duties in decreasing order of obligatoriness. It arranges them in descending order of stringency, from strict legal duties (leftmost column) all the way to heroic supererogation (rightmost column). It is a gradation of duties and obligations ranked according to the strength of their claims against obligors, if any.[20]

Our first category of duties and obligations in terms of obligatoriness comprises legal dues. The next two categories are moral duties. Note that there is a continuum of moral duties – from the more stringent moral duties (arising from bonds and ties, community expectations, and common praxis) [column 2: particular moral duties] to the less stringent moral duties (beyond community expectations and praxis) [column 3: general moral duties]. Particular moral duties are much more stringent than general moral duties because in addition to the basic obligations owed to all as part of humanity, they impose additional responsibilities stemming from the community's expectations and ethos. After all, people are expected to abide by and follow the common praxis of the particular communities and various groups to which they belong, from which they draw benefits, and to which they are supposed to contribute. As we have seen earlier, these moral dues are aptly called particular moral duties to underscore their origins from the particular communities and groups from which they arise. Recall that they are also referred to as relational, primary, or *sui generis* obligations. In contrast, general moral duties arise by virtue of our duties to one another as fellow humans.

Caveat #1: Alternative Criteria

We could use alternative criteria in juxtaposing the claims of justice and agape vis-à-vis each other in Table 1.2. Two come to mind. As we have seen earlier, for Cicero and Singer, the cost of the beneficence is an important consideration. For them, the obligatoriness of an action is diminished the heavier the burden imposed on the benefactor. Thus, recall Cicero's strict

[20] Duties are sometimes distinguished from obligations. Duties arise from one's station or role in life. Thus, one has duties as a parent, as a police officer, etc. Obligations arise from commitments (Beran 1972, 216; Mish'alani 1969). Despite not being told by law to do so, people nevertheless buy voluntary carbon offsets or recycle because of their commitment to preserve the ecology. Duties are ongoing, while obligations may be one-time commitments, although people often have long-term commitments. For purposes of this study, we do not distinguish duties and obligations but use them interchangeably.

stipulation that the duty of beneficence is binding only if it is costless. Or recall Singer's qualification that there is a duty to prevent harm, but only if it does not entail the loss of comparable significant moral value on the part of the rescuer. Hence, it has been called the "duty of easy rescues." Thus, duties of agape and justice could also be lined up in the following decreasing order of obligatoriness:

No-cost beneficence > Low-cost beneficence > Costly, but affordable beneficence

The rightmost end, of course, is that of supererogation. This alternative rank ordering of duties can easily be superimposed on Table 1.2's triage. As mentioned earlier, the easier or the lower the cost of the beneficence or rescue, the more communities will expect their members to accord that to each other.

Another possible criterion is St. Thomas' distinction between legal and moral duties and their importance for the rectitude of virtues. St. Thomas distinguishes two types of moral dues. The first are those that are necessary if there is to be rectitude of virtues within the community (moral debt 1). Truthfulness, gratitude, and resistance to evil are three examples. These are indispensable and obligatory. In contrast, the second type pertains to those that are not strictly necessary for virtue to exist but will nevertheless greatly enhance such virtue (moral debt 2). These add joy and pleasantness to life. Liberality, friendship, and pleasantness are some examples.[21]

> [T]he moral due ... has two degrees. For one due is so necessary that without it moral rectitude cannot be ensured: and this has more of the character of due .... There is another due that is necessary in the sense that it conduces to greater rectitude, although without it rectitude may be ensured. This due is the concern of "liberality," "affability" or "friendship." (II-II, 80.1)

Moral debt 1 is much more stringent and demanding than moral debt 2. After all, moral debt 1 is necessary if there is to be virtue at all. In contrast, moral debt 2 merely adds to the quality of the virtue but is not essential for the virtue's existence. For St. Thomas, the degree of obligatoriness is:

legal dues > moral debts 1 > moral debts 2

Caveat #2: Overlapping Boundaries

Readers are reminded that in terms of obligatoriness, these duties form a seamless continuum. Table 1.2's division into four discrete categories is

---

[21] O'Brien (1971, vol 41, Appendix 1, 316–320) makes the distinction moral debt 1 and moral debt 2. See also Dewan (1992, 49–51) for a further elaboration of the varying degrees of *debitum* in St. Thomas.

artificial and is done only for ease of exposition. The problem with such discrete categorization arises when it comes to the boundaries of the resulting groupings. We see this difficulty, especially when it comes to our third category of general moral duties.

General moral duties are important for this study because this is where the claims of justice and agape overlap. It is also where the obligatory overlaps with the nonobligatory, the superperfecterogatory with the supererogatory.[22] This category requires careful discussion. Two questions immediately arise:

- Why does this category fall under agape if it is a moral debt? Since it is a debt, should it not fall under justice?
- Why are general moral duties a moral debt if they are beyond community praxis and expectations? Would that not make it supererogatory?

We examine each of these questions in what follows.

Why under Agape?
General moral duties fall under agape rather than justice because they go beyond community expectations and common praxis. These acts of kindness, goodness, and generosity are freely given out of empathy and a genuine concern for the well-being of our fellow humans, including the distant and the stranger. (Think of Outka's agape as equal regard.) Goodwill (benevolence) animates these deeds. They are properly classified under agape because they are motivated not by a duty imposed by the expectations, ethos, or common praxis of our local community but by sheer benevolence and a desire for the good of a fellow human. Nevertheless, such beneficence can be said to be a moral debt in a qualified manner, as we see in the next section.

Why a Moral Debt?
Why are general moral duties considered moral debts if they are beyond community expectations and exceed common praxis? As we have just seen, these are gratuitous acts freely given from one's heart. Nevertheless, they are still considered to be duties because of the basic expectations that

---

[22] Sinnott-Armstrong (2005, 204) has a threefold distinction between (1) erogatory [that which is required by perfect duties], (2) superperfecterogatory [above and beyond the call of perfect duty but not beyond imperfect duty], and (3) supererogatory [above and beyond the call of both perfect and imperfect duty]. Column 1 is erogatory, and column 3 is superperfecterogatory. Column 4 is supererogatory. Column 2 is a mix of both erogatory and superperfecterogatory.

come with being a human person – membership in the larger community of humanity and its attendant obligations. Thus, recall Cicero's duty of beneficence, Hume's duty of humanity, Kant's duty of benevolence, and Peter Singer's duty of easy rescues. Using Kant's universalizability rule, if we expect to receive assistance in our moment of need from others, we should see ourselves also readily extending to others the same kind of assistance we expect or hope from others. This is the categorical imperative – acting in such a way that the principle of one's action can be generalized for everyone else, with no exceptions. This duty stems from our common humanity – to assist others. Recall, too, the Golden Rule. Nevertheless, it is a heavily qualified duty depending on the cost it imposes on the benefactor. Thus, from a secular viewpoint, its obligatoriness is inversely proportional to the cost incurred.[23] It is a weaker duty relative to particular moral duties (column 2).

In contrast, Christian theology imbues these general moral duties with a much stronger obligatoriness (relative to its secular counterpart) because of the divine command to love one's neighbor. People owe such beneficence to one another because of God, and they are merely requiting and returning what they themselves have individually received from God. It is merely "paying forward" to other fellow humans the same favors that they themselves had received gratuitously from God. Recall the motive clauses of the Mosaic economic laws (e.g., Dt 15:15).

Thus, while this beneficence exceeds community praxis and expectations, it is nevertheless still a duty because of the divine command to love one's neighbor. This is a precept and not merely a counsel. Note, for example, the punishment in the case of those who were indifferent to the plight of their neighbors, as in the parable of the sheep and the goats (Mt 25:31–46) and in the case of Lazarus and the rich man dressed in purple (Lk 16:19–31). While there are no legal sanctions from the community for noncompliance in these biblical examples, there is nonetheless divine punishment because caring for one another is a commandment.[24] It is a divine expectation. It is the same point underscored in the letter of James. St. Paul's argument on reciprocity and mutual assistance in his collection for the poor of Jerusalem (2 Cor 8: 13–15) brings to mind Kant's universalizability rule or the Golden Rule. This is a duty as members of God's family, the One Body of Christ (1 Cor 12).

---

[23] Recall Cicero's strict standard of costless beneficence.
[24] In contrast, there is no punishment for the rich young man for not selling all he had and giving to the poor (Mk 10:17–31). This is a counsel rather than a precept.

Note the contrast between secular and Christian views on the strength of general moral obligations. For Cicero et al., costly but affordable beneficence are weak duties, at best. For Christian thought and praxis, these general moral duties are strongly binding even if they are costly, for as long as they are within the means of the benefactor. It is a duty owed to God. This is the divine precept to love our neighbor as ourselves (Lev 19:18; Mt 25:31–46).

Is there not a jarring inconsistency here? Is love not supposed to be spontaneous and freely given? It cannot be compelled or coerced. How can love (and its consequent beneficence) be commanded and thereby be made a duty, a debt?[25] Is the duty to love an oxymoron?

God can command humans to love one another because everything, including people's very existence, comes from God. God's sovereignty and creation-providence make the resulting human duty to do as God commands a matter of justice. St. Thomas classifies what is owed to God under the category of "religion," which is only a potential part of justice because humans are unable to reciprocate fully everything that God had given humans (II-II, 81). That would otherwise be commutative justice, an equality in that which is exchanged.

Humans are commanded to love God and their fellow humans.[26] Just as in the case of the Chosen People, God can ask us to be each other's keeper. This is a strong duty of justice owed to God. It is always to be observed when well within the means of the giver. Examples of this include the parable of the sheep and the goats in Mt 25:31–46, the Mosaic economic laws, and part two of the principle of subsidiarity. In contrast, the claim for love that humans can make against their fellow humans is due only to the divine precept to love one's neighbor, and not because of any rightful, meritorious rights-claims on their part. Thus, relative to God, humans' duty to love is a demand of justice (religion as a potential part of justice). However, relative to fellow humans, such a duty to love falls outside the scope of justice proper (Cicero's *iustitia*) and into the realm of agape and its concomitant beneficence.[27]

---

[25] This is over and above the duties of our natural loves, such as love for parents and family (*storge*) and love for ourselves (*philautia*).

[26] Albert Plé (1986, 343–344) views this "commandment" as more of a teaching on a way of life or on the general principles of life rather than a directive. After all, "love is spontaneous; it proceeds from the innermost personal depths of the subject."

[27] Some do not believe that there is a duty to love. For example, Bernard Gert (2005) does not hold that benevolence is a duty. For him, the only duty is the duty of nonmaleficence – to do no harm. It is a negative duty. He denies there is such thing as a positive duty – that is, the duty to act to prevent harm or to do things for others. Thus, the duty of beneficence is attached to a role in society or is assigned by institutions or cultural practice, but it is not a general obligation for all. See also Buchanan (1987) for a discussion of this issue.

We can make a further distinction using Cicero's differentiation between requiting and bestowing beneficence (I, xv [47–48]). For him, requiting beneficence is about reciprocating an act of goodness received in the past. In contrast, bestowing beneficence is a pure gratuitous gift. The former is much more stringent than the latter. And so it is when speaking of God and humans. From a theological viewpoint, we requite God's love via our love and care for our neighbors, but we bestow beneficence on our fellow humans.

One further consequence of this distinction is that humans' agape (for God or for one another) can never be supererogatory vis-à-vis God. However, humans' agape for one another can be supererogatory. Consequently, even as this affordable beneficence is still properly a moral duty (owed to fellow humans by God's command), it is nonetheless far less stringent compared to those that are low-cost and expected by public morality (column 2). Thus, costly but affordable beneficence can be called a quasi-obligatory beneficence.

A general moral duty (column 3) is an obligation of agape. This is agape as a moral duty commanded by God, a precept. Self-sacrificial beneficence (column 4) is supererogatory. That agape is an aspirational moral ideal, a counsel, to be discussed at greater length in Chapter 7.

Another Distinction: Gratuitousness

We could make one further distinction in terms of corollary obligations that are created. Kant distinguishes two types of obligations. The first type of duty is one that creates obligations on the part of the recipient. For example, love creates an obligation on the part of the recipient to reciprocate, to requite that love. These duties and obligations are beyond community expectations and praxis (the third and the fourth columns). For Kant, this duty is meritorious. In contrast, the second type of duty is one that does not create a duty to reciprocate on the part of the recipient because it is something expected, something that is owed (Kant 1991, *Metaphysics, Doctrine of Virtue*, Part II, Ch I, Sect I, #23). These duties and obligations are expected by law or community praxis (the first two columns). For example, corporations' efforts to be green in their operations do not create obligations to reciprocate on the part of their host communities because climate change mitigation is now an expected common practice, a duty for these firms to begin with.

Utility of This Continuum

This continuum of obligatoriness clarifies the nature of the clashing claims of agape and justice. It allows us to distinguish claims according to their premises, strength, and sources. The greater the degree of the duty's obligatoriness, the stronger is its claims. Undoubtedly, this is relevant for resolving such conflicts. In fact, some would argue that it is the nub of the issue. Being able to categorize the nature of the claims is also helpful in understanding what is at stake and who is at risk.

A second use of this continuum of obligatoriness is to show graphically the disparity in the relative strengths of the clashing claims. We can locate conflicts within a spectrum of obligatoriness to show the relative demands of the various clashing obligations. This continuum underscores the lop-sided strength of the claims presented respectively by agape and justice in those instances when they compete over the use of resources. It graphi-cally shows the degree of accommodation that will be needed to meet the demands of agape. It shows how much sacrifice or foregone claims will be necessary to satisfy the needs of agape.

Consider the case of the parable of the prodigal son (Lk 15:11–32). On the one hand, the older brother could claim the sore lack of proportional-ity in the father's treatment of the two sons – not even a goat for the long-suffering obedient older son versus the slaughtered fattened calf for the impudent younger son. The older son's claim is that of distributive justice based on community praxis and its ethos (column 2). In fact, the younger son's reprehensible disrespect for his father may even merit censure from the spirit of the law (Ex 20:12) (column 1). On the other hand, the father was exceedingly generous, to a fault, in his treatment of the wayward son. This reception is well beyond community expectations and common prac-tice (the finest robe, a ring on the finger, and a lavish party feasting on the fattened calf). This liberality is right on the edge of the supererogatory end of column 3. This wide disparity only goes to underscore even more the generosity of the father in his willingness to incur even more criticism from kin, neighbors, and even his older son for what would appear to many to be foolish, extravagant big-heartedness.

Third, this continuum provides a ready framework for understanding the development of moral thinking. As we will see in the next chapters, the boundaries separating these different types of duties, obligations, and beneficence shift over time. They are not fixed, but are subject to changes in society's underlying customs, law, and usage. The public's ethos evolves, and with it, the community's expectations of what constitutes acceptable conduct. Acts of beneficence move from one category to the next, gener-ally from the less stringent to the more stringent categories over time. At some point, what used to be supererogatory may become the standard community practice and the public expectation, to the point of being codified in law. As mentioned earlier, the Mosaic teachings on lending without interest, forgiving debt, and slave manumission were nomadic practices that they had practiced as a strategy for mutual survival in the face of the harsh conditions of the ancient world. These nomadic practices were eventually adopted in the Mosaic laws when Biblical Israel eventually engaged in settled agriculture (von Waldow 1970). What might have started out as supererogatory became a matter of practical necessity in reciprocal aid, which the people eventually turned into common practice. In the modern era, recall the national provision of an old-age social security safety net that Otto von Bismarck initiated in nineteenth-century Germany and that has now become an expected part of national laws in most countries (Sigerist 1999).

There was a time when debt forgiveness was an exceedingly generous, supererogatory act. In contrast, chapter 11 today puts debtors under the protection of the law. Prior to the Internet, cross-border assistance was probably deemed to be an act of liberality or supererogatory. Today, with globalization and the possibility of crowdfunding, such cross-border assistance is most likely expected – a general moral duty given our greater capacity to send aid with the click of a mouse. The provision of a universal basic income today would most likely be considered an especially generous supererogatory act. In the future, it might even be codified in law as a legal due. It is a similar case for Brazil and Mexico's successful conditional cash transfer programs. Indeed, gratuitous transfers in an earlier age eventually become legal dues for succeeding generations (e.g., social security, Medicaid, Medicare). Muhammad Yunus' supererogatory beneficent microfinance initiative among the poor in his neighborhood in the 1970s bloomed into a global phenomenon. It is now codified as a standard element in many poverty-alleviation programs for nations and multilateral institutions, such as the World Bank and the US State Department's USAID. Indeed, Table 1.2 helps account for the development of social philosophy, moral theology, and public policy as practices and expectations move toward greater obligatoriness over time. Legal duties are select moral duties that have been codified given the need for a high rate of compliance to ensure order and the smooth functioning of the community. They are essentially moral duties that have been raised to a higher level of visibility and enforcement.

Another example of this phenomenon is Stephen John Duckett's (2023) *Healthcare Funding and Christian Ethics*. His call for greater public funding for healthcare is an illustration of the shifting position of the public ethos in increasingly acknowledging the community's obligation to assist individuals in meeting this universal human need. It is, in effect, codifying this moral obligation into a legal due.

Fourth, Table 1.2's continuum of obligatoriness provides us with a rough measure of the heroic degree of people's supererogation in giving generously of themselves, even in the absence of any claims at all. We examine this in greater depth in Chapter 7, when we deal with infused agape and *caritas*.

Fifth, this continuum flags the gray areas of agape-justice conflicts when the relative strengths of the competing claims are not clear. This model highlights those clashing claims that will have to be resolved with prudential judgment and a lot of goodwill. This, in fact, is the case in most agape-justice conflicts that emerge from unattended past wrongs (Chapter 5).

Finally, this continuum shows us where the fault lines are whenever justice and agape clash in their claims. This allows us to categorize these conflicts into sub-groups with similar characteristics. This is helpful for future studies of these conflicts.

Sample Application

In the case of the parable of the vineyard owner, the earlier hires were complaining about the violation of distributive justice – the absence of proportionality in pay based on contribution, equal work for equal pay. In contrast, the vineyard owner paid the last hires according to his concern for their well-being. He was motivated by agape in his generosity. Matthew 20:1–16 is a clash between the claims of distributive justice, on the one hand, and agape, on the other hand. Looking at Table 1.3, what we have is a clash between the claims of the earliest hires who expected to be paid proportionately based on the tenets of distributive justice at that time. These fall under the quasi-lawful debt based on what we could call the informal, unspoken law of common practice (column 2). In contrast, the demands of the vineyard owner's duty of love fall under agape. His generosity goes well beyond community praxis and expectation (rightmost end of column 3). The earlier hires have very strong claims compared to the last hires, who had none. This disparity in claims underscores even more the utter generosity of the vineyard owner toward the last hires.

Consider some of the cases that the following chapters will briefly examine. How generous to make social safety nets is a perennial debate between those who call for personal responsibility and those who call for compassion. It is a clash between distributive justice and agape. Looking at Table 1.3, we see that this is a clash between the legal and moral due of personal responsibility from all (columns 1 and 2), on the one hand, and costly beneficence beyond community praxis (column 3), on the other hand. The greater the generosity in interpreting and implementing the provisions of the law, the more likely it is to be situated toward the right-most end of column 3.

The row between the advanced nations and the World Health Organization regarding vaccine distribution in the early deadly days of Covid-19 was in effect a struggle to balance the needs of one's nearest and dearest vis-à-vis the needs of the distant and the stranger. It is a tension between legal dues to one's own citizens (column 1) and moral dues to one's natural loves (*philautia, storge, philia*) (column 2), on the one hand, and agape for the distant and the stranger (columns 3 and 4), on the other hand.[28] It is a similar tension when it comes to using international trade or untied aid as a way of ameliorating poverty across the world, but at the expense of domestic workers. These are conflicts between strict legal dues (column 1) and claims from agape (columns 3 & 4).

Angela Merkel braved political backlash and eventually lost her chancellorship of Germany in opening her nation to war refugees fleeing the Syrian civil war in 2015 (Mushaben 2017). Many local citizens complained that it disrupted their local way of life and culture and put their jobs and wage growth at risk. It is a similar resentment seen in many other countries, especially when migrants make no effort to assimilate into their host communities. Migration is a contentious issue that pits the needs of local constituencies versus the needs of the displaced. This is yet another case in which national leaders must walk a fine balance between the legal dues to their own citizens and the moral dues to their natural loves (national *philautia* and *storge*), on the one hand, and compassion and agape for the noncitizen and the nonkin, on the other hand. Angela Merkel's outreach was far beyond what the law stipulated and was beyond common expectation. Table 1.3 gives us an idea of just how beneficent she was with her bold response to the crisis (column 1 versus columns 3 and possibly 4).

Countries in a debt crisis invariably must face IMF conditionality, which entails restoring macroeconomic balances in the short- to medium-term. This generally includes severe cuts to social spending.

---

[28] It goes up to column 4 – self-sacrificial supererogation – because sending vaccines and N95 masks overseas during the early deadly phase of the pandemic of scarce vaccines and medical supplies means incurring more deaths locally that could have been averted.

Table 1.3 *Sample of agape–justice conflicts*

Justice		Agape	
Legal due	**Particular Moral Duties**	**General Moral Duties**	**Supererogatory**
Codified in law	Relational obligations Community expectations	Duty of humanity Divine expectation	
		Agape as a precept	Agape as a counsel

X*-----Whether to expand social safety net expansion?------- X

X*-------Whether to share Vaccine/N95 during early, deadly Covid phase? ---------X

X*-------------Angela Merkel's 2015 welcome of Syrian refugees --------------------X

X*----------Whether to loosen IMF conditionality? ---------- X

X*----------------------Tied-in Aid -------------------------- X

X*-----------International Trade as Foreign Aid --------------- X

                   X*------Parable of vineyard owner------X

X*------Shareholder vs Stakeholder business model------------- X

X*--------Aid workers/citizens prosecuted for humanitarian assistance------------X

X* = status quo that fails to prevent an imminent harm
X = ameliorative agapic act that averts or mitigates a looming harm

The poor often bear a disproportionate share of the cost of such adjustments. Advocates note that strict adherence to long-standing bank rules and capital market practices is essential to avoid creating moral hazard problems for other fiscally negligent nations. In contrast, IMF critics call for a more humane timetable and a more accommodating approach. This is a tension between the demands of distributive justice based on law and long-standing practice in capital markets (column 1), on the one hand, and agape's call for leniency beyond standard practice (column 3), on the other hand.

Aid workers and ordinary citizens who were arrested, prosecuted, fined, or jailed for their benevolent assistance to endangered migrants in the Mediterranean, the Italian-French border, or in the Southwestern deserts of the USA lived up to their general moral duties to humanity (column 3, perhaps even 4). However, this came at the expense of violating their legal obligations (column 1).

These are but a sampling of actual cases of clashing claims between agape and justice. There are many more once we raise issues in corporate

Table 1.4 *Three fault lines*

	Justice		Agape	
Legal due	**Particular Moral Duties**		**General Moral Duties**	**Supererogatory**
Codified in law	Relational obligations Community expectations		Duty of humanity Divine expectation	

```
X------Legal vs. Moral Duties ---x---------------------- X
            X---Particular vs. General Moral Duties---X
X----------------------x-------------------------------x----Duty vs. Supererogation-------X
```

governance, social enterprises, and extra-market compensation in the following chapters. It is sufficient to note for now that Table 1.4 shows that the fault lines in conflicts between agape and justice run along one of these axes:

• Legal debt (column 1) versus moral debt (columns 2 and 3)
• Particular/relational moral duties (column 2) versus general moral duties (column 3)
  ○ Expected beneficence (column 2) versus unexpected beneficence (column 3)
  ○ Stringent moral debt (column 2) versus less stringent moral debt (column 3)
• Legal and moral debt (columns 1, 2, and 3) versus supererogatory, self-sacrificial beneficence (column 4)

In sum, justice requires; it demands. In contrast, agape does not require or demand but elicits and entices. Justice is driven by externally imposed standards, while an internal compass that works with fevered intensity for the highest good of one's beloved, the Thou, impels agape. Justice renders the moral agent accountable to the ones who set and imposed the external standards (both human and divine laws). Agape renders the moral agent answerable to God and to oneself as part of the quest to reach the heights of integral human development.

CHAPTER 2

Deference to Justice

Social philosophers, theologians, and even saints prioritize the demands of justice whenever they conflict with agape's claims. They do so based on the following implicit rules, namely:

- Perfect duties take precedence over imperfect duties.
- Subsistence test: Whatever is critical for society's existence has primacy.
- Legal debt takes priority over moral debt.

We examine each of these in what follows.

Primacy of Perfect Duties over Imperfect Duties

The strength of competing claims is partly a function of whether they are perfect or imperfect duties. The duty of justice is a perfect duty. It must always be observed. Moreover, it produces perfect correlative claim-rights. My duty to render you what I owe you creates a correlative perfect claim-right on your part to receive what is due to you from me. Justice is clear and precise as to who the obligor(s) and the obligee(s) are and what the obligor owes to the obligee. Moreover, justice specifies exactly when, how, and in what manner the obligor ought to discharge these duties owed to the obligee(s). This exactitude makes for accountability and liability in cases of nonfulfillment because there is no ambiguity as to who is at fault and what is owed.

In contrast, the duty of beneficence is an imperfect duty because it need not always be observed. Individuals are free to choose the time and the place to exercise such beneficence. It does not produce correlative claim-rights (Floyd 2009, 461–462). My duty to give alms does not mean that you have a claim-right to my benefaction. It is a virtue that cannot be extracted or forced but is given freely. One is to be beneficent, but not to anyone in particular. One need not be beneficent all the time given the finitude of our resources. People choose at their discretion when, in what manner, to whom, and how much they are to be generous to others. Even as the community expects people to be charitable toward one another, it is up to individuals to pick the time and manner of their beneficence as their circumstances permit. Imperfect duties provide their obligors wide latitude.

This distinction should not come as a surprise because of differences in the nature of justice and love. Justice is precise, not less just or more just, but simply just. In contrast, love comes in varying degrees, from genuine concern all the way to complete self-sacrifice.

Adam Smith notes the significant differences between perfect and imperfect duties and their implications for failing to discharge these obligations.

> In the Theory of Moral Sentiments, Adam Smith compared duties of humanity with duties of justice. Duties of humanity, he said, are "vague," "indeterminate," "loose," "inaccurate," filled with exceptions, impossible to learn by rules, an "ornament." Omitting them causes no "positive evil." On the other hand, duties of justice are "exact," "precise," "accurate," "exceptionless," "stricter," the "foundation" and "main pillar." The last terms in the comparison suggest that while justice is absolutely necessary, humanity [beneficence] is an optional extra. (Shaver 1992, 545)

Thus, perfect duties trump imperfect duties.[1]

Thomas Pogge (2008) admonishes advanced countries not to view their assistance to less developed countries as an act of charity and an imperfect, positive duty. Far from it. According to him, these nations' assistance is in fact a negative duty, and a perfect one at that. They should cease their practices and policies that skew global trade rules to their benefit at the expense of poor countries. Moreover, they should desist immediately. Describing their act as one of charity gives them latitude and discretion. Not so. Pogge is adamant that what is at stake is an act of justice that produces a perfect obligation.

Does the duty to aid come from love or from justice? Why does it even matter whose duty it is? It matters because the source determines the strength and urgency of the claim. The duty to aid takes precedence over the duty of benevolence because justice demands that we treat people as equals and bring them up to the level of sufficiency (duty to aid) rather than merely improve their welfare (duty of benevolence) (Igneski 2007, 328). Justice's claims are more binding because of their immediacy for the survival of society (duty to aid), while duties of love have more leeway and are viewed as discretionary (duty of benevolence).[2]

---

[1] See Buchanan (1987, 569–571) for a critique of this rule.
[2] For a critique of this customary differentiation between perfect and imperfect duties, see Campbell (1965, 285) and Rainbolt (2000, 233) for their alternative distinctions. See also Sinnott-Armstrong (2005).

The Subsistence Test

Conceptual Arguments

Cicero

For Cicero, *iustitia* must always and everywhere be satisfied because it is essential to maintaining societal order. He submits that the most basic of *iustitia*'s requirements are to do no harm and to employ common resources to promote common interests (I, vii [20]). Such a rule of law enables people to live and function together in harmony as a polity. This rule of law comes about only as community members satisfy the demands of *iustitia*. Legal dues actualize public order, the most fundamental building block of any society. In contrast, moral dues are about effecting public virtue – the qualities that make living together as a community congenial, happy, and good. Thus, he accords much greater latitude in the fulfillment of the duty of beneficence.

St. Thomas

St. Thomas differentiates a legal due from a moral due. In his discussion of the potential parts of justice, St. Thomas contrasts legal from moral debt in that the former deals with satisfying the requirements of the law, while the latter pertains to the rectitude of virtues.[3] Legal debts impose strict binding duties that carry the weight of the law. These impose stringent obligations without which the community cannot survive (e.g., payment of taxes). This is the proper realm of justice (Cicero's *iustitia*). There is immediacy to satisfying the demands of *iustitia* because a body politic is a human creation. It does not arise spontaneously from nature. As a human creation, such body politic requires both the articulation and the enforcement of clearly defined statutes, procedures, and expectations from its membership. Relative to moral dues, legal dues are precise in what they require. They create perfect duties. The difference between perfect and imperfect duties must be considered in deciding the clashing claims between agape and justice. St. Thomas notes that there is greater latitude in paying a moral debt unlike a legal debt, which must be paid when it is due. He notes, "*A legal debt must be paid at once, else the equality of justice would not be preserved*, if one kept another's property without his consent. But *a moral debt* depends on the equity of the debtor: and

---

[3] "The legal due is that which one is bound to render by reason of a legal obligation; and this due is chiefly the concern of justice, which is the principal virtue. On the other hand, the moral due is that to which one is bound in respect of the rectitude of virtue" (II-II, 80.1).

therefore it *should be repaid in due time according as the rectitude of virtue demands"* (II-II, 106.4.ad 1, emphasis added).

Adam Smith et al.

The social philosophers of the Enlightenment subscribed to what may be called the *subsistence test*, which states that the strictness of an obligation depends on whether it is necessary for the subsistence of society (Shaver 1992, 552). We could reformulate this and say that the strength of an obligation's claims is a function of how important it is for the existence, survival, and growth of the community.

In section II-II.1 of his *Theory of Moral Sentiments*, Adam Smith specifically contrasts the virtues of justice and beneficence (humanity). Beneficence adds to the quality of life and happiness of all in the community. People laud those who treat others in such a manner, and they may think ill of those who do not. Nevertheless, people cannot demand this virtue from one another, nor can anyone be penalized for its nonobservance. In contrast, the virtue of justice does not produce the same felicity as beneficence. Nonetheless, people expect this virtue from one another. People are punished for its violation. One difference, of course, stems from how justice gives rise to a perfect duty in contrast to beneficence's imperfect duty.

These critical differences led Smith to conclude that despite the joy and happiness that beneficence effects, society can nevertheless exist without it, although a bit cheerless. For him, the virtue of justice can singlehandedly still sustain society even in the absence of beneficence.

> Where the necessary assistance is reciprocally afforded from love, from gratitude, from friendship, and esteem, the society flourishes and is happy. All the different members of it are bound together by the agreeable bands of love and affection, and are, as it were, drawn to one common centre of mutual good offices.
>
> But though the necessary assistance should not be afforded from such generous and disinterested motives, *though among the different members of the society there should be no mutual love and affection, the society, though less happy and agreeable, will not necessarily be dissolved. Society may subsist* among different men, as among different merchants, from a sense of its utility, *without any mutual love or affection*; and though no man in it should owe any obligation, or be bound in gratitude to any other, *it may still be upheld by a mercenary exchange of good offices according to an agreed valuation.* (Smith 1790, II-II.III, emphasis added)

In contrast, the community cannot do without justice. It immediately disintegrates without it.

> Society, however, cannot subsist among those who are at all times ready to
> hurt and injure one another. The moment that injury begins, the moment
> that mutual resentment and animosity take place, all the bands of it are
> broke asunder, and the different members of which it consisted are, as it
> were, dissipated and scattered abroad by the violence and opposition of
> their discordant affections. If there is any society among robbers and mur-
> derers, they must at least, according to the trite observation, abstain from
> robbing and murdering one another. *Beneficence, therefore, is less essential*
> *to the existence of society than justice. Society may subsist, though not in the*
> *most comfortable state, without beneficence; but the prevalence of injustice must*
> *utterly destroy it.* (Smith 1790, II-II.III, emphasis added)

Justice is indispensable for there to be any community at all because it
prevents a descent to a Hobbesian state of nature in which might is right.
Justice is the glue that holds the social contract together. Unless the social
contract is enforceable and enforced, there is no reason for people to stay
in it. To put it bluntly, Smith contrasts emphatically the ornamental function of beneficence versus the foundational role of justice.

> It [beneficence] is *the ornament which embellishes, not the foundation which*
> *supports the building,* ... Justice, on the contrary, is the main pillar that
> upholds the whole edifice. If it is removed, the great, the immense fabric
> of human society, ... must in a moment crumble into atoms. In order to
> enforce the observation of justice, therefore, Nature has implanted in the
> human breast that consciousness of ill-desert, those terrors of merited pun-
> ishment which attend upon its violation. (Smith 1790, II-II.III, emphasis
> added)

Smith argues that this differential importance is embedded within natural law itself in that those who fall short of their duties of justice merit
punishment but not so for those who do not live up to their duties of
beneficence. The duty of beneficence is optional, while the duty of justice
is imperative.

Robert Shaver (1992, 545) views the *Wealth of Nations* as Smith's further
extension of this point. Indeed, the brewer, the baker, and the butcher
were not being beneficent but were acting out of their own self-interest
when they inadvertently promoted the good of all by provisioning the
community of its needs. The invisible hand did not seem to require beneficence, but it definitely needed the virtue of justice to ensure that the baker,
brewer, and butcher kept at their craft.

Hugo Grotius, Samuel von Pufendorf, Lord Kames, and John Stuart
Mill all argue along the lines of Smith's differentiation between justice
and benevolence. Justice creates perfect duties that are necessary for the
existence of society. The duty of justice is essentially an obligation not to

harm anyone. This is the most fundamental tenet of any community. In contrast, beneficence produces imperfect duties that simply improve existence. While the beneficent person may win the affection of others, the just person will nevertheless be considered just and moral, even without the affection of others (Shaver 1992, 551; Schneewind 1987, 141).[4] The duty of justice is an existential matter and supersedes the duty of beneficence.

Even the staunchest advocates of a duty of benevolence affirm the priority accorded to justice. As we will see in the next chapter, David Hume disagrees with Adam Smith's conclusion that society can subsist only on justice (Shaver 1992). For Hume, the duty of humanity (benevolence) is also a necessary building block of community. Nevertheless, despite his vigorous defense of this duty, he is silent on whether the duty of humanity supersedes the duty of justice. While he does not concede the priority of justice, he does not close the door to such a possibility. In fact, Hume himself acknowledges that society cannot exist without justice.

> Hume argues that failures of justice can lead to the demise of society, that justice is "absolutely requisite to the well-being of mankind and existence of society," and that justice is "of all circumstances the most necessary to the establishment of human society, and that after the agreement for the fixing and observing of this rule, there remains little or nothing to be done towards settling a perfect harmony and concord" … for Hume "while all the positive virtues are an 'extra' which makes society flourishing and happy, social life is quite possible without them, but … there can be no society without justice." (Shaver 1992, 555)

Kames is critical of Hume for failing to distinguish between what is necessary (justice) and what is meritorious (beneficence). For those who privilege the claims of justice over agape, justice is necessary, while agape is merely meritorious (Shaver 1992, 555). The necessary has priority over the meritorious.

Kant (1991) also articulates a duty of beneficence. This is understandable and expected considering his categorical imperative. Nevertheless, he acknowledges the difference between the perfect nature of justice's duty and beneficence's imperfect duty. Furthermore, unlike Hume, Kant explicitly rank orders the claims of justice and beneficence relative to each other in the event of conflict. He accords priority to the duty of justice, which, after all, is a perfect duty to begin with and having always to be observed.

---

4 Observe that in contrasting the duty of justice and the duty of beneficence, Adam Smith et al. believe they are drawing from natural law. For example, they compare the visceral reaction of people vis-à-vis those among them who are deficient in either virtue.

Humans must work together if they are to be effective collectively. However, large-scale coordinated action does not arise naturally. It requires deliberate and well-thought-out action, culminating in the promulgation and enforcement of positive law.

> It begins with the facts agents do not naturally coordinate their use of things and yet require coordinated conditions of use to act effectively. To meet this need, the first principle of right secures the moral idea of positive law: that a part of morality (the conditions and norms of externally free action) is to be worked out in terms of civic order and legal sanction. These conditions make the institutions of property and contract morally possible, and provide a framework for institutional rules that dictates their consistency with the (external) freedom of all. (Herman 2001, 236)

St. Vincent de Paul

St. Vincent de Paul, in a letter (June 27, 1659) to Jean Barreau, a confrere who was the consul in Algiers, seems to be responding to an inquiry about the permissibility of using restricted funds for charity.

> I thank His Divine Goodness that, [by His grace], you have maintained [all your influen]ce with the slaves, for whom you h[ave so much charity]. It is of the utmost importance for [you to be careful] always to do the same. [Avoid] diverting sums of money for anything other than the int[ention for which] they have been sent to you. [Do not take] from one to give to the other, [but keep for] each one what belongs to him so that you [will be in a position to] give it to him whenever he wishes. *The ob[ligations of] justice have priority over those of c[harity].* (Vincent de Paul 1997 [CCD:VII:633], emphasis added)[5]

One cannot be beneficent at the expense of justice. In the event of having to choose being either charitable or just, as seems to be the case in this correspondence, justice takes precedence. This is yet another illustration of how perfect duties trump imperfect obligations.

Reinhold Niebuhr

In his book *Love and Justice*, Reinhold Niebuhr tackles the issue head-on. He is unwavering, indeed passionate, in his position that justice must take priority over charity. For him, the ethic of Jesus is perfectionism. It is unrealistic and unachievable in actual life (1) because of self-interest and sinfulness at the individual level and (2) because such individual sinfulness and selfishness are compounded and magnified in collective self-interest.

[5] The letter is partially torn, which accounts for why there are gaps that Vincentian scholars and archivists had to fill. My thanks to Vincentians James Claffey and Robert Maloney for this material.

The most that can be hoped for is to approximate these ideals. However, they cannot be achieved in their fullness. Niebuhr gives many examples of how unrealistic it is to expect to operate fully out of love, as Protestant liberalism tells us. The whole point of justice is to counter these selfish tendencies and inclinations. Human existence is littered with sin and brokenness. We must be honest, clear-eyed, and realistic in acknowledging this. Ours is a world that needs to be restrained by the demands of justice, and it is far from the ideals of love. We cannot expect moral suasion and love to solve very real social problems (Niebuhr 1957, 29–41).

> It is just this kind of realism that the church has been failing to supply in the social struggle .... [W]hat a world of nature this human world is and how necessary it is and remains to establish basic justice in it by the contest of interest with interest .... Moral idealists are incapable of recognizing that fact. They will *live under the illusion that they can be so unselfish that they will be able to grant other people justice without any pressure on the part of the latter.* (Niebuhr 1957, 42, emphasis added)

For Niebuhr's Christian realism, achieving justice is messy because it entails the shoving and pushing of one interest versus another. This is the reality of the marketplace. It is neither antiseptic nor clearly defined by right or wrong. It is a chaotic place of never-ending conflicting claims.

For Niebuhr (1957, 26), philanthropy is lower than the highest form of justice. After all, philanthropy is given to those unable to make claims, while justice acknowledges that others do have a claim on us. Philanthropy connotes and projects power, prestige, and preeminence in rank, while justice is a humble acknowledgment that we owe something to those who can make a legitimate claim on us.

In his book *Agape and Eros*, Anders Nygren concludes that agapic love is extended to all and is therefore oblivious to justice. Agape trumps justice. Niebuhr takes a diametrically opposed position by noting that justice trumps agape. One cannot ignore the realities of the world in which we live. Agapic love is possible only in the Messianic age. Christian realism must acknowledge the reality of sin and its destructive power. Society will not be viable at all if agapic love were to be oblivious to justice, as Nygren suggests. Justice takes priority over agape because the world is mired in so much injustice (Wolterstorff 2011, 62–74). Many contemporary social philosophers hold that justice is obligatory and all else is optional, including agape (Shaver 1992, 546, fn 3).

H.L.A. Hart
H.L.A. Hart (1961, 168–176) differentiates legal from moral rules and obligations in terms of their importance. He measures importance according

to the personal sacrifice entailed or what is asked of individuals to curtail, the effort to communicate the rules and ensure conformity, and the dire consequences that will follow with noncompliance. In general, legal obligations surpass moral obligations in these areas. Legal duties were erstwhile moral duties that have now been codified and made enforceable with accompanying sanctions for noncompliance. Evidently, there is a communal desire for a much higher compliance rate among the population. Enacting legal duties requires much work and coordination, in addition to generating debate and disagreements. Thus, legal duties would not be lightly promulgated unless the subject obligations are deemed to be essential to the community as to warrant the time, effort, and contentious discussions in codifying these and making them mandatory, rather than simply leaving them uncodified and up to the individual's voluntary compliance. In other words, legal dues carry much greater heft.

Practical Role of Justice in the Economy

As mentioned in the Preface, most agape-justice conflicts transpire in socioeconomic life because of the competing demands for its finite resources. The arguments presented thus far by social philosophers, theologians, and economists have been theoretical in nature. Do economic history and empirical evidence bear them out? Can the economy function without justice? What is the practical role of justice in the economy?

It is not surprising for Adam Smith et al. to emphasize the importance of justice. Justice is indeed important, a necessary foundation for social life. This is particularly true in economic life, in which there is fierce competition, limited resources, unlimited wants, and the zero-sum phenomenon. Justice is a necessary condition. The economy would otherwise descend into chaos.

Justice and the Institutional Preconditions of Markets

Enforcement and the rule of law: Justice is entirely dependent on its underlying formal and informal laws that specify what is due to people. Laws, no matter how well written, are only as good as their execution and enforcement, which are the functions of justice. No community, or market for that matter, can exist without the rule of law. Cicero repeatedly stresses in *De Officiis* that justice is essential for the conservation of organized society (e.g., I, v [15]) and the fulfillment of past obligations assumed. For him, the "common bonds" of people unravel without justice. Enforcement is the most fundamental role of justice. Justice is self-policing and catches instances of injustice according to its underlying statutes. Justice holds people accountable.

Allocation and distribution: Allocation-distribution of burdens and benefits is at the heart of socioeconomic life. Justice is about giving people their due or assigning them their duties. This is multifaceted: to whom to give, what to give, how much to give, when to give, in what manner, and for how long to give. Justice gives a rudimentary structure (a skeletal framework, so to speak) that holds together a complex, chaotic, and often messy set of interpersonal exchanges transpiring simultaneously across various levels – familial, local, national, and global. Not surprisingly, even staunch advocates of laissez-faire capitalism acknowledge the need for institutional pre-conditions, such as the rule of law, if markets are to exist at all. Moreover, the efficacy of market operations will be a function of the quality of these institutions. Certainly, justice rather than benevolence or agape plays the central role in this regard because it ensures that people get their due.

Economic goals: Allocative efficiency is the principal goal that markets pursue by their nature. After all, they allocate merely according to the price mechanism and the parties' purchasing power. Communities choose the criteria that govern the allocation of shared resources among their members. Besides allocative efficiency, other overarching goals of the economy that the community triages are equity, need, harmony, growth, stability, and sustainability. Distributive justice implements the criteria set by the community. Its task is the orderly distribution of scarce communal resources according to the standards set by the community. In other words, justice serves as the enforcer of the community's will. On its own, the marketplace is unable to do so because it is not designed for such a function. As mentioned earlier, this is the role of its underlying legal institutions.

Exchange and justice: Commutative justice is at the core of economic morality. Economic life is at its heart founded on economic exchanges or transfers. As mentioned earlier, commutative justice is about parity in economic agents' exchange with one another. This is particularly so in the modern economy of equality in exchange in contrast to reciprocity in earlier times. People will trade with one another only if they feel that the transactions are fair. Aggrieved market participants will ultimately lead to the decline, even the disintegration, of the marketplace for want of participants. The perception of fairness in exchange is a necessary condition if there is to be a market at all. Socioeconomic life can be peaceful and sustainable only if people see equity in the exchanges they have effected and received in the marketplace. Commutative justice provides such standards and expectations.

Governance: Beyond the marketplace, justice is an important instrument of "Leviathan" in preventing descent into a Hobbesian state of nature in which people are at war with everybody else, and mutual predation is the norm. It is a shared vision of justice that allows people with differing visions of the good to live together in harmony. Justice is at the heart of any social contract. Its enforcement determines whether such a social contract endures. Rule of law (justice's forte) is a necessary condition if governance is to be sustainable and credible.

Justice and Collective-Action Problems

Collective-action problems pertain to the difficulty of reaching the best mutually beneficial outcome for all parties either because of the lack of a formal mechanism for people to coordinate their actions or because of the incentive to free-ridership. An example of the first instance is the case of people choosing which side of the road to drive. Unless set by an authority, large groups of people will find it difficult to coordinate their driving. Note, too, the traffic chaos that ensues when traffic lights do not function during power failures. Another example is the recent problem of convincing people and nations to wear masks, to socially distance, and to be vaccinated to cut off the transmission of the Covid-19 virus and prevent a further mutation. The millions of avoidable Covid deaths worldwide are an indictment of people's inability to work together. Without a credible central global or national authority, getting to the optimal arrangement in fighting the pandemic will be difficult, if even possible at all.

A second instance of collective-action problems is the case of the prisoner's dilemma or Hardin's (1968) tragedy of the commons.[6] The optimum solution is for people to cooperate with one another. The problem arises if individuals gain by going it alone. In such a case, others will be less inclined to work together, and everybody ends up being worse off.

In both instances of collective-action problems, justice and its underlying rule of law play an important role in getting around these hurdles for everyone's mutual benefit. Consider the following examples.

---

[6] Prisoner's dilemma is the phenomenon whereby individuals choose a sub-optimal outcome by pursuing their own interest despite knowing that cooperating with others produces a much better outcome for all. The "tragedy of the commons" is where the communal fields are overgrazed because individual farmers have no incentive to curtail voluntarily their own herd's use of these fields.

Cross-border exchange: With the benefit of hindsight, most economists agree that the protectionist response of nations to the Great Depression only deepened and prolonged the economic malaise of the interwar years (e.g., US Smoot–Hawley Tariff Act). Nations closed their borders to each other's goods to shore up their domestic employment. In response, the United States took the lead in setting up a rules-based global marketplace to ensure that this mistake was avoided in the post–World War II era. The General Agreement on Trade and Tariffs (GATT) and its replacement, the World Trade Organization (WTO), led nations to mutually beneficial cross-border exchanges of goods, services, and even capital. This rules-based mechanism created a vibrant global marketplace that led to the greatest boom in economic history with its string of economic miracles, from war-torn Japan to the Asian Tigers and then to China. The much-touted global economic integration that has lifted hundreds of millions out of poverty would not have been possible at all without people and nations feeling that they get their due from the global marketplace. Rules and their enforcement (justice) matter, and they matter enormously as we have seen from empirical evidence.

Global commons: In contrast to the orderly success of global international trade in the post–World War II era, note the tragedy of the global commons that is unfolding. The oceans are heavily polluted with plastic to the point where micro-plastics are now in the food chain and are commonly detected in major body organs and even in newborns. Fish stocks are dangerously depleted because of overfishing by industrial fleets. Climate change continues to wreak havoc via extreme weather events. These troubles reveal a serious collective-action problem. Collective-action problems arise because it is not clear to all the parties involved what they will get from cooperation versus going it alone. This is the consequence of not knowing or not being able to enforce what is due to people. Justice is essential in preventing what has been widely called the problem or the tragedy of the commons (Hardin 1968). Our current problems in the global commons reveal the importance of the rule of law, with justice as its enforcer.

Justice and Market Protection

Economic guardrails and blocked exchanges: The marketplace does not second-guess people's economic decisions. Markets consummate exchanges for as long as the buyer has the purchasing power to effect the exchange and the seller is in possession of the good or the service to be sold. Markets do not evaluate whether the good or the service should be provided, exchanged, or consumed at all. Whether the good or service is harmful to begin with is not a concern for the marketplace. *Caveat emptor, caveat venditor* (Buyer beware, seller beware). Justice prevents people from getting what is not their due or what ought not to be their due. For example, local laws direct legal institutions to slap sin taxes on alcohol, tobacco, and sugary drinks. These taxes are meant to change personal behavior into more healthful choices. Justice blocks problematic exchanges, such as the sale of public office, of one's kidney or other major body organs, or of oneself or others as slaves. Justice provides guardrails for blocked exchanges (Sandel 2012).

Market destruction: Justice prevents the destruction of markets because of asymmetric information or power among their participants. The classic problem of the market for lemons (Akerlof 1970) is a case in point. Used car sellers know the true condition of the vehicles they sell, in contrast to buyers, who have limited knowledge about the quality of the pre-owned vehicle they are buying until they have bought and driven it. Unscrupulous sellers take advantage of this asymmetric information at the expense of unwary buyers. However, this situation is unsustainable because word eventually gets around that used car dealers sell "lemons." This becomes a self-reinforcing phenomenon because wary buyers will offer lower prices even as people with used cars in good working condition will not want to sell to these dealers. This is the destruction or the severe curtailment of the market for used cars because it has turned into a "market for lemons." Five years after the publication of George Akerlof's path-breaking study, Congress enacted "Federal lemon laws" that provide buyers with recourse. Local communities followed suit. Justice prevents the destruction of markets because of its systemic problems.

Related to this is the problem of fraud and market destruction. Markets are fraught with incomplete, imperfect, and even fraudulent information, unlike the perfect knowledge of the hypothetical perfectly competitive markets. Suppliers and manufacturers mislead people with partial or even erroneous information. Fake goods, postings, and reviews abound on online platforms. The proliferation of fake KN95 masks on Amazon.com during the Covid-19 pandemic led to the creation of alternative shopping sites for masks that vetted sellers. Markets are destroyed or greatly diminished if participants cannot be trusted. Not surprisingly, online platforms have been generous with their return policies. Herein is the role of justice once again in ensuring that people get their due.

Capital markets are especially prone to fraudulent information or unfair practices, which, if left unaddressed, lead to these markets' rapid destruction. The Enron Scandal of 2001, the Bernard Madoff Ponzi scheme discovered in 2008, the Theranos medical-testing device fraud revealed in 2016, the collapse of the cryptocurrency exchange FTX in 2022, and the perennial problem of insider trading are cases that underscore the inherent vulnerability of markets – they are heavily reliant on participants' word of honor. Reparative and restorative justice provide relief and recovery to victims. This assurance keeps capital markets viable. Not surprisingly, the Securities and Exchange Commission sets strict reportorial requirements for publicly listed firms. Note, too, the Sarbanes–Oxley Act in the wake of the scandals of the early 2000s. Justice protects markets' integrity. Justice compensates for imperfect or incomplete information in the marketplace.

Asymmetric bargaining power and market destruction: Besides information, asymmetric power can also destroy markets. Dodgy businesses ignore consumer grievances for their shoddy services or goods. Financial institutions impose onerous conditions or one-sided contracts on retail consumers who put up with these impositions because they desperately need such services (e.g., credit card, check-cashing services). To mitigate this problem, the Federal government established the Federal Trade Commission and, more recently, the Consumer Financial Protection Bureau. These are yet further illustrations of the practical role of justice in shoring up and restoring the credibility of markets. Big Tech holds enormous power over people's personal data and the information shared and posted online. Governments have had to step in and legislate safeguards against these firms' misuse of data and their unwillingness to moderate social media content. Justice levels the playing field.

Competition and anti-trust: Survival of the fittest is the logic of capitalism. Successful market participants accumulate ever more resources and power and eventually absorb the weaker players. This is part of the much-touted allocative efficiency of markets – placing scarce resources in the hands of those able to put them to their best use. Unfortunately, an unintended consequence of this dynamic is market concentration. Nevertheless, capitalism can defend itself through anti-trust legislation. Justice and its underlying statutes protect markets from self-destruction and safeguard the competition that is at the heart of the market's dynamic "creative destruction."

Justice and Market Creation

During the Commercial Age of the pre-Modern era, merchants quickly realized that they could not finance or bear the entire risk all by themselves for outbound inter-continental trading journeys. The peril of losing a single ship to piracy or severe weather could wipe out their entire life savings. Thus was born the limited-liability corporation, in which people could pool their resources together to fund projects that would have been too big or too risky for any single person to undertake (Harris 2020). Such cooperative risk sharing was possible only because participants believed in the statutes governing such joint undertakings and their enforceability. In other words, justice allows for risk-taking that otherwise would not have been possible. This is an instance of justice paving the way for market creation. This role of justice continues to this day, as seen daily in the international global capital markets. Justice allows for large-scale cooperative ventures (IPOs and public corporations) that could not have been pursued without the assurance that justice and its standards provide.

Foreign direct investment: Foreign direct investments are vital for any local economy, but especially for poor communities and countries. This type of investment opens the door to jobs, international markets, skills, technology, and access to credit, among many other benefits. Empirical evidence shows that there will be under-investment if contracts are unenforceable, under-enforced, or expensive to enforce (Văduva 2008). Justice guarantees such enforcement, but only to the extent that the laws are on the books, and there is a bureaucracy able and willing to enforce them. Once again, we see the practical difference that justice can make on the ground.

Justice and Market Outcomes

Taking responsibility: Justice compels people, both as individuals and as a community, to take responsibility for market processes and outcomes. For example, tort laws compel people and firms to be careful in their provision of goods and services. Property owners ensure that they keep up with maintenance and safety precautions to prevent injuries for residents or passersby. Sin taxes on cigarettes, alcohol, and sugary drinks partially compensate the community for the added healthcare costs due to these products. The continual need to evaluate fairness in a fast-changing marketplace and to revisit current standards of justice provides excellent occasions for people to take individual and collective ownership for the marketplace. For example, legislators constantly adjust emissions standards, oil drilling in ecologically sensitive areas, and gasoline-ethanol mandates. Constantly shifting markets mean that people are directly affected by the resulting redistribution of burdens and benefits. Most have a direct and immediate interest in changing market processes and outcomes, and many people will act to effect such change. Collective oversight of justice and its standards provides occasions for civic engagement and political dialogue, although they can admittedly also be a source of division.

Diagnostic tool: Justice serves as an early warning sign of things that may have gone awry in market operations beyond the guidelines set by customs, law, and usage (CLU). Justice provides a ready set of standards that facilitate such moral reflection by identifying the "dues" that people ought to get but do not. For example, citizens and NGOs have won court cases that hold to account the United States and the EU for their laxity, failure, or wrong implementation of environmental laws meant to protect the health and safety of their citizens (Erickson 2017; Quell 2021). The bipartisan US law *No Child Left Behind* (2002) held local school districts accountable for their students' lagging performance. This was an effort to close the achievement gap between well-off and underprivileged children. Justice and its underlying CLU ensure that citizens have recourse in compelling national and local governments to give citizens their due.

Human rights protection: Justice restrains economic life from its dehumanizing tendencies. Left on their own and operating only by their own rules, markets will deal with humans merely as labor, and no differently from the way capital, raw materials, credit, and so on are treated as factors of production. Without restraints, markets will view humans merely as economic agents – as potential customers, partners, or investors, who might provide profitable exchange. They will treat people as means rather than as ends. They will exclude and marginalize people who do not have the requisite purchasing power or useful skills to contribute. Unrestrained markets will dehumanize people. Justice provides extra-market mechanisms for correcting markets from their amoral[7] feature. Justice defines the lines that markets may not cross. We have empirical evidence for this by looking at the abuses and appalling working conditions during the early stages of the Industrial Revolution prior to the enactment of protective social legislation and their enforcement. Justice is a necessary condition if human rights are to be upheld. Note, for example, the importance of labor market regulations, including health and safety standards.

Justice brings to the fore the reality of social structures themselves as sources of injustice. The marketplace is supported by social structures that are vital and at the heart of its operations. Social justice calls for the reform

---

[7] I use "amoral" to mean that markets are not concerned with the rightness or wrongness of economic transactions.

of these structures when they become problematic. For example, the Community Reinvestment Act promulgated by the US Federal government in 1977 compels financial institutions to serve the credit and banking needs of low-income communities that they had avoided all along for want of profits. Developing countries have had to enact similar laws to compel their financial institutions to serve money-losing rural and agricultural sectors. Even poor and low-income people are entitled to access credit and financial services. Other examples include anti-discrimination laws in hiring, school admission, or the awarding of contracts.

Agape Needs Justice

Justice serves agape in many critical areas. First, justice is an indispensable guide for agape when it comes to issues related to allocation. Clinton Gardner (1957, 217–219) presents a particularly good example of this in his exposition of the parable of the Good Samaritan. Meeting the needs of the victim on the roadside was not a problem because there was only one. However, had there been two of them and he had the resources to assist only one but not both, then this is where agape and justice will have to work in tandem to arrive at the fullness of agape in such a situation. Justice will be helpful in knowing how to divide the resources on hand and, as a result, satisfy the moral demands of agape.

As mentioned earlier, Anders Nygren argues that agape is oblivious to justice. It is indiscriminate in extending its solicitous care. This is most likely possible only when talking about agape and justice in the abstract. Nygren's position is difficult to hold in practice because we must deal with third-party effects (externalities), not to mention the accumulative costs that will inflict real injustice or adverse consequences against love. For example, overly generous social welfare can spawn injustice by imposing undue burdens on taxpayers. Given the fluidity of social life and its many zero-sum phenomena, the community constantly adjusts the distribution of burdens and benefits among its members precipitated by agapic acts, as in the case of tax-funded, generous social safety nets. Justice and its standards are important for this task.

Second, structures of justice are needed because we cannot realistically live on love alone, not even in the Church or as a family. We also need the foundational structures provided by justice. For example, among the early Christians, despite their agape and *koinōnia* (fellowship) that enabled them to hold everything in common (Acts 4:32), they nevertheless encountered problems of allocation. The Greeks complained that their widows were not properly cared for (Acts 6:1), thereby leading to the appointment of deacons to ensure fairness and better service. This is an example of justice at work. It has a practical function to it. Niebuhr (1953, 451) notes that justice is not about "'eternal norms to which life must perennially conform' but pertains rather to 'ad hoc efforts to strike a balance between the final moral possibilities of life and the immediate and given realities'."[8] Note that since justice shapes the "ad hoc" structures and rules through which love has to operate, it is all the more important to have a hand in how these public norms of justice are formed. (We will examine this in the next chapter on value formation.) If justice provides the practical rules of society, it is love that provides the ultimate norms of justice (Gardner 1957, 220–222). This is yet another example of agape and justice working as a tandem.

Third, justice is an instrument of love. Justice sensitizes us at the individual level to the needs of our neighbors. Then, justice also shows us how to extend such sensitivity from an individual neighbor to a group and then even to the entire community. Moreover, justice facilitates the comparison of people's differing responses to meeting each other's needs. It provides an occasion for dialogue within the community.[9]

Finally, agape is prone to a moral hazard problem. Justice is helpful in this regard. Love imbues people with laudable virtues, such as commitment, internalized norms, empathy, and many others, as we will see in the next chapter. Nevertheless, it would be naïve to think that all members in the community are animated by agape. This is a vulnerability of love because it opens the door to all sorts of moral hazard problems whereby people take advantage of the generous accommodation of those who act according to love. Herein is an important function of justice in mitigating the limitations of love.

St. Paul provides a good example of this contribution of justice to love. Despite his hymn of love (1 Cor 13) in which he lauds its longsuffering nature, St. Paul is nevertheless hard-nosed enough to know that there are necessary limits to such compassion. In his second letter to the Thessalonians (2 Thess 3:10–12), he reprimands those who refuse to work and then instructs the community not to feed these people. Paul notes that such sloth harms the rest of the community because its scarce resources are diverted from those who genuinely need such aid. Moreover, through gainful employment, idlers could have been earning income that could have been used to aid others. This is not a one-off example from Paul. He

---

[8] Gardner (1957, 221)
[9] Gardner (1957, 217–219) discussing Niebuhr's Gifford Lectures.

is also adamant that widows should be supported by their families and not be put in the charge of the community, whose resources are best used for those who are truly bereft of any support (1 Tim 5:1–16). In his Jerusalem collection for the poor, Paul encourages the faith communities to be generous, but not to the point of impoverishing themselves. St. Paul is clear-eyed about how justice is a necessary condition for love.

St. Paul is not alone in this hard realism and appreciation for justice's critical role in protecting love at its most vulnerable points. Chapter 12 of the *Didache* acknowledges the moral obligation of extending hospitality. Nevertheless, it also stresses the duty to be intelligent and critical in providing such hospitality so as not to be abused. Anyone asking to stay with the community beyond two or three days of hospitality must work and not be idle.

Doctors without Borders is remarkable for its agape, the equal regard for all that makes it embark on even the most dangerous missions. Nevertheless, even *Doctors without Borders* has set rules that it imposes on combatants and errant nations to allow for its effective assistance. Even *Doctors without Borders* has withdrawn from the neediest situations when the minimum conditions it requires are violated.[10] We find similar requirements in charitable programs run by NGOs and religious communities. Mexico and Brazil impose requirements on needy recipient families in their conditional cash transfer programs. Workfare has been made an integral part of welfare entitlements in some communities. These are all cases in which policies cannot be based entirely on agape alone. There is also a need for justice.

Justice prevents love from being abused by opportunists. This is important because love's work on the ground would otherwise not be sustainable. Many have likened it to a hard head bringing discipline and rigor to a soft heart. Justice ensures that love, for all its mercy and compassion, nevertheless calls for accountability. St. Thomas describes justice without love as cruelty, while love without justice is blindness, irresponsible, or hurtful sentimentality (Perricone 2012, 71).

Love is the fulfillment of and never a replacement of justice (Gardner 1957, 214–217). "[J]ustice is the matter that individuates love" (Mongeau 2013, 296). Justice cannot be merely subsumed under love because justice has its own unique set of contributions and independent claims to make (Porter 2002). After all, as we will see later, grace builds on nature and does not substitute for it or destroy it.

---

[10] See, for example, their withdrawal from Cameroon. www.doctorswithoutborders.org/latest/msf-forced-withdraw-teams-cameroons-north-west-region last accessed April 18, 2022.

In sum, both economic history and praxis validate the Enlightenment philosophers' subsistence test for justice. Justice is essential to the workings of the marketplace. It is indeed foundational.

Summary and Conclusions

There is no consensus on how to settle agape-justice conflicts. It is still an unsettled question. Nevertheless, there is a predisposition to privilege justice because of its perfect duties compared to agape's imperfect duties. For St. Thomas, there is a descending order of obligatoriness: legal debts, moral debts 1, and moral debts 2. For Kant, justice's perfect duties must always be satisfied, while moral debts' imperfect duties may be satisfied as circumstances permit. Moreover, justice is foundational if any community is to exist at all. In fact, even defenders of agape also defer to justice when the two come into conflict. For example, Hume defends the duty of humanity as a necessary condition for justice, but then, not even Hume closes the door to justice taking precedence over love. Wolsterstoff (2011) unites love with justice in his care agapism. In cases of conflict, the presumption is to accord priority to the demands of justice relative to agape's claims. Of course, the assumption here is that the laws that justice implements or enforces are morally valid. After all, laws themselves are often unjust or immoral (e.g., slavery, segregation, apartheid).

CHAPTER 3

Agape in the Marketplace

Introduction

Justice is based on laws and rights to determine what is due; agape is based on friendship. In what follows, we summarize laws, rights, and their enforcement mechanisms as *customs, law, and usage* (CLU) to include informal laws, the public ethos, and long-standing practices since these are also significant determinants of what is due to people. Justice only implements instructions it receives from CLU. Consequently, justice is only as good as its underlying CLU. For all its contributions to making the marketplace work as we have seen from the preceding chapter, justice is nevertheless limited in critical areas of socioeconomics that affect the quality of life.

The economy cannot run on justice alone, *pace* Adam Smith et al. David Hume argues that agape is needed if there are to be virtuous and just people to begin with. This chapter extends Hume's argument by showing that the nature of the economy itself requires agape. In other words, agape is just as foundational as justice for the existence, proper functioning, and sustainability of socioeconomic life. In the same way that justice has a crucial function in the marketplace, agape also has its unique and important role to play. The marketplace, especially its modern variant, requires the tandem of agape and justice working together if it is to exist at all, much less thrive. We see this in the following essential areas that shape the character and quality of socioeconomic life:

- Institutional preconditions
- Value formation and development of customs, law, and usage
- Triage and pursuit of economic goals
- Frictional and transaction costs

This chapter finds that just like justice, agape also easily passes Adam Smith et al.'s subsistence test, that is, society cannot exist without it.

Institutional Preconditions: Legal Framework and Mutual Trust and Goodwill

Even the most ardent laissez-faire advocates acknowledge that markets require institutional preconditions. In the first place, a legal framework is vital in establishing and enforcing private property rights. Moreover, markets need enforceable contracts. Surely, justice plays *the* central role in maintaining such a legal framework. Without enforceable private property rights and contracts, it is not possible to have modern markets at all in which complete strangers from geographically distant places engage in economic exchange.

Mutual trust and goodwill are other institutional preconditions that are essential for functional markets. David Hume is backed by empirical evidence in arguing that society cannot run on justice alone without an accompanying duty of humanity. Adam Smith's world that is driven purely by justice may be possible, but only in the idealized setting of perfect competition, in which there is perfect information for all, there are no frictional costs, and adjustments are instantaneous across all sectors. These are heroic assumptions that are far from what we have in practice.

Justice has three limitations regarding the institutional preconditions that are essential for functional markets. First, the tenets underlying justice do not arise in a vacuum. How do they come about? Who gives rise to them? Where do they get their underlying values? Second, it turns out that even plainly spelled out contracts, laws, and rights nevertheless still require mutual trust and goodwill among market participants. Third, justice can only go as far as what CLU tell it is due to people. Socioeconomic life is fluid and complex; it is fraught with chance and contingencies for which CLU might not provide guidance. As a result, justice is helpless in dealing with these cases.[1] Ultimately, mutual accommodation based on trust and goodwill is key to resolving these. Engendering mutual trust and goodwill is not the forte of justice but of agape.

---

[1] H.L.A. Hart (1961, chapter 5) notes that society has clear and commonsensical laws that are geared for the survival of the community. However, three problems make such a set of primary laws insufficient, namely:

- a problem of uncertainty – which block of laws and standards will apply to whom and how, etc.?
- a problem of the static nature of primary rules – these rules may change only ever so slowly and may not be able to respond to urgent new conditions.
- a problem of inefficiency – because the social pressure is diffused in the way it is exerted.

David Hume's Duty of Humanity

David Hume's (1896, 1902) insight on the duty of humanity as a precondition of justice sheds much light on these questions. The duty of humanity precedes justice. Hume staunchly defends the duty of humanity and disagrees with Adam Smith et al., who claim that only justice is needed and everything else, including love, is either merely optional or an add-on.[2] In his books *Treatise of Human Nature* and *Enquiries Concerning the Human Understanding and Concerning the Principles of Morals,* Hume submits that the duty of humanity is just as necessary as justice for the following reasons.

First, Hume argues that the duty of humanity passes the subsistence test, which states that the strictness of an obligation is a function of whether society can exist without that obligation. Hume himself acknowledges that society cannot exist without justice. However, he goes further than Smith, Grotius, and Pufendorf et al. to argue that justice in its own turn presupposes the duty of humanity. Justice needs the duty of humanity if there is going to be any justice at all.

Life is a web of "unequal relationships." An example of this is that of a parent and a child. Justice is at risk amid unequal relationships either because it will not be applied at all in the absence of any viable resistance or because the rules of justice themselves will be set to the advantage of the strong and the powerful. Recall how the great empires of the pre-modern world were built on the blood and sweat of the ruled. Note the modern history of colonialism and the common lament of the poor regarding their lack of voice and power in shaping the decisions that determine their fate (e.g., the World Bank's *Voices of the Poor*).

Hume argues that the duty of humanity serves as a check, a restraint that governs relationships between unequals and between equals as well (Hume 1902, 190–191, 186; Shaver 1992, 547). Take the case of children. Book III, Section II of his *Treatise* deals with the question of how the rules of justice come about. Hume notes that the most fundamental principle of life is not justice, but the love that is learned within the family. Parents do not abuse their authority over their children, despite the disparity in power. This restraint is due to parents' natural affection for their children. In fact, far from taking advantage of such an unequal relationship, parents shower their children with love and all the good things within their power to acquire. Out of this nurturing family life, children grow up

---

[2] Hume means "benevolence" whenever he uses the term "humanity" (e.g., *Enquiry*, pp. 278–282. See also Shaver 1992, p. 546).

e that they themselves had received
ced for themselves the happiness
bility, and benevolence. Indeed,
1 without having to be told to
in nature – to maintain order
.ast, benevolence is sought for
.ot to mention its attendant joys.
, beneficence, affability, and all the
y the family supply the people (now
.nape the rules of justice. In other words,
are people of virtue and goodwill who are
..uce, enforcing them, and most of all, living up
..iumanity makes all these possible, and more (Hume

se of e-commerce.
payment, as in the
.d dishonest
. workers are
.linger in
and

Requisite Mutual Trust and Goodwill

Even as ordinary economic transactions are covered well by laws and contracts, businesses, nevertheless, expend both time and company resources in developing camaraderie among their workers and with their customers. Japanese men, for example are expected to join their colleagues for after-work drinks, often until late evening. *Guanxi* (social networks and personal relationships) is standard in the conduct of Chinese business. The same is true for the team-building retreats common in Western corporate life. These examples are all geared toward building mutual trust and goodwill. It turns out that mutual benevolence is much more effective than justice even in what are supposed to be contractual relationships.

Despite well-written contracts and a whole host of enforcement mechanisms and institutions, there will be gray areas in socioeconomic life that are ill defined by contracts or legislation. Moreover, CLU enforcement can be expensive or ineffective, thereby discouraging market participants from relying solely or heavily on these, if they even have recourse to them. In the end, people will have to trust one another, live up to their word, and care for others' welfare and not only for their own self-interest. In particular:

- Contracts cannot always be comprehensive to the point of covering all aspects or eventualities affecting a transaction (e.g., unexpected disruptions due to the Covid pandemic).
- Timing of transactions and exchanges do not match in which delivery and payment occur at different times. Advance payments are

often made for subsequent delivery, as in the ca
Alternatively, deliveries are made for subsequent
case of consignments.

- Extending credit lines is standard business practice, a
  people can simply walk away and swindle their credito
- Employers are unable to monitor labor and ascertain tha
  in fact giving their best. Workers can be half-hearted or m
  their jobs.
- Credence goods and services (e.g., teachers, plumbers, doctors
  ministers) abound, and customers simply rely on providers' adv
  on the need for or the quality of the goods and services supplied.
  Customers often do not have the expertise to evaluate the need for
  the quality of these goods or services.
- Generous returns policies of retailers presume trustworthiness on the
  part of customers.
- Claims for insurance, welfare, and disability payments cannot always
  be fully verified.
- It is up to taxpayers to declare what they put in their tax returns.
  Government audits only a small percentage of these.

There are many more transactions in socioeconomic life that rely on the
moral integrity of people. In the above cases, it can be expensive or even
impossible to monitor and close off loopholes that enable fraud. At some
point, there is need to rely on mutual honesty and trust.[3] Mutual trust
and goodwill provide the order for matters or contingencies that contracts
fail to or are unable to cover. Goodwill and generosity are the strong suits
of agape rather than of justice. Many economists find the self-interested
homo oeconomicus model to be inadequate because it does not capture the
compassion, beneficence, and love that animate people (Geest 2021).

To be sure, there are many instances of deceit. While there have been
abuses stemming from the above market limitations, economies are nevertheless still able to function largely because of the honesty and benevolence
that people show each other. In fact, that markets are still functional despite
gaps in laws, rights, and their enforcement suggests that market participants
are for the most part trustworthy. Otherwise, the marketplace will of its
own shut down or limit economic practices that are unsustainable (e.g.,
experimental restaurants in which people decide how much to pay).

[3] Thomas Reid argues similarly in acknowledging that even contracts need mutual trust if they are to
be viable in the long run (Shaver 1992, 552–553, fn 19).

Limits of CLU and Therefore the Limits of Justice

Even the most detailed laws and rights are subject to differences in interpretation. People who avoid their responsibilities through their rogue or unreasonable interpretation of legal provisions make this problem even worse. While courts can sort through these disagreements, they take time and can be expensive.

A far more serious dilemma, however, arises when laws, rights, and contracts are not able to cover unforeseen exigencies. Socioeconomic life is much too complex and dynamic for that. Moreover, there are important matters that are outside the scope of established CLU. Take the collective-action problems in the preceding chapter. As mentioned earlier, the depletion of fish stocks due to overfishing is a contemporary instance of the "tragedy of the commons" (Hardin 1968). It is a similar dilemma for many aspects of our shared economic life, such as, the plastic pollution of the oceans, climate change, satellites' increasingly crowded use of space, and the global distribution of limited supplies of life-saving vaccines and medical equipment. The Amazon has been described as the lungs of the world, and yet, the world can only watch on the sidelines as it is slashed and burned in the name of Brazilian economic development. Public health officials have repeatedly warned that uncontrolled widespread infections provide the occasion for further mutations of the corona virus. The international community can only stand by helplessly as national and local government leaders precipitate widespread infections due to their permissive hands-off policy of noninterference regarding their populations' behavior and autonomy. Justice has been impotent in all these instances because there are no established CLU in these cases, much less global rules. And even if there were, there will most likely be a problem of enforcement or the lack of will to do so.

Need for Agape: Nonpecuniary Motivation

Markets and even national governments are unable to deal with the abovementioned problems because they are outside the scope of CLU. Global grassroots outrage has emerged to shame and push national governments to act on climate change. Nonetheless, global warming has exposed the helplessness of nations even with their near consensus on the urgency of the problem. In the absence of a global CLU, even the most powerful and the most willing nations are unable to make a dent in the problem. The marketplace, too, has significant limitations. Economic life is about presenting the right set of incentives to get people to act in such a fashion as to effect allocative efficiency. Unfortunately, the marketplace could not set these price signals appropriately because it is beset with many market imperfections. In the end, contracts cannot cover all possible contingencies, governments have significant limitations in what they can command due to the lack of means or political will, and markets do not always provide the necessary or correct price incentives.

In such cases, moral suasion is a noneconomic, nonpecuniary incentive that can move economic agents to choose that which promotes the general welfare. Examples of this are the campaign for voluntary restraint in fishing, fair trade, recycling, voluntary carbon offsets, and debt forgiveness for environmental conservation. Agape makes people much more receptive to such moral suasion than justice could. Agape provides the impetus for people to take responsibility for themselves and others, even at great personal cost. Moral suasion is often effective because of fear, social pressure, sense of duty, one's conscience, and one's own sense of decency. Love[4] provides an additional, and powerful, venue for moral suasion.

Justice can also privilege or even impose nonpecuniary reasons for acting, depending on its underlying CLU. However, nothing in the nature of justice requires it or even equips it for such a task. In fact, justice would most likely fail in eliciting nonpecuniary motives because it operates by coercive fiat. The impasse of nations over climate change illustrates this. In contrast, by its nature, agape is much more effective in imbuing people with nonpecuniary motives. Compared to justice, agape is much more potent in achieving moral suasion in economic life. As mentioned earlier, justice commands while agape elicits compliance.

Agape is effective in addressing the many limitations of justice. Agape has the agility, the motivation, and the *telos* (universal human well-being) to fill in the gaps in CLU. Unlike justice that is wedded to CLU and can only do what CLU direct it, agape is constrained only by the need to care for the well-being of others. By its nature, agape engenders mutual trust and goodwill, the other critical institutional preconditions of a functional socioeconomic life.

Agape makes reciprocity more likely. Markets do not always operate with precision and equal exchange. There will be mismatches and disequilibria in which equal exchange is not possible or fail to materialize despite

---

[4] Readers are reminded that agape is a subset of love. What is said of love in what follows applies also to agape. We use "love" instead of "agape" in those instances when what is said is also pertinent to *philautia*, *storge*, *pragma*, and *philia*.

people's best efforts. Capitalism and market exchange need not always be the coincident exchange of goods of equal value. Such exchanges of equal value have been modern. Most exchanges in human history have been based on reciprocity. For example, note the Mosaic laws of mutual assistance. We find this too in the medieval Franciscan economic exchanges. To this day, we find such reciprocity in rural areas and small communities (e.g., corner-store purchases on credit until payday). Agape makes such reciprocity possible (Zamagni 2021; Bruni and Zamagni 2007). Where reciprocity is not possible, agape engenders generous accommodation. Such generosity is not the realm of legal dues and claims, but of big-heartedness and philanthropy. For example, note Merck's commitment to provide Mectizan, its drug for river blindness, free for as long as needed to eradicate this disease. Or, recall Warren Buffett's commitment to give away the bulk of his wealth to charity.

Agape fills in the gaps in global, national, local, and interpersonal relationships that justice does not. Justice does not tell us how to relate to everyone in our lives, and even if it did, it has only rudimentary guidelines that must still be fleshed out. In contrast, agape, by its nature, is about interpersonal relationships (Pope 1997). However, it gently guides in a most general way and is not deontological in the way justice is. Love can fill these gaps not by micromanaging, but by presenting the ideals and the possibilities of our various relationships. Thus, it has the advantage over justice of not needing a lengthy or detailed CLU because it is bound only by its concern for human well-being for all.

For example, justice might be able to compel consumers to change their carbon footprint through mandated emissions standards and government taxes or subsidies (e.g., electric vehicles). Similarly, justice might be able to curtail overfishing through international treaties. These require significant coordinated action. In contrast, agape elicits voluntary compliance by appealing to people's conscience. It provides for a faster and a more enduring solution to our shared problems. Agape averts the well-known prisoners' dilemma because individuals are moved to think beyond their own interests. Agape can reproduce the early Christian community of Acts 2:44–45 and 4:32–37 in which everything is held in common, with people voluntarily giving with alacrity what they have and taking only what they need.

Agape automatically provides guidance for the unforeseen. Law and rights cannot provide guidelines for all possible contingencies. Agape can because it simply provides an overarching principle to govern all moral choices – the promotion of human well-being. For example, we have property owners voluntarily foregoing rents during the pandemic lock-down. Recall, too, Mr. Aaron Feuerstein of Malden Mills continuing to pay his workers' salaries during the rebuilding of their factory after it burned down in 1995 (CNN Money 2001). In these cases, note the speedy response that agape can inspire.

Mutual trust and goodwill as institutional preconditions are not binary (1, 0) but come in varying degrees. The quality and functionality of socio-economic life are dependent on the quality and depth of these institutional preconditions. The deeper and the more profound the mutual trust, the more likely it is that we can take collective action in resolving the above-mentioned problems.

Furthermore, individuals' trustworthiness mutually reinforces one another to produce a synergy in which the resulting whole is greater than the mere sum of its parts. This dynamic is empirically verified in the litera-ture on corruption. Less developed and poorly functioning economies are often marked by widespread graft in which trust is minimal, and bribery is not only rife but is the norm. In contrast, the economy is more func-tional and performs much better the greater the trust and compliance of its people.[5] A good example of this is Denmark in which there is a high social trust. People are willing to pay as much as 50 percent of their GDP in taxes because they trust government to return these funds to them in public services. For its part, government trusts its citizens to do that which is for the common good, even as people trust one another to do what is good for everybody. As a result, Danes are said to be among the happiest people in the world (Behsudi 2022).

Economic life, in practice, functions because people trust one another, are mutually empathetic, and think of others' well-being and not only their own.[6] David Hume's argument for the duty of humanity's necessity and preeminence is supported by actual experience. The duty of human-ity can indeed be defended based on the mutuality of interest. It is in the mutual interest of market participants to embrace and to live up to the duty of humanity for their individual, but especially for their collective well-being. The duty of humanity lends itself well to resolving the conun-drum in the prisoners' dilemma – the solution being always to think in terms of universal human well-being and not only of the self.

In sum, agape makes up for the limitations of justice in:

---

[5] Note, for example, Transparency International's list of the most corrupt countries. www .transparency.org/en/cpi/2021 last accessed April 18, 2022.
[6] See, for example, the empirical work of Niazi and Hassan (2016).

- Matters not covered by CLU.
- Attending to unfolding problematic market processes & outcomes.
- Adjusting to shifts in the socioeconomic terrain.
- Providing leniencies, exemptions, and special cases outside the purview of CLU.
- Identifying boundaries and actions that should not be crossed but which are permitted by CLU.

Moreover, agape accomplishes these in a much speedier manner than justice because the latter must wait for CLU to catch up with constantly changing economic requirements. One could liken the tandem of justice and agape to a human body. Justice provides the skeletal framework holding up the body politic, including the marketplace, while love fills in everything else. Justice deals with whatever can be identified ahead of time, while love deals with all else for which the community is not prepared. Paul Tillich (1954, 25) proposes an ontology of love and justice with justice as its form and "love as the moving power of life."

Agape's critical role stands out even more once we bring in the notion of social capital. Modern society is keenly aware of the different types of capital that have driven human achievement in the last three hundred years. Economic capital is the most visible and well-known type. This includes financial wealth and physical and social infrastructure – critical inputs in the modern economy. Human capital pertains to the quality of the population – its education, literacy, skills, health status, life expectancy, tacit knowledge, and many other qualities that directly affect people's capacity to pursue their life goals and contribute to the community. Social capital pertains to the quality of interpersonal relationships within a community (Fukuyama 1999). Social capital is both a cause and effect of people being able to work together for the common good. Like economic and human capital, social capital is extremely difficult to build up. It requires much commitment, collaboration, and mutual goodwill from people and only grows incrementally over time. Agape is a major contributor to developing social capital.

Value Formation and Shaping the Public Ethos

Importance of CLU

Socioeconomic life is fraught with competing claims. After all, human wants and needs far exceed the finite resources of the earth. People's rival claims must be resolved. This is obviously a daunting task considering the volume of such competing demands. No bureaucracy or civil service will be able to do so effectively or sustainably (e.g., Soviet-style economies). Herein lies the strength of the marketplace. No other social institution to date can handle the volume of competing claims as the marketplace, and in a timely way at that. At the heart of this unique ability is its price system.

Nevertheless, as we have seen, the marketplace requires institutional preconditions if it is to function at all. Among these is the set of CLU that provides order within the marketplace. Justice is the implementing arm of these CLU. Thus, as we have seen in the preceding chapter, many social philosophers and theologians defer to justice's claims when they come in conflict with agape's claims.

H.L.A. Hart (1961, 168–176) notes that one difference between legal and moral debt is what he calls the contrast in the immunity to change. Legal laws are enacted and can change at will. In contrast, moral rules are not changed by human fiat but are discovered and internalized over time rather than enacted. Agape is important in shaping community values. It plays a pivotal role in discovering moral rules and then transforming the public ethos. Agape can shift the lines of division in Table 1.2's continuum of obligatoriness. In effect, one way of settling agape-justice conflicts is to change the underlying laws or public ethos that in turn alter what is considered a legal due, a moral debt, or a pure gift.

Moral duties and obligations evolve over time along with shifts in the public's ethos. Community expectations and practices, in general, are not subject to sudden or quick alterations. Nevertheless, CLU are not static. They continually evolve and develop, for better or for worse, but they never stand still. Three institutions are at the heart of the modern industrial society: the marketplace, government, and civil society. These interact with one another in shaping and implementing CLU.

Government undoubtedly plays a substantial role in this regard because it codifies rules and procedures for socioeconomic life, including the marketplace and civil society. It not only formalizes such regulations, but it also provides the coercive fiat and the legal institutions to enforce these. Nevertheless, government does not have the last word because it is itself subject to change and merely follows the direction given it by its citizens, at least in democratic states. Thus, civil society is just as important as government. Civil society is comprised of the country's varied associations, institutions, local communities, non-governmental organizations (NGOs), and other social entities that do not fall under the government or the marketplace. Civil society is the larger cocoon that nurtures the community. It shapes the all-important public ethos, the uncodified and informal moral tenets held by the public. This shared ethos is built up over time, even across generations – best-practices and mores that have survived the test of time and that are known to work and thereby handed down from generation to generation. The informal, uncodified tenets of public ethos ultimately make their way to being part of the community's CLU. The public ethos infuses its values to shape both the government and the marketplace.

Civil society is the incubator for the public ethos that eventually finds expression in market praxis and in the laws and regulations codified and enforced by government. Public ethos shapes practices in the marketplace that are not covered by formal government regulations. This includes the markets' informal laws or customary praxis (e.g., 15–20% tipping). Civil society engenders the public ethos that in turn sets what people may or may not expect of each other, of what is acceptable or unacceptable conduct. While justice plays an important role in building civil society, agape plays an even more significant part. Civil society is animated by agape and its mutual respect and goodwill. It is through civil society that agape can make its contribution to both the marketplace and government.

The Marketplace's Potency in Shaping CLU

Both government and civil society are important in the formation and implementation of CLU that govern the rules and procedures in the community, including markets. Nevertheless, it turns out that the marketplace itself is an important determinant of its own rules, procedures, and expectations.

In addition to government and the public, the marketplace turns out to be a significant player as well in shaping CLU. In fact, the marketplace enjoys distinct advantages over both government and the public in the race to shape the de facto ground rules and the overall expectations regarding proper conduct in the marketplace and beyond. Markets are powerful determinants of economic ethos and praxis because of their agility and responsiveness and because of the phenomenon of network externality.

To begin with, democratic government policymaking takes time and effort, especially in nations with bitterly divided political parties. Getting the public to act collectively requires even more lead-time and effort because of the requisite campaigning and organizing. In contrast, the marketplace is in a constant state of flux, adjusts quickly to accommodate changing conditions, and is adept at altering the economic terrain itself. Second, the marketplace is the ultimate crowd-sourcing phenomenon. Government legislation and public grassroots campaigns often depend on a few key people. In contrast, the marketplace reflects the dynamism and energy of its massive pool of participants. Not surprisingly, the marketplace is often the cutting edge of new initiatives and innovations, the Internet e-Revolution and its generative artificial intelligence (AI) being a case in point.

Third, the phenomenon of network externality makes the market an even more potent determinant of CLU compared to government or even civil society. The easiest way to explain network externality is to look at the keyboard. The QWERTY configuration of the keyboard is inefficient and prone to errors. Innovators have long proposed even better replacements since the late nineteenth century. Nevertheless, none of these attempts has succeeded because of the enormous cost of replacing keyboards worldwide, and more importantly, the unimaginable expenditure in time and effort for everyone to retrain on a new keyboard configuration. QWERTY, despite all its imperfections, is simply the standard. The more people get used to it, the more it gets to be entrenched in its dominant position.

We can also explain network externality in the choice and use of currencies, such as the US dollar. It is the leading international currency of exchange and is used even by the most bitter enemies of the United States. This is so because the US dollar is accepted anywhere in the world and is, in fact, the predominant currency used in cross-border trade. The more people use the US dollar in international transactions, the more it is ensconced as the standard. We see the same phenomenon with the use of English as the predominant language for the Internet. Non-native English internet users invest time and effort in learning English because much of internet materials are in English. And as non-native English users do so, the more English gets to be the dominant language on the Internet. Note, too, the use of English by pilots in international aviation and by air-traffic controllers. In other words, network externality is the phenomenon whereby the more people subscribe to a particular rule, product, or service, the more dominant it becomes until it eventually serves as the de facto standard.

And so it is in socioeconomic life as well. Markets are not immune to this dynamic. In fact, markets reinforce and even give rise to new network externalities. Cases in point – Amazon.com has become the go-to site in searching for a book. Microsoft WORD has become the dominant word-processing software. Similarly, Google has become the most dominant search engine. Successful social media apps have become even more attractive to use and are nearly the standard because of their widespread adoption – Facebook, TikTok, YouTube, and WhatsApp, among many others. Marketplace practices become the standard practices as more people depend on and participate in the market.

The marketplace has become potent also because of the phenomenon of bounded rationality. Mainstream neoclassical economic theory's *homo oeconomicus* conducts a maximization or optimization exercise for every economic choice. After all, it is how allocative efficiency is achieved whereby economic actors constantly adjust their economic choices in accord with changes in the price signals and their shifting constraints. Such ceaseless maximization-optimization exercises work only in perfectly competitive markets in which there is perfect information, perfect mobility, and frictionless markets. Of course, we have none of these in practice. It is impossible in real markets for economic agents to be doing a maximization-optimization exercise for every economic choice they make. That would not only be tedious and time-consuming, but it is beyond the person's capacity. Besides, even if it were possible, the person would have no time left for anything else. Thus, in practice, market participants use rules of thumb in their decision-making. People simply replicate what worked well in previous rounds of economic activity. They "satisfice" rather than maximize or optimize (Simon 1957). This is bounded rationality whereby people make choices based on rules of thumb.

Both network externalities and bounded rationality strengthen markets in their ability to set the CLU that govern market participants. For example, the flight from farms and rural areas to urban centers is an example of network externality at work. Urban areas become much more vibrant and stronger with this infusion, but at the expense of the rural sector. Examples also abound in the case of bounded rationality. Many young people see going to college as the gateway to good-paying jobs. In South Korea and China, it has become standard for families to send their high school-age children to expensive after-school tutorials and cram-schools in preparation for the national exams that determine their college or university placement. These placements in their own turn determine the prospects of their graduates by the sheer heft of the school's reputation. These practices have become well-entrenched rules of thumb. Another powerful example of such rules of thumb that have become ingrained is the new path taken by young women – college, a career, delayed marriage, and delayed childbearing until they are well-established and secure in their profession. These have become nearly standard market behavior in some countries.

Indeed, the marketplace is not merely an important determinant in shaping CLU; it is often even more powerful and more agile than government or civil society in this role. Take globalization as an example. The global integration of the last half century is primarily an economic phenomenon driven principally by a technologically transformed marketplace. Markets have turned the world into a single integrated workshop. The worldwide supply disruption in the wake of Covid-19 is proof of this shift.

Globalization has made the market even more dominant as a source or key determinant of public economic morality. Globalization has demonstrated that the marketplace can singlehandedly force alterations even in long-standing national CLU. Poor developing nations have toned down their nationalistic rhetoric and have bent over backwards, even amending their constitutions on foreign ownership, to solicit international investments. Nations and even NGOs that have traditionally been vocal defenders of human rights have been restrained, even silent, in criticizing errant nations or autocrats for fear of losing lucrative export markets or contracts.

Indian national economic policy has been rooted in the Ghandian philosophy of self-sufficiency and an appreciation for the local. Thus, the country has been a relatively closed economy. Globalization compelled India in the 1990s to start moving down the path of openness to trade, precipitating changes in its domestic CLU, including its retail trade. An even earlier and even more stunning example, of course, is China voluntarily exchanging its communist economic philosophy to embrace capitalism, although with a heavy dose of the government's visible hand. Despite its state capitalism, China is nevertheless a demonstration of the potency of the marketplace in shaping not only an entire nation's CLU, but also the socioeconomic terrain itself. Markets gave birth to a public ethos of entrepreneurship in China since 1979.

Marketization of Values and Practices

To be sure, the marketplace is merely a social institution that facilitates interpersonal exchanges through its price system. Nevertheless, the marketplace generates and promotes certain values.[7] It is not value-free because its institutions are undergirded by CLU that are themselves the product of philosophical commitments of the people, institutions, or social processes that generated these CLU to begin with. In other words, markets propagate their underlying values among their participants. The network

---

[7] See McCloskey (2007) for an exposition on the positive benefits of markets in helping people acquire virtues.

externality and bounded rationality of the marketplace can eventually make these *the* standard for all to follow.

Note how market-generated values seep backward, permeate, and alter the public ethos itself. It is the marketplace itself that changes civil society and the public ethos, and not the other way around as we would expect. Take marketization, as an example. This is the phenomenon whereby market rules and economic thinking are applied even in the noneconomic realms of life.[8] Market-generated values become ascendant, privileging allocative efficiency, growth, and stability over equity, harmony, and sustainability. Moreover, market discipline prevails with competition, survival of the fittest, and cease-less cost-cutting efficiencies becoming the norm. Pecuniary externalities, no matter how damaging, are left unmitigated (e.g., trade-related layoffs), as are technical externalities (e.g., climate change). Anti-social consumer preferences, wide individual autonomy, and commodification (e.g., paid surrogacy) are permissible given the reluctance to interfere with the workings of the marketplace. Market rules creep into the noneconomic spheres of socioeconomic life, such as the privatization of traditional government services in prison and school management, postal services, water and sanitation provision, and tax collection. The public accepts even the most lopsided inequality. Human labor is viewed and treated as a mere factor of production and therefore hired and fired at will or as economic conditions dictate without regard for the uprooted lives of workers and their dependents. There is nothing wrong in flaunting one's wealth and opulent lifestyle.[9]

Markets do not merely alter national or community CLU; they have transformed even their core foundational cultural mores. China, Singapore, and South Korea are steeped in Confucian values that prize family, marriage, children, filial respect, and elderly care. It took only one generation for the marketplace to upend these centuries-old traditional values, to the point where women have delayed or even foregone marriage or childbearing altogether in favor of pursuing careers that markets have now made available to them. Fertility rates in these East Asian countries have dropped precipitously below replacement rate. Moreover, the problem has gotten so bad to the point where China and Singapore have had to legislate formally children's filial obligation to care for their aging parents and even enact laws that mandate them to visit or get in touch with their parents

---

[8] Even altruism has been explained in economic terms (Becker 1981). Viewing the world through economic spectacles has become so common to the point that critics have called it the "imperialism of economics."

[9] See, for example, Wang and Dong (2021).

(Serrano et al. 2017). Indeed, markets can alter not only economic policy and national ideology, but they can also overturn deeply held traditional values at both the collective and personal level.

Even wealthy nations have had their CLU altered by the marketplace. The sharing economy has shifted views regarding the need for property ownership, such as cars for example. The gig economy has upended traditional employer-employee relationships. Just-in-time inventory and outsourcing have changed traditional business practices. The potency of markets in changing values overnight is seen in how the e-market has singlehandedly convinced large segments of the public to exchange their privacy for the great convenience and variety of services now made available by apps.[10]

Indeed, the marketplace has outpaced both government and civil society in the speed, effectiveness, and depth with which it has influenced and shaped CLU. In fact, governments and civil society often find themselves having to catch up and react rather than lead in such an important role.

These are but some examples of how the marketplace generates its own values, practices, and rules that shape public ethos and ultimately CLU. They arise spontaneously as part of market operations, and they fill the vacuum left by the inaction of civil society and government. Unless there is political consensus, vigilant and competent leadership, or strong grassroots activism, many nations are often not intentional in shaping their CLU. This is particularly true in countries with weak institutions. In the absence of extra-market initiatives from government or civil society, the marketplace fills the vacuum and shapes the public's economic CLU.

These market-generated values, practices, and rules become the default position because no extra or costly effort is needed at all on the part of markets, unlike civil society and government where action requires significant commitment and expending time and resources. The momentum and the inertia are in favor of these market-generated values and practices. Nevertheless, government and civil society can have the last word. They can always trump market-generated practices and values through legislation (e.g., China & Singapore on filial visits) or through public naming and shaming (e.g., price gougers). Local governments have had to legislate

---

[10] See also George (2004) on how markets shape our preferences and Elster (1983) on adaptive preference formation and how people are unwittingly shaped by external influences. See also Frank et al. (1993) on how exposure to self-interest models makes students much less cooperative and more self-centered.

ordinances to restore some of the traditional employer obligations (e.g., employee benefits) that had been lost with these new market arrangements. Similarly, public officials have curbed market-created changes in food delivery services, Airbnb rentals, and their fees. Civil society, too, has had its share of successes, as in the public outcry against Martin Shkreli, the pharmaceutical executive who bought the exclusive rights to the antiparasitic drug Daraprim in 2015 and then promptly raised its price to $750 from $17.50 a tablet, a 4,286 percent increase.

In sum, among the triad of government, civil society, and markets that shapes society's CLU, the marketplace is the most potent, the most agile, and consequently, the most dominant determinant of CLU. If government or civil society is not pro-active in steering CLU, market influence prevails. Market-generated values fill the vacuum that government or civil society leave unattended. This is so because markets, by their nature, are engaged 24/7 with CLU, they are crowd-sourced (recall the value of network externality), and they provide *the* terrain where much of social interpersonal interactions transpire. The default position is where market rules become the de facto customs, law, and usage in socioeconomic life. Economism, the belief in the preeminence of economic factors, takes root. In effect, market rules govern most of social life, and market values direct personal lives. Market practices and market values prevail as status quo, unless government or civil society steps in. Such interventions are few and far in between because they entail substantial investments of time and effort. Consequently, we might as well assume that the perennial or main task of economic ethicists and policymakers is to reshape or perhaps undo market-generated practices and values. Herein lies an important function for justice and agape.

Agape Mitigates the Limitations of Justice

As we have seen in the preceding chapter, justice is essential for the existence and proper functioning of the human community. It ensures order among people who have differing visions of the good, but who must nonetheless live together. Justice lays down the ground rules for what community members may or may not do, and what they may expect from one another. Justice steps in to correct market-generated practices and values that deprive people of what is rightfully their due as per CLU. Thus, for example, China and Singapore have been compelled to ensure that children render the filial solicitude they owe their parents. Local governments and courts have had to define what it means to be an independent contractor in the gig economy. Nevertheless, justice is limited in what it can do vis-à-vis problematic market-generated practices and values. Justice is only as good the underlying philosophical commitments of the CLU that direct it and determine what are due to people.

A second important contrast between justice and agape underscores an even more worrisome limitation of the former. As we have seen earlier, the marketplace is in fact the much more dominant and effective determinant in shaping CLU compared to government and civil society. Thus, it becomes a self-reinforcing dynamic: market-generated practices and values seep into CLU, which in turn determine the norms for marketplace operations.

Justice is unable to check this inbreeding because justice is supposed to be at the service of CLU. Justice is vulnerable to cooptation by the encroaching marketization of social life, including the public's ethos. Justice often simply goes along and reinforces the prevailing CLU that it is supposed to implement. Justice can go so far as to reinforce marketization.

For example, since many deem the marketplace to be amoral, various troubling practices have not merely become commonplace but have even been enforced under the auspices of justice. British American Tobacco and other big international tobacco firms have threatened litigation against at least eight African countries intending to follow the example of wealthy countries in safeguarding their people's health and restricting cigarettes and tobacco use (Boseley 2017). Or, note the export of dirty industries and even toxic garbage from wealthy to poor countries, one-sided mining contracts for poor host countries, and exploitative infrastructure projects that saddle poor nations with unsustainable loans – all sanctioned by CLU and enforceable in a court of law.

Cicero himself acknowledges that justice could paradoxically become an occasion or a tool of injustice through the manipulation of its underlying laws, their deliberate misinterpretation, or inappropriate enforcement. Even as early as the ancient world, people described such chicanery in the maxim "More laws, less justice" (*De Officiis*, I, x [33]). Indeed, justice, on its own, is vulnerable and can be used for ill purposes.

Thus, a major limitation of justice is that it is only as good as the philosophical commitments undergirding the CLU it is supposed to enforce. There is nothing in the nature of justice that requires it to recognize universal norms, that is, intrinsically morally unacceptable acts that set boundaries to what humans may or may not do. In contrast, agape is bound by such limits because its object is human well-being. Agape questions and prevents marketization's encroachment.

Role of Agape in Value Formation

Justice is an ethics of right action. Its concern: What is the right (just) thing to do? Its object: Give people their due according to what laws and rights prescribe. In contrast, love, including agape, is an ethics of being. Its concern: What kind of person others and I need to be or can be? Its object: actualizing such personhood. Thus, Justice : doing :: Love : being.

John Oesterle (1970) concludes that there is a connection between being morally good and doing what is morally right in which the latter is more likely to happen with the former.[11] Nevertheless, the latter is not always an automatic outcome of the former because people must have 'appetitive rectitude,' that is, the will to do the right action at every moral choice. Thus, compared to justice, love has greater breadth in the scope of its moral deliberations and concerns and addresses questions that are far more profound & consequential in their implications. No one would claim that justice could represent the totality of one's ethical orientation. In contrast, many would say that love could be the totality of one's ethical orientation (Wolterstorff 2011, 1).

Love can provide vision and change. Justice is unable to do so because it is about execution of standards already given. It is not in its place or role to change laws unless specified in CLU itself. However, love is a different story. It not only can change CLU, but it will necessarily do so because of the nature of its task – transforming hearts and minds and serving as the wellspring for moral action. Love can and does change the standards. For example, justice and its deontological fixation with what is due would have prevented the Gentiles from becoming Christians without first practicing the Mosaic Law. However, mutual love in the Council of Jerusalem where this issue was settled allowed them to see the *epikeia* of what Christ did and to come to the consensus that observance of the entirety of Mosaic Law was not a necessary condition to be a follower of Christ, as the early Jewish Christians thought and initially demanded (Acts 15).

Love rather than justice provides responsiveness to changing times and circumstances. Justice is precise in its requirements, expectations, and adjudications. It provides structure to community life by providing guidelines on what we may or may not expect from one another, even while identifying lines that CLU specify should not be crossed. Justice provides order, structure, and strength to community life. However, adversity and unforeseen contingencies buffet communities for which no clear

---

[11] See Williston (2006, 567, fn 11) for a further useful distinction between character and integrity.

guidelines are available from justice. In such moments, it is love that binds and holds the community together and provides it with the flexibility to bend along with the winds to accommodate one another as needed and for as long as necessary. Love after all brings about compassion and the readiness to trust others. Justice provides the basic rules for interpersonal dealings, while love fills out and provides the richness and vibrancy that allow these interactions to bloom into relationships. Love provides staying power and pliability to justice's order and structure. The survival of the Christian Church in its first 500 years of struggle with persecution, disagreements over dogma, and governance is an example of love in action along with grace.

Agape, as an ethics of being, shapes CLU that are foundational for justice. This is particularly so with the *telos* that it presents in the case of infused agape. Consequently, we can expect love to be pro-active in shaping CLU and not leave a vacuum, which market-generated values fill by default. Love is powerfully transformative and life-changing. Justice can be transformational too, but not to the same degree and same power as love.

We find numerous examples of agape at work as it shapes and changes the public ethos and justice's underlying laws. As we have seen in Table 1.2's continuum of obligatoriness, the boundaries between and within legal and moral debts shift over time. What was once considered supererogatory may at some point be widely expected in public ethos and then ultimately be codified in law. For example, we have affirmative action in university admissions, hiring, public contracts, public office, and even certain economic activities. Such affirmative action ranges from general common practice (e.g., university admissions) to being codified in law (e.g., Malaysia's Bumiputra Program).[12] As mentioned earlier, we have seen a similar trajectory from the supererogatory to codified law for the US Affordable Care Act and Muhammad Yunus' microfinance initiative. Carbon offsets are currently voluntary, but there is already talk of widespread carbon taxes, not only for domestic production, but also even for imports. In December of 2022, the EU announced its plan to impose a tax on its imports based on the greenhouse gases emitted in manufacturing them.

Urban fresh food deserts that are currently mitigated by NGOs may eventually be addressed by law, just as redlining in banking and insurance was eventually rectified via legislation – the Community Reinvestment Act.

---

[12] Azmi and Daniele (2021)

Social enterprises and triple bottom line accounting are currently deemed supererogatory but may eventually be the norm for community praxis. Warren Buffett's philanthropy is supererogatory by today's standards but may eventually become a moral debt via community expectations. Recall the phenomenon of bread and circus in the ancient world's limited-goods worldview whereby the rich were expected to circulate their wealth by underwriting public games, services, and even monuments (Gregory 1975). In sum, agape moves the boundaries between the various categories of legal and moral debt in the continuum of obligatoriness (Table 1.2). It accomplishes this by shaping CLU.

Triage and Pursuit of Economic Goals

The major economic goals pursued by nations in the modern era are allocative efficiency, growth, equity, stability, harmony, and sustainability. All are necessary for an economy not only to survive but also to thrive. Unfortunately, these goals, no matter how laudable, cannot all be pursued to the same degree given the finitude of time, effort, and resources. Nations vary in their emphases and rank ordering of these goals based on their philosophical commitments and politics. Governments and the public rank order their preference for these values and then embed them in the CLU that will run their marketplaces. Common examples include public programs on healthcare provision and taxation (equity as a goal), fiscal and monetary policy (stability and growth as goals), and minimal market regulations (allocative efficiency as a goal).

Nothing intrinsic to justice requires it to choose any particular goal(s). Its selection depends on the decision makers' views as to whether distributive justice should be based on merit, utility, potential, contribution, need, or any other criterion. Distributive justice according to utility (greatest good for the greatest majority) will prioritize allocative efficiency, growth, and stability. In contrast, those who believe in gross national happiness, such as Bhutan, will emphasize equity, harmony, and sustainability.

Thus, depending on the underlying philosophical commitments of CLU, justice may itself affirm and, in fact, reinforce market-generated practices and values. Note, for example, the difference in the more market-oriented economy of the United States versus the more socially democratic political economy of the EU. Or, consider the UK and Canada's single-payer universal healthcare system versus the more market-driven approach in the United States that leaves many without access to healthcare or in bankruptcy on account of their medical bills. Alternatively, observe the differing visions of what constitutes economic justice between Republicans and Democrats in the US Congress. Justice is only as good as the philosophical commitments underlying its CLU, and it is entirely possible for justice to focus primarily on a handful of goals (allocative efficiency and growth) and give short shrift to the others (e.g., equity). The object of justice is to give people their due. What this "due" entails is dependent on the criteria of justice undergirding CLU. In contrast, by its nature, agape privileges the centrality of human well-being above everything else in social life. This is nonnegotiable for agape.

The Person and the Economy

How does one treat the human person in the marketplace? Is the human person viewed merely as a factor of production, a potential consumer, a potential contractual counterparty, or a potential competitor? Markets and CLU need not accord primacy to human well-being.

Primacy of Human Well-being

Justice's priority is giving people their due according to CLU and not necessarily their well-being. Nothing in its nature requires justice to prioritize or be oriented to promoting people's welfare, unless specified by CLU. In fact, justice may even give priority to private property rights protection, individual autonomy, or procedural requirements over the promotion or protection of human well-being depending on its underlying CLU. For example, in April 2022, a Florida district court vacated the US Center for Disease Control's (CDC) two-week extension of the Federal mask mandate for transportation because it was beyond CDC's statutory authority and did not follow procedures set forth under the Federal Administrative Procedure Act (APA). CDC, for its part, argued that given the exigencies and urgency of the ongoing public health crisis, the "notice-and-comment" phase under the APA was "impracticable and contrary to the public's health" (National Law Review 2022). Note that this Florida district court was able to singlehandedly vacate what CDC, in its best scientific assessment, thought was a needed short-term public health precaution for the entire country, thereby putting vulnerable people such as the immunocompromised at greater risk. Agape would have decided this case differently and given human well-being the benefit of the doubt. This is by no means an isolated case. Government regulations over clean air and water, food and drug safety, and restrictions in the use of chemicals have been routinely challenged and litigated in courts vis-à-vis businesses' freedom of commerce (e.g., Tsang and Wyatt 2017). Despite the innumerable mass shootings and deaths in the United States, courts and legislatures have routinely blocked even commonsensical and the least intrusive gun control measures. Indeed, justice need not necessarily promote human well-being. Its object is due process and rule of law according to its underlying CLU.

In contrast, agape (concern for others), by its nature, prioritizes human well-being over other considerations. Agape seeks the good of the object of its love. In effect, agape acknowledges the overriding importance of the beloved. As we will see in Chapter 7, the object of agape is sometimes accorded such worth and significance as to elicit even self-sacrifice and self-giving from one another.

Scope of People Covered

Justice's concerns are limited only to those specified by CLU. Thus, it can be parochial by virtue of its limited mandate. It will accept Smithian individualism if told to do so by CLU. It will accept and serve even self-interested nationalism, such as the 45th US president's "America First" policy. In contrast, agape, by its nature, is universal in its coverage. Agape transcends borders because its concern is human well-being, regardless of who or wherever they may be. Agape makes nations better global citizens.

Storge (kin love) builds on *philautia* (self-love) and expands the circle of people's concerns to include their family. In its own turn, *philia* expands to include friends in what people desire and expect for themselves and their family members. Finally, agape prevents an exclusive focus on the self or on people's closed circle of family and friends. Agape makes for a much wider circle of concern, as we will see in Chapter 6.

There is nothing intrinsic in the marketplace or in socioeconomic life that compels market participants to work for the welfare of strangers or the distant. Natural love and affinity by blood, association, or proximity lead people to conduct their economic lives with an eye toward promoting the well-being of people within their tight circle of family, friends and associates. Agape pushes them to go to "deep waters" beyond the circles that are familiar, comfortable, or dear to them. It serves as a counterweight to the natural inclination of self-interest or of safety amid the familiar. Agape expands the horizons of economic agents. Just like *philautia*, *philia*, and *storge*, agape leads people to the expectation that their personal economic choices should also promote others' well-being. In the case of agape, this includes that of strangers, indeed, of as many people as possible. Agape brings about a readiness to transcend oneself and to fulfill all the objective requirements that will bring this about.

In sum, one could view a set of ever-larger concentric circles centered on the self and then expanding outwards from *philautia* as the innermost circle closest to the self, followed by *storge, philia*, and *agape*. This is the ever-widening circle of concern-empathy-solidarity to which love invites them. *Love makes peoples' circle of concern, empathy, and solidarity coincident with their circle of economic exchange. It imbues their circle of economic exchange with a like circle of concern-empathy-solidarity.* Thus, the human person, especially the stranger, cannot be viewed merely as a factor of production, a potential customer, a potential contractual counterparty, or a potential competitor. The human person is simply viewed as a human being, one's equal and worthy of respect and compassion. Besides, this is how people would want others to treat them as well. It is the Golden Rule or Kant's universalizability law.

Intertemporal Moral Cosmopolitanism

Justice can be concerned with future generations, but only to the degree that it is told to do so by CLU. In contrast, by its nature, agape is concerned with universal human well-being. Such concern transcends not only space, but also time. By its nature, agape is necessarily attentive to the welfare of future generations. This is a significant contribution. In Smithian self-interest, economic agents act only to promote their own well-being. They will care for the next generation or two, but only with the expectation that their children and grandchildren will care for them in their old age. Beyond that, there is no incentive for the economic agent animated by Smithian self-interest to care for future generations. In a contractual mindset, future generations beyond the third have no benefits to confer on current economic agents. Not so, for agape. Since its object is human well-being, agape will work toward, and even self-sacrifice for generations yet to be born. Agape does not seek a return for its beneficence, and thus, it does not cease to care just because future generations are unable to requite such benevolence. By extension, such concern for future generations means better care for the earth and a greater interest in sustainability as a goal of socioeconomic life.

Universal Norms and Objective Moral Standards

Because justice is undergirded by the philosophical commitments of the decision makers behind CLU, it need not subscribe to any universal norms. For example, in a purely positivist political economy, right or wrong is essentially what the law says is right or wrong. In a positivist world, legislators or autocrats have full rein over whatever it is they want to legislate. Only their values and philosophical commitments restrain them. In other words, nothing in CLU formation necessarily identifies certain acts as intrinsically morally unacceptable. There are no moral absolutes. Thus, for example, unlike the EU, the United States does not see capital punishment to be an intrinsically morally unacceptable act. For its part, the EU does not see physician-assisted suicide to be an intrinsically morally unacceptable act. In other words, justice and its underlying CLU need not necessarily respect any universal norms. The deficiency of this, of course, is evident in the legalized enslavement of peoples practiced until the late nineteenth century and in the anti-Jewish laws of Nazi Germany.

Not so for agape. Anything that endangers or demeans human dignity and welfare is an unacceptable moral act, regardless of wherever people may be in the world or whatever century they may live in. There are moral absolutes for agape. This is a noteworthy feature of agape vis-à-vis its impact on the economy. Consumer sovereignty is the standard in most political economies. Neoclassical economic theory's *homo oeconomicus,* who has complete autonomy in choosing what to consume and how much to consume, is replicated in real life. Markets do not second-guess consumers in their choices. Needs and wants are not differentiated nor triaged. Consumers are sovereign for as long as they have the purchasing power with which to back up their preferences. Most governments respect such consumer sovereignty, excepting some products and services that are harmful to self or to society per CLU's determination, such as tobacco, alcohol, prostitution, vote-buying, and so on. Justice simply follows whatever CLU ordain is or is not permissible in people's choices. Note the wide variation in what CLU permit across nations and local communities regarding abortion, physician-assisted suicide, online gambling, and legalized recreational drugs.

The key difference here is substantial. For as long as they stay within the limits of CLU, justice will allow open-ended consumer utility or firm profit maximization. Market participants enjoy wide spheres of autonomy in which they have untrammeled freedom of action. In contrast, agape will have a more circumscribed freedom of action with universal norms defining boundaries that people should not cross. Agape will block anything that debases human well-being. For example, as mentioned earlier, for as long as CLU permit it, justice will not interfere with the export of toxic garbage or dirty industries from wealthy countries to poor countries that are willing to accept them to generate jobs or to earn foreign exchange. Tobacco multinational firms have used international trade treaties and domestic litigation to fight vigorously tobacco-control policies instituted by low- and middle-income countries protecting the health and safety of their citizens (Gilmore et al. 2015). Justice and its CLU can be used for purposes beyond their original intent. None of these cases would be morally acceptable to agape.

Telos and the Instrumental Nature of Economic Life

Agape's universal norms presuppose a larger backdrop from which such norms are drawn. The notion of human well-being itself connotes that the human person has an end, a *telos*. Given agape's commitment to the well-being of the beloved, the object of agape is to support the beloved's pursuit of such *telos*. Different religious and philosophical worldviews propose different *teloi*, such as Buddhism's *nirvana*, Hinduism's *moksha*, Islam's paradise, Christianity's *caritas* (friendship with God), and Judaism's *tzedeq* (righteousness). Human flourishing in any of these worldviews entails the attainment of this *telos*. It is what should preoccupy human beings in their moral agency. Thus, economic life, indeed earthly life itself, is merely instrumental. It is but a stepping-stone, a means, to attaining the even greater state defined by the *telos*.

There is nothing in the nature of secular agape that defines what human life's *telos* or even *teloi* ought to be.[13] Nevertheless, despite the lack of a consensus on human *telos* or *teloi*, we know enough to be able to conclude that such *telos* (or *teloi*) means that far from being an end in itself, economic life is but a means to a much larger end(s). Thus, agape views economic life as a venue for working toward such human *telos* (*teloi*). In contrast, nothing in its nature requires justice to hold that there is a human *telos* (*teloi*), much less a requirement for economic life to assist in attaining such a human end(s). To be sure, justice could be used for this purpose, but it will only do so if its underlying CLU tell it do so.

An implication of all this is that under agape, socioeconomic life will not only have a much more circumscribed freedom of action – negative duties that proscribe activities harmful to human well-being – but it will go further and impose positive duties, that is, actions and initiatives that promote human welfare. Justice will be able to replicate all these that agape requires, but only if CLU mandate it to do so. Nothing in the nature of justice requires these duties. In contrast, it is in the nature of agape to expect these from economic life, indeed, from earthly life. Agape presumes that economic choices are meant to advance human welfare.

---

[13] As we will see in Chapters 6 and 7, for Christified agape and St. Thomas' *caritas* or infused agape, the human person's *telos* is friendship with God.

Dealing with the Chance and Contingencies of Life
Economic life is fraught with chance and contingencies. Despite one's best efforts and good intentions, one may yet end up in destitution and want. How then does the community deal with people who suffer from these life events? Justice has proven to be effective in this task as demonstrated by the social safety nets instituted by nations in the modern era. In addition, some of the philosophical schools of thought competing to shape CLU prioritize those who have been disadvantaged in life. Note, for example, John Rawls's (1971) justice as fairness in which inequality in the community is permitted only to the degree that it benefits the most disadvantaged.

Despite justice's record of accomplishment in addressing this problem, it has significant limitations. In particular, justice is able to protect the disadvantaged, but only if its mandating CLU tell it do so. While there have been many examples of national social safety nets, there are even many more nations without or with minimal safety nets. In this regard, justice is only as good as its underlying CLU, as we have seen on so many other issues. Furthermore, even if justice reaches out to the margins, justice can be impersonal even as it provides aid. Note, for example, the complaint of poor people in how they are treated with disdain by civil servants dispensing government assistance or healthcare (Naraya et al. 2000). There is nothing in the nature of justice that calls it to be caring and empathetic when giving people their due. In fact, whenever this happens, it is highly likely that such care and empathy came about because the administrators of justice were animated by their agape.

Regardless of whether the prevailing CLU provide a social safety net, agape by its nature reaches out to those who are in distress. Love acts on multiple fronts in this regard. It helps directly by providing material relief, to the extent possible, and it also assists indirectly whereby love works to shape CLU to make taking care of the marginalized a matter of justice (e.g., welfare, Medicaid, US Affordable Healthcare Act). Agape also provides hope and perspective because of its empathy and compassion. Love provides hope and perspective that one is deeply loved despite such a hard life. Thus, love (*storge, philia,* agape) makes hardships not only bearable, but also provides real avenues for the relief of such adversities. Love provides mechanisms and structures within which to rise above such chance and contingencies.

Related to this concern and outreach to those at the margins is the question of inequality. Nations have different tolerance levels for relative inequality depending on their philosophical commitments and public economic ethos. This is evident in differences in these nations' policies on taxation, subsidies, business regulation, social service provision, and social safety nets. Justice will simply follow what CLU specify. In contrast, agape, by its nature, will call for smaller relative inequalities and will advocate for a more pro-active approach in minimizing these relative inequalities. Agape as equal regard is the least demanding of the variants of agape. Equal regard means treating others as peers and giving them the respect and care people expect for their own person and their loved ones. This strong solidarity and empathy will not allow neighbors to be left too far behind to the point of being unable to participate and contribute meaningfully to the shared common life. Not surprisingly, religions have been among the most vocal critics of large wealth and power inequalities. Other variants of agape, such as *caritas*, will demand even more as we will see in Chapter 7.

Selection of Economic Goals

The preceding differences on universal moral norms, human *telos*, and the instrumental nature of economic agency have ramifications for the all-important selection of the economy's goals. Justice only follows what CLU mandate, and its implementation is heavily dependent on the philosophical commitments of whoever dispenses justice. The decision makers' and the enforcers' values prevail in what justice does. For example, numerous environmental groups urged the ban of the pesticide chlorpyrifos based on studies that link it to lower IQ, reduced birth weight, attention disorders, and other health problems in infants and children. This is a pesticide used for US-grown fruits and vegetables. The Obama Administration banned its use in 2015, giving the benefit of the doubt to protecting children's health. The Trump Administration reversed this ban in 2017 because the neurodevelopmental toxicity of the pesticide has not been definitively established. It deems that the burden of proof is to show that it actually causes harm. Moreover, it argued that chlorpyrifos was "currently the only cost-effective choice for control of certain insect pests" (Volcovici 2019). Indeed, standards of justice can swing 180-degrees overnight with a change in administration.

We see this in a wide range of issues in environmental protection, fossil fuel use, food-and-drug safety regulations, gun control, mask/vaccine mandates, and many other matters with direct and substantial impact on human well-being. Such swings in the CLU underlying justice are ultimately driven by the value commitments of decision makers and enforcers, such as small government versus big government, individual freedom versus common welfare.[14]

This is a global phenomenon and not limited only to the United States. The standards of justice change with every new national or local leadership. In contrast, agape-based decisions are much more consistent because it has a single and clear standard – human well-being. To be clear, there will still be differences even with agape because of disagreements over what constitutes well-being and how to measure it. Nevertheless, these differences will be much narrower compared to those from justice. Moreover, the human person will always be the primary focus.

Thus, it is entirely possible and in fact quite common in the more capitalistic nations for justice to focus exclusively, if not primarily, on allocative efficiency, economic growth, and economic stability. Private property rights may even trump other human rights essential for human well-being (e.g., Covid-era evictions, mortgage foreclosures). It is entirely possible to prioritize property rights over people depending on the leadership's and courts' philosophical values and ideologies. In contrast, agape by its nature is committed to human well-being. Thus, agape will always call for a proper mix and rank ordering of economic goals that promote human welfare.

Given their underlying philosophy of maximizing the creation of economic value, free-market proponents will prioritize allocative efficiency, growth, and stability. They will pursue equity, harmony, and sustainability, but only to the degree that these serve the larger purpose of maximizing economic value. Note, as an example, the package of reforms pushed by the IMF on poor developing nations in a foreign exchange crisis. The push to restore macroeconomic balances (especially a reduction in fiscal deficits) comes at the expense of cuts in social spending that are disproportionately borne by the poor.

In contrast, agape will triage economic goals according to their contribution to maximizing human well-being, regardless of the philosophical commitments of CLU, indeed, regardless of what CLU may say. In fact, agape will go against prevailing CLU if human well-being is at risk or ill-served. This is because the object of agape is human flourishing and the attainment of its most promising possibilities in its *telos*. Thus, equity, harmony, and sustainability would unlikely be short-changed given agape's

---

[14] The Executive Order from the White House on President Biden's first day in office reviewing the previous administration's policies on health, safety, and the environment is also illustrative of these wild swings in policy that are critical for human well-being (White House 2021). See also Popovich et al. (2021).

commitment to human welfare. In the face of the powerful economic forces unleashed by globalization, agape serves as an important ballast to the market's bias toward allocative efficiency and growth as the preeminent, if not sole economic goals for the community. The marketplace, by its nature, will prioritize the creation of economic value above everything else, even human values. In contrast, agape, by its nature, necessarily puts human welfare ahead of economics.

Agape's input in the selection and pursuit of economic goals is accomplished through civil society, that is, through the public's ethos and through individuals and groups advocating and actively working to infuse the economy with agape. As we have seen earlier, agape balances and addresses justice's limitations through civil society.

Frictional and Transaction Costs

The paradigm of perfectly competitive markets is characterized by perfect knowledge, perfect mobility, and instantaneous adjustments. Thus, they can achieve allocative efficiency in the blink of an eye. In contrast, participants in real-life markets must deal with missing or imperfect information, much uncertainty, and obstacles to moving resources and factors of production around the economy. As a result, they are saddled with difficulties that have challenged economists and policymakers alike, such as moral hazard, collective action/coordination problems (e.g., prisoners' dilemma, problem of the commons), principal-agent problems, and technical and pecuniary externalities, among others. These impose additional costs on the economy that we could call frictional or transaction costs.

Justice can mitigate these costs for as long as CLU specifically address these problems. For example, justice can address pollution as a technical externality through CLU-mandated pollution abatement regulations or tax-subsidy schemes. Unfortunately, justice is limited in its ability to respond to these market imperfections because enforcement itself can be extremely costly. Moreover, many of these problems cannot be legislated away or mitigated through contracts. For example, both CLU and justice cannot monitor people's intentions and intensity of effort.

Love is much more effective than justice in addressing frictional costs because of at least three of its distinct advantages over justice:

- Love internalizes enforcement.
- Love is animated by commitment rather than mere duty.
- Love views community as familial rather than contractual in nature.

Internalized Enforcement

H.L.A. Hart (1961, 168–176) differentiates legal from moral rules and obligations in terms of moral pressure. Legal duties are enforced externally and by coercion. In contrast, moral duties appeal to the internal forum, that is, the individual's conscience. Moral debt is discharged out of one's sense of decency rather than out of any legally binding obligation (Pieper 1990, 56–57). People bind themselves voluntarily to their duties because of their love of neighbor or of God. Hence, duties of love are endogenous rather than exogenous unlike justice. Charity comes from within; it is voluntary. In contrast, justice is imposed from without.

Without love, the application of norms would otherwise be content with the minimum that is required and entail costly enforcement mechanisms. Justice is ultimately dependent on external enforcement and coercive power.[15] Thus, it has significant limitations. Justice is only as good as its enforcement mechanisms. Compared to love, it has high monitoring and implementation costs. It engenders many losses in what are called "directly unproductive activities," such as lobbying and legal and accounting maneuvers to exploit tax loopholes. It is unable to deal effectively with moral hazard problems, ownership externalities, credence goods, principal-agent problems, and labor shirking, among many other problems. After all, what is more important for justice is to be legal in one's actions rather than moral.

Love as an ethics of being versus justice's ethics of right action internalizes moral behavior. Agape is internally enforced.[16] It does what is right and pursues what is good on its own. Agape internalizes and enforces autonomously (coming from within) that which justice enforces heteronomously (meaning imposed on the person). In justice, people give out of duty. They are compelled heteronomously. In contrast, love even goes beyond the minimum requirement with spontaneity and alacrity. Justice is guided and measured from without. It is exogenous to the person. Love wells from within (whether it is an act of the will or an emotion). It is endogenous to the person. There are consequences for economic life from these differences.

Smaller Government and a Larger Sphere of Autonomy

Agape greatly reduces monitoring and transaction costs because people internally (voluntarily) enforce their obligations. The degree to which the

15 In contrast, for Cicero, an act has to be voluntary rather than compelled if it is to be just (*De Officiis*, I, ix [28]).
16 Besides, external enforcement of the duty of beneficence would be too prohibitive, if even possible at all. It is an imperfect duty and therefore imprecise, and it would lead to a loss of individual liberty (Shaver 1992, 554).

community is animated by agape is inversely proportional to the monitoring and enforcement costs of society. For example, there will be high compliance with tax payment and other government rules. There will be less litigation; there will be less need for courts, law enforcement, and lawyers. An example is the early Church community that held everything in common (Acts 2:44–45; 4:32–35).

We have a paradoxical outcome: Justice is tasked with protecting the scope of individual autonomy. However, it is agape that creates more freedom, less oversight, less rules for all because of a familial community and internalized moral behavior. Justice will have to surrender a much more significant amount of personal autonomy to Leviathan. Agape leads to less need for Leviathan and, consequently, more freedom for everyone.

Minimize Opportunism and Exploitative Conduct

As we have seen in the preceding chapter, justice and its underlying statutes provide safeguards against the most egregious forms of opportunism. Enforcement of laws dealing with truth in advertising, food labelling, and consumer product protection prevents unscrupulous people from taking advantage of others. Nevertheless, justice can only go so far because there are loopholes in laws no matter how well written they are. Note, for example, the tax avoidance of firms and people with the wherewithal to employ accountants and lawyers to reduce their tax liability. This underscores the distinct advantage of agape over justice vis-à-vis the prevention of anti-social behavior. Justice prevents such conduct through its statutes and external enforcement mechanisms (e.g., regulatory agencies, audits). These are expensive to conduct and maintain. In contrast, agape enforces internally – in people's hearts. It is practically costless.

Love minimizes opportunism. Love makes people self-policing and self-starters. They take responsibility on their own and for themselves. Genuine love engenders responsible behavior. This is a boon, especially as globalization makes policing complex markets much more challenging and expensive.

There are additional economic benefits to reducing opportunism besides lowering monitoring and transaction costs – it precipitates more investments. As mentioned earlier, there will be under-investment if contracts cannot be enforced or are expensive to administer (Văduva 2008). Thus, justice is clearly important in providing institutional safeguards. However, agape is even more effective because it internalizes moral behavior and generates a much higher level of compliance. Moreover, agape makes investments and collaboration possible even in activities that cannot be covered by contracts and are reliant entirely on people's goodwill. Note the many successful crowd-funding appeals for small business enterprises.

Commitment Rather than Mere Duty

Related to internal enforcement is another major difference: Agape : commitment :: Justice : duty.[17] Justice is motivated by duty. The claims of justice stem from what people owe to others because of their station, role, office, or relationships. Common examples include the payment of taxes and government disbursing unemployment or disability insurance benefits. They are well-defined and measurable expectations. Note, for example, how the Hebrew Scriptures define *tzedeq* as the righteousness that people attain once they satisfy all the demands of their relationships.

In contrast, love is animated by a commitment. Unlike justice, love goes beyond duty, beyond what is laid out by CLU, beyond what is expected. It is committed to the well-being of others for their sake alone, without thought of return or gains for oneself. Unlike justice whose charge is accomplished as soon as the due is rendered, there is no completion for the work of love because its commitment is both total and open-ended as we will see in Chapter 7. Its object is the well-being of the beloved. Its task is never completed. It is forward leaning and restless as it seeks the further improvement of the good of the beloved. More than just being forward-leaning, it has ardor and intensity.

By its nature, love brings singular focus, intensity, dedication, and motivation to whatever it is that must be pursued and accomplished for the beloved's well-being. Justice need not have this kind of passion. Love is, by its nature, about the pursuit of the Good. There is need and room for such intensity and passion in the community.

Duty to Do Our Best

Michael Ferry (2013) asks whether there is a duty in morality that demands our very best. This is yet another difference between justice and agape. We can ask a pair of questions instead. First, is there a duty to do one's

---

[17] See Beran (1972, 216) and Mish'alani (1969) for insights on differences between duty and commitment.

best? Second, is there a duty to give the very best to others? Justice may not be able to demand these but love always does because it is self-giving and diffusive by its nature given its innate concern for others' well-being. Love settles for nothing less than the best from us and for others.[18] After all, justice is the duty to give what is due to others, while agape, especially Christified agape, is the duty to give of oneself as a constitutive element of integral human development. Thus, agape rather than justice is much more effective in promoting general-legal justice.[19]

Inner dispositions and motivations matter, and they matter enormously. Commitment includes the interior disposition and not merely the external acts. This is where many of love's duties fall compared to justice. The interior forum is important for love. The duties of justice are satisfied once the external acts are fulfilled. The duties of love are not necessarily fulfilled even after the external acts are performed because they may have been done grudgingly or only out of fear. Love requires a particular motivation – care for the other for his/her own sake.

The underlying reason for moral obligation is much more important for love than for justice because of the nature of the enforcement. Justice can compel conformity because of fear of sanction. In contrast, for love, fulfilling duties out of fear of punishment is not good enough. The underlying reason for one's external action is just as, if not even more, important. Motivation is critical in moving people to act (Pink 2004, 166).

One difference between justice and love is that the latter requires an inner disposition that is consistent with external acts. It requires a change in interior disposition. This is a necessary condition. The exterior act must match the interior disposition. In contrast, justice does not require the interior disposition to mirror external acts. One can do the just act grudgingly because one is fearful of consequences from the law. Even as a virtue, there is no need to internalize the external act in justice, unlike benevolence, which requires something much deeper than just acting benevolently, such as a deep-seated goodwill. In Kantian terms, people can conform to duty in two ways: (1) outward conformity alone because of fear, or (2) outward conformity because of a real desire to do one's duty. The external acts are the same. Justice requires only the external acts, but love requires an internal disposition to match – truly done with ease, alacrity, and spontaneity.

---

[18] For Perricone (2012, 73–74) love demands much for the beloved – to be the very best that he/she can be, by the nature of love.

[19] Recall from chapter 1 how general-legal justice pertains to individual acts and virtues directly or indirectly advancing the good of the whole community.

Recall, too, Cicero's position that an act is just only if it is voluntary and not compelled (*De Officiis*, I, ix [28]).

To be sure, commitment also requires the fulfillment of duties. It is a necessary condition. Love requires the fulfillment of justice. Justice is a necessary condition of love. However, the fulfillment of duty does not necessarily mean the fulfillment of the commitment. In other words, there is more to commitment because duty does not exhaust everything that there is in commitment. Commitment is much more profound and all-encompassing as we will see in Chapter 7.

In sum, love directly shapes motivation and therefore affects so much of social life and economic agency. It makes a significant difference, from specifying the content of our utility function, all the way to how we maximize this utility function. Love changes how we view and treat other economic agents (as means or as ends), our attitudes toward the use of the earth and the ecology, our views on future generations, and our acceptance or correction of resulting market processes and outcomes. Anything in economic life that depends directly or indirectly on the economic agent will necessarily be subject to love's influence. After all, love is a distinctively human quality – one that is potent and transformative.

Beyond the Minimum and Maximizing Behavior

Justice is necessarily precise and measured by its nature (giving people their due). Therefore, the limits of CLU also determine the limits of justice. Justice does not go beyond the limits of its mandating/underlying CLU. After all, it acts only according to what laws and rights tell it to do. Its goal is to uphold and implement laws and rights. Consequently, justice is fulfilled even as people stick only with the minimum requirements. More important, justice is fulfilled even if the minimum requirements specified by and acceptable to CLU are in fact deficient by the standards of public ethos or of civil society (e.g., healthcare access in the United States).

In contrast, love is unmeasured by its nature. Love is marked by a relentless maximizing and optimization exercise very much like neoclassical economic theory's *homo oeconomicus*. Just as *homo oeconomicus* maximizes preferences in its utility function and the firm maximizes its profit function, *homo caritatis* maximizes the well-being of the beloved. Just as there is no satiety to *homo oeconomicus* or to the firm in such a maximizing exercise, there are also no limits with *homo caritatis* promoting the good of the beloved. Just as *homo oeconomicus* and the firm are engaged in an optimizing exercise of creating the most value given available resources, *homo caritatis* ceaselessly optimizes the promotion of the beloved's well-being given life's constraints. Just as *homo oeconomicus* and the firm are forward-leaning and constantly prowl for *pareto*-improving and *pareto*-optimizing alternatives, *homo caritatis* is also forward-leaning and proactive in searching for ways to further serve and promote the well-being of the beloved. Love takes initiative beyond what CLU mandate.

Take the case of healthcare access. Justice, by its nature, need not go beyond the precise measures given it by CLU. In fact, justice cannot even give beyond what CLU specify because it would be unjust to those who would have to bear the opportunity cost of justice's liberality. They, too, must get their due. Thus, the status quo in healthcare is good enough from the point of view of justice based on existing CLU. Not so for agape. Stephen John Duckett's (2023) strong case for greater public funding for healthcare is founded ultimately not only on social justice, but on agape's call for greater mutual compassion. That many are hard-pressed in meeting a fundamental need such as healthcare is deeply disturbing and problematic for agape.

Nevertheless, agape is not merely about compassion. It also pursues justice, and with alacrity as well. It necessarily overflows into just acts. More than that, it is a "forward-leaning" observance of the law – not only of its letter but also of its spirit. Love will not allow the subject to be complacent with the mere satisfaction of justice but invites the subject to move beyond that. Love entices the subject not to be content with the mere satisfaction of the minimum.[20] Love's maximizing and optimizing behavior stems from its underlying commitment. Minimum is not good enough. It gives nothing but its best and wants nothing but the best for the beloved by virtue of its genuine concern for the well-being of the object of its love. There are clearly defined limits for justice; there are no limits for love. As St. Paul writes, there are no limits to love's forbearance, to its trust, its hope, and its power to endure (1 Cor 13:7).

Interpersonal Relationships: Contractual or Familial-Empathetic?

For this section, "justice" refers to commutative and distributive justice, while "love" pertains to *philia*, *storge*, *pragma*, and agape. Operating in the economy all by itself, justice will form impersonal, contractual interpersonal relationships. Justice, by its nature, fosters and is content with

---

[20] Harrelson (1951, 177 column B) notes Matthew 5 as a good example in which adultery, lust (even in thinking in the heart), or hatred for a brother are incurred at a much lower threshold than what the law stipulates.

contractual relationships. Tolerance is its highest social virtue. There is no need to care for others. The Smithian self-interested behavior of the butcher, baker, and brewer is good enough. The minimum acceptable interpersonal behavior is that which is specified in contracts or is expected by CLU. Thus, Adam Smith holds that justice by itself suffices for the economy to subsist (Smith 1790, II-II.III).

As we have repeatedly seen, justice is concerned only with people giving each other their due and receiving their due. It is not in its purview to deal with other aspects or even with the quality of relationships, unless mandated by CLU. In such a transactional world, people are viewed no more than as a potential customer, business-trading partner, worker, or competitor. Justice is merely concerned with a straightforward contractual relationship. Anything beyond that is left to private individual choice. Justice is measured in its giving or taking.

Justice or even its sources (CLU) cannot legislate or coerce people into mutual benevolence. Moreover, socioeconomic life is fraught with unequal relationships, roles, power, and endowments that become the occasion for opportunism or exploitation, or both. Justice protects against these, but only as specified by CLU.

In contrast, agape calls for solidarity and empathy, at the very least. As we will see in Chapter 7, biblical (Christified) agape goes even beyond these to call for a familial, rather than a contractual community. The minimum acceptable interpersonal relationship is not merely living up to our contractual obligations, but agape and friendship. Agape as equal regard is the minimum social virtue. For Christians, *caritas* is the highest of virtues: to love as Christ loves us and to be one with the Father and the Son as they are one (John 10:29–30). This is the antithesis of a Hobbesian contractual community of wary mutual accommodation to prevent a life that is nasty, brutish, short, solitary, and poor.

Agape builds civic spirit and virtue more than justice does, by the nature of the mutual concern it fosters. Agape generates sharing and generosity. It completes the interstices of community and interpersonal relationships that justice does not or cannot fill. Justice does not tell people how to relate to everyone in their lives, and even in those cases when it does (e.g., Chinese and Singaporean laws that permit parents to sue their children for filial attention and care), it can provide only rudimentary guidelines that ultimately depend on people's goodwill.

Agape makes people see their neighbors as more than just a possible customer or potential contractual partner, but as a human being. Agape teaches and enables people to empathize. It is unmeasured in its giving, unlike justice. Agape compels people to go beyond mere duty and supererogate for others' well-being. Agape prevents the ill consequences of unequal relationships. Justice is also able to do this, but it needs external enforcement unlike benevolence, which is internalized moral action. As a result, compared to justice, agape is much more protective against opportunism because of its central premise of care for others. However, there is more. Agape serves a dual function of (1) avoiding exploitation, and (2) goes even further and in the opposite direction by proactively helping. Foundational for agape is being able to treat others as an equal, at a minimum. *Caritas* demands even more as we will see in Chapter 7.

Agape compels people to have more to do with one another and to be more intense and profound in their mutual regard. It adds quality to the relationship established by justice. People cannot relate to each other only by justice. It would otherwise be such an impoverished community. To be sure, justice is vital for interpersonal relationships, but it is love that fills them out to the fullness of their potential. Agape builds even stronger communities than justice would have been able to do on its own because of agape's spirit and dynamic (self-giving, friendship) and its lofty goals (*koinōnia, caritas*). *Caritas in Veritate* (Benedict 2009, #19) observes well that globalization has made us neighbors, but not necessarily brothers and sisters.

Pragma prevents the community from fracturing in the face of justice's unmet demands.[21] It is the "shock-absorber" that allows people and the community to survive and to rise above the resulting disappointments and even the acrimony from injustice. Agape, *philia*, and *storge* even lead people and communities to overlook the unfulfilled demands of justice from family, friends, or others, and nevertheless still love them and work for their well-being.

By its nature, agape answers even more profound questions than justice does. Since justice is about giving people their due, it merely specifies the minimums and the boundaries, while agape describes the possibilities going forward. Agape significantly affects the quality of community life, and by extension, economic life. Selfless concern for others' well-being leads to volunteerism, philanthropy, a wider and more generous social safety net in public policy, and paying forward acts of kindness. Goodwill is extended to all.

---

[21] *Pragma* is the love that has gone through life's disillusionments and has learned to accept what cannot be changed. It is a committed, flexible love that can "roll with the punches."

Mitigating Evil

Agape is even better than reparative and restorative justice in mitigating evil. Agape allows both victims and perpetrators to rise above the evils that economic agency often precipitates. Socioeconomic life is fraught with danger in that it can be used as a venue for inflicting harm on others and on oneself, as in the inordinate pursuit of wealth. This is detrimental to the good of such economic wrongdoers; it also impedes and puts obstacles for those on the receiving end of such injustice. Agape allows all affected parties (the oppressor and the victims) to rise above such injury. It provides the possibility of forgiveness and a new life for the oppressor (e.g., Zacchaeus in Lk 19:1–10), even as it provides hope to the downtrodden and the suffering (e.g., Lazarus and the rich man-Lk 16:19–31; beatitudes–Mt 5:1–12). Agape provides hope for both the oppressor and the victims – that such is not their permanent condition and that they may yet enjoy a different life free from wrongdoing.

Agape can mitigate evil in another way. Agape's compassion should not be equated with softness, or worse, coddling. Niebuhr (1957) assumes that love requires the absence of coercion. Not surprisingly, he is led to the conclusion that justice must trump love if society, beset with wickedness, is to survive at all. For him, love is incapable of dealing with the realities of human life; only justice can. Agape is best reserved for the Messianic Age to come. Not so. Agape can discipline when it should. After all, its goal is to promote the good of the object of one's love. For Christians, Jesus is the paradigm of agapic love. Jesus did not indulge the scribes, the elders, and the Pharisees. He spoke plainly in calling them thieves and hypocrites (Mt 23). He drove out the money changers from the Temple (John 2:13–16).

Result: Lower Frictional and Transaction Costs

Stefano Zamagni (2022) observes that what is important in arriving at a consensus is not so much the agreement itself, but the participation and commitment of the people involved in bringing about such accord. What is critical is the lived "narrative traditions" that instantiate such consensus. Such commitment is the forte of agape.

Internalized norms, deep commitment, and a familial community mutually reinforce one another to produce synergistic effects that greatly enhance the quality of socioeconomic life and interpersonal relationships. In particular, economic life will have lower frictional and transaction costs. There is peace and goodwill in the economy. People's word of honor is reliable. Community members step up and do more than just the minimum. Greater innovation and productivity result from closer collaboration and division of labor. It is a friendly competition and not a buccaneer capitalism. There is minimal deadweight loss due to directly unproductive activities (e.g., lobbying). People's energies are better channeled toward work that is more productive. The strain on the social safety net is less because moral hazard problems and abuse are avoided.

Civil society substitutes for government in addressing market failure. Government is much smaller than would have otherwise been the case. The nation becomes a more attractive investment environment and enjoys higher returns because of self-enforcing contracts, better harmony, and lower taxes. There is a better chance of actualizing Deuteronomy 15:4's vision of there being no poor. Generous retail returns policies are sustainable, and pilferage and policing costs are minimized. Tax compliance is much higher, as is volunteerism, especially for public services, such as firefighting. Credence goods and services are provided honestly and with the best quality. People internalize the Lockean proviso of leaving "enough and as good for others" in appropriating property for themselves. There is greater trust and simplicity of life all around. Indeed, agape has great instrumental value and benefits for the economy. Using the language of economics itself, we can say that agape creates tremendous economic value as it reduces monitoring and enforcement costs.

Theological Affirmation

The preceding sections present the case for why agape easily passes Adam Smith et al.'s subsistence test, just like justice. No community can exist without agape. It plays a central role in essential areas that shape the character and quality of socioeconomic life: institutional preconditions, the triage and pursuit of economic goals, frictional and transaction costs, value formation, and the development of customs, law, and usage. Note that these arguments are all based on reason and experience, including economic history, empirical evidence, and economic thought.

Chapters 6 and 7 present theological arguments on the need for agape not only in the marketplace, but in life as a whole. Benedict XVI (2005, #26, 28–29) brings up the Marxist claim that what the poor need is not beneficence but justice. In rectifying unjust social structures, there will be no need for mutual acts of charity. Benedict XVI acknowledges injustice as a source of much human suffering. Nevertheless, the claim that

just social structures render agape superfluous is a materialist concep-
tion of the human person and "disregards all that is specifically human"
(#28b). Even if we were to assume, for the sake of argument, that there
are no longer any instances of injustice, humans will still need to be
benevolent and beneficent to one another because agape is at the heart
of what it is to be human. Even in the most just society, the state cannot
provide what the human person needs most – to love and be loved. We
examine more of these theological warrants for agape in the later chapters. Agape is indispensable in human life and is not merely ornamental,
pace Adam Smith et al.

PART II

How and Why Agape-Justice Conflicts Arise

CHAPTER 4

Socioeconomic Disequilibria

The preceding chapter had argued that agape makes up for justice's limitations. Justice by itself is not a sufficient condition for socioeconomic life. Social life needs agape working alongside justice. Thus, in resolving agape-justice conflicts, we cannot always defer to justice's claims over those of agape.

Nevertheless, lest we err in swinging too far to the other extreme, we cannot assume either that in settling agape-justice conflicts, agape must always have precedence over justice's claims because of the former's manifold contributions. Recall, for example, Anders Nygren's position that agape trumps justice and is oblivious to it. This may be an extreme position because from a purely pragmatic viewpoint, agape needs justice. Thus, agape and justice are necessary complements. They mutually reinforce each other. They are distinct but inseparable. Agape and justice are symbiotic in what we may aptly describe as a socioeconomic *homeostasis*.

Socioeconomic Homeostasis

Economic agency is fundamental in personal life because humans are corporeal beings. They need material inputs for both body and soul. Economic agency is also a constitutive element of community life because the goods of the earth are finite, even as people have unlimited wants and needs. There will be a consequent clash of competing claims and a need to allocate scarce resources to their competing uses. Besides, there is rival consumption[1] and consequent opportunity costs to every economic choice. Thus, mainstream economic thinking views economics as a science of allocation.

The allocative task is challenging. Market exchange is complex, fluid, and ceaseless. It is comprised of an extensive web of interdependence. It

---

[1] Rival consumption means that a good or service cannot be consumed or used simultaneously by more than one person at a time.

leaves in its wake both salutary and adverse ripple effects that are inter-woven. It produces accumulative harms that require collective action for mitigation. It creates a constant stream of new problems and concerns, even as people are yet grappling with how to respond to past and current difficulties. Not all claims can be satisfied. And all this is not even to men-tion the intergenerational dimension of economic life, in which economic choices today have a consequential impact on future generations. Then, there are the consequences for the ecology that must be taken to account.

Such clashing claims can be resolved in a variety of ways:

- anarchically, as in a Hobbesian state of nature where might is right, and everyone is at war with everybody else.
- by the fiat of an elite ruling class (e.g., ancient, medieval, feudal eras).
- in a reasoned and orderly fashion, to the extent possible, as in the case of the marketplace.

Economic history provides abundant and robust empirical validation to the claim that there is, to date, no other social institution that can match the efficiency of the marketplace in allocating scarce goods.

Markets do not arise in a vacuum, nor are they self-sustaining. As we have seen earlier, they are undergirded by a foundational set of institu-tions, such as government and civil society. They are sustained by formal and informal rules that are enforced through legal means or through public moral suasion (forte of justice). There is a requisite minimum level of trust and mutual solicitude among its participants (forte of agape). Markets are both an outcome and a contributory cause of culture and civilization.

Justice and agape are among the building blocks of these institutional preconditions that hold together and sustain socioeconomic life. To be sure, the requirements of justice and agape are not homogeneous, nor do they always harmonize. Justice and agape have their respective constitutive elements, each with their own demands and prescriptions. These often present competing claims in economic life. Justice and agape are not the panacea that can sort through the allocative challenges posed by economic life. Justice and agape will not satisfy all claims, nor will they lead to a consensus. Nevertheless, justice and agape provide vital conceptual tools that enable people to talk with one another about how best to allocate burdens and benefits among themselves. It may not be the best or even the second-best, or the umpteenth-best solution, but what matters is that justice and agape permit an orderly and reasoned adjudication of clash-ing claims. The great moment here is that grappling constantly with such intractable problems of allocation may strengthen people's commitment to and appreciation for one another, or it may occasion the demise of such a community. These are the stakes facing justice and agape as they make their case with their respective clashing claims.

The two preceding chapters have argued that socioeconomic life needs both justice and agape. Each of these is a necessary condition without which the economy cannot survive, much less thrive. Chapter 2 has shown how justice provides the fundamental framework for economic life. This is evident to most people. What may not be obvious to many, however, is how agape performs critical functions without which people cannot have an economy. Love is also essential for the smooth functioning of the marketplace (Chapter 3).

The difficulty, of course, arises when it comes to satisfying the claims of agape and justice while simultaneously considering rival consumption and limited societal resources. Whose claims take precedence, and why? Obviously, there is a need to mix the demands of both agape and justice depending on the time and place. To borrow the term "homeostasis" from biology, there is a delicate balance that must be maintained between agape and justice, just as the human body needs a delicate balance of various fluids, cells, and organisms to function properly. Significant deviations from the requisite balance lead to illness. So it is with socioeconomic life. Agape and justice complement each other – mutually reinforcing, substituting for, or correcting each other's limitations. Imbalance leads to socioeconomic dysfunction. *Agape-justice conflicts may in fact signal an imbalance in the market's homeostasis, that is, its institutional preconditions, its rank ordering of its goals, and its underlying customs, law, and usage.*

History of Economic Thought

The notion of a socioeconomic homeostasis that requires balancing both agape and justice in the community should not come as a surprise to scholars of the history of economic thought. Italian thinkers of the 15th and 16th centuries point out that markets are in fact underpinned by a public ethos of reciprocity and civic virtues and not by modern economic theory's self-interested, utility-maximizing *homo oeconomicus* (Bruni and Zamagni 2007). Such reciprocity and civic virtues in the economy are examples of Civic Humanism on full display. Antonio Genovesi in the 18th century describes the central importance of *philia* for a functional economy. This chapter's appeal for a socioeconomic homeostasis of justice and agape parallels the literature on the civil economy paradigm that Stefano Zamagni (2021) describes along a tripartite axis of Community – Market – State versus modern mainstream economics' paradigm of a bipartite axis of Market – State. The Franciscan economy of the pre-modern era is an example of such a tripartite dynamic that relies on civic virtues and values.[2]

Consider, too, how Adam Smith's *Wealth of Nations* is complemented by his earlier work *Theory of Moral Sentiments*. While the *Wealth of Nations* touts the power of the "invisible hand" in harnessing the butcher's, baker's and brewer's self-interest to promote the good of the community, the *Theory of Moral Sentiments* accentuates human values and virtues, including prudence, sympathy, and self-control, that underpin economic life. In other words, the much-touted self-regulating mechanism of the market in the *Wealth of Nations* is in fact dependent on the mores discussed in the *Theory of Moral Sentiments*. Even by Adam Smith's standards, both agape and justice need each other to produce a functional economy.

Note Francis Fukuyama's (1995) conclusion regarding the necessary foundations of the postindustrial society:

> The liberal democracy that emerges at the end of history is therefore not entirely 'modern.' If the institutions of democracy and capitalism are to work properly, they must coexist with certain premodern cultural habits that ensure their proper functioning. Law, contract, and economic rationality provide a necessary but not sufficient basis for both the stability and prosperity of postindustrial societies; *they must as well be leavened with reciprocity, moral obligation, duty toward community, and trust, which are based in habit rather than rational calculation.* (Fukuyama 1995, 11, emphasis added)

Indeed, regardless of the era or type of economy, agape serves an indispensable role in socioeconomic life.

The need for both agape and justice is consistent with the earlier observed differentiation between justice and agape. Justice is an ethics of right action. It is concerned with what is the right thing to do. Agape is an ethics of being. Its focus is on what it is to be a whole person. What does it mean to be human and a member of a community? What kind of person or community do we want to be (Flanagan and Jackson 1987)? Undoubtedly, an ethics of right action and an ethics of being are complementary. They need each other.

Philosophical and Biblical Warrants of Agape-Justice Homeostasis

Socioeconomic homeostasis – the delicate balancing of both agape and justice for a functional socioeconomic life – is merely a reflection of the

[2] "Franciscan Economy." https://franciscanoted.com/franciscan-economy/ last accessed April 19, 2022.

larger complementarity of agape and justice in life. Not surprisingly, we find such agape-justice homeostasis affirmed in social philosophy, theology, and Sacred Scripture.

Practical Wisdom

Socrates in *Republic*, Book I, Chapter 2, views Polemarchus's definition of justice as incomplete because Socrates believes that benevolence is a part of justice. There has to be benevolence if justice is to be justice at all (Socrates 1941; Koutsouvilis 1976, 430). Love and justice are not contradictory. They are not merely supplements to one another in which we are to love others in addition to treating them justly. Love and justice are not a restriction, a constraint, or a brake on one another. Rather, they are one whole piece (Wolterstorff 2011, 80–84).

Justice provides the "ad hoc" structures in how to deal with the messiness of the claims of the here and now (temporal life), while love provides the wisdom that gives us a glimpse of where we are headed or supposed to be headed (the not yet of the Messianic Age) (Gardner 1957, 221). Indeed, both justice and love are needed for proleptic living, that is, living in the here and now how we are to live in the transcendent life.

Note the complementarity in the differing objects of justice and love. The object of justice is societal order – the orderly allocation of scarce resources (e.g., time, roles, material goods, power, attention). It directs the proper ordering and adjudication of competing claims. Justice is about getting people to live together side by side without rancor. However, the absence of rancor is such a low bar, just as the absence of war is not necessarily meaningful peace. Nevertheless, low bar as it may be, it is essential – a precondition. This is because justice makes possible a wary living together as a group, a Hobbesian social contract in which people will have to be constantly defensive and protective of their rights and claims. Justice deals with the immediate existential question for the community – will it survive as an assemblage of people living together? Nevertheless, such collective co-existence is not a community. It is love that turns it into a genuine human community. The object of love is *koinōnia* (fellowship).

Both love and justice serve the social nature of the person. However, love goes further than justice in that love also addresses the very core of personhood – integral human development. Love is not satisfied with just living together with others. Love goes further with a deeply fulfilling friendship with others and with God.

Sacred Scripture

In the prophetic literature, love and justice form one single piece: *misphat*, *chesed*, and *tzedeq*. Love and justice mutually reinforce one another and come as a single unit. This justice-love tandem is the model for humans (Gardner 1957). God's *tzedeq* comprises both justice (*mishpat*) and mercy (*chesed*). Justice and love, while distinct, are in fact inseparable. They are constitutive of righteousness (*tzedeq*). Biblical Israel experienced first-hand such divine justice and mercy multiple times when it had turned away from God and got into trouble, only to be saved by God. God's righteousness is the basis and the model for human righteousness (*tzedeq*). Humans are righteous when they fulfill the demands of their relationships. Among these are the love of God and neighbor. Thus, as part of their Covenant with God, Israelites were to care for one another, especially those who were marginalized. They had to live up to the laws given by God if they were to be righteous.

The prophetic literature is emphatic that Biblical Israel's injustice is an impediment to love. The wisdom literature repeatedly underscores the link between love, justice, and human flourishing.

> I have been young, and now am old,
> > yet I have not seen the righteous forsaken
> > or their children begging bread.
> They are ever giving liberally and lending,
> > and their children become a blessing.
> Depart from evil, and do good;
> > so you shall abide forever.
> For the LORD loves justice;
> > he will not forsake his faithful ones. (Psalm 37:25–28)

Biblical Israel shows us that justice is a necessary condition of love. It is a building block of love. Justice is instrumental for love. Thus, the God of Abraham, Isaac, and Jacob found Biblical Israel's holocausts despicable because of its injustices. The Chosen People had to be just to love. To love is to be just – both for Biblical Israel and for God. Thus, the nation had to be chastised in the evil it brought down upon itself. For the Hebrew Scripture, divine love and justice form a single package. Love comes with the Law.

Lawrence Toombs (1965) submits that the Book of Deuteronomy illustrates well how love and justice is a relationship of continuity and reinforcement. Love is the motive that gives rise to justice. Justice flows from love. After all, God gave the Law to Israel not for God's sake but for the sake of Israel out of God's love for them.[3]

The Covenant between Biblical Israel and God was characterized by a triangular bond in which (1) God loved Israel and initiated the Covenant relationship and in which (2) Israel, in its own turn, responds to God's love and initiatives, (3) overflowing into interpersonal relationships within the nation. Thus, it is a three-sided relationship. Only the first of these two relationships are characterized by love: Deuteronomy 7:6–11 for relationship (1) and Deuteronomy 10:12–22 for relationship (2). For the third leg of the triad, relationship (3), the Deuteronomist is quiet. The writer of Deuteronomy is realistic enough to see that getting the Israelites to love one another may be a tall order. Toombs (1965) captures the tension between justice and love well. How can love be given to the undeserving and the reprehensible?

> The book, it should be reiterated, was designed to deal with the hard and often unattractive realities of a society in decay. Israelite society, as the Deuteronomist knew it, contained its full quota of false prophets, aggressive landlords, greedy merchants, corrupt judges, witches and wizards, thieves, adulterers, and insensitive parents, and they all appear in the legal sections of the book. How, as a practical matter, does one love this motley and repulsive crew? Can love for our fellow man really be a reliable guide amid the ambiguities of life in human society? (Toombs 1965, 407)

It was Leviticus 19:18 that eventually characterized relationship (3) in terms of love. Meanwhile, justice filled the lacuna.

> [T]he purity of one's feelings is not as important as the nature of one's deeds. One does not have to feel for one's fellows the intense, total sympathy and community which love implies in order to treat them as fellow members of the Covenant, under the Covenant. In society, justice is what is demanded, and not necessarily the full range and power of love. Indeed, in the thought of the Deuteronomist, justice and love are closely akin, *for justice is nothing less than love with its coat off, in action in society.* (Toombs 1965, 407–408, original emphasis)

Love and justice are close to being identical to one another, albeit in a different guise. In fact, Leviticus 19:11–18 shows the relationship of justice and love as one of continuity and reinforcement (Allbee 2006).

Justice is the manifestation of the minimum requirements of love. Justice is love at work. It is the instantiation of love.

---

[3] Toombs (1965, 402) notes the Deuteronomist's use in Hebrew of *'ahab*, in contrast to Hosea's *hesed*. He suggests that this choice of word for love implies intensity, interiority, totality, and a familial bond.

[T]he Deuteronomist offered a concept of justice which would carry the *minimum* claim of love into action in society; but he was fully conscious that justice is a minimal expression of the operation of love – a floor, as it were, upon which love walks and below which it cannot descend... when he has done this he has transmuted love into justice and justice into the minimum activity of love. (Toombs 1965, 411, emphasis original)

Justice is in the very essence of God. This is evident in Biblical Israel's liberation from her slavery in Egypt. Justice is the same quality and essence that God now passes on to Israel – not as a burden, but out of God's love for Israel. Justice is not an imposition. The Law is in fact a divine gift flowing from divine love. Biblical Israel was invited to love and to be just so that she might be holy as God is holy (Lev 19:2). Justice is in fact a gift of love and flows from love. They form a seamless whole. It would be wrong to think of justice or love as being simply an add-on to the other. The inseparability of justice and love is best seen in the abhorrence God had for all the sacrifices and holocausts Biblical Israel was offering in observance of the Law, even as they were oppressing the weak and defenseless in their midst. Rather, they were invited to let justice roll down like a river (Amos 5:21–24).

Jesus Christ in the New Testament also provides an example and completes this link between justice and love. We witness justice at work when Jesus confronts the scribes, elders, and Pharisees for their hollow observance of the Law, following it to the letter, but not its spirit. He warns them of the great reversals about to befall them (Mt 21:28–46). Law (and justice by extension) must be observed from the heart and not grudgingly or half-heartedly. This means that justice/law must be observed with and from love. Justice is animated by love! This is the only genuine obedience that is fitting for the Covenant relationship, which was given by God out of love for Israel after all. It is the Chosen People's way of requiting God's love. In this regard, the scribes, elders, and Pharisees of Jesus' time failed in their Covenant obligations. This is the point of contention between Jesus and the Jewish religious leadership.

Nevertheless, we also see love at work in Christ as he heals, forgives, and shows mercy to all, but especially those who were undeserving of such love and mercy, like those responsible for his arrest, torture, and death (Lk 23:34). In his own person and in his own deed, Jesus demonstrates the inseparability of justice and agape. The letter of James affirms that one cannot claim to love God without being just to the poor and one another.

Sample Cases of Homeostatic Imbalances

The discussion thus far has been purely theoretical. Real-life agape-justice conflicts arise when the abovementioned economic homeostasis is under stress, imbalanced, or is adjusting. For example, as we have seen earlier, economic life is a mixture of goals pursued: allocative efficiency, equity, growth, stability, harmony, and sustainability. The community assigns various weights to this variety of objectives. However, circumstances, needs, political commitments, and values change, as does the public ethos. Agape-justice conflicts arise during the process of debate and consensus building in changing or rebalancing the mix of priorities.

How Generous to Make the Social Safety Net

Clashing claims may in fact signal the need to adjust the dividing line between justice and agape (Table 1.2) because of a shifting economic terrain, problematic market outcomes, or unsustainable market processes, or all of these. Conflicts may indicate the need to tweak customs, law, and usage (CLU). It is very likely that the more severe the disequilibria or the threat to this delicate socioeconomic homeostasis, the more severe is the conflict between justice and agape. A good example of such severe disequilibrium and dissatisfaction is the long-running struggle in dealing with the US healthcare infrastructure and restrictive access. Prior to the Affordable Care Act of 2010 (aka Obamacare), many had no access to healthcare. Anecdotal accounts abound of stricken individuals and their families having to choose between getting lifesaving treatment and being driven into bankruptcy. Despite spending so much more of its economy on healthcare compared to other developed countries, the United States trails many other nations in health outcomes. The political debate is fierce on whether US healthcare provision should be left to the marketplace or to government, or to both. Republicans stress individual responsibility, while Democrats call for greater mutual assistance. Obamacare is an example of how the United States opted through the political process for more mutual compassion and assistance as an important collective goal. Republicans' continued efforts to rescind the law or pare it down shows this as a socioeconomic homeostasis that is still contested, at least around healthcare.

The debate over US healthcare provision reflects the much larger and longstanding issue of how large and how generous to make the social safety net. Even the most market-oriented political economies have some form of social assistance for their citizens and residents who fall to the chance and contingencies of economic life. Thus, we see a wide assortment of government programs, such as unemployment insurance, social security, disability pay, assistance for the elderly, medical care for the poor, food stamps, and housing assistance, among many others. Such aid is consistent with nations living up to the obligations imposed by distributive justice. There is also an element of commutative justice in many of these cases because of the premiums paid by people into these programs such as social security, healthcare, and unemployment insurance. The provision of such safety nets is a demand of justice.

Currently, it is a foregone conclusion in most nations that there is need for such safety nets. However, the contentious debates are primarily about the scope and the generosity of these social protective measures. For how long, what kind, and how much assistance should be provided? What are the criteria to qualify for such help? How restrictive should eligibility be? What conditions must be imposed on recipients to ensure that they exercise personal responsibility and not be completely dependent on the rest of the community?

The laws instituting these social programs spell out the general rules that will apply to all, including guidelines governing exemptions or leniencies. Unfortunately, no matter how detailed these statutes may be, legislation will not be able to cover all possible contingencies nor consider the particularities of people's circumstances and needs. There will be people who will still fall through the cracks and not qualify for these ameliorative measures or not have their needs adequately met. The number of such cases falling through the cracks can be minimized by being generous in terms of benefits, criteria for eligibility, exemptions, etc. However, this causes program costs to rise as will the requisite taxes to fund these safety nets.[4] An example is the Medicaid expansion as part of the US Affordable Care Act to minimize the number of people who will be excluded. Ten states, as of March 2023, refused to avail of matching Federal funds for this expansion so as not to increase their state-level taxes thereby leaving 2.1 million people without healthcare coverage.[5] In effect, these 10 states chose not to assist people unable to access healthcare rather than raise taxes for the rest of the community.

---

[4] In addition, critics argue that it also increases the moral hazard problem of people taking less responsibility for their own upkeep given the generosity of these programs.

[5] These are the people who are too poor to avail of the Affordable Care Act (ACA) market assistance even as they do not qualify for Medicaid because their states declined the ACA Medicaid expansion. (Center on Budget and Policy Priorities. www.cbpp.org/research/health/the-medicaid-coverage-gap last accessed May 21, 2023.)

Compassion and regard for the well-being of the vulnerable and marginalized in the community would call for a more unstinting and a more inclusive approach. However, questions from distributive and general-legal justice will arise, at some point, as to whether the threshold of what is reasonable and just in taxation has been crossed. After all, social safety nets are de facto transfer programs. They redistribute burdens and benefits among community members. In addition, distributive and general-legal justice will also address, at some point, the even more difficult issue of fostering a moral hazard problem in which unscrupulous people take advantage of these generous government transfers and reduce their work effort. Thus, it is not surprising that the design of such social programs is fiercely contested.

Take the case of US unemployment insurance. "Workfare" was introduced as a condition for receiving unemployment insurance, food assistance, and other types of aid (Wiseman 1986). On the one hand, proponents of workfare wanted to ensure that people were exercising their personal responsibility in improving their condition in life. They point to anecdotal accounts of able-bodied people who have abused such state largesse. On the other hand, critics of workfare give compelling accounts of people whose circumstances are so dire as to be unable to meet this condition.

The debates surrounding the design of these assistance programs reflect the tension between the demands of agape and the demands of justice. Commutative and distributive justice demand that taxpayer funds are used properly and judiciously, lest tax-paying citizens and residents bear more burdens than they should. General-legal justice demands that people take responsibility for their own upkeep, to the extent of their abilities, and not be dependent on the community. They owe this obligation to the community and to themselves. However, agape calls for greater generosity and compassion both in the design and administration of these programs to minimize the number of people excluded. Adjudicating these clashing claims is made much more difficult because no matter how detailed legislation may be, there will be both unforeseen circumstances and hardship cases for which the law has not made provisions.

The same tension is also seen in the design and implementation of trade adjustment assistance programs.[6] As we will soon see in a later section, international trade displaces some segments of the population who will

---

[6] See *Trade Adjustment Assistance Reauthorization Act of 2015*, U.S. Department of Labor. www.dol .gov/agencies/eta/tradeactn last accessed April 18, 2022.

need assistance re-training and relocating as they are reintegrated back into some other sectors of the economy. The hard choices are the same: How high should the bar be set for people to qualify for these programs? For how long should assistance be provided? How much help should be given? What conditions should be attached in exchange for receiving these benefits? Who should bear the cost of such aid?

Chronic fiscal deficits and ballooning government debt open another front in the clashing claims between agape and justice. Consider the case of the US Covid-19 stimulus package. There was much disagreement over the extension of the supplemental unemployment insurance and the size of the stimulus package that eventually totaled $5 trillion. Critics were against the total amount set and the threshold income for eligibility for these stimulus benefits. Many US citizens and residents did not need these payments. Nevertheless, both the supplemental unemployment insurance and the stimulus package were made generous for the sake of those who truly needed them. This illustrates yet again the need to be extra generous in an effort to minimize the number of people whose needs will be inadequately met. A consequence of all this is the aggravation of already swollen budget deficits and the national debt (Parlapiano et al. 2022). This is not to mention contributing significantly to the forty-year high inflation rate that ensued (Labonte and Weinstock 2022, 17–22) and the costs that such high prices inflicted on all, especially the poor. It is an example of how one can be too beneficent to excess.

Compassion today will in effect be paid for by higher taxes on the next generations. It is the same trade-off for all the other programs mentioned earlier, including Medicare, Medicaid, and social security that saddles the US government and future generations with multi-trillion-dollar unfunded liabilities (Scott 2010). This does not even include the issue of government bailouts for unfunded or failing private pension funds. One cannot adjudicate contemporary clashing claims between agape and justice in favor of compassion and then simply pass on the bill to future generations. Most reasonable people would say that this is neither just nor even genuine compassion. General-legal justice, intertemporal distributive justice, and part one of the principle of subsidiarity[7] demand that the bill for today's compassion must largely be shouldered by current generations, to the extent possible. Otherwise, it is the easy way out of resolving these contemporary clashing claims of agape and justice.

---

[7] Part one of the principle of subsidiarity calls on people to do what they can do for themselves instead of passing on responsibility to others or a higher body. See Pius XI (1931, *Quadragesimo Anno* #79).

In sum, the compassion that argues for generous government social safety nets to mitigate distress and minimize the people who fall through the cracks will bump up against the demands of justice on behalf of the people and the next generations who will have to shoulder the cost of these programs. Agape and justice clash both during the legislative phase of these programs when they are designed and during their execution when agencies and local governments have wide discretion in writing the implementing rules at the local level on how restrictive or how generous these safety nets will be in actual practice.

Market versus Government Mix

Closely related to the issue of social safety nets is the even larger debate on the right mix of market versus government in economic life. This debate also reflects the clashing claims of agape and justice. Take the case of the political divide in the United States. Republicans believe that government should let private initiative take the lead in the marketplace, intervening only as needed. People ought to take personal responsibility for their own upkeep, and this is best done in the marketplace where people exercise their autonomy in setting and pursuing their own life goals and be compensated accordingly. Risk-taking, education, initiative, and an excellent work ethic are rewarded appropriately. People are remunerated for their efforts. Distribution is according to their contribution and merit. People get their just deserts. Not surprisingly, justice-oriented people who prize personal responsibility call for a more market-oriented political economy.

In contrast, Democrats focus on the marketplace's shortcomings and call for government to be pro-active in setting and achieving worthwhile social goals that could not be achieved via the marketplace alone. They are more empathetic to the plight of the people at the margins and see a communal responsibility toward them. Thus, there is a widespread public perception that Republicans are hard-hearted, embrace a law-and-order approach to governance, and are averse to government involvement. In contrast, Democrats are deemed more compassionate and empathetic, especially as they champion large government programs that serve the marginalized. They have been labelled as the "tax-and-spend party." Note how President George W. Bush, Republican, had to go so far as to tout his own political philosophy of "compassionate conservatism."[8] Similarly, there is a common view that Europeans are more compassionate with their

---

[8] See George W. Bush Institute (2018).

social economy and its sizable government role, in contrast to the just-deserts emphasis of the US market-oriented approach in which personal responsibility is uppermost.

In practice, extra-market intervention is often required to correct market failures. Thus, we see government and NGOs rectifying or mitigating market failures (e.g., aforesaid social safety nets, social enterprises, soup kitchens). Extra-market interventions are often required by justice itself to correct flawed market processes and outcomes (e.g., unemployment insurance). Nevertheless, many more of such extra-market interventions are motivated by and called for by compassion.

A good example of this is the EU's stance regarding healthcare provision, childcare, and labor market regulation. EU governments take a much bigger role in regulating these areas of social life with an eye toward improving the well-being of their citizens. Of course, all these are accompanied by a much higher tax bill. Arguments from distributive justice can be made to justify such an approach (distribution according to need and contribution according to means). Nevertheless, compassion and an equal regard for all (agape) provide a major impetus for this more pro-active extra-market intervention in economic life. This is in sharp contrast to the United States and its more market-oriented approach in which distributive justice underscores personal responsibility.

In sum, agape is not only more inclined but would in fact advocate for a much larger government economic role to protect the vulnerable.[9] In contrast, more justice-oriented moral agents who underscore personal responsibility tend to be more market-oriented in their political philosophy because markets are believed to reward according to people's merit and contribution.[10]

Agape-Justice Tensions at the Executive Level

It is not only in legislatures that we see the tension between agape and justice play out. We also witness similar hard choices in the executive arm of

[9] This is not to say, however, that extra-market intervention is the exclusive domain of agape. Social justice and some of the criteria in distributive justice also call for extra-market interventions, as in the case of egalitarianism.

[10] This tug-of-war between compassion's greater reliance on collective action, on the one hand, and justice's call for greater individual responsibility, on the other hand, plays out as well in the perennial debates in the EU on how its initiatives are to be funded. Northern European countries such as Germany and the Netherlands call for greater national responsibility, while southern European countries such as Greece and Italy call for joint action and shared funding. Note, for example, their constant wrangling over mutualized debt.

government. Take the case of Dreamers in the United States. The Obama Administration took a more compassionate approach in 2012 by providing legal paperwork to undocumented adults who had been brought to the country as children. Such documents allow them to participate more fully and openly in the larger community, such as getting a job, going for higher education, securing a driver's license, and availing of public services, among others. This is not even to mention relieving them of the constant fear of deportation. Critics have successfully challenged this executive action in courts. Dreamers have been on a roller coaster ride. Compare the differing stance taken by the Trump administration, and then by the Biden presidency (Nieto del Rio and Miriam Jordan 2021).

Or, consider the debate over student debt forgiveness. Advocates have been pushing for executive action in providing generous debt relief. In contrast, critics have been adamantly opposed as it causes moral hazard problems, is unfair to the preceding generations and students who worked hard to pay off their debt, and goes against people taking greater personal responsibility (Mulhere 2021).

In both cases, there is leeway for immediate action, either for more compassion or for a stricter observance of the law, through executive action.[11] Agape-justice tensions are most likely a common dilemma facing executives at all levels of governance – national, state, or local. After all, laws are subject to interpretation when it comes to implementation, not to mention the leniencies and exemptions that can be invoked.

Corporate Governance: Shareholder versus Stakeholder Model

Milton Friedman's (1970) famous article on the social responsibility of business is unambiguous. Its primary responsibility is to do what it does best: earn as much profits as it can. After all, this is the contractual agreement between shareholders and corporate managers. The latter have been hired not to solve society's problems but to run the business enterprise. Moreover, a successful business sector redounds to the benefit of society. This is reminiscent of Adam Smith's butcher, baker, and brewer who end up producing much social good even as they pursue their own private interests.

---

[11] Many would argue that both cases of the Dreamers and student debt forgiveness are intra-justice conflicts, that is, differences in the criteria used for what constitutes justice rather than agape-justice conflicts. This is not the place to settle this claim. It is sufficient for our purposes to note that, at the very least, both cases can also be argued from the point of view of agape – for more compassion. Recall the earlier discussion in the Preface on the methodology used in this study of opting for the argument of last resort – compassion.

Commutative justice supports Friedman's call to protect shareholders' interests. In prioritizing allocative efficiency, merit, or contribution as essential goals of the economy, one can argue that distributive justice also supports Friedman's position on the social responsibility of business. In contrast, agape will disagree, as it is more in line with a triple bottom line approach. It will call for a stakeholder rather than a shareholder model of corporate management.

This tension between a shareholder and stakeholder approach was evident in the sale of Ben and Jerry's to Unilever in 2000. The original founders of this successful ice cream brand preferred to let a more socially oriented firm take over their company but had no choice. They could have been sued because selling to Unilever provided much better pecuniary value for shareholders (Hays 2000). Because of the Ben and Jerry's case, numerous US states have since then enacted what have been called B-Corp laws. These laws now make it possible to prioritize the claims of agape over those of justice without fear of being sued by shareholders. This tension between a stakeholder and a shareholder mode of governance mirrors the fault line between the claims of agape and justice.[12]

In sum, agape-justice conflicts are symptomatic that there are disequilibria in the community's socioeconomic homeostasis that need to be addressed. As we have seen in the preceding cases, such disequilibria can be rectified by amending laws, adjusting goals set for the economy, or altering the public ethos. The following chapters examine other causes of agape-justice conflicts. These present many other cases of disequilibria in the socioeconomic homeostasis requiring changes in customs, law, and usage. Agape-justice conflicts get to be much more complicated when their multiple causes mutually reinforce and aggravate each other to make the resulting conflict that much more difficult to resolve.

Settling Agape-Justice Conflicts

Not a Binary Choice

As we have seen earlier, Adam Smith et al., argue that only justice passes the subsistence test, that is, society cannot exist without justice and that everything else is merely ornamental, an optional add-on, including agape. The preceding chapter disputed their claim. The community cannot exist

---

[12] Again, note that the stakeholder model can also be argued based on justice. I have opted to bypass this and to go directly to its fallback argument – based on agape as equal regard for all.

without agape either. Agape passes the subsistence test as well. Given that both justice and agape are essential for the community's subsistence, it makes no sense to ask which one is more important at a general level, a priori. Both are needed. One can only do a triage at the level of particulars and only after having weighed the context, the current state of balance or imbalance in socioeconomic homeostasis, and the need to adjust accordingly. Imbalance in socioeconomic homeostasis serves a useful diagnostic function in revealing whether the current state of the community needs to settle pending agape-justice conflicts in favor of one or the other.

Thus, resolving clashing claims of agape and justice is not a case of either one or the other but not both. The choice is not as stark as that. In fact, there are problems both with the presentation of the issue in the literature and with the public's perception of these clashing claims.

First, in his comparison of justice and beneficence in the *Theory of Moral Sentiments,* Adam Smith equates justice with the duty to do no harm to others. Note, once again, his reason for why the virtue of justice takes precedence over the virtue of beneficence:

> Society, however, cannot subsist among those who are at all times ready to hurt and injure one another. *The moment that injury begins, the moment that mutual resentment and animosity take place, all the bands of it are broke asunder,* and the different members of which it consisted are, as it were, dissipated and scattered abroad by the violence and opposition of their discordant affections. (Smith 1790, II-II.III, emphasis added)

For him, foregoing justice opens the door to people preying on each other and, consequently, descending into Hobbes' state of nature. He is adamant that society can exist without benevolence, but it cannot exist without justice. The latter is foundational for any community. John Stuart Mill uses the same argument to arrive at the same conclusion.

> '[t]he moral rules which forbid mankind to hurt one another ... are more vital to human well-being than any maxims,' ... because '[i]t is their obedience which alone preserves peace' and because 'a person may possibly not need the benefit of others, but he always needs that they should not do him hurt.' (Shaver 1992, 551)

Grotius, Pufendorf, and Kames also follow Smith in making the duty to do no harm to others the centerpiece of the duty of justice. Not surprisingly, they also base their defense of the preeminence of justice on the existence of society itself. They view justice as primarily about people not harming each other. The virtue of justice not only passes the subsistence test but is also accorded the strongest claim (the strictest of obligations).

Smith et al., are right that the duty of justice is a necessary condition for society's existence. It is an existential matter. Nevertheless, this is an incomplete view of justice. There is much more to justice than the duty to do no harm, important and central as this is. Besides giving people their due by not inflicting injury on their life, liberty, or pursuit of happiness, justice is also about giving people their due in the manifold interpersonal exchanges characteristic of human life. In fact, the bulk of justice's enforcement deals with disputes on fairness in the allocation or exchange of resources, burdens, and benefits. Commutative and distributive justice are its workhorses. Thus, as we see in the cases presented in this study, conflicts between justice and beneficence are not about life-and-death harm to others but about entitlements and transfers. Foregoing justice in these cases in favor of beneficence need not immediately nor necessarily lead to the destruction of society, as would have been the case if the issue on hand were exclusively or principally about the duty of not hurting others, as in the exposition of Smith et al. In comparing the virtues of justice and beneficence, one cannot pose the problem merely as a choice between preventing life-threatening harm to others (justice) and being charitable. There are many other constitutive elements of both justice and love. Both virtues are richly heterogeneous.

The second problem has to do with the common impression that what is at stake in agape-justice conflicts is the stark choice of foregoing *in their entirety* either agape or justice. The issue gets to be an all-or-nothing proposition. Society loses justice altogether in favoring beneficence, or vice versa. This is to fall for the fallacy of composition, in which what is true for a part is necessarily true for the whole. Thus, one must be cautious with the sweeping conclusions of the social philosophers and theologians reviewed in Chapter 2 who favor duties of justice over duties of agape as a universal rule.

Furthermore, clashing claims between justice and agape are generally not one-time events but repeat over time. In fact, many of the cases considered in this study are in chronic agape-justice conflict (e.g., migration, social safety net, foreign aid). Thus, one can accommodate the claims of justice or agape in these various iterations, taking into account the state of their homeostasis and previous resolutions of their claims, and then adjusting accordingly for any disequilibria. The most appropriate analogy to use is that of riding a bicycle. The adjustments are constant and expected in order to stay upright and move forward. So it is with maintaining equilibrium in the socioeconomic homeostasis.

We see examples of such adjustments when nations reform or institute new social welfare safety nets in response to shifting needs and challenges in the community. Note, for example, Brazil's and Mexico's successful conditional cash transfer. The US Affordable Healthcare Act is another instance, as are the US Social Security program instituted in the 1930s, its expanded welfare programs in the war against poverty in the 1960s, and its reform in the 1990s. Note, too, the tweaks to these programs and to taxes with every change of administration and the composition of Congress, reflective of shifts in the public ethos.

An example of the never-ending, delicate process of balancing the demands of agape and justice is Stephen John Duckett's (2023) *Healthcare Funding and Christian Ethics*. He calls for greater public funding of healthcare. This is a universal human need that many are unable to access under current CLU. The community cannot stand idly in the face of this moral problem. Greater public funding is justified based not only on agape, but also on justice itself. There is need to change CLU accordingly to reflect this shift in public thinking and to justify such public policy response. Nevertheless, this is neither a simple nor a smooth process. In his Chapter 5, he acknowledges the need to sort through three competing demands that arise in healthcare, namely: a compassion – social justice tension, a compassion – stewardship tension, and a social justice – stewardship tension. This is not the place to delve into the intricacies of these trade-offs and his proposed solutions. It is sufficient to note for our purposes that agape-justice conflicts are often not straightforward and that the key lies in balancing the demands of both, as circumstances warrant, instead of a blanket rule of prioritizing the claims of justice over agape or vice versa.

Temporal Dimension

People do not acquire virtues overnight.[13] They do so over time through repeated choices. Moral choices have a reflexive dimension to them because they come back to define and shape the character and personality of the moral agent. Thus, if one makes the effort to be kind and loving even to difficult people, he/she eventually becomes a virtuous person of kindness and love. Being kind and loving eventually becomes second nature to that person, a defining feature of his/her character and personality. Technically, this is the *habitus* (Aristotle's *hexus*), which has been variously described as the state of character, a disposition, or even a power. Every act of kindness reinforces and strengthens this *habitus* even further, while every act of unkindness erodes it a bit, but not completely.[14]

---

[13] Unless, of course, one is talking of infused virtues as we will see later.
[14] For social scientists, recall the stock-flow distinction from introductory economics courses. Think of a bathtub of water and with its spigot open. The stock tells us the total amount of water stored in

This dynamic in virtue formation applies just as well at a collective level. Consider, for example, the problem of corruption. Transparency International presents an annual ranking of graft among nations. Such dishonesty did not arise overnight but was widely practiced over time and across various sectors of the nation until it became endemic. People routinely expect grease money, from the highest public officials, all the way to the lowliest bureaucrat processing paperwork. Every act of bribery reinforces this practice and public ethos as part of the national *habitus*.

The notion of *habitus* and the dynamics of virtue formation apply just as well to the virtues of justice and love. They explain why agape-justice conflicts are not an all-or-nothing proposition. The discipline of economics has an analytical method to contribute in this regard – its marginal analysis. The famous early twentieth century economist Alfred Marshall (1890) observes, "nature does not make a big leap" (*Natura non facit saltum*). Changes are, for the most part, incremental. It is the same for economics and its marginal analysis by which economic agents incrementally adjust the disposition of their resources based on the most recent price changes. For example, consumers curtail their driving, rather than totally give up their vehicles, in response to an increase in gasoline prices. Families dine out less in the face of inflation, rather than completely give up on their favorite restaurants. People adjust their decisions incrementally.[15]

The key insight here is that agape-justice conflicts can be similarly weighed "at the margins." Love and justice are among the highest of human values. They are instantiated in our customs, laws, and usage, indeed, in our individual and collective lives. They are part of the warp and weft of society, our collective *habitus*. Thus, agape-justice conflicts are not an all-or-nothing proposition of having one or the other but not both. Settling such conflicts is not about doing a triage of love's and justice's intrinsic

the tub so far, while the flow from the spigot tells us the amount of water being added at any single point in time. A net inflow adds to the stock, while a net outflow (open drain, for example) depletes the stock. The stock (of water in the bathtub) is the *habitus*, while the flow (from the spigot or drain) is every instance of moral choice that adds to or diminishes the stock. Another helpful distinction is the interaction between microeconomics and macroeconomics. It is the microeconomic decisions of innumerable consumers and firms that eventually shape the macroeconomics of the nation.

[15] Or, consider the well-known water-diamond paradox. Water is essential for life, and yet its price is an infinitesimal fraction of that of a diamond. This difference, of course, is due to the relative scarcity of diamonds. Water is relatively abundant, so much so that it is used, and even wasted, for nonessential purposes (e.g., water fountain displays). Recall that the downward sloping demand curve shows the quantity demanded at every price point. The price of water is ultimately determined by the price at which the last gallon of water was sold in the marketplace. For those who have taken a course in economics, recall that the rule of thumb in arriving at the optimum disposition of resources is marginal cost = marginal revenue (benefit), not the average cost or benefit.

worth or overall utility, contribution, or role in society, as we have seen in Adam Smith et al.'s thinking. Rather, deciding the clashing claims of agape and justice is about weighing their relative merits *in this particular case and with this specific set of circumstances at this particular moment*. In other words, the claims of agape and justice ought to be weighed in their particularities – "at the margins" and not be lumped together as an issue of agape *per se* versus justice *per se*. The competing claims of agape and justice have a history behind them and a context around them. They cannot be resolved as hypotheticals, nor can they be resolved with universal rules. Context is important.

Equally important, to resolve these conflicts in favor of one or the other is not to be dismissive of or to repudiate altogether the other. Favoring the duties of benevolence in one case over the duties of justice does not mean forswearing completely the rule of law. At best, one could take it as an exception to the rule of law or tweaking the application or the nature of the rule of law at the margins. It could also point to the need to change the underlying CLU of justice, as we have seen earlier in the shifting boundaries between legal and moral dues in Table 1.2 on the continuum of obligatoriness. What used to be supererogatory eventually becomes a legal due (e.g., universal broadband access in Finland).

Consider Jubilee 2000, the grassroots debt forgiveness initiative that appealed to advanced nations to write off the debt of poor countries in celebration of the new millennium. Advocates were motivated by benevolence and appealed to our mutual duty of compassion. Nevertheless, there was significant opposition. Critics adamantly warned of moral hazard problems and the erosion of the global rules of finance with such action. We have a clash in the claims of beneficence versus those of justice (as rule of law). Thus, the turn of the millennium came and went with no debt forgiveness. It took time, but at their summit in Gleneagles, Scotland in 2005, the G8 nations pledged the debt cancellation of highly indebted poor countries (HIPC) over the misgivings of critics. In this case, the G8 leaders finally accepted, after much lobbying, that their duty of beneficence outweighed the demands of justice in preserving the rule of law in the global capital marketplace.

Forgiving the debt of the HPIC countries in 2005 along with the other initiatives that followed did not mean throwing out altogether the rules of international finance. It simply meant carving out exceptions to established rules or incrementally altering long-established global rules, procedures, or expectations for a specific set of cases (HIPC) for a particular time. Surely, justice and agape are distinct from one another, but they are inseparable. Whether at a conceptual or practical plane, justice and agape can only work if they function as a tandem. Favoring one or the other in particular conflicts does not mean getting rid of the other altogether.

In sum, settling the competing claims of agape and justice is ultimately not a binary choice (1,0). In the first place, it is not a clash of agape *per se* versus justice *per se*. Rather, it is a conflict between the demands of certain elements of agape versus the claims of certain elements of justice, and only at the level of particulars. Thus, one must assess the specifics of every case. Second, resolving such conflicts in favor of one or the other does not impugn the intrinsic worth or need for the other. All it says is that there is greater need or greater merit in fulfilling the claims of agape or justice *for this particular instance* under these unique circumstances *at this particular time* given *the current disequilibrium in the social homeostasis*. Such incremental adjustments are how the societal structures of agape and justice are built up over time, strengthened, or evolve for good or for ill. One must resolve such conflicts at the margins on a case-by-case basis, and always with an eye to balancing the social homeostasis. There will be occasion to prioritize the claims of justice over those of agape and vice versa depending on the needs of the moment. One must distinguish between the overall state or condition of justice or love in the community, on the one hand, and individual instances of just or loving acts, on the other hand. Agape-justice conflicts pertain to the latter rather than the former.

Ecclesiastes 3:1 says it well, "For everything there is a season and a time for every matter under heaven." So it is with agape and justice as we weigh their competing claims. At the end of the day, communities can be both just and beneficent overall, as many are or at least strive to be.

Finding the All-Important but Elusive Balance

Can one be too compassionate to excess? Is there a point beyond which compassion must be curtailed for its own sake? Similarly, can one be excessively just? Is there a point beyond which justice must be curtailed for its own sake? In both cases, where do we draw the line and why?

Sustainable Compassion

Consider the case of Aaron Feuerstein. On December 11, 1995, a massive fire destroyed Malden Mills in Lawrence, Massachusetts. It must have been tempting for Mr. Feuerstein to take the insurance money, retire, or build new factories overseas, just as other mills had already done in the previous decades. Not so for Mr. Feuerstein. Not only did he keep paying his 1400 workers in the months after the fire, but he also rebuilt his operations with a $130 million plant within twenty months, with financing assistance provided by GE Capital. Unfortunately, despite his best efforts and good intentions, he could not get around the demands of the marketplace. Malden Mills had to declare bankruptcy five years later in 2001 due to the high cost of bank financing and rebuilding, and he eventually had to leave the company in 2004 after new management had to take over. There was a second attempt at rehabilitating the company, with even more loans secured. Unfortunately, the outcome could not be changed. The firm had to declare bankruptcy again in 2007 and had to be sold to new owners because of the unaffordable cost of financing and the much higher labor cost in the United States compared to other countries (Associated Press 2007). Ultimately, the Lawrence plant had to be shut down and operations moved to Tennessee in 2016 (Whittaker 2016).

Mr. Feuerstein wanted to save the livelihood of his workers, knowing that many families depended on it, not to mention the well-being of the local community. He was heeding the call of agape in his persistence to do both what was right and what was compassionate. Unfortunately, the market is an unforgiving place. In this case, compassion had to be grounded in the hard realities of the laws of demand and supply. His act of both beneficence and righteousness could not be sustained because of the exacting economic terrain. From a purely economic angle, some would describe Mr. Feuerstein's compassionate-just act as going against the requirements of allocative efficiency.

Mr. Aaron Feuerstein and Malden Mills are not examples of an agape-justice conflict. Far from it. Mr. Feuerstein was in fact both compassionate and just. By his own admission, he sought to satisfy the demands of both righteousness and agape. Justice and agape converge in their claims in this instance. Nevertheless, despite this strong mutually reinforcing dynamic, it could not be sustained. This reveals to us that there is an important, indeed constitutive, economic dimension to this chapter's much-touted homeostasis. It turns out that socioeconomic homeostasis is not merely about balancing the demands of justice and agape, it is also about including in that delicate balance the demands of economics, politics, culture, and the many other dimensions of human life. The question of whether one is too compassionate to excess is answered ultimately by whether such compassion is sustainable. In this case, not even its convergence with the demands of justice (righteousness) was good enough. Even social enterprises themselves cannot be all compassion if they are to be sustainable.

Generally, social enterprises are different from nonprofit organizations in that the former are attentive to the requirements of the marketplace. Social enterprises aim to make profits in order to sustain their continued good work. Economics also matters in deciding agape-justice conflicts.

Prudent Compassion

Is there a limit beyond which compassion is misguided or excessive? Consider the hard choice pharmaceutical firms face in their expanded access programs. As part of the drug approval process, clinical trials are held in which carefully selected patients are enrolled to test the efficacy and the safety of drugs under development. Many desperately or terminally ill patients, who could not qualify for inclusion in these clinical trials, nevertheless appeal to the pharmaceutical firms to give them access to these drugs because it is their last recourse. No other existing treatments or drugs work for them, and time is not on their side. Many pharmaceutical firms grant them "compassionate use" of these drugs under an expanded access program.

Other firms, however, are reluctant to give such access based on their fear that adverse results even for the "compassionate use" of these drugs will still have to be reported to the Food and Drug Administration (FDA) and might delay or even endanger the subsequent approval of these drugs (Bishop 2015). After all, patients who are at the stage of having to request for compassionate use are terribly ill to begin with, thereby increasing the odds of adverse results for the drug. Moreover, the drugs may turn out to be unsuitable for these desperate patients who ask for them nonetheless as "a shot in the dark" for want of any other alternative. Such "compassionate use" is deemed by some as an unnecessary risk for pharmaceutical firms who are accountable to their shareholders. Most of all, it jeopardizes future patients for whom these drugs are more appropriate and effective but who would be negatively affected by the delay or, worse, even rejection of such drugs by the regulatory agencies based on the adverse events of such "compassionate use."

Thus, on the one hand, agape calls for allowing generous "compassionate use" for terribly ill patients who are desperate for anything that might work. Agape calls for taking the risk even for the added adverse results that will have to be reported in the drug approval process. On the other hand, justice demands not taking needless risks that might delay or even imperil the subsequent approval of the drugs to the detriment of many other patients who could benefit from their timely approval. Others will add that it unnecessarily risks the time and money already devoted to the drugs' development and is not the best or even a just use of shareholders' or society's resources.

Consider, too, the dilemma of the National Health Service (NHS) of the United Kingdom that routinely denies drugs or treatment that are deemed medically ineffective or too costly. This is a demand of both justice and prudence, given the limited medical resources that must be used wisely and well for the good of the whole nation. Nevertheless, for desperately ill patients who are fighting for their lives, they appeal for compassion (Samuels 2019). Another dilemma for NHS trusts in England is their mandate to require upfront payment from people who are ineligible for free healthcare, such as, failed asylum seekers and visitors overstaying their visas. As a result, many have had to forego treatment, leading to their further suffering, health failure, and even death (Jayanetti 2018). Both unpleasant hard choices entail safeguarding the fiscal discipline and financial viability of the NHS (demand of justice), on the one hand, versus extending compassionate care to those who need it (demand of agape), on the other hand.

Caveats

In the same way that one can be excessively just, can one also be too compassionate to excess? Yes. There are at least two caveats worth noting. First, one cannot choose to be solely compassionate and disregard the rightful claims of other stakeholders, such as shareholders or other patients and affected parties as in the case of the NHS. This goes against commutative justice (not living up to contractual obligations), distributive justice (shareholders or other affected parties not getting their rightful share of societal goods), and general-legal justice (contributing to the stability and growth of the community). Compassion is laudable, but people must nevertheless still fulfill their responsibilities to all the other stakeholders.

Second, despite all their good intentions and good work in addressing social needs, compassionate people are nevertheless still bound by the obligation to contribute to the goal of sustainability. This includes contributing toward the efficient use of scarce resources for the benefit not only of contemporary but also of future generations. The case of the NHS in having to make hard choices in declining drugs or treatment to desperate ill patients is one such example.

A compassionate motive is not good enough. Intelligent, critical design and execution are just as important. Misplaced compassion can end up wasting scarce societal resources that could have been better used to promote the well-being of so many others. With the benefit of hindsight, the unstinting 2020–2021 US Covid fiscal and monetary stimuli and their contribution to the consequent runaway inflation are good illustrations.[16] The US Federal Reserve had to drastically increase interest rates to tame a forty-year high inflation rate in 2022, thereby adding even further to the economic burdens already borne by poor developing countries. General-legal justice demands that even compassion must be sustainable and avoid generating terribly injurious effects. Part of sustainability is being efficient in the disposition and use of resources. Commutative and distributive justice are critical in reaching such allocative efficiency. Moreover, even the most agapic social enterprises cannot long endure without commutative and distributive justice.

Sustainable, Prudent Justice

Can one be excessively just? Yes. The example of Police Inspector Javerts in *Les Miserables* is an excellent example. Justice demands that he implement CLU. It is his duty as police inspector. On two separate dire occasions (rescuing orphan Cosette and getting medical assistance for dying Marius), probation-breaker Jean Valjean pleads with Javerts not to arrest him right there and then but to permit him to finish his mission of mercy. Javerts adamantly refused the first request. He accommodates the second request, but he is so distraught in having failed to live up to his duty (and broken the law himself). Moreover, Javerts could not live being indebted to a convicted thief (Valjean) who had just saved him from execution. This is an example of a clash between distributive-retributive-restorative justice in holding Jean Valjean to account for breaking his parole, on the one hand, and on the other hand, agape-mercy-compassion-beneficence in letting Jean Valjean assist Cosette and get medical aid for Marius.[17]

Ecclesiastes 17:16 says it well when it hints that one can cause harm in being excessively just: "Do not be too righteous, and do not act too wise; why should you destroy yourself?" As we have seen in this chapter, so it is for our shared economic life. Justice operating by itself and not complemented by agape leads to problems of being just to excess.

One practical measure to guard against such excess is to check whether such justice is sustainable. Take the case of Truth and Reconciliation initiatives in the wake of South African apartheid, the Colombian rebel-government strife, and the Rwandan genocide of the 1990s. Some of the crimes committed in these cases were unimaginably heinous. Yet, one common feature

---

[16] See Labonte and Weinstock (2022, 17–22) on the impact of the Covid fiscal and monetary stimuli on the resulting inflation.

[17] Javerts should have recognized that in-extremis cases always trump all other claims.

of these initiatives is the willingness to forego retribution and punishment in exchange for truth and the possibility of moving forward together as a nation and living in peace and harmony. Many victims and their families feel terribly aggrieved and robbed of justice by this initiative. Those who had inflicted them so much harm, including the loss of their loved ones, are walking free, unpunished, and rejoin the community. In some cases, they live as neighbors amid the very people whom they had harmed so grievously.

Nevertheless, to insist on adhering to the demands of justice means years, perhaps even decades more of unending strife, violence, suffering, and death. For the sake of peace, if not for genuine reconciliation, national leaders have sought to forego the demands of justice if the polity is to be sustainable at all.

Truth and reconciliation initiatives are another illustration of how social homeostasis may require foregoing the demands of justice for the sake of peace or even compassion. At the very least, these are instances of expedient reconciliation, even if not genuine forgiveness. Humans have repeatedly demonstrated that they can rise above what seems to be unforgivable or unbearable and be just and humane at the same time. Instances of heroic and saintly supererogation prove this. In so doing, people reach their most promising possibilities and higher purpose. Many agape-justice conflicts, no matter how difficult or painful, are well within the human's capacity to resolve, especially with divine grace. All these cases are yet again another illustration of my earlier conclusion that agape-justice conflicts cannot be resolved at a general, abstract level with a universal rule. They must be decided at the level of particulars with their all-important context.

Conceptual Tools

Acknowledging that agape and justice need to complement each other, even in those cases when they present competing claims, is easy and straightforward. The difficulty lies in identifying where this much-desired balance lies. How does one know, for example, as to whether one is excessively just or too beneficent to excess? What then is the metric for determining whether one has crossed the line to excess?

Key Considerations

Three considerations present themselves in searching for the balance between agape and justice in socioeconomic homeostasis: the diachronic nature of the task, differentiating the periods under consideration, and the redistribution of burdens and benefits across the community.

Diachronic Task

In settling the competing claims of agape and justice, it is important to know what we have today and how we got to where we are today. History matters because context reveals the degree to which justice and agape are lacking, how long they have been deficient, who have been adversely affected by such deficits, and which shortfalls are most urgent to mitigate or correct. The next chapter on unattended past wrongs underscores the need for a diachronic approach even more. There is no set formula for the ideal balance. It will ultimately be the prudential judgment of leaders and the community that will be critical, as in the case of Angela Merkel's decision to accept over a million Syrian war refugees in 2015 or the Marshall Plan after World War II.

Time Horizon under Consideration

The time horizon also matters. In deciding the clashing claims between agape and justice, for which period are we looking for a solution – the immediate-, short-, medium-, or long-term? Clearly, the requirements and results of balance or imbalance between agape and justice will vary between these time periods. Immediate and short-term solutions, while usually expedient, need not necessarily be best for the long term either because they do not address the deep-seated causes of problems, or because they do not even address the immediate problems at all. For example, in the case of pensions and social safety nets, legislative action that simply increases the budget allocation to satisfy constituencies in the immediate term may be setting up huge unfunded liabilities for future generations and either sizable tax increases or drastic cuts in promised pensions in the future. Thus, the task of balancing agape-justice claims is complicated even further in having to consider the period for which balance in socioeconomic homeostasis is sought.

Redistribution of Burdens and Benefits

In resolving agape-justice conflicts, claims will be satisfied but at the expense of other claims that will have to be foregone. These disexternalities should not bar the exercise of agapic love. We simply must accept that given the nature of economic life (finite resources, rival consumption), there will be opportunity costs with every choice. Not all claims can be satisfied. There will be a consequent redistribution of burdens and benefits. The key is to ensure that those who are unfavorably affected by agape's disexternalities are the ones best able to bear the opportunity cost. This was the case for the G8 Gleneagles HIPC debt forgiveness, as in the other cases in this study as well.

One could also follow liberalism's rule in settling competing claims over freedom by affording the individual with the maximum freedom that is consistent with everyone else enjoying the same degree of freedom. We are limited in the freedoms we enjoy to the degree that our exercise of such freedoms runs up against others' exercise of the same freedoms. In balancing the competing claims of justice and agape, we could adopt a similar liberal approach to resolving moral dilemmas.

> [W]henever a moral obligation is party to a conflict of obligation and it is necessary to determine which obligation is the actual one: One ought to recognize as the actually right course of action that one which contributes most to the realization of the good life (a wide range and frequent occurrence of intrinsic values) in the lives of all persons implicated in the problem, and one ought to recognize as the actually right course of action that one which makes the same relative contribution to the goodness of the lives of all persons involved. (Crawford 1969, 318)

In other words, Berry Crawford proposes that the adjudication of moral dilemmas must observe the following two principles, namely:

- Principle of utility or beneficence: the solution maximizes the chances of all the parties involved in the agape-justice conflict in attaining a life full of the best of human values.
- Principle of egalitarian justice: the solution makes the "same relative contribution" of goodness in the lives of those who are party to the agape-justice conflict.

"Same relative contribution" is vague and will still need to be worked out, but the intent is clear – there should be proportionality in the distribution of burdens and benefits in living together as a community.

Thomistic General-Legal Justice as Overarching Framework

St. Thomas' general-legal justice (II-II, 58.5 and 6) is a good framework in working out the proper balance between the claims of agape and justice. General-legal justice is founded on the premise that virtues/vices and acts at the level of individuals necessarily ripple through the whole community itself, for good or for ill. Thus, temperance, prudence, and fortitude on the part of individuals or commutative justice in the interpersonal exchange of individuals generally redound to the ultimate good of the whole community. While specific virtues pursue their respective particular ends,[18] they also simultaneously and ultimately contribute to the common good. The exercise of these specific virtues is imbued with the additional virtue of general-legal justice to the degree that it will also likely promote the good of the community. Hence, it is called general justice because it directs all human acts to the common good. The end of general-legal justice is the common good. Thus, even agape satisfies general-legal justice. In fact, in many of the above cases, agape, rather than commutative or distributive justice, better serves general-legal justice, such as the Medicaid expansion under the US Affordable Healthcare Act.

St. Thomas' general-legal justice, then, is an ideal conceptual metric to use in deciding the clashing claims of agape and justice. Competing claims are settled in favor of those that satisfy general-legal justice best, that is, those that greatly advance the good of the community in addition to satisfying the particular claims or ends of the virtue itself.

The imprecision of claims and counterclaims in social life also makes general-legal justice an ideal guide to resolving agape-justice conflicts. Rights are often difficult to identify, justify, or satisfy in the marketplace. There is often a problem of assigning and measuring obligations with precision. All these are compounded in a rapidly changing complex marketplace that spawns many imperfect duties. Noncontractual (extra-market) economic obligations are poorly specified. And even if these duties can be identified and assigned, there are few enforcing social mechanisms to compel people to discharge them. Thus, duties are often enforced only in the internal forum, out of people's goodwill. Thus, general-legal justice is vital in having people voluntarily own up to their duties and obligations. People must weigh in their conscience what they can contribute according to their means. General-legal justice pushes people to live up to widely ignored or ill-defined obligations or imperfect duties. It is a voluntary compliance out of concern for the good of the community. For this reason, it is an ideal reference point in arbitrating agape-justice conflicts.

Principle of Double Effect

To be sure, general-legal justice as a conceptual framework will still turn out to be inadequate because it does not provide precise measures and

---

[18] For example, the virtue of temperance keeps unruly passions at bay. Fortitude makes for perseverance in the face of great odds. Commutative justice ensures equality in the value of exchange.

criteria. In the end, prudential judgment is still needed in ascertaining whether agape's or justice's claims satisfy the common good best. The principle of double effect will be a useful tool in making such judgment. After all, agape-justice conflicts are about satisfying a moral obligation but at the expense of violating another moral obligation as an unintended consequence. The requisite prudential judgment will ultimately redound to balancing the ill and positive effects of compliance or noncompliance with agape's and justice's moral claims.

Chapter 1's distinctions on the varying degrees of obligatoriness vis-à-vis legal and moral debts will be useful for the principle of double effect in weighing the competing claims. Consider the following triage in order of diminishing priority of claims:

- Bedrock priority is that of the survival of society and maintaining the integrity and cohesion of society [balance in the socioeconomic homeostasis]
- Enhancing the quality of life in the community and leading it to flourish
- Impact on particular individuals for their flourishing at the individual level

Finally, the principle of double effect is also an ideal framework to use because however we resolve agape-justice conflicts, this principle requires that we mitigate the resulting ill effects. That is a moral obligation that both agape and justice will also most likely demand.

Summary and Conclusions

Can one be excessively just? Can one be too beneficent to excess? In both cases, the answer is yes, especially when we talk of socioeconomic life because of the finitude of material goods, time, public office, or societal roles. Anything that needs to be allocated will incur opportunity costs. That means that one can satisfy the claims of agape but only at the expense of justice's claims, and vice versa. Thus, whose claims take precedence?

No doubt about it, justice is foundational for economic life. In beginning any shared undertaking, people must set the rules first by which they live and collaborate with one another. Justice is critical in ensuring order without which there can be no community. However, even as justice takes precedence in the establishment of a community, agape is also necessary and not dispensable. Justice and its limitations reveal agape's critical practical role in socioeconomic life.

Agape shapes the character and the quality of life within the community that is forming. Because agape is transformative for both its subject and its object, it changes the exercise of justice as well. Love makes one more assiduous in wanting the beloved to get what is his/her due, at a minimum. Then love goes beyond that. Since love is also an act of the will, it provides the necessary courage in the pursuit of justice even if its demands are difficult. It provides the end for which justice is exercised – not for self-satisfaction or retribution, but for the well-being and welfare of the beloved. Love, including agape, is needed for sustainability.

Contrary to Adam Smith and others' claim that economic life can operate based on justice alone, agape is needed as well. Both justice and agape are necessary if there is to be a shared common life at all. Agape does not replace justice, or vice versa. Each has its unique contribution. Agape and justice are distinct, but they are inseparable because they are necessary complements in socioeconomic life. Justice and agape form a tandem. You cannot have one without the other, not especially in social life. Therein lies what we can call socioeconomic homeostasis. This delicate equilibrium requires constant balancing, akin to riding a bicycle. Achieving such a balance is more an art than a science. Nevertheless, difficult as the task may be, we can prepare for it and understand its requirements.

Perhaps, this accounts for why Cicero had long observed that beneficence is in fact a part of justice as a cardinal virtue and that beneficence strengthens the common bonds that make society. Recall that for Cicero, the second duty of justice proper itself (*iustitia*) is to conserve the common interest (*De Officiis*, I, ix [30]). As we have seen in the preceding chapter, beneficence plays an essential role in the conservation of society as a partner of justice.

Agape-justice conflicts must be settled at the level of particulars, on a case-by-case basis. There is no single a priori universal rule that can be used. Finding the balance in this socioeconomic homeostasis between agape and justice is clearly a matter of prudential judgment. Nevertheless, the gradation of love makes that task a little easier. Love and its differing degrees provide us much greater flexibility in being nuanced and incremental in how we balance the clashing claims of agape and justice. General-legal justice is a good reference point for this balancing task. After all, it is called a general virtue because it directs all human actions and virtues to advancing the good of the entire community. Not surprisingly, general-legal justice can also be used in the next two chapters in settling agape-justice conflicts from past wrongs (Chapter 5) and from an expanding circle of responsibility (Chapter 6).

Agape-justice conflicts may turn out to be an important part of socioeconomic life. They become the occasion to adjust to changing circumstances and needs. Such conflicts, contentious and painful as they may be, can be likened to a fever or pain that alerts one that something is awry in the body and needs remedial action. The clashing claims of agape and justice are indicative of where these adjustments are needed. Paradoxically, these conflicts turn out to be a necessary part of a flourishing community life.

CHAPTER 5

Unattended Past Wrongs

Agape-justice conflicts can arise from unattended past wrongs and previous disequilibria in the socioeconomic homeostasis. We see this both in theory and in practice. This is sometimes called "prior-fault" moral dilemmas. This includes cases in which the underlying customs, law, and usage (CLU) are unjust, such as the legalized enslavement of people.

Theory

Time-and place-utility: There is an important time- and place-utility to the claims of justice and agape. Take the case of justice. It is about giving people their due. However, what is due has multiple dimensions: giving the right claim, the right amount, at the right time, to the right recipient, from the right payer, at the right place, and in the right manner. Violations or deficiencies in any of these contribute to disequilibria in the delicate socioeconomic homeostasis described in the preceding chapter.

Agape also has dues, and just like justice, it has multiple dimensions that must be satisfied simultaneously. Even St. Ambrose acknowledges the precise nature of these obligations in his exposition on liberality: "148. Perfect liberality is proved by its good faith, *the case it helps, the time and place when and where it is shown* .... 152. We notice how the Apostle includes both good-will and liberality, as well as *the manner*, the fruits of right giving, and *the persons concerned*" (Ambrose 1952, Book I, Ch 30, emphasis added). Indeed, our shorthand for this is time- and place-utility in the claims of justice and agape.

There are real consequences to failure to live up to the claims of justice and agape. Among these are the disequilibria in socioeconomic homeostasis. Moreover, there is moral injury inflicted on both the subject (moral agent, person/community) and the object whenever we fail to live up to the obligations of agape and justice, whether by commission or omission. Such moral injuries ultimately adversely affect the well-being of the community as well. We produce the opposite dynamic of general-legal justice.[1]

To make matters worse, three other social dynamics aggravate these resulting disequilibria. First is the accumulative phenomenon whereby individual instances of disequilibrium or wrongdoing coalesce to produce a synergy – the resulting whole being greater than the sum of its individual parts. An example of this is the series of events and flawed decisions by different leaders building on each other and eventually spinning out of control to trigger what was then going to be World War I (Tuchman 1962).

A second aggravating dynamic is network externality, whereby a particular social practice or state of affairs is widely adopted or accepted and ultimately becomes the norm for everybody else to follow.[2] Recall our earlier example on petty corruption in some nations, whereby grease money is needed to get anything done, even in hospitals (Riley 1999).

The third dynamic is path dependency, in which the past determines the options going forward. Social practices or states of affairs take a life of their own and create a momentum that requires effort to change. For example, agricultural subsidies have been a regular part of advanced countries' policies despite their adverse ripple effects. Farming sectors have come to view them as an "entitlement" and the status quo, with the burden of proof falling on those who want to rescind or reduce these subsidies.

These social dynamics mutually reinforce each other to magnify the disequilibria and past wrongs that arise with the failure to meet the claims of justice and agape in a timely manner and at the right place in previous rounds of socioeconomic life. The result is a cascading downward spiral of further disequilibria or wrongs going forward into the future. Left unaddressed, these create ever more problems that are serious. There is a snowballing effect that creates flawed social structures that will continue producing ill results and magnifying problems down the road, as we will see in the following examples. Unaddressed past disequilibria lead to more intense and much more difficult agape-justice conflicts in the future.

The distinction between primary and secondary obligations from Chapter 1 is helpful in dealing with agape-justice conflicts precipitated by previous disequilibria and past wrongs. The duties we owe to those under our charge or those associated with us are called primary obligations, while those that we owe to others unaffiliated with us are called secondary

---

[1] Recall that in general-legal justice, individual virtues or actions eventually redound to the overall good of the community.

[2] This phenomenon was discussed in Chapter 3 as part of the market's ability to shape its own values.

obligations. Secondary obligations are also called "inherited obligations." We "inherit" the latter duties because of the failure of others upstream to fulfill their primary obligations, thereby creating a need for others to fill in for their deficiency (Herman 2001). This distinction is important because as we will see shortly, most of the duties of agape are in fact "inherited obligations." Let us examine actual examples of "inherited obligations" from agape-justice conflicts in real life that stem from such unattended disequilibria or past wrongs.

A word of caution before we examine these cases. There are some who argue that these "inherited obligations" are duties of justice rather than duties of agape. For them, it is an intra-justice clash whereby the conflict lies in the selection of which criterion of justice takes priority. As mentioned earlier in the Preface, this is not the place to debate whether these "inherited obligations" are demands of justice or of agape. They may in fact be claims from justice. However, this study takes the position that it is best to argue the claims of "inherited obligations" from their fallback position, indeed their weakest position, of having no claims at all except for their appeal to our shared humanity. Thus, winning their case based on agape makes their case much more compelling. It shows that they can stand on agape alone without even having to bring in their claims from justice. Of course, there is nothing to prevent arguing their case as a demand of justice. However, that is a topic for another work.

Immigration

Criminalizing Humanitarian Assistance

Cédric Herrou extended assistance and provided haven on his property to desperate, exhausted Eritreans, Sudanese, and others crossing over from Italy to find refuge in France. This French farmer's property lies along the route used by migrants fleeing to Europe. For his humanitarian outreach to people in desperate straits, Monsieur Herrou was charged in court for "helping undocumented foreigners enter, move about and reside" in France, a crime that carried a possible five-year sentence and a €30,000 fine. Prosecutors asked for a suspended six-month sentence. Monsieur Herrou was convicted and sentenced to a suspended €3,000 fine. This was by no means a unique case. Two others had been fined earlier for similar actions – a 73-year-old academic, fined €1,500 for a comparable violation, and a university researcher prosecuted after having been caught in Nice providing a lift to three Eritrean women shortly after arriving from Italy.

Unable to keep up with the relentless surge in the number of asylum seekers since 2015, Italy and Greece legislated stricter laws criminalizing assisting seaborne undocumented migrants and bringing them to port, no matter how endangered they might have been at sea. Both countries have arrested, jailed, and prosecuted nongovernmental organization (NGO) ship captains and aid workers for violating these statutes regarding providing succor to distressed migrants at sea and then landing them ashore. Italy and Greece argued that their navies' previous rescues of migrants floundering in the Mediterranean backfired as they inadvertently encouraged even more migrants to make the sea journey, now deemed to be less dangerous. It was also a boon for human smugglers. Some have even claimed that migrants had been intentionally put in rickety boats to hasten their rescue.

In response, Italy and Greece stepped back from patrolling the Mediterranean and assisting distressed migrants. NGOs stepped in to fill the void by providing search-and-rescue missions to prevent migrants from drowning in the Mediterranean (Trilling 2020; Kitsantonis 2021). On the one hand, NGOs accuse the Italian and Greek governments of abandoning migrants to the dangers of the sea to dissuade further immigration. On the other hand, the Italian and Greek authorities fault the NGOs and other volunteers for aggravating what is already an unmanageable problem by inadvertently encouraging even more people to make the dangerous sea journey.

It is a similar tussle between law enforcement and NGOs along the borders of the United States. Many migrants have perished crossing the inhospitable desert along the southwestern border with Mexico. Volunteers and NGOs have responded by leaving water supplies and food across the desert and the most likely routes used by migrants. US Border Patrol officers have arrested many of these volunteers and aid workers. Courts have convicted, fined, and sentenced them to probation for violations of multiple Federal laws including trespassing in restricted areas and even aiding and abetting illegal human smuggling. In certain cases, there were even threats of significant jail time (Ingram 2019; Phillips 2019).

Syrian War Refugees

At the height of the 2015 surge of migrants from Syria into the EU, Angela Merkel opened the borders of Germany to these war refugees out of compassion and empathy. She heeded the duties of humanity in overriding EU protocols whereby asylum seekers were supposed to be returned to the first country they entered and register there. The dissension from within

Germany itself was swift and fierce. The sudden influx of over a million migrants exacerbated tensions on domestic issues, such as cultural assimilation and social spending. Allegations of crime and a surge in the sexual abuse of women by migrants in Cologne in December 2015 added even more tinder to the backlash (Mushaben 2017).

We see similar economic objections and pushback in Turkey and in Lebanon, the country that has borne a larger share of these refugees as a proportion of the local population. Hungary and Poland are concerned with the erosion of their culture and way of life, especially when faced with migrants who have no intention of assimilating into their host countries. Permits and resident certificates are needed to secure employment, thereby driving refugees into dangerous jobs in the underground economy and made vulnerable to exploitation.

The nub of the tension falls again along the fault line of the claims of agape versus the claims of justice. On the one hand, agape calls for compassion and empathy for peoples, who through no fault of their own, have had to flee war and violence. On the other hand, justice calls for safeguarding the well-being and preserving the lifestyle and culture of local citizens, or at the very least, imposing some prudential limit on the number of refugees absorbed without negatively affecting the community. The interests of fleeing refugees are pitted against the interests of local citizens and residents. It is the same dynamic in the case of Venezuelan migrants fleeing to Colombia, but on a much smaller scale.

Refugees from War, Persecution, and Climate Change

It is a similar phenomenon and the same fault line unfolding along the southern borders of the United States vis-à-vis refugees from Haiti and Central American countries, and to a lesser extent between Mexico and its southern neighbors. Families from Haiti, El Salvador, Guatemala, and Honduras flee from gang-war violence and the ravages of extreme weather events from climate change. The influx of large numbers of unaccompanied minors has forced the US Federal government to ratchet up its spending to house, clothe, feed, and provide for migrants, especially the unaccompanied minors. This has been bitterly decried by critics who argue that such taxpayer funds are better devoted to taking care of poor children right within the borders of the United States itself. Many children of US citizens and residents are also poor and deficient when it comes to food, childcare, housing, and education, and they do not receive sufficient aid from the state or the Federal government. Consequently, critics angrily complain that their taxes that are sorely needed by poor US children themselves are being spent instead on unaccompanied migrant minors at the southern border. Once again, we see the collision of claims attributed to agape and to justice.

Many migrants have been accepted into the United States on humanitarian grounds due to natural disasters, as in the case of the 2010 Haitian earthquake, Hurricane Mitch in Central America in 1998, and the Ebola crisis in Liberia. Regular extensions of these migrants' temporary visas have allowed them to live in the country, some for more than three decades. They have sunk their roots and established their lives along with their children in the United States. Their temporary visas have been extended, thus far, but there is always the threat that a new administration may not be as sympathetic to their plight.

Many have argued for a path to permanent residency and citizenship for these groups, as had happened in the case of Liberians under the 2019 Liberian Refugee Immigration Fairness Act (LRIFA) law. This humane approach also gives greater peace of mind to these families. In contrast, critics stick with the demands of justice that protect the claims and concerns of local citizens.

It is a similar debate and dilemma for children who were bought into the United States without proper documentation by their parents. These "Dreamers" have known only this country as their home. They are also in the same predicament and experience the same uncertainty and fear of deportation. They are unable to participate fully and contribute to the community for lack of documentation. Compassion calls for a path to citizenship for these "Dreamers." In contrast, critics argue for a strict adherence to the law of the land in which lawbreakers should not be rewarded at all. Moreover, they are concerned that it creates a moral hazard problem. The tension between the claims of agape and justice are in full view in the wrangling between Republicans and Democrats in the US Congress on this issue. Contrast the diametrically opposed positions taken by the Obama administration versus the Trump administration. Which should take priority – the claims of agape or the claims of justice?

Compulsory-education laws were enacted as early as the colonial era in the United States. Since the nineteenth century, every state has required children to attend school. However, since the 1970s to the present, various Southern states have attempted to prevent undocumented children from enrolling in public schools, as did the administration of the 45th US president. There is resentment over the use of taxpayer money to pay for public services for undocumented migrants. Courts have blocked such attempts (*Economist* 2022a).

These agape-justice migration conflicts are not recent phenomena either. Recall the M.S. St. Louis in 1939 with over 900 European Jews denied landing rights in Cuba, the United States, and Canada, and then ultimately sailing back to Europe. Two hundred forty-five of these fleeing refugees eventually died in the Holocaust.[3] Or, recall the Swedish diplomat Raoul Gustaf Wallenberg, whose name will forever be associated with great courage, compassion, and humanity in saving innumerable Jewish lives by bending and even breaking laws.

Less well known and only recently acknowledged is Hiram Bingham IV, one of the US vice-consuls in Marseille, France at the start of World War II. Mr. Bingham deliberately violated official US State Department policy and instructions from the highest levels of government by liberally issuing visas to endangered Jews, even going so far as to provide shelter and replacement travel documents to desperate migrants. In just ten months, he is believed to have saved over 2,500 Jews, among whom were people who eventually contributed much to society: Marc Chagall and Max Ernst, famous artists, and Hannah Arendt, one of the most influential political thinkers of the twentieth century. Mr. Bingham's humanitarian work was a blatant violation of policy and procedures, and the US State Department transferred him out of Marseille (Eisner 2009). His is an example of bending the rules or perhaps even breaking the law for the sake of compassion. It is also an illustration of how agape-justice conflicts are consequential in the number of lives affected and in the ripple effects down through the next generations.[4]

This tension between compassion for the endangered, on the one hand, and the call for status quo in protecting national interests, on the other hand, is evident not only on the issue of Jewish migration but also on the issue of providing vital war materials to a teetering Great Britain standing all alone at the outset of World War II. The America First Committee and Charles Lindbergh staunchly opposed such assistance.[5] Indeed, migration-related agape-justice conflicts are not recent phenomena.[6]

---

[3] www.history.com/news/wwii-jewish-refugee-ship-st-louis-1939 last accessed May 3, 2022.

[4] Three decades after these life-and-death decisions, in 2002, US Secretary of State Colin Powell lauded Hiram Bingham IV's readiness to put his own life and career at risk in saving lives. Mr. Bingham was honored as "Courageous Diplomat" by the American Foreign Service Diplomats. In addition, the US State Department also revised the official biographical entry for Mr. Bingham, underscoring his humanitarian work (Eisner 2009).

[5] See Ken Burns' 2022 documentary *The U.S. and the Holocaust* for a recent exposition on this issue.

[6] Critics note that migration issues are tainted with race discrimination, just as opposition to assistance to Jewish refugees at the outset of World War II was partly driven by anti-Semitism. This is a topic beyond the scope of our study, which is limited only to examining the current tension over refugees as a compassion-justice conflict.

Economic Migrants

The clash between agape and justice becomes even more fraught when it comes to economic migration.[7] In fact, host nations and anti-immigration groups are even more hostile to this type of migrants.

The rationale for welcoming refugees from war, natural disasters, or political persecution is based not only on humanitarian grounds, but also on justice and reciprocity. Nations have long accepted that people under such distress ought to be given sanctuary and assistance. It is even a human right ensconced in the UN Universal Declaration of Human Rights (Articles 13, 14, and 15). One can appreciate why and how this can be justified as a claim of justice and not only of agape by looking at the Mosaic laws whereby mutual assistance was deemed to be a rational strategy of mutual survival. The help I give you today may in fact be the very help that I myself may need someday. The Golden Rule and Kant's universalizability rule also provide justification from justice for the welcoming of refugees from war, political persecution, or natural disasters.

Not so for economic migrants. Economic migration is driven by the search for a better life. Most nations do not accept this to be a valid reason for extending asylum or assistance. Undoubtedly, there are stark differences between these two sets of migrants. War, political persecution, and natural disasters are an immediate threat to life. They are in-extremis cases. Not so for economic migration. Furthermore, economic migration is generally viewed as putting the less-skilled citizens and residents of host countries at risk because it means competition for their jobs and, consequently, lower wages as well. Even the more-skilled workers feel threatened by such type of migration. In addition, residents and citizens fear that the influx of these migrants will crowd them out of the public services they enjoy, such as health, education, and other social services that in many cases are already inadequate.

There is yet no consensus on the empirical evidence concerning whether economic migrants adversely affect the economic well-being of citizens and residents of the host countries.[8] Nevertheless, two things are clear. First,

---

[7] There are two types of economic migration. The first is the economic migration caused by natural disasters like drought, hurricanes, pandemics, etc. These are better lumped together with the war and political refugees because there is an immediate threat to life and limb. The second type is where migrants seek a better life to escape poverty and hardship in their native birthplace. The following discussion covers only this type of economic migration.

[8] Numerous empirical evidence have been presented that support both sides of the debate as to whether migrants benefit local workers in terms of job security, employment creation, and wage growth.

regardless of what studies say on the empirical impact of such migration, the fear of job loss and lower wages is real and widespread. Local workers and residents feel directly threatened. Second, such economic migration produces unambiguous economic benefits not only for the migrants and their immediate families, but also for their extended families back home and their native countries as well. Global remittances have become a major source of much-needed foreign exchange and income for many poor developing countries as part of globalization (World Bank 2019). Economic migration has a track record of alleviating poverty for untold millions. It is an effective way of improving the well-being of the poor in developing nations. The benefits and the dynamics are akin to those generated by rural-urban migration within countries.

Given this effective assistance to the poor, agape would call for a more sympathetic hearing for economic migrants. Nevertheless, receiving countries would be wary of such generous accommodation and find it contrary to their duties of distributive justice to their local citizens and residents. Since economic migration stands on much weaker and less urgent humanitarian grounds than migration from war, persecution, or natural disasters, it becomes an even better measure of host countries' generosity and response to the call of agape.

Withholding Public Medical Care

As of October 2017, NHS trusts in England have been mandated to ask for advance payment from those ineligible to receive free healthcare, such as, failed asylum seekers or visitors overstaying their visas before they are given elective care. In a study by the *Guardian*, one out of every seven who were asked to pay upfront was not treated, and there have been anecdotal accounts of people failing further in their health and dying as a result.[9] After all, many of those affected by this new rule were people of limited means (Jayanetti 2018). Some claim that this rule was part of the "get tough" approach to immigration. Others, however, say that justice demands safeguards to prevent the abuse of the system which ultimately harms everybody else receiving poor or inadequate healthcare because of the strain on national resources, the NHS in particular.

---

[9] The study was conducted between October 2017 and June 2018 with 84 out of England's 148 acute hospital trusts participating. In that time, of the 2,279 patients who required advance payment, 341 (15%) did not pursue their treatment. This is most likely a significant undercount because 64 hospital trusts (43% of the total) did not participate in the study (Jayanetti 2018).

Past Disequilibria and Unattended Wrongs

The duties from agape and from justice clash on so many migration-related issues. Common to all the aforesaid cases are agape's call for communities to share voluntarily some of their own substance (jobs, pay, resources, way of life) with those who have nothing, or who are poor, or who are in trouble – people who have no legal rights at all to claim any of these. However, local citizens and residents of the host countries also present their fears and just claims and rights over the same jobs, pay, resources, and way of life. The perception of a zero-sum phenomenon due to rival consumption is evident in these fears and claims. Extending hospitality and compassionate succor to distressed neighboring populations runs up against the demands of justice from local citizens who feel that their own needs, distress, and concerns have yet to be met by their own governments. These aggrieved local citizens or residents believe that their jobs and wages are at risk with the influx of plentiful, cheap labor. Moreover, they resent having to pay higher taxes to fund the resulting higher social spending to settle and integrate these new arrivals. It also puts additional strain on the social services of the local community, with adverse impact in terms of the longer wait times and the decline in the quality of service because of the heavier usage. Furthermore, the erosion of their cultural homogeneity and way of life angers the local populace especially in view of migrants who make no effort to assimilate into the host community.

The backlash from residents and citizens has been substantial and fierce so much so that domestic politics have singlehandedly upended the loftiest values and public pledges of solidarity and common humanity even among nations that pride themselves to be the bastions of liberal Western values, such as the United Kingdom, the United States, and the European Union (Fisher 2022). Domestic realities and pressures from constituents, not the duty of humanity, have the ultimate say in agape-justice conflicts pertaining to migration. As we have seen, some EU nations have gone so far as to criminalize and prosecute what many see as humanitarian acts of solidarity in aiding desperate migrants (*The Guardian* 2017, 2020; Trilling 2020). Migration is arguably the most contentious but also the most poignant of all agape-justice conflicts.

Herein lies the clash between the duties from agape and the duties from justice. Note that the aforesaid migration issues are different from the Old Testament duty of extending hospitality to strangers because the latter hospitality does not demand a similar costly sacrifice and is only for a limited time. These modern migration issues ask for sharing from one's substance, and their cost will be immediately incurred, even as their benefits are unseen, uncertain, or arise only in the long term. Not surprisingly, migration-related clashing claims from agape and justice are worldwide. The EU has been grappling with the influx of refugees from Syria, Afghanistan, and Africa. The UK has become so desperate with the Channel crossings to the point of reaching an accord with Rwanda to send migrants to the latter (UK Home Office 2022). The US ideological divide bitterly contests policy over migrants at its southern border.

South Africa occasionally expels economic migrants from its neighboring sub-Saharan countries. Colombia has been overwhelmed with Venezuelans fleeing government repression. Mexico has been trying to stem the flow of migrants from Central America. Chile has provided haven to Haitians but has been unable to meet their needs and expectations, so much so that many Haitian migrants are now on the move again, this time to the United States (McDonnell and Poblete 2021). Australia has sent asylum seekers to Papua New Guinea at one point and then to Nauru for offshore processing of their claims, much to the criticism of human rights activists (Kwai 2021). Myanmar's neighbors, even those that are predominantly Muslim, have been wary of providing refuge to fleeing persecuted Muslim Rohinga refugees. Rural migrants from the Chinese interior are unable to secure the all-important *hukou* in Shanghai, the residence permit that will allow them and their children to avail of vital urban social services despite years, even decades, of working in the city.

A common feature in all the above cases is that people are compelled to migrate, whether because of war, political persecution, natural disasters, or poverty. Refugees and migrants seek a better life or a safer environment because of hardships and dangers encountered in their original domicile. Their national and local governments that had been responsible for them had failed them (primary obligations). Consequently, secondary, "inherited obligations" have been created and are now incumbent on the receiving nations and local communities. Indeed, migration-related issues are an excellent example of how agape-justice conflicts arise from unattended past wrongs or disequilibria. As evidence, note the instability and the chronic, even egregious, failures of the countries marked by emigration. This repeated clash between the requirements of the law and the duties of humanitarian assistance are the predictable outcomes of unattended past wrongs and disequilibria in the national social homeostasis of the sending countries.

However, the failures are not limited to the leadership of the sending nations. Advanced nations also bear their own share of failures in this regard. In the first place, their failure to extend assistance to their flailing neighbors is now coming back to haunt them. A genuine attempt to help these poor developing countries in the past could have precluded or at least minimized the exodus from these now failing economies. The EU could have been more attentive and forthcoming in providing development aid and collaboration with their neighboring African and Middle Eastern nations. Similarly for the United States and Canada vis-à-vis their poorer neighbors in the Americas. A more sustained and generous outreach in the past could have preempted the even bigger and more intractable problems that will have to be resolved today to keep their populations from uprooting themselves to go north. The Marshall Plan is an example of a successful preemptive assistance that headed off even bigger problems in a struggling war-torn Europe in the aftermath of World War II.

Similarly, failed states, such as Syria, Libya, and others, might have been avoided if nations with the military, economic, diplomatic, and political power had been more forthcoming in preventing these countries from unraveling. To be sure, such intervention and assistance are not always welcome or successful, as in the case of the US, UN, and international efforts in Somalia, Haiti, Iraq, and Afghanistan. Moreover, there is only so much that even powerful nations could do. Nevertheless, we cannot ignore repeated historical lessons that failures by omission or commission in heading off past disequilibria or past wrongs will inevitably produce even more dire consequences going forward. There is an element of self-interest in the duty to prevent harm. These unattended past wrongs and disequilibria create agape-justice conflicts downstream for everybody else. This is yet another collective-action problem (recall Chapter 2) in which nations are unable to act together to head off their shared problems.

Balance of Payments Crises and IMF Conditionality

Another good example of agape-justice conflicts due to past disequilibria and unattended earlier wrongs is the role of the International Monetary Fund (IMF) in dealing with balance of payments crises. The IMF has been at the center of controversies surrounding foreign exchange (forex) crises worldwide. On the one hand, it is the lender of last resort, and its assistance is much sought by nations going through a balance of payments (BOP) crisis. It has a reputation for rigor, and its stamp of approval is a prerequisite for these nations' return to international capital markets. Not surprisingly, the EU insisted that the IMF be a party to any assistance package provided by the EU to one of its members – Greece (Dijsselbloem n.d.). On the other hand, the IMF is the poster child for heartless capital-ist greed in the eyes of its critics because of the very tough conditions it imposes as a requirement for any assistance.

The dilemma of IMF decision makers and the country in BOP crisis is challenging. On the one hand, like any bank, the IMF is accountable to its shareholders (the member nations of the IMF) in ensuring that the funds they lend will be repaid. This is a demand of commutative and distributive justice. It is the IMF's responsibility as banker to nations to exercise fidu-ciary care for the funds entrusted to its management. Furthermore, since the IMF stamp of approval is taken by global commercial banks as the signal that it is now safe to lend to these failing nations, the IMF has the obligation, like any auditing firm, to be accurate and truthful in its public pronouncements on the financial health of the borrowing, ailing nation in crisis. This is the IMF's obligation to the rest of the global banking system. Commutative and distributive justice demand such due diligence and oversight.

These demands of justice often clash with the demands for compassion. Among the prescriptions and conditions that are required by the IMF is the restoration of fiscal balances within a short period. This often entails drastic changes by raising taxes and cutting spending because immediate results are needed. Social expenditures are usual targets, especially sub-sidies for food, fuel, and other basic needs. Furthermore, raising inter-est rates is another step required to stanch the country's bleeding foreign reserves. All these substantive and overnight changes lead to inflation, recession, and the cut-off of public assistance. There is a severe impact on the local economy. More worrying, the burdens of the IMF conditions fall disproportionally on the poor. Thus, critics of the IMF call for greater leeway, if only out of concern for the well-being of those adversely affected by such reforms.

This is not the place to weigh the merits or demerits of the IMF condi-tions. It is sufficient to note that we have ample historical evidence from the numerous foreign exchange and banking crises in the post–World War II era to witness this clash of claims between justice and agape.

A related issue is the question of debt forgiveness. Before the turn of the millennium, a global grassroots movement appealed to wealthy coun-tries to forgive the debt of poor developing countries (Busby 2007). This initiative took inspiration from the Jubilee Law of the Hebrew Scriptures (Lev 25). Some debts were eventually forgiven but only for a select group of highly indebted poor countries (HIPC). This was after the turn of the millennium and only after significant urging by UK Prime Minister Tony

Blair among his fellow leaders at the 2005 Gleneagles G-8 meeting. A major obstacle to such debt forgiveness was the concern over fostering a moral hazard problem. Besides, there was also the question of holding nations accountable for their fiscal indiscipline. Such debt forgiveness did not seem fair in the eyes of their critics, not for global distributive, commutative, or general-legal justice.

Proponents of debt forgiveness also appeal to the duties of justice in calling for writing off such debt. This is not the place to weigh these competing claims of justice. It is sufficient to note that proponents of debt forgiveness could always fall back on an appeal to compassion. Poor nations earn very little foreign exchange. What little they earn must be used to pay back interest on these loans, not to mention the principal. This is vital foreign exchange that could have been used for their development. Their huge debt overhang puts them in a poverty trap. This is yet again another example of the tension between the demands of justice and the demands of agape. How strict or how much latitude ought the IMF give to cushion people's suffering? Should it adhere to banking standards as it always has (justice), or should it be less bank-like and be more accommodating for a change (agape)?

Common to most nations in BOP crisis and seeking IMF assistance is their fiscal negligence. These BOP crises were foreseeable based on the unsoundness and even recklessness of the macroeconomic policies pursued by these nations. They end up in BOP or banking crises because of chronic economic mismanagement. These are examples of subsequent agape-justice conflicts that arise from unattended past wrongs and earlier disequilibria. They are aptly called "prior-fault" moral dilemmas.

Responsible Giving

From 2013 to 2015, twenty-six cities in the United States banned food sharing in public spaces. In a study of 187 cities, 9 percent banned food sharing in public. Police have charged violators with misdemeanor offenses, most of whom were providing food to homeless people. Public health is the justification for these statutes, such as the prevention of the spread of hepatitis A. However, critics and NGOs believe that these statutes were enacted to drive away homeless people from these public spaces (Guarnieri 2018). Feeding them was seen as making it easier for homeless people to dwell in the city's public spaces (National Law Center 2019, 46, 106).

The Montgomery (Alabama) city council unanimously passed an anti-panhandler law in July 2019 whereby even those who give to such solicitation can be jailed (MacNeil 2019; Associated Press 2019). Earlier in 2014, San Antonio Police Chief William McManus wanted to go beyond the city's 2011 ordinance banning panhandling and to ratchet it further by criminalizing even giving to such appeals for money (Solomon 2014). City leaders were desperate to prevent car accidents at street intersections, protect pedestrians, preserve local tourism, and heed the complaints of local businesses (Solomon 2014; MacNeil 2019). Giving money to such street solicitation facilitated what was deemed an urban blight.

In April 2022, the Montgomery City Council discussed an ordinance supporting a citywide campaign with the slogan "Don't enable panhandling, give smart Montgomery" (Martin 2022). In New Haven, signs on "responsible giving" went up on streets with heavy pedestrian foot traffic. In brief, "responsible giving" asked good-hearted people who gave to individuals asking for loose change to give their donations instead to local established groups to ensure that their benefactions get to the truly needy. Furthermore, these groups can address the root causes of the problem and help as part of a much larger program to improve the lives of those who are compelled to solicit loose change from students and shoppers. It is a much better use and disposition of societal resources. It also encourages those who are driven to ask for loose change to seek assistance from these specialized groups. In effect, "responsible giving" prevents good-hearted donors from enabling people to avoid seeking professional help. Furthermore, there is an accumulative dynamic in this case in that the combined giving of passers-by de facto institutionalizes and encourages such practice. For example, note the proliferation of people with signs asking for loose change sitting on the sidewalk in the tourist stretch of Fifth Avenue in mid-town Manhattan, New York or the proliferation of people standing at street intersections with signs soliciting money in many urban areas. "Responsible giving" can be cast as a demand of distributive justice, and perhaps even of agape, as tough love.

Nevertheless, this is not always an easy decision in practice for some passers-by. Proponents of responsible giving make sense. It is the better way of almsgiving and addresses root causes rather than mere symptoms. However, for some people, compassion cannot make them simply ignore the person asking for some change, especially if the person is obviously in distress. Unfortunately, even people in severe distress often refuse to seek assistance from groups that are specifically set up to provide such aid, for one reason or another. Moreover, social agencies are fraught with problems themselves, such as ill treatment that drive potential beneficiaries to avoid them altogether. At any rate, "responsible giving" works by drying up the source of alms so that people who fall on hard times finally seek assistance from the social agencies set up specifically for their needs. Some passers-by will find it difficult, out of agape, to walk or drive by, heedless of these people's pleas. They would not want to drive them to such dire need as to compel them to seek assistance from social services. This is too hurtful for some passers-by. The initiative of "responsible giving" will work only if most passers-by cooperate.

This dilemma of whether to give or not is another instance of an agape-justice conflict. Just like in the earlier two cases on migration and IMF conditionality, people are driven to have to ask passers-by for loose change because their families, friends, or local communities have failed to provide a safety net for them. Some might have even brought these problems upon themselves. These primary obligations have been unmet. As a result, "inherited" secondary obligations are now incumbent on passers-by to fill in for the former's failures. "Responsible giving" is yet another example of an agape-justice conflict that arises because of unattended past wrongs or disequilibria.

In all these cases, nations and local communities have been overwhelmed by a surge in migration or by street solicitations and have responded by making it illegal to provide assistance that is deemed to facilitate or enable these activities. National and local leaders seek to deter people from crossing the Mediterranean, sneaking into the United States through its southern deserts, engaging in street solicitation, or living in the community's public spaces by making them much more difficult to pull off successfully. As a result, ordinary citizens and NGO aid workers who were arrested, jailed, prosecuted, fined, charged with misdemeanor, or sentenced to probation faced an unpalatable choice – to be beneficent but be deemed a lawbreaker or to follow the law but fail to prevent harm in turning a blind eye to people in need. Some have called their deeds "crimes of solidarity." They are faced with having to choose between living up their duties as law-abiding citizens and their duty of humanity or duty to prevent harm. This is not the place to debate and resolve the question of whether the previously mentioned laws are just to begin with. It is sufficient for our study to note that even in democratic societies steeped in liberal values, moral and legal obligations can present incompatible claims. How did we get to the point whereby acts of kindness have come to violate the law?

Compassion and Material Cooperation in Wrongdoing

Nations and NGOs are often confronted with the dilemma in which they must enable wrongdoing in order to do good. The Taliban takeover of Afghanistan in August 2021 is an example of tension between agape and justice. Nations and NGOs had underwritten 70 to 80 percent of the Afghan government's budget prior to the Taliban takeover. Just to underscore the severity of the country's needs, note that the World Bank considers a country to be aid-dependent if 10 percent of its GDP comes from foreign donors. Pre-Taliban Afghanistan's GDP was 40 percent from foreign aid (Lawder 2021; Nagesh 2021). Thus, the Taliban takeover not only precipitated an economic, health, and food crisis for the country, but it also presented nations, multilateral agencies, and NGOs with a moral dilemma on whether to continue providing aid.

To continue such assistance is to enable an unreformed Taliban with its problematic treatment of women and its violation of human rights. Besides, the West repeatedly warned during the peace negotiations that it would cut off aid if the Taliban forcibly took over the country, which they did. To withhold aid in exchange for reforms, however, is to fail to prevent the starvation of millions of Afghans and the implosion of its healthcare system. How should one adjudicate these clashing claims between agape and justice?

It is a similar question in the case of food aid for North Korea. Massive food aid had to be brought into the country in the 1990s to prevent widespread starvation and death. To this day, a good part of the 30 percent of its food supplies coming from foreign sources is aid. There is food insecurity in the country, as reflected in the various measures of malnutrition, including stunted growth for its population (Chisolm 2018). Even as steps were taken to ensure that the aid in kind went to the vulnerable people for whom they were intended, there is nonetheless still the problem of having enabled a regime that has brought such a chronic food crisis on itself with its misdirected spending. Besides, funds and resources are fungible.

Even if the aid in kind did go entirely to the starving population, it nevertheless relieves the state from using its own resources to alleviate the disaster. It could keep misusing its resources. To make matters worse, such misuse entails devoting its resources to the development of nuclear arms and their delivery system. This presents a serious moral dilemma. To stop food aid altogether is to inflict even more suffering on the population. However, to continue providing such assistance is in effect to support its nuclear weapons program and hasten its acquisition of arms that endanger the whole world.

It is a similar predicament for many NGOs. This includes *Doctors without Borders*. In working in the most horrific war zones to attend to unaddressed needs, they incur the risk of enabling wrongdoing. By working with brutal regimes or warlords, these NGOs are in effect relieving pressure on these errant states and actors to change their ways. Of course, NGOs are more concerned with relieving the immediate threat to life and limb. Compassion demands nothing less than this. Nevertheless, global distributive and general-legal justice also caution these NGOs to be mindful of their enabling these states or warlords in their wrongdoing. Justice calls for greater sensitivity to not being complicit to wrongdoing. Compassion, however, would willingly accept such material cooperation if it is the only way to do good, especially if they pertain to in-extremis needs. Indeed, these are moral dilemmas in which one must enable wrongdoing to do good. The questions for compassion are whether it should draw a line it will not cross, and if so, where it will set that threshold. How egregious is the wrongdoing that one is willing to tolerate?[10] All these cases are "prior-fault" moral dilemmas.

Occasions to Update Underlying Public Ethos

Besides showing how they are the result of past unattended wrongs, the cases presented in this chapter also illustrate another vital role of agape-justice conflicts – they signal the need to modify society's underlying CLU in line with changing circumstances and needs. The cases of "Dreamers" and children outgrowing their parents' visas underscore a gap in legislation that needs to be addressed. The NGOs' sea captains and aid workers who are willing to be jailed for rescuing distressed migrants in the Mediterranean and bringing them ashore have brought to the public's attention the recently enacted laws criminalizing such assistance. In the face of significant public outcry, city leaders in Montgomery, Alabama and San Antonio, Texas have had to back off from the city council's statutes and the police chief's proposal to penalize even those who give to people soliciting assistance.

The perennial calls for compassion in the IMF's adjustment package for countries in BOP distress have led to greater caution and sensitivity within the IMF on the impact of its structural adjustment programs on the poor. Similarly, the International Monetary Fund (2017) built on the G-8's 2005 Gleneagles debt-forgiveness for highly indebted poor countries (HIPC) by providing new programs for poor countries in debt distress. These new initiatives were the direct outcomes of the agape-justice clashes behind the grassroots Jubilee 2000 campaign to forgive these debts.

---

[10] Recall the third condition of the principle of double effect that weighs whether the good effects outweigh the resulting ill consequences.

The moral dilemmas in cases where compassion enables wrongdoing may in fact present unique occasions for agape to effect much-needed reforms in the underlying CLU of nations that violate human rights. The seeming hardheartedness of cutting off international aid from a Taliban-ruled Afghanistan may turn out to be the Afghan women's best hope of retrieving their hard-earned gains from the last two decades.

Recall from the preceding chapter how the moral and legal dilemma precipitated by the sale of Ben & Jerry's to Unilever eventually led to ben-efits corporation legislation in more than half the US states. Such B-Corp legislation protects corporate directors from lawsuits when they pursue nonpecuniary goals in their decisions, such as protecting the ecology and the larger society (Lowenstein 2013). Similarly, the tension between Friedman's (1970) shareholder model (demand of justice) versus the stakeholder model (demand of agape) of business governance ultimately spawned socially responsible investing in finance and social entrepre-neurship in business management with its triple bottom line accounting. This includes the revision of MBA curricula that broaden the horizon and the skills of future executives well beyond mere profit maximization (*Economist* 2022b).

Note that agape-justice conflicts are not always about agape making justice much more humane. There have also been cases of agape-justice conflicts leading justice to impose limits on compassion. We see this in the much harder line that the Scandinavian countries have taken in accept-ing immigrants in the wake of their new domestic social problems after the 2015 migrant surge. Even the most generous and welcoming of these nations have imposed restrictions that stress greater personal responsibility from would-be migrants including a genuine desire and effort to assimilate into and contribute to the local community (Traub 2021). This is a case of the demands of justice making the necessary corrections to a compassion that had been abused.

In all these cases, we see that agape-justice conflicts become the catalysts or occasions for communities to adjust their underlying CLU in response to shifts in the socioeconomic terrain. Equally important, agape-justice conflicts may in fact bring to the surface the unjustness of the underlying CLU that justice seeks to enforce. On these occasions, agape may be chal-lenging the underlying premises of justice (e.g., panhandling laws, laws on rescuing migrants at sea). Agape-justice conflicts may in fact be an integral part of social life rather than be viewed as aberrations. Besides bringing about hard choices, clashing claims from agape and justice may in fact be opportunities for improvement.

Summary and Conclusions: Adjudicating "Prior-fault" Moral Dilemmas

The goal of this chapter has been to show that agape-justice conflicts arise because of unattended past wrongs or disequilibria in the social homeostasis of preceding periods. Using Herman's (2001) terminology, we see the emergence of secondary, "inherited" obligations because of the failure of primary obligation holders to live up to their duties or to maintain the delicate balance in their social homeostasis. Thus, in the case of migration, unattended past ills in Africa, the Middle East, Asia, Latin America, and Central America have finally driven huge numbers to migrate to the more prosperous and safer regions of the world, such as the EU, the United States, Australia, and Canada. Such large-scale migratory movements have precipitated competing claims between local citizens (demanding their legal and moral dues from their governments), on the one hand, and migrants and asylum seekers (asking for compassion), on the other hand. We find agape-justice conflicts in actual cases of humanitarian assistance being criminalized by law and then prosecuted.

In our second example, note that nations get into BOP crises because of their past fiscal indiscipline, economic mismanagement, and other national ills. This creates secondary, "inherited obligations" on the part of the IMF and its constituent member nations because of the earlier failures of the leaders of these distressed nations. Again, the IMF will be confronted with competing claims from justice (follow standard IMF conditions), on the one hand, and claims from humanity to be more accommodating (agape).

In our third case, people are faced with the dilemma of responsible giving. On the one hand, justice demands that the well-being of the entire community be safeguarded by minimizing dangers to pedestrians and car accidents and protecting local businesses and tourism from the proliferation of people soliciting loose change from passers-by. Moreover, there is a fear that generosity might cause more harm than good by enabling people to forego necessary change or to avoid the professional help they require. On the other hand, compassion calls for extending assistance to those who have truly fallen on hard times.

In our fourth case of compassion being in material cooperation with wrongdoing, such moral dilemma would not have arisen had it not been for the failures of so many of the primary obligation holders. Recall the graft of the previous Afghan governments, the colonial occupation of the Korean peninsula and its division and subsequent war, the rogue North

Korean regime and its enablers, and the many causes behind failed states' descent into chaos and war.

In all these cases, agape-justice conflicts arise because there is need to mitigate past wrongs or unattended past disequilibria in socioeconomic homeostasis. We face two difficulties in adjudicating these conflicts. First, there is no clear-cut method on how to go about resolving these clashing claims. All we know is that they are secondary "inherited obligations" that have emerged and are now incumbent upon us because the primary obligation holders (nations, institutions, and people) had failed to live up to their duties and obligations to begin with. There is no universal, blanket solution given the complexity and fluidity of these cases. One can only deal with them in their particularities and in their context.

The second problem is even more difficult. Correcting or mitigating past wrongs or unattended disequilibria in social homeostasis may itself create even more instances of new wrongs or disequilibria. Solutions to any of the four preceding cases are fraught with risks of creating new imbalances and grievances.[11] Yet, doing nothing and maintaining the status quo is in itself also a choice that may create such new wrongs or further disequilibria. In other words, both problems essentially leave us with the unpalatable choice of having no clear path going forward. To make matters worse, whichever path we take may create even more problems than solve them.

We can adopt the general rule from the preceding chapter – we resolve agape-justice conflicts in a diachronic manner, that is, conscious of the past, but with an eye toward maintaining the delicate balance in social homeostasis going forward. Keenly aware of where we have been and the state of our current social homeostasis, we simply balance these competing claims at the margins with small corrective measures – just like riding a bicycle as mentioned earlier. To mitigate or correct the consequences of past wrongs or past disequilibria, one can only do so within the larger social homeostasis described in the preceding chapter. We must look at its current state and needs and its most likely future trajectory. Lest we be too pessimistic, let us conclude this chapter with an actual example of such adjudication that considers the past and the present state.

Recall the case of Monsieur Herrou who was prosecuted for "helping undocumented foreigners enter, move about and reside" in France, a crime that carried a possible five-year sentence and a €30,000 fine. He was convicted and sentenced to a suspended €3,000 fine (*The Guardian* 2017). In July 2018, the French constitutional court ruled that Monsieur

---

[11] Court challenges to affirmative action in university admission in the United States is an example.

Herrou's action was not a crime, given the foundational principles of France — "liberté, égalité, fraternité." It ruled that "crimes of solidarity" cannot be prosecuted. The French court of final appeal (*Cour de Cassation*) overturned Mr. Herrou's conviction in December 2018 and sent the case back to the appeals court in Lyon, which eventually declared in May 2020 that all charges against Mr. Herrou were void (*The Guardian* 2020). This is an example of agape taking precedence over the demands of justice based on a keen awareness of the past and the current state of the social homeostasis. It is a similar resolution of the other cases of NGOs' ship captains prosecuted for their humanitarian search-and-rescue missions.

No doubt, agape-justice conflicts arising from unattended past wrongs or unaddressed past disequilibria in social homeostasis are daunting and difficult to adjudicate. Nevertheless, they are manageable and can spawn improvements. Note the examples cited above of more socially sensitive IMF conditional packages and the institution's new debt relief programs in the wake of the G-8 Gleneagles response to the grassroots Jubilee 2000 Millennium debt forgiveness campaign. Recall, too, the B-Corp legislation in more than half of US states to head off future Ben & Jerry's legal dilemmas. Similarly, note the broadening of MBA curricula and the emerging fields of social entrepreneurship and socially responsible investing in the wake of Friedman (1970)'s claim of shareholder value maximization as *the* social responsibility of business. These examples illustrate how people, from the top leadership to the grassroots, eagerly put in their share in settling agape-justice conflicts, both past and present. After all, as mentioned earlier, most people strive to be both loving and just.

CHAPTER 6

Grace Building on Nature
Love Is Diffusive

Introduction

Many agape-justice conflicts reflect the competing demands of universal love (agape), on the one hand, versus kin-particularistic love (justice), on the other hand. It is a clash between impartial and partial love. Consider the following illustrative case on vaccine and personal protective equipment (PPE) distribution.

Misplaced Nationalism or Just Allocation?

On April 2, 2020, as the infection rates and deaths soared in the United States and the implications of the corona virus were beginning to be understood, President Trump invoked the Defense Production Act to halt the export of domestically produced N95 respirator masks to Canada and Latin American countries.[1] The dissent from 3M (the manufacturer) was swift and strong, and it warned of "significant humanitarian implications of ceasing respirator supplies to healthcare workers in Canada and Latin America, where we are a critical supplier of respirators."[2] N95 respirator masks are the gold standard in preventing infection from the corona virus because of its ability to filter out effectively the air-borne virus. They are vital for frontline workers caring for those afflicted with the virus. At this time during the crisis, empirical evidence from China and then Italy already underscored both the deadly nature of this virus and the high mortality rate among doctors, nurses, and other support staff caring for the infected patients. It was also clear by this time that the whole world, including the United States, was woefully unprepared and did not have sufficient supplies of such PPE. Medical personnel had to improvise or recycle such PPE, which were

---

[1] Breuninger and Wilkie (2020) and Swanson, Kanno-Youngs, and Haberman (2020).
[2] 3M (2021)

supposed to be for single use only. Many healthcare workers in the United States were falling seriously ill and even dying.

With the country having recorded over four hundred thousand Covid-related deaths, the new Biden administration (January 2021) ultimately had to continue the previous administration's severe restrictions on the export of Covid vaccines from the United States, including all the critical materials to produce such vaccines (Martell and Rocha 2021; Wingrove 2021). The EU also imposed export controls on vaccines when it ran into trouble securing supplies for its own citizens (Stevis-Gridneff 2021). India hosts the world's largest producer of vaccines (Serum Institute), and it had pledged at the onset of the pandemic that it was going to share at least half of its vaccines with other poor nations, purchased largely by the World Health Organization's (WHO) Covax program. In March 2021, India had to renege on its earlier pledge and suspend all exports of vaccines as the virus ravaged its cities and countryside with severe illness and death. This, in effect, put other poor countries dependent on Covax in a lurch. The pandemic was wreaking unimaginable death in Indian cities and its countryside at that time (Roy and Agarwal 2021).

The issue is straightforward: There are not enough supplies to go around, and people will be put at great risk or even die. The question is whose citizens will die. This is not even to mention the question of whose economy will get back to normal first, with implications for which populations will ultimately bear the economic brunt of the pandemic and be even more impoverished coming out of the pandemic. Note that such export controls are not limited to medical supplies alone. During the uncertain, early period of the pandemic, Southeast Asia's biggest exporter of rice, Vietnam, banned all exports of rice (Reuters 2020).

The moral arguments on both sides of the debate are compelling. On the one hand, national leaders uniformly deemed their primary obligation to be to their own citizens first. They are tasked with safeguarding the well-being of the people who had been entrusted, legally and morally, to their care and leadership. In his collection for the poor of Jerusalem, St. Paul explicitly said that people should not give to the point of impoverishing themselves, thus implicitly acknowledging their overriding duty to themselves and those dependent on them. As we will see later in this chapter, our natural loves do prioritize those who are nearest and dearest to us relative to those who are farther or who are strangers. Besides, these citizens could rightfully claim that their taxes had paid for the socioeconomic infrastructure that now makes the production of these vital medical supplies possible. Commutative and distributive justice and *philautia, philia,* and *storge* all support the actions of these national leaders in prioritizing their citizens.

On the other hand, there are also strong moral arguments that would call for sharing these vital medical supplies. Our duty of humanity will not allow us to be indifferent to the plight of those who are farthest or who are strangers to us, especially if they are in grave distress just as we are. They, too, are human beings, and they too are dependent on these lifesaving resources.

Moreover, they have far less means than US and EU residents to mitigate the impact of Covid. US-based 3M had a point in framing the question as a humanitarian issue, made even more serious by Canada and Latin America's heavy dependence on 3M's US-based factories. Agape calls, at the very least, for equal regard for all – our dearest and nearest, alongside those who are strangers or who are more distant to us.[3]

The difficulty of adjudicating this conflict between agape and justice is evident in the 180-degree turn of the nations that had initially stayed on the moral high ground. India started with a voluntary 50-50 split, only to have to backtrack when faced with a severe national outbreak. The EU with its liberal, universalist values eventually buckled and prioritized its own interests when its supply of vaccines dried up. They imposed export controls in March of 2021 (Stevis-Gridneff 2021). The Biden administration started with a much-heralded turn away from the "America First" policy of the preceding administration and took back its place as a good global citizen. It nevertheless ended up banning the export not only of vaccines but also of the critical ingredients to produce these vaccines, much to the chagrin of the EU, India, and other vaccine-producing nations. In all three cases, note that the sudden turnaround only goes to show that in practice, the demands of justice (including *storge, philia,* and *philautia*) eclipse those of agape, even if they weigh heavily on and go against our personal or national conscience. Self-preservation is important, but, at the same time, so is compassion for our neighbors equally in distress. Indeed, these are extraordinary examples of a moral dilemma, or, more accurately, a moral tragedy. In-extremis arguments cannot be used in these cases because all face the same danger of infection and death.

The competing claims over the limited global supplies of vaccines and PPE during the early stages of the pandemic redound to a clash of duties

---

[3] The World Health Organization (WHO) calls the advanced nations' conduct as misplaced "PPE/vaccine nationalism." This international body appealed to these nations' self-interest by noting that the pandemic will end only if it is stopped at the global level.

from justice vis-à-vis those from agape. Which claims should we prioritize? Dividing supplies between these two sets of claims does not solve the fundamental question because of the dire shortage. For as long as there is need to allocate between these two competing sets of claims, our duties from *philautia, storge, philia*, and commutative and distributive justice can be satisfied only at the expense of turning our back on our duties from agape. Agape calls for giving out of one's substance rather than merely from one's surplus.

PPE and vaccines are only a sample of many more similar issues, admittedly not with such urgency but with similar life-changing consequences nonetheless. We can think of the dispute over sharing the headwaters of the Nile between Ethiopia, Egypt, and Sudan; the headwaters of the Mekong River between China and downstream countries such as Cambodia and Vietnam; and the headwaters of the Jordan River between Israel and Jordan (Milne 2021).

A similar issue is the case of foreign aid. The UK had set 0.7 percent of its gross national income (GNI) for foreign aid. However, in response to the pandemic, it reduced this to 0.5 percent, generating protest, including from the Prime Minister's own party. This is approximately four billion pounds a year. The retort was that it was temporary. Moreover, they had to do it because the UK government was already borrowing money for its day-to-day operations. Note that poor developing countries were in an even deeper hole than the UK was at that time. These poor countries were losing aid when they needed it most. The UK was the only G7 country that curtailed its aid during the Covid pandemic, even as other advanced countries increased their assistance (Barber and Boycott-Owen 2022; Mason 2021).

In all these cases, we have a clash of claims between justice (obligations to one's own citizens) and the duty of agape. These cases also illustrate the time- and place-utility of legal and moral debts, that is, there is a specific time and place where these duties need to be fulfilled. For example, sharing excess vaccines and PPE in the later stages of the pandemic is laudable, but not as praiseworthy had they been shared when they were most needed – during the deadly early phase. Nevertheless, some will argue that collectives do not inherit obligations in the way individuals do. Collectives are not bound to promote the happiness of other collectives. Barbara Herman (2001, 252) observes:

> [I]t is hard to see how a society, whose raison d'etre and authority derive from its role in securing the fair distribution of the burdens and benefits of social cooperation for its members, would inherit failures of obligation from other cooperative schemes and so warrant to tax its own members on their behalf.

Particular, Partial Love versus Universal, Impartial Love

A clear thread that goes through many of the real-life conflicts between agape and justice is that most involve a clash of claims between those who are within our immediate circle, on the one hand, and those who are not associated with us, except for our common humanity, on the other hand. Who has first claim on our affection, attention, assistance, and finite resources – those who are nearest and dearest to us, or the neediest even if they are strangers or distant to us? Whom should we prioritize? On one end of the spectrum are people like Cicero, St. Thomas, and many others who argue that human life is comprised of special relationships and their attendant obligations. It is part of human nature for people to be closer, indeed, to be bound by stronger obligations to their kin, friends, dependents, neighbors, and fellow citizens compared to those who are unrelated to them or who are strangers, even if they are relatively needier. This is an order of charity that is rooted in human nature itself. On the other end of the spectrum is moral cosmopolitanism, including Outka's agape as equal regard, which is characterized by universality and impartiality. The New Testament provides vivid illustrations of this in the parable of the Good Samaritan and in Jesus Christ meekly laying down his life even for his enemies and for people who were undeserving of his love (cf. Matt 5:43–47). We are to be just as undiscriminating in our love and beneficence.

At first glance, it seems that this is merely an intra-love conflict and not a clash between agape and justice. After all, *philautia* is self-love, *storge* is the love of our kin, and *philia* is the love of our friends. Thus, the conflict seems to be between different types of love that are simultaneously operative. Love of self, family, and friends (*philautia, storge, philia*) demand priority for the nearest and the dearest, while *agape* demands priority for the neediest based on an equal concern for all. Indeed, these competing claims seem to be intra-love conflicts. A deeper look, however, suggests that these are not intra-love conflicts but genuine clashes between justice and agape.

As we have seen in Chapter 1, the respective claims of *philautia, storge,* and *philia* properly fall under justice. For example, justice requires filial solicitude for one's parents. Similarly, children have rightful claims on their parents' and relatives' love and care as a matter of justice. *Philautia, storge,* and *philia* are not optional but obligatory. These are instances of love commanded by natural law itself. Thus, the salient clash in the previously mentioned cases is primarily a conflict in the demands of justice from *philautia, storge,* and *philia* (our nearest and dearest) versus the demands of agape on behalf of the distant and the strangers. Choosing to save the lives of one's own citizens to whom one owes legal and moral duties rather than neighboring or distant noncitizens is not only an act of love for one's own but is also a demand of justice. Thus, nations and their political leaders have banned the export of vaccines and PPE. Similarly, prioritizing the well-being of distressed and needy citizens over that of neighboring or distant noncitizens when it comes to immigration or international trade is a demand of justice and not of love. Indeed, the abovementioned cases are ultimately a clash between agape and justice. On the one hand, justice presents the claims of kin love. On the other hand, agape presents the claims of the distant and the stranger based on nothing but an appeal to equal regard (Outka) or the duty of benevolence (Kant), humanity (Hume), or beneficence (Cicero).

The nub of the issue is how wide a net do we cast in taking people within the ambit of our care. How expansive should our circle of love and responsibility be? Who should be included in it? What we have is a clash between the strong, legitimate claims of kin-particularistic-preferential-natural love, on the one hand, and unconditioned-stranger-universal-impartial love, on the other hand.

This issue of priorities is a long-standing, difficult problem in social philosophy and moral theology (Hallett 1998). The complexity and fluidity of social life make sorting through the competing claims of justice and love that much more difficult. Would that we had to deal only with a small circle of people. Gardner (1957, 218) describes the problem well:

> [J]ustice may be used as an instrument of love in relationships involving only two individuals by way of assisting us to discern with greater clarity and objectivity the neighbor's true needs, but as soon as a third person is introduced into the relation love *requires* some calculation of conflicting needs and interests. Even within the family some rational estimate of conflicting claims and interests is necessary in the interest of love. The Samaritan may not have to employ the concept of justice in dealing with the single neighbor by the side of the road, but the moment he becomes confronted with two neighbors both of whose needs he is unable to meet[,] he must evaluate their respective claims in the interest of *agape* (emphasis original).

The need to allocate immediately raises a parallel need to scrutinize the rank ordering of the loves within our circle of responsibility. Equally important, it also underscores the need to examine the scope of the circle of love and responsibility that we have drawn around ourselves.

Can universal, all-inclusive agapic love coexist with the natural-preferential-selective-particularistic loves? There is no consensus among philosophers and theologians. Nygren (1953) says no, Pope (1997) says yes, while Wolterstorff (2011, 30–35) claims that there is no conflict at all. In what follows, we first examine justice's case for prioritizing the claims of our nearest and dearest. We then weigh the arguments that have been presented to expand this circle of love-responsibility beyond our natural loves. We conclude the chapter with an exposition on how to balance these two seemingly incompatible sets of claims.

The Case for Prioritizing Our Nearest and Dearest

Thomas Aquinas argues that as a matter of justice, humans owe *love of benevolence* (*amor benevolentiae*) to their fellow rational beings because (1) every person is an *Imago Dei*, and (2) every person has the potential for eventual union and friendship with God. Moreover, in St. Thomas' twofold order of the universe, every person is part of a much larger whole from which (s)he draws benefits and to whose good (s)he contributes (II-II, 65.1). This includes promoting the good of the human community through the solicitous care of fellow humans. Furthermore, humans accord affection to other humans because they recognize their likeness in their shared humanity (I-II, 27.3). People can identify with their fellow humans, and love them accordingly (Pope 1990, 120).

Given that such universal benevolence is a matter of justice owed to all, there should be no conflict at all between the demands of agape and justice. Not so. Despite this universal love owed to all, clashing claims nevertheless still arise because of (1) a practical reason – scarcity constrains us to rank order the material expression of our universal love of benevolence – and (2) a moral reason – our natural loves have attendant duties.

Argument #1: Practical Reason Due to Material Finitude

Material scarcity compels us to allocate to particularistic love instead of giving indiscriminately to all. Even if we were to assume in the most generous manner that our interior affection should be equal for all, nevertheless, the outward material expression of that affection will be unequal because of the insufficiency of our time and material resources. In his work *On Christian Doctrine*, St. Augustine acknowledges the duty to love all (universal benevolence). However, he is realistic enough to concede that putting this love into action will have to be unequal given the need to allocate our limited resources. In other words, St. Augustine calls for universal benevolence but realistically accepts that beneficence[4] will necessarily be unequal according to our socio-historical location.

> [A]ll men are to be loved equally. But *since you cannot do good to all, you are to pay special regard to those who, by the accidents of time, or place, or circumstance, are brought into closer connection with you* .... Just so among men: since you cannot consult for the good of them all, you must take the matter as decided for you by a sort of lot, *according as each man happens for the time being to be more closely connected with you.* (Augustine 1998, I. 28, emphasis added)

St. Thomas diverges from St. Augustine and takes an even stronger position by noting that both benevolence and beneficence cannot realistically be given equally to all. He accepts St. Augustine's position that beneficence, the outward expression of our love, will be unequal due to our material finitude. St. Thomas concludes: "As regards beneficence we are bound to observe this inequality, because we cannot do good to all" (II-II, 26.6, ad1). Charity does not oblige us to be beneficent to every person because it is impossible given the constraints of our resources and our finitude (II-II, 25.8).

However, St. Thomas goes further to note that even benevolence itself, the interior love, cannot be given equally to all our neighbors because human nature itself makes us more inclined to love and favor those who are closest to us. In responding to the question whether one ought to love one neighbor more than another, St. Thomas responds:

> [S]ome have said that we ought, out of charity, to love all our neighbors equally, as regards our affection, but not as regards the outward effect. They held that the order of love is to be understood as applying to outward favors, which we ought to confer on those who are connected with us in preference to those who are unconnected, and not to the inward affection, which ought to be given equally to all including our enemies.
>
> But this is unreasonable. *For the affection of charity, which is the inclination of grace, is not less orderly than the natural appetite,* ... the inclination also of grace which is the effect of charity, must needs be proportionate to those actions which have to be performed outwardly, so that, to wit, the affection of our charity be more intense towards those to whom we ought to behave with greater kindness.
>
> We must, therefore, say that, *even as regards the affection we ought to love one neighbor more than another. The reason is that, since the principle of love is God, and the person who loves, it must needs be that the affection of love increases in proportion to the nearness to one or the other of those principles.* (II-II, 26.6, emphasis added)

---

[4] Recall from chapter 1 the distinction between benevolence and beneficence. Benevolence refers to the interior goodwill we have for others. Beneficence is the outward, material expression of that benevolence.

In other words, St. Thomas allows for loving our neighbors unequally, both interiorly and outwardly. Our beneficence will have to be unequal since we do not have enough for all. Nevertheless, he also sees inequality in benevolence (interior affections) because humans by nature are inclined to love those who are closest to them. These are their natural loves.[5]

The reality of material finitude has consequences in the way we dispense our beneficence:

Consequence #1: To be Responsible for Nothing
The first consequence of our material finitude is the need to acknowledge that if we are to be benevolent at all, we need to allocate our beneficence. In other words, we must resign ourselves to accepting that we cannot help everyone, even those who may be meritorious or in distress. For example, Aelred rank orders the claims of six categories of humanity and their descending priority: relatives; special friends; those bound to us by obligations of duty; fellow Christians; those outside the Church such as Gentiles, Jews, heretics, and schismatics; enemies (Carmichael 2004, 77). Thus, "Aelred demonstrates a practical concern not to allow ourselves to be taken in by *'a love which in addressing itself to all, reaches no one'*" (Carmichael 2004, 96, fn 77, emphasis added). Similarly, it has been said, "if we are all responsible for everything ... then we are equally responsible for nothing" (Aronson 1990, 59).

Common sense tells us that beneficence must be necessarily limited to be workable. We cannot overstretch ourselves in helping everyone. Self-love (including love for our nearest and dearest) is also an obligation and is a precondition for universal benevolence. Because of our corporeal nature and the finitude of the earth, there is a natural limit as well to the material expression of supererogation. Otherwise, unrestrained self-giving in economic life eventually turns into self-annihilation. Even religious traditions with much-touted teachings on almsgiving and universal love acknowledge this practical limitation. Because of the obligations to oneself and one's family, Judaism limits almsgiving to no more than 20 percent of one's property.[6] In his collection for the poor of Jerusalem, St. Paul is careful to

---

[5] See also Pope (1990, 128, fn 29).
[6] Rabbi Yirmiyohu Kaganoff, Kislev 5768: "After the destruction of the Second Beis HaMikdash, the Sanhedrin relocated several times and was once situated in a town name Usha. While in Usha, the Sanhedrin made several important takanos (permanent rulings). One of these takanos forbade a person from distributing more than twenty percent of his property to tzedakah lest he himself become needy (Gemara Kesubos 50a). This ruling is referred to as the 'Takanas Usha'." www.yeshiva.co/midrash/6482 last accessed April 26, 2022.

remind the various church communities not to give to the point of impoverishing themselves (2 Cor 8:1–15). Kant is also realistic in his acknowledgement of limits to the duty of beneficence. He notes, "How far should a man expend his means in practicing beneficence? Surely not to the extent that he himself would finally come to need the beneficence of others" (Kant 1991, *Metaphysics, Doctrine of Virtue*, Part II, Ch I, Sect I, #31).

Consequence #2: Duty of Beneficence Becomes an Imperfect Duty

As we have seen, the limitations of our resources constrain us from being beneficent all the time whenever we encounter need. Since we are unable to help everyone and will have to allocate, we exercise our discretion in exercising such duty of beneficence as circumstances permit. Thus, the finitude of resources is a proximate reason for why the duty of beneficence is an imperfect duty. Had we infinite resources available to us, we would have faced a perfect duty of easy rescues.

Consequence #3: Distinguish Duty and Supererogation

Prudential judgment balances duty and supererogation in expanding our circle of responsibility; it knows when and where to stop widening the circle. We cannot enlarge such circle indefinitely (affectively at most, but not materially) because of the limits of our resources.

For example, in commenting on the precept to love our neighbor, Kant acknowledges that to wish others well (benevolence) costs us nothing. Benevolence can be unlimited. Not so for beneficence. It is far more difficult to do good (Kant 1991, *Metaphysics, Doctrine of Virtue*, VIII, 2 a, #393). There are limits to what we can provide given our inadequate means, and as such, we are permitted to use our discretion on whom to bestow such beneficence, presumably those who are nearest and dearest to us. We can only do so much when it comes to beneficence. We are hemmed in by limits, which is why we vary the range and degree of our beneficence.

When and where do we stop the expansion of our circle of beneficence? Jean Porter concludes that it is the order of charity that will determine whether widening the scope of our beneficence is due to duty or supererogation. Referring to St. Thomas, she notes:

> [I]n his discussion of beneficence that while we should be prepared to help out anyone at all, "if we have time to spare," charity does not require that we try literally to do good to each individual person. Rather, the strict obligations of beneficence are specified by the requirements of time, place, and circumstance (2a2ae 31.2). He then goes on (in 32.3) to explain that the obligations of beneficence are specified by reference to the different degrees

of proximity of the persons whom we might help; and these degrees are specified in turn by the different kinds of connection, and proximity that persons have to one another. *In other words, the order of charity determines (roughly) the concrete circumstances in which positive promotion of another's good is obligatory rather than supererogatory.* (Porter 1989, 206, emphasis added)

Therein lies the clash between agape and justice. Therein lies the centrality of economic life as the terrain where we see the competing claims of agape and justice play out.

Argument #2: Moral Reasons for Prioritizing Our Nearest and Dearest

Philosophical Rationale
Human reason and experience show how and why it is perfectly reasonable to prioritize the claims of those who are nearest and dearest to us relative to those who are strangers or distant to us, even if latter's needs may be relatively greater (but not in extremis). Consider the following arguments.

Order of Generosity: In *De Officiis*, Cicero affirms beneficence as an essential part of justice. Such charity and generosity bring out the very best in human nature and strengthen the bonds of society (I, xiv [42]). Cicero repeatedly affirms that this generosity cannot be indiscriminate. There is an important order of generosity to be observed. In the first place, such beneficence should be within the means of the benefactor. To give beyond one's means is to inflict injury to the next of kin and to give to others what should have been given or bequeathed to them (I, xiv [44]). Furthermore, justice requires that beneficence must be proportionate to the merit of the recipient. Such worthiness includes the closeness of the recipient to the giver and services that the recipient might have rendered to the giver in the past (I, xiv [45]). Obviously, these are considerations that apply to one's kin, friends, and associates rather than to complete strangers or to distant beneficiaries.

Cicero discusses at length a triage in one's generosity in the following descending order of priority: country, parents, children, family, and kin (I, xvi, [50]; I, xvii, [53–58]). In addition, justice requires that we do the most for those who love us most and for those to whom we owe a debt of gratitude for past favors and acts of kindness received (I, xv [47]). Thus, it is not surprising that country and parents rank highest in Cicero's proposed order of generosity. One cannot rob those to whom we owe a primary obligation in order to be generous. For Cicero, "nothing is generous, if it not at the same time just" (I, xiv [43]). Observing this order of beneficence is important in both maintaining and strengthening the bonds and ties that make society possible.

Nature of Obligations and Relationships: David Owens (2012) makes a strong case for why special relationships take priority. Life is a web of obligations and relationships. On the one hand, obligations are inherently relational. They call for accountability and bespeak of a relationship between the imperator and the addressee and between the addressee (subject) and the object of the obligation. "Obligation enters human life as one of the building blocks of relationships that we value" (Owens 2012, 211). F. Earle Fox (1959, 174) goes so far as to claim that "obligation is the relationship itself." On the other hand, relationships, for their part, create obligations. Relationships define how agents are bound to one another and what they owe each other. In fact, obligations and relationships are corollaries in that one can infer obligations from relationships and vice versa.

Owens (2012, 200) makes a distinction between relational and general moral obligations. He defines *relational obligations* as those we owe to specific parties who will be wronged if we do not fulfill these obligations. They are duties that are grounded by virtue of our special relationships to those to whom we owe these obligations. In contrast, *general moral obligations* are grounded by virtue of how we ought to treat others as persons (e.g., telling the truth, promise keeping, etc.). Thus, relationship obligations are partial and entail interested forms of duties, whereas general moral obligations are supposed to be impartial and entail disinterested responsibilities.

Owens argues that the grounds for relationship obligations are founded on the normative value that the subject reaps with the fulfillment of these obligations. The example he presents is friendship. These have underlying obligations. Nevertheless, we do things for our friend, not because we are obligated to do so, but because (s)he is a friend. We just do it without even being conscious that it is an "obligation" we are fulfilling. It is part of who we are and our self-understanding. It is part of our self-actualization. We are just much better persons for it. It is second nature to us to do such for our friend. I propose that an even better example is that of a parent-child relationship. Parents do many things for their children by virtue of their maternal and paternal love. They neither see the obstacles or the difficulties, nor do they consider the things that they do for their children as impositions at all. In fact, it is a pleasure, a delight to do so. It is similar for the people we love in our lives – the people who are special and mean a lot to us, our dearest.

As Owens puts it, such *sui generis* obligations are good for us. The "[o]bligation is valuable in the context of this relationship and the relationship is valuable (partly) in virtue of the obligation" (2012, 203 and fn 7). This is well said and, again using the parent-child relationship, we can say all that parents do for their children define and form who they are as parents, even as their being parents is partly defined by their obligations. These duties are not received as burdens at all.

In other words, relational obligations take precedence over general moral obligations because of the reflexive dimension of these responsibilities in forming who we are. These duties build up relationships that become the warp and weft of life. Relationships and their attendant obligations are important reference points for who we are. How well (or badly) we live up to these relationship obligations significantly influences our character and our personality, our very self-understanding of who we are. Consider the time spent with family and the people we love. It is an "obligation" for us to spend time with them, but we do it not because we are required to do so, but because it builds us up; it is who we are. Similarly, in the earlier examples, our primary focus is the friend or our child, and the "obligations" are merely incidental. In fact, we do not even think of them as obligations. We take delight in satisfying these "obligations" because of our child or friend. This is an important reflexive impact of special relationships.

Thus, Owens can claim that obligations from special relationships carry extra weight in that they are grounded in the "normative value" of fulfilling these duties. They are normative because of the reflexive impact of living up (or failing to live up) to these relationship obligations for all the parties concerned (Wallace 2012).

In contrast, general moral obligations (non-special relationships) are grounded in the instrumental (nonnormative) value of living up to their obligations, such as promise keeping, being truthful to one another, or treating each other with respect. Thus, Owens (2012, 213) argues that modern liberalism is in effect reductionist in its insistence of an equal treatment for all in an impartial manner without regard for the special obligations that are characteristic of every human life. Owens (2012, 210) unambiguously responds affirmatively to the question of "whether relationship obligations, those grounded in our normative interests, can claim some sort of explanatory priority over those rights and duties which we have simply in virtue of our non-normative interests." In other words, the claims of those nearest and dearest to us take priority over those who are distant or strangers to us. Special relationships create additional normative value for the subject and the object.

Kant: At first glance, it seems that Kant's moral theory does not accord priority to the claims of our nearest and dearest relative to the distant and the stranger. Recall that for Kant, only autonomous, self-legislation is a valid ethical method. This self-legislation must be reasonable, and it is reasonable only to the degree that it is disinterested. This means that self-legislation cannot focus exclusively on one's own self-interest but must weigh the needs and interests of the entire community. Impartiality is central to Kantian ethics. We see this impartiality in one of the common formulations of the categorical imperative: Act in such a way that the principle of your action can be generalized for everyone else, with no one excluded. Not surprisingly, some conclude that special relationships (as in the case of the ethics of care) have no place in Kantian moral theory (Held 2006). Furthermore, note how Kant poses the duty of benevolence:

> [T]he maxim of benevolence (practical love of man) is a duty of all men toward one another, whether or not one finds them worthy of love .... I want every-one else to be benevolent toward me (benevolentiam); hence *I ought also to be benevolent toward everyone else ... which includes the whole species* (and so myself as well) in its Idea of humanity as such, *includes me as giving universal law along with all others in the duty of mutual benevolence,* in accordance with the principle of equality, and permits you to be benevolent to yourself on the condition of your being benevolent to every other as well; for it is only in this way that your maxim (of beneficence) qualifies for a giving of universal law. (Kant 1991, Part II, chap I, section I, #27 [451], emphasis added)

Plainly, this calls for impartiality in the way we view others.

It seems that there is no room for special relationships in Kant's impartial moral theory given his requirement of universalizability. However, this is not the case. Immediately after stating the need for universal benevolence, Kant addresses the question of whether one ought to be equally benevolent toward all despite being closer to some.

> Yet one man is closer to me than another, and in benevolence I am closest to myself. How does this fit in with the precept "love your neighbor (your fellow man) as yourself"? ... it would seem that I cannot, without contradicting myself, say that I ought to love every man as myself, since the measure of self-love would allow for no difference in degree ... what is meant is,

rather, active, practical benevolence (beneficence), making the well-being and happiness of others my end. *For in wishing I can be equally benevolent to everyone, whereas in acting I can, without violating the universality of the maxim, vary the degree greatly in accordance with the different objects of my love (one of whom concerns me more closely than another).* (Kant 1991, Part II, chap I, section I, #28 [451–452], emphasis added)

As we have seen earlier, Kant distinguishes between benevolence (wishing others' well-being) and beneficence (acting on such benevolence). Kant calls beneficence practical benevolence. For Kant, one must be benevolent toward all in accord with the universalizability requirement. This is the duty of benevolence. However, one need not be beneficent toward all nor be impartial in such beneficence. Beneficence could be limited only to a small circle.

Furthermore, Marilea Bramer (2010) argues that Kant's categorical imperative itself requires special treatment for family and friends. The categorical imperative requires that we treat others as ends in themselves.[7] However, we would be remiss in treating our families and friends as ends in themselves if we do not consider our special relationship and our bonds with them. We cannot abstract from these unique ties in treating our families and friends as ends in themselves. Humans are distinct from each other precisely because of their web of relationships that is unique to them and them alone. Far from being impartial in order to treat them as ends in themselves, we are dissolving what makes them as ends to us (Himmelfarb 1996, 77). For example, when people visit their parents in a nursing home, they do not divide their time equally among all the residents on their floor (including their parents) to bring everyone some cheer and company. To do so is to rob their parents of their end as parents. Their special relationship to their families and friends is constitutive of their personhood. Partiality turns out to be essential if we are to treat them as ends in themselves. Thus, even Kant's much-touted impartial moral theory turns out to affirm the special regard that we owe to our nearest and dearest relative to the distant and the strangers.

Natural loves are perfect duties because obligors and obligees are specific and precise. They must also always be observed and not only some of the time when it suits the obligor. This contrasts with the imperfect duties that we owe those outside the circle of our natural loves.

---

[7] Bramer (2010, 125) notes that the categorical imperative and its all-important Formulation of Humanity as an End (FHE) asserts, "Act in such a way that you treat humanity, whether in your own person or in the person of another, always at the same time as an end and never simply as a means" (Kant 1993, 429).

Primacy of the Local: Barbara Herman (2001, 229–232) argues for the "primacy of the local." For example, people who know that they will readily aid others in their circle of friends and kin will have no qualms themselves about asking these others for assistance. They are comfortable with each other because of their relationship. It is just a normal act to ask for assistance as needed. Mutual aid in such cases is in effect a constitutive element of an existing, ongoing moral relationship. This is descriptive of our relationship with kin and friends. People simply go to their circle of kin and friends first before going to strangers for help. Mutual support is first a localized phenomenon before it goes farther afield.

Herman distinguishes primary obligations to our relations from the secondary obligations we owe to the stranger and the distant. Our primary obligations (our local circle) are duties of justice. In contrast, our secondary obligations are merely inherited obligations. They are duties of beneficence. We inherit them because of others' failure (individually or collectively) to live up to their primary obligations. For example, the distant poor are destitute and in need of our assistance because their own circle of kin, friends, and the local communities to which they belong had failed them. Primary obligations take precedence over secondary (inherited) obligations. Furthermore, our primary obligations are perfect duties – they are fully determined. In contrast, our secondary obligations are imperfect duties. We enjoy wide latitude in living up to them, choosing the time, place, circumstances, and degree of assistance we are going to provide when the time comes.

Theological Arguments

Theology, too, presents its own set of arguments as to why our nearest and dearest have priority in non-in-extremis cases. As we have seen earlier, Jewish teachings limit almsgiving to no more than 20 percent of one's assets. St. Paul reminds the Corinthians not to impoverish themselves in giving to the poor of Jerusalem. We see an order of charity too in St. Paul's admonition to the Galatians to work for the good of all, but especially of their fellow Christians (Gal 6:10).

As we have also seen earlier, St. Augustine is realistic in acknowledging that even as we must love everyone (benevolence), we cannot do good to all of them (beneficence) given our limited means. Thus, in response to the question to whom we should give aid, St. Augustine notes that we must prioritize our kin or those who are closest to us (*On Christian Doctrine*, I. 28). St. Ambrose also notes that there is an obligation to assist one's kin who would otherwise be compelled to seek succor from others (*De Officiis*, I, 30, #150).

St. Thomas follows St. Augustine's position but provides a much more extended and sustained argument in his position that there is in fact an order of charity (II-II, 44.8; 25.12; 26.1 and 2). Natural loves and their claims are in accord with Divine wisdom itself. Despite the need to love all, human nature nevertheless imposes different layers of particularistic loves on such universal benevolence based on the web of relationships into which we were born and which we develop and nurture as we grow into adulthood. In other words, over and above the expected benevolence for all fellow humans are added obligations of special loves that are by their nature selective and partial. Humans are bound by varying degrees of love, with kin, friends, and close associates enjoying greater claims compared to strangers or distant neighbors. How much we love someone is influenced by our relationship to that person or by what that person means to us. The depth and profundity of the love extended are a function of the underlying relationship between the lover and the beloved. Thus, in his exposition on the order of charity, St. Thomas notes that our bonds and ties from blood, citizenship, or shared undertaking are relevant considerations both in the degree of our affection and our beneficence (II-II, 26.7 and 8).

As we have seen earlier, there are different types of love, namely: *philautia* (love of self); *eros* (sexual passion); *philia* (profound friendship); *storge* (e.g., love of parents for child; sibling love); *pragma* (long-standing love; compromising to make relationships work; e.g., long-married couples); *agape* (universal love). These loves have their proper place in life. Each has a specific role to play in human flourishing. Thus, one cannot have all *philautia, philia,* or *storge* (favoring the nearest and dearest) nor can one have only *agape* (equal regard for all and favoring the neediest).

Moreover, as we have seen earlier, there is a time- and place-utility for each of these loves. Each has a specific role to play at the right time, at the right place, and with the right people and dispensed in the right degree. Lacking that constitutes a privation of something good, as we have seen in the preceding chapter on past wrongs. It is a failure by omission. Furthermore, human freedom cuts both ways – it can be misused and abused just as it can be used wisely and well. One can love improperly the wrong object or love in the wrong place at the wrong time or in a wrong manner, or all the above. This, too, causes a privation. It is a failure by commission.

These various loves mutually reinforce each other, for good or for ill. There are varying degrees of excellence to all kinds of love, including *philautia, philia, storge,* and *agape.* St. Thomas goes further than St. Augustine who merely argues for the priority of natural loves based on the practical necessity of allocating finite resources. St. Thomas bases his arguments heavily on Divine Providence and human nature itself. In response to the question of whether we should do good to those who are most closely united to us, he notes that:

> Grace and virtue imitate the order of nature, which is established by Divine wisdom. Now *the order of nature is such that every natural agent pours forth its activity first and most of all on the things which are nearest to it* …. Therefore *we ought to be most beneficent towards those who are most closely connected with us.* (II-II, 31.3, emphasis added)

St. Thomas prioritizes natural loves in the order of charity based on human nature itself as part of the Divine governance of the world (II-II, 26.6; 44.8). This means that natural justice can put limits on charity. For example, almsgiving should not be to the point of hurting one's own kin to whom one has obligations. After all, the precepts of natural justice come from practical reason (e.g., taking care of one's kin). Agape, even infused agape, does not go against reason. As we will see shortly, grace does not destroy nature but builds on it. St. Thomas, unlike St. Augustine and modern Christian moralists like Gene Outka, holds the position that our loves (both our interior affection and outward action and the material manifestation of this interior affection) cannot be equal across all, but must follow the natural order of love. Jean Porter (1989, 200) agrees that "the order of charity is not less reasonable than the order of nature, since both spring from the divine wisdom."

St. Thomas views the claims of these natural loves to be so strong that despite the New Testament mandate to love our enemies (Mt 5:43–48), he nevertheless states that when we love as we love our neighbor, loving a friend is better than loving an enemy:

> [L]ove of one's friend surpasses love of one's enemy, because a friend is both better and more closely united to us, so that he is a more suitable matter of love and consequently the act of love that passes over this matter, is better, and therefore its opposite is worse, for it is worse to hate a friend than an enemy. (II-II, 27.7, response)

Just to demonstrate how strongly St. Thomas believes in this rank ordering of love, he then goes further to note that if we, however, look at the reason why we love, then we should love our enemy more than we should love a friend because loving our enemy entails a greater love of God. Nevertheless, even after having acknowledged this, St. Thomas goes back to reiterate the strength of the claims of loving those who are near and dear to us:

> Yet just as the same fire acts with greater force on what is near than on what is distant, so too, charity loves with greater fervor those who are united to us than those who are far removed; and in this respect the love of friends, considered in itself, is more ardent and better than the love of one's enemy. (II-II, 27.7, response)

One way of making sense of these seemingly contradictory or indefinite answers from St. Thomas is to note that his first distinction (love as in loving our neighbor) pertains to our love in the natural realm, while his second distinction (why we love) refers to excellence in the supernatural realm. We prioritize kin love as part of our natural excellence, while love of our enemies and the undeserving is called forth in our supernatural excellence.

The Case for Expanding Our Circle of Love and Responsibility

Let us examine the arguments of the other side of the debate that calls for universalistic love. Economic, philosophical, and theological arguments justify the expansion of our circle of love beyond our natural loves.

Arguments Based on Justice

Economic Reasons

Considering shifts in the socioeconomic terrain, justice itself may require that we widen our circle of love and responsibility. As we have seen in the preceding section, obligations are a function of our relationships. These relationships change over time and may either strengthen or weaken previous obligations. Porter (1989, 208) notes, "Thus, neighbor love is stable and permanent for Thomas, as it is for proponents of equal regard; *the degree of love appropriate to a particular person may change, if the relationship to that person is legitimately changed*" (emphasis added). Relationships also change in light of global and intertemporal allocative efficiency.

By the 1960s, the Second Vatican Council already observed that global relations had changed radically due to the advances in transportation and communications at that time. In response, the bishops boldly proclaimed a major expansion in the scope of people's mutual obligations:

> [C]haritable enterprises can and should reach out to all persons and all needs. Wherever there are people in need of food and drink, clothing, housing, medicine, employment, education; wherever men lack the facilities

necessary for living a truly human life ... there Christian charity should seek them out and find them, console them with great solicitude, and help them with appropriate relief. *This obligation is imposed above all upon every prosperous nation and person.* (Vatican II 1965a, #8, emphasis added)

If there is a moral obligation for universal beneficence because of the technological strides achieved in the 1960s, how much more in the era of globalization. The Microelectronics Revolution and its consequent globalization have been a paradigm shift for the late twentieth century, just as the Industrial Revolution was for the eighteenth and nineteenth centuries. Because of the economic integration of nations, people are now ever more interdependent regardless of their geographic distance from one another. The world has been turned into a single workshop with an intricate division of labor. Furthermore, people have better information on the plight of strangers and the distant given the Internet. Moreover, they are now in a much better position to help easily, with the click of a mouse (e.g., crowdfunding). Thus, unlike an earlier age, people now have ever-greater duties toward one another's well-being.

F. M. Kamm (2000) argues that it is our means rather than our physical distance from one another that drives the duty to rescue. At any rate, not only has globalization brought about the "death of distance," but it has also greatly enhanced our capacity to provide aid to the needy even if they are distant or are strangers. Based on both distance and means, justice demands the expansion of our circle of love beyond kin-love because of changes in the socioeconomic terrain in the last half century. As we enlarge our circle of exchange, so should we expand correspondingly our circle of love and responsibility. This is a conclusion that emerges not only from theological sources (as in Vatican II) but also from economic theory and praxis as well. Moreover, as early as 1776, in his *Wealth of Nations*, Adam Smith argued for greater interdependence considering the gains from specialization and the division of labor.

Agape-justice conflicts may in fact be merely reflecting this need to expand our circle of love in response to changes in our social relationships. For example, agape (compassion) may alert us to preferential trade as an effective form of foreign aid for less developed countries. Agape brings to the fore the role of trade in alleviating poverty among the distant and the stranger.[8] We will discuss this at greater length shortly.

---

[8] There is much in Development Economics that can be used to make the case for agape and international trade, such as the flying-geese pattern of development, the well-known mutual benefits of trade, the ladder of comparative advantage, and many other insights.

Based on In-extremis Need

Justice itself requires that we go beyond our immediate circle of natural loves and prioritize those with in-extremis needs. Life-and-death needs trump all other claims. Even St. Thomas himself, who expounds at length on the order of charity and on the priority of those who are nearest and dearest to us, nevertheless subscribes to this position (Porter 1989, 206; Pope 1990, 120). Responding to the question on whether we ought to do good to those who are most closely related to us, St. Thomas affirms the priority of our natural loves. However, he quickly qualifies his response:

> [W]e ought in preference to bestow on each one such benefits as pertain to the matter in which, speaking simply, he is most closely connected with us. And yet this may vary according to the various requirements of time, place, or matter in hand: because *in certain cases one ought, for instance, to succor a stranger, in extreme necessity, rather than one's own father, if he is not in such urgent need.* (II-II, 31.3, emphasis added)

St. Thomas reiterates the overriding claims of in-extremis needs in his exposition on who ought to receive our almsgiving.

> On the part of the recipient it is requisite that he should be in need, else there would be no reason for giving him alms: yet since it is not possible for one individual to relieve the needs of all, *we are not bound to relieve all who are in need, but only those who could not be succored if we did not succor them. For in such cases the words of Ambrose apply, "Feed him that dies of hunger: if thou hast not fed him, thou hast slain him"* ... *give alms to one whose need is extreme.* (II-II, 32.5, response, emphasis added)

The extreme needs even of those who may be distant or strangers to us override even the strongest claims of our natural loves. Need becomes the primary criterion in resolving agape-justice conflicts under in-extremis conditions. Two implications immediately follow from this. First, this is consistent with the bedrock Judeo-Christian teaching on the preferential option for the poor. Under normal conditions, our beneficence radiates outward, beginning with those who are nearest and dearest to us and then moving on to those beyond our circle of natural loves. This order of charity is upended, indeed reversed, in the face of in-extremis needs (Pope 1993, 163).

Second, claims arising from in-extremis needs do not fall under the demands of agape. Rather, they become the claims of distributive justice – proportionality in the distribution of our shared resources. Proportionality here is measured in terms of the fundamental claim of natural law for the basic needs satisfaction of all. "[A]ll persons are owed equal regard at least in the sense of equal immunity from serious harm and certain kinds of coercion, *and equal claim on the necessities of life in situations of dire need*" (Porter 1989, 208, emphasis added).

Philosophical Arguments: Common Humanity

Moral Cosmopolitanism

Moral cosmopolitanism is the antithesis of St. Thomas' order of charity. It is characterized by impartiality, individualism, universality, and generality. To begin with, moral cosmopolitanism frowns on limiting our attention only to our own group, affiliates, and relations. Rather, it calls for equal regard and weight assigned to all based on the like moral worth of every person. In contrast to the "ethical particularism" of kin love, moral cosmopolitanism espouses a "moral universalism" (Miller 2011, 394). Impartiality is a characteristic feature of moral cosmopolitanism.

Second, individualism means that the individual is the basic unit of analysis and concern, and not family, clans, nations, or any other groups (Pogge 1992, 48). The individuality and uniqueness of every person cannot and should not be subsumed within the group or community of which that individual is a part.

Third, universality means that the previously mentioned individuality and uniqueness that must be acknowledged and respected are to be accorded to every human being, and not merely to a privileged or select subset of humanity (e.g., men vs. women, Gentile vs. Jew, poor vs. rich). This is the universality of the individual as the basic unit of concern. It applies to every human (Pogge 1992, 48).

Fourth, generality means that everyone is bound by the duty to accord to other individuals the respect that their individuality and uniqueness require (Pogge 1992, 48–49). This is a general obligation that applies to all. The difference between Pogge's universality and generality is that in the former, the individual is the object, the obligee, while in the latter, the individual is the subject who is bound by the obligation to be attentive to the individual as the ultimate unit of concern.

Given its four characteristic features of absolute impartiality, individualism, universality, and generality, moral cosmopolitanism in effect brings everyone and all into one's circle of love and responsibility. There is no distinction between kin, neighbor, or close associates, on the one hand, and the distant and the stranger, on the other hand. Such distinctions are irrelevant. The allegiance of moral cosmopolitanism is to "the worldwide community of human beings" (Nussbaum 2002, 4).

Cicero, Kant, and Hume
Readers are reminded of Cicero' duty of beneficence, Hume's duty of humanity, Kant's duty of benevolence, and Singer's duty of easy rescues. These were discussed in Chapter 1 when we examined particular and general moral obligations. We do not discuss these again to avoid repetition. Nevertheless, they call for expanding our circle of love and responsibility. General moral obligations are in effect a call to expand our solicitude beyond our circle of natural loves.

Theological Arguments

Principle of Subsidiarity, Part Two
The second part of the principle of subsidiarity argues that higher bodies or individuals with the necessary resources have the moral obligation to intervene and assist individuals or lower bodies who are no longer able to function on behalf of the common good (Pius XI 1931, *Quadragesimo Anno* #79). This is a positive obligation and is not merely a counsel (i.e., optional). It is akin to Cicero's duty to prevent harm (I, vii [23]). This calls for going beyond our circle of kin love.

Developmental Nature of Love
The moral faculties of reason and will are not given to humans in their perfected form at the time of their birth. These moral faculties develop and grow over time in a process of learning by doing. People generally get better in the use of their reason and will over a lifetime, although it is entirely possible for them to regress in the use of these faculties, as when they misuse or abuse them or when they become vicious rather than virtuous. This developmental nature of the moral faculties means that love also evolves in terms of its object, scope, intensity, and motivation. It can grow or regress, but it never stands still. Love either moves toward perfection or it retreats, but it never stays the same. Thus, people's circle of love-responsibility expands or contracts rather than be in a long-term stasis. An expanding circle of love-responsibility, the topic of our chapter, is well within the dynamics and realm of human experience. Such an expansion is not reserved merely for the supernatural realm or for infused love.

Love is Diffusive by its Nature
Love is relentlessly expansive and spontaneously diffusive by its nature. It cannot be contained as it spills over into the lives of the people around

us and beyond. It is akin to light, which, by its nature, diffuses entirely to dispel darkness.

Love is ceaseless in its movement until it reaches its Final End. St. Augustine (*Confessions*, Bk 1, 1) describes this dynamic well, "[Y]ou have made us for yourself, and our heart is restless until it rests in you." In addition to this touching articulation of love's innate hunger, St. Augustine himself exemplifies the source of this deep yearning – grace! For this chapter, we can identify distinct stages in love's trajectory of diffusion: from natural loves to agape to *caritas* where we see grace building on nature.

Responding to the objection to St. Thomas' order of charity as neglecting love for the distant and the stranger, Pope (1991, 175) is confident that this is not so because of the expansive nature of love:

> One might address this criticism first of all by recalling *the essentially centrifugal and expansive nature of charity: like the good which it loves, charity is inherently diffusive of itself.* While it is true that the precepts of the natural law instruct us as to the most basic requirements of morality, the New Law of grace calls us to a life of ever-deepening, self-giving love (I- II, lo7, 1; I-II, 108, 3). *Charity tends of its very nature to overflow rather than to withdraw, spontaneously to give away rather than retain and conserve. Charity tends towards (even if it does not always attain) its own perfection, which includes the love of the remote as well as proximate neighbour, not only friends and family but also strangers and enemies* (II-II 184.2, ad 3). (Pope 1991, 175, emphasis added)

We could build on Pope's image of love's diffusiveness as a centrifugal force and argue for the complementarity of our natural loves and our love for the distant and the stranger. It turns out that not only do these two types of love complement each other, but they are necessary conditions to each other's sustainability and perfection. Natural love can be likened to the centripetal force that keeps the circle intact, while the love that reaches out for the distant and the stranger is the centrifugal force that gives dynamism to that circle. Both centrifugal and centripetal forces feed off each other in a delicate balance. We examine this complementary, balancing act in how (1) natural love is the springboard for agape, while (2) agape perfects natural loves. Theology's characterization of love as diffusive reinforces Kant's observation that the duties of benevolence and beneficence are in fact wide duties because people are naturally drawn closer to each other (Kant 1991, *Metaphysics, Doctrine of Virtue*, Part II, Ch I, Sect I, #24–25).

Natural Loves as Training Ground for Agape: More than just being expansive, natural love turns out to be the training ground for love of the distant and the stranger. *Love is diachronic* because it builds on itself by acquiring even greater depth and then expanding its scope. In securing their just claims, natural loves can reach out beyond themselves.

We learn to love others (agape) because we have loved ourselves and our own. *Philautia* (self-love), *philia* (love for friends), and *storge* (familial love) are the incubators, indeed, the school for agape (universal love). After all, you cannot love others if you do not love yourself. You would otherwise not know what love is and what it entails. Not surprisingly, the Hebrew Scriptures call on people to love their neighbors as they love themselves (Lev 19:18).

Love does not emerge from nowhere but is received and then internalized over time. Children experience for themselves and learn what love is from their parents' love for them and its accompanying safety and warmth. These children, in their own turn, are then able to love, not only their parents but others as well. Recall that Hume bases his duty of humanity on this very argument – the family nurtures and supplies the very people who will be virtuous and just (*Treatise* 1896, 486–487).

The different types of love complement and mutually reinforce one another as they push jointly toward love's perfection. *Philautia* (the healthy variant) is necessary for *storge* and *philia,* both of which in their own turn are necessary for *pragma* and eventually for agape. There is progression and growth. They build on one another. The earlier ones can be called the foundational loves while *pragma*, but especially agape, are the perfective ones.

Agape is the call to love the stranger and all of humanity. It is universal love. *Philia* and *storge* present agape with a concrete pattern of how to love others, not as a stranger but as a friend or even as family. *Philia* and *storge* are stepping-stones to agape. In fact, *storge* with its long-suffering nature may be a good training ground for the even more demanding *caritas*, which calls for love of one's enemies.[9] We can help the neediest or even our enemies out of a genuine desire for the common good, but only if we have a healthy self-love. This self-love encompasses family, friends, and close kin. These natural loves are the first schools that teach and provide us with "learning-by-doing" occasions to love. After all, "[t]hese relations allow the special kind of personal knowledge and the profound identification with one another's good that make possible more highly attuned and sensitive expressions of love, compassion, and concern than are afforded

---

[9] This is not to say that *caritas* is something humans can earn on their own. It is an infused virtue as we will see shortly.

in impersonal relations" (Pope 1990, 110). There is a complementarity between *philautia, philia,* and *storge* vis-à-vis agape. They are necessary conditions for each other. Love develops relationships. It is the medium of growth for relationships (Kolodny 2003).

Stephen Post (1994) concludes similarly in noting that the love learned, experienced, and nurtured within the family becomes the seed for subsequent loves, including the love of strangers and even of enemies. Heroic love of enemies or strangers does not arise spontaneously. It is slowly built up over time. And, as we will see later, even for infused love, grace builds on and works through nature. John Baker (1984) argues similarly on the complementarity of the different types of loves as they mutually feed off each other. In reflecting on what biblical theology teaches on romantic love, he goes so far as to argue that even *eros* itself is a school of learning for agape.

> According to Scripture man learns and finds his *true fulfilment within the disciplined security of committed relationship,* …. 'The first principle of a Christian sex ethic is that this side of life should *be so ordered, disciplined* and released, that sexual love *becomes a creative aspect of the life of agape, the giving of each person in service to God and neighbour*'. (Baker 1984, 127, emphasis added)

Baker identifies important contributions of natural loves in the lead-up to agape. In the first place, a committed relationship (such as family, friends, and kin) provides a protected, secure, and reassuring space within which one can receive and internalize love that is bestowed. This very same space nurtures that love through its various stages of growth. Second, Baker also correctly notes such committed relationships imbue order and discipline in the loves learned. What he says about *eros* is in fact also applicable to all the other natural loves. In other words, for Baker, *philia, storge,* and *eros* shape and form how people will live up to the demands of agape.

Agape Draws Natural Loves to Their Completion: Natural loves grow toward their completion and perfection in their love for the distant and the stranger. Without this outward orientation, *philautia, philia,* and *storge* run the danger of shriveling into narcissistic self-absorption. We can appreciate this dynamic better by looking at the major obstacles to friendship. In writing on St. Thomas' thoughts on friendship, Daniel Schwartz (2007, 69–93) observes that vainglory and pride are major impediments to the necessary concord of will if there is to be any friendship at all. Overestimating one's own excellence and downplaying others' potential obstruct the possibility of a vibrant, meaningful interaction with them. *Philautia, philia,* and *storge* face the same risk if they are trapped in thinking that they are self-sufficient with no need for others and therefore content to stay within the confines of their comfort zone. Friendships blossom because of the friends' realization that such relationships complete and perfect them. They are better people because of such friendships. *Philautia, philia,* and *storge* need a similar openness to the "other" that blooms and blossoms in agape.

There is a second damage inflicted by vainglory and pride. An exaggerated sense of one's accomplishments and excellence coupled with looking down on others' capabilities lead one to think that there is nothing to be gained or learned from others. Thus, in the end, the vainglorious and the prideful themselves are the ones who are hurt the most because they have closed off a significant avenue for learning and growth. It is a self-inflicted wound.

It is a similar dynamic for *philautia, philia, storge,* and agape. As we have seen in the preceding section, natural loves are the training school for the subsequent loves, such as agape. However, the contribution also goes the other way. Agape feeds back to strengthen *philautia, philia,* and *storge.* After all, agape is the school for further selfless, sacrificial love. Agape is the school for love not as an emotion, but as an act of the will. In effect, agape gives flight to its subject in being able to reach greater heights of love that are not always available even to *storge* or *philia.* Agape prevents *philautia, philia,* and *storge* from being trapped in self-absorption. Like any other type of love, *philautia, philia,* and *storge* cannot stand still. They either wither or flourish. Distant loves perfect self-love.

Philautia comes to its fullness only as one encounters the other and blooms in agape. Once again, we can use friendship to understand how this comes about. Friendship is "constitutive of an individual's own subjectivity: someone comes to a full awareness of their existence only as they become aware of the existence of their close friend .... '*The friend is not another I, but an otherness immanent in self-ness, a becoming other of the self*'."[10] Others have observed similarly: "Since I am human and you are human, to love other humans is to love myself as well as you. In giving myself to you in love, I am fulfilling myself" (Olthius 1983, 112).

One could go so far as to say that *philautia* and agape are inseparable. They are necessary conditions for each other. There are attendant

---

[10] Vernon (2004, 129, citing Giorgio Agamben, emphasis added)

obligations to *philautia* that arise in the course of being "a self" (Lippitt 2009). These are strong natural obligations and not something that is commanded heteronomously or by divine command. They come from our nature as part of self-actualization. *Agape is constitutive of the formation of "the self."*

These insights describe the same dynamic as Christian social teachings' understanding of the nature of integral human development (IHD). Contrary to most people's thinking, integral human development involves more than just one's own holistic development of body, mind, and spirit. It necessarily also entails the integral human development of one's neighbor. Integral human development is a journey that is taken jointly and can only be completed together. One's IHD is realized only and simultaneously as the IHD of my neighbor. It is through working for the IHD of my neighbor that I reach my own IHD and that I become aware of the fullness of self-love blooming to its healthiest form. In other words, *philautia* blossoms to its fullness in agape. This is consistent with what has long been established regarding how humans can only flourish within community. The individual is actualized only in community (Maritain 1947).

Gaudium et spes makes the same point when it argues that far from being at odds with each other, the individual and the community are necessary conditions for each other's good (Vatican II 1965b). The individual flourishes only to the degree that (s)he is oriented toward others. To be sure, *philautia* is a necessary but not a sufficient condition for human flourishing. Humans, by their nature, are about transcending themselves to find completion in reaching out beyond the self via love. It is a necessary condition for integral human development.

Besides *philautia* and agape's inseparability and complementarity, it is important to note their constitutive economic dimension. In contrast to the self-esteem and self-worth that modern psychologists say is the definition of self-love, Scripture talks of self-love in concrete practical terms – taking care of ourselves and procuring our physical and other needs for survival, growth, and development. Hence, this kind of self-love (*philautia*) is also the kind of love that we should extend to our neighbors. This is the context of the second greatest commandment's reference to self-love stemming from Leviticus 19:18 (Makujina 1997).

Agape has an important reflexive dynamic that strengthens and deepens natural loves and special relationships. Partial, particularistic love blooms to its perfection and completion as it expands to impartial love. It is the harvest of natural loves nurtured well.

God-like Love for the Stranger, the Distant, the Unworthy, or the Enemy
Aristotle's understanding of friendship entails (1) a desire for and actively
working for the good of the other; (2) mutuality and reciprocity in such
concern and work; and (3) communication and actual exchange of goods
between the parties. To this, St. Thomas tacks on two additional features:
(4) charity is friendship between unequals, specifically between God and
humans, and (5) following the example of such unequal and unmerited
Divine-human friendship, charity is loving those who are enemies, who
are not virtuous, or who do not share the same values (Mongeau 2013,
290–91). Kin or particular loves are well within Aristotelian friendship.
Moving toward agape that includes the stranger and even one's enemies
and those who are difficult to love falls within the friendship described
by St. Thomas. Humans are invited by God to follow the paradigm of
the radically unequal Divine-human friendship. It is to extend friendship
and love even to those whom one may deem to be unequal or unworthy
of such love or friendship. St. Thomas' charity (*caritas*) captures the utter
gratuity of unequal friendships and love.

This thoroughly unequal Divine-human relationship provides another
lesson. Love appraises value in the beloved. Love also confers value. Indeed,
love "creates a new value" (McClure 2003, 27). Love bestows value on
the marginalized, the distant, the stranger, and the ignored. Love imparts
value on those who are at the fringes of my world. Love bequeaths value
on the object of its love.

Clearly, the paradigm of this is divine love. God loves humans and as
a result affirms the goodness of humans (McClure 2003, 24). So it is with
agape. The lover affirms the goodness that is inherent in the object of one's
love and which the beloved communicates or radiates. Such appraisal is
an interpersonal connection made and highlights the goodness for others
to see. This second-order effect confers an additional bestowal – that of
shining light on the goodness of the beloved. To love someone is to affirm,
appreciate, and hold up for the rest of the world to see and appreciate for
themselves the goodness of the beloved. Here is the one I love. Let the
whole world see! We could call this the "calling-attention-to" function
of love. Love provides the occasion for others to appreciate the object of
one's love.

As we have seen earlier, in weighing which love should take precedence
(friend or enemy), St. Thomas answers that if we are talking of the reason
why we love (because of our love of God), then loving our enemy is much
better and should take priority. This is because it requires much more
effort and goes against our natural inclination and comfort (II-II, 27.7).

Such love reveals the extent of our love of God and deepens it, with the help of grace. One is willing to do what is distasteful or even abhorrent.

So it is with agape. It is much easier not to venture beyond our comfort zone and the safety of our circle of natural loves. However, we are invited to expand our natural loves to a much larger circle as a way of deepening and making our love even more profound. In other words, our circle of natural loves must extend to the loves that do not have a human or natural claim on us, no matter how unequal the relationship might be or how unworthy the object of our love. After all, recall the paradigm of all unequal relationships – the Divine-human relationship that is nevertheless given and nurtured. There is greater merit in loving what goes against our inclination or comfort. There is great moment in loving the stranger, the distant, and even the undeserving. Indeed, agape is prima facie evidence of our natural loves blooming and producing abundant harvest.

We are better people, in terms of human flourishing, for these expanded relationships. After all, these obligations (whether from justice or love) make us who we are. The obligations we take on ourselves, the alacrity, spontaneity, and the virtue with which we perform them determine their reflexive impact on us, including the extent of their effects, their depth, and their lingering quality.

Finally, note that the clash in the competing claims between our natural loves and agape gets to be more intense in proportion to the severity of the relative unmet needs of those at the fringes of our circle of responsibility. Most agree that St. Thomas' order of charity is trumped by in-extremis contingencies. As mentioned earlier, life-and-death needs take precedence even over those who are nearest and dearest to us (II-II, 31.3). Most cases, however, pertain to non-in-extremis clashes of claims. Nevertheless, in these cases, the relative severity of needs will still be a relevant consideration from a theological viewpoint because of the preferential option for the poor.

The more deprived the plight of the distant and the stranger outside the circle of our natural loves, even if non-in-extremis, the more intense will be the pushback of and the claims presented by agape. Agape's claims and urgency are directly proportional to the severity of the deprivation it seeks to fill. This leads to an intensified clash of claims between agape and justice. After all, people are incorporated into one's circle of responsibility not only because of natural love or special relationships but also because of compassion. Benevolence, by its nature, is sensitive to suffering and deprivation, even if non-in-extremis. Love, by its nature, cannot stand idly by. Love appreciates the intrinsic worth of the object on which it lavishes its benevolence. And in so doing, love acknowledges the recipient's value as it welcomes that person into one's circle of responsibility.

Agape-Justice Conflicts as Occasions for Grace Building on Nature

The clashes between the claims of justice (kin-particular loves), on the one hand, and the claims of agape (for the distant and the stranger), on the other hand, may in fact be instances of grace building on nature. These conflicts provide occasions by which grace perfects natural loves and agape. In particular, it may be grace bringing these loves to their crown and perfection in *caritas*, charity defined as friendship with God (II-II, 23.1). To avoid repetition, it is sufficient for now to provide a thumbnail description of infused grace and *caritas*, which we examine at greater length in the next chapter. Infused agape is not earned or achieved but is given as a gift. It empowers even as it directs and leads recipients to their Final End – God. Thus, infused love is of a higher quality than acquired love. There are no limits to how high infused love can soar. Not even physical death contains it (Rom 8:35). Infused love simply radiates joy, peace, goodness, kindness, generosity, faithfulness as an effect of love – the uncontained and uncontainable overflowing heart aflame with divine love (Gal 5:22–23).

As mentioned earlier, Outka's agape as equal regard prevents natural loves from being parochial or narcissistic by widening their horizon to include the stranger and the distant. Grace transforms these natural loves.

> [E]ros, storgē, philia, and epithymia are different natural ways of loving which belong to the structure of being human. However, agape [*caritas*] is not just another—albeit higher—kind of love. Agape [*caritas*] is the quality of obedience to God and neighbor which is to color, direct, and motivate all our natural ways of loving .... [E]ros, philia, epithymia, and storgē need to be enjoyed and exercised in Christ, that is, in the spirit of love. Then they are agape [*caritas*]. (Olthuis 1983, 111)[11]

Outka's agape as equal regard differs from St. Thomas' *caritas* (charity) in that the latter is a general virtue that orients people to their Final End in God. Infused agape's obligations and relationships are oriented toward the supernatural realm. Infused agape sees all as children of the one family of God. *Caritas* builds on natural justice to expand one's circle of responsibility to include the stranger and the distant and to treat them as a brother or as a sister. One can even go so far as to say that infused agape (*caritas*) dissolves the natural divisions defined by natural loves. In his letter to the

---

[11] Olthuis's *agape* refers to *caritas* rather than Outka's *agape* as equal regard.

Galatians (3:28), St. Paul writes, "There is no longer Jew or Greek, there is no longer slave or free, there is no longer male and female; for all of you are one in Christ Jesus." Love reveals what is yet possible over and beyond what justice requires (McClure 2003). In effect, love provides the larger overarching backdrop and sets the spirit within which socioeconomic life and justice unfold and develop further going forward.

Grace Builds on Nature

"[G]race does not destroy nature but perfects it" (I, 1.8, ad2). As an example, St. Thomas notes how sacred doctrine employs human reason to make clear that which faith reveals. Grace builds on nature. Grace works through nature. Thus, grace uses natural loves as the building blocks to that Final End of friendship and union with God – *caritas*.

> [G]race heals, corrects, and restores fallen nature to its right and proper order; it also elevates nature by supernaturally "infusing" a new form proportionate to its new, supernatural end (I-II.109.2; I-II.112.1; II-II.23.2). It is in this sense that in grace God "draws the rational creature above the condition of its nature to a participation of the Divine good" (I-II.110.1) .... For Thomas, as A. P. d'Entreves notes, "the natural order is only the condition and the means for the attainment of a higher order." (Pope 1990, 114)

Thus, the circle of natural loves expands to encompass a much wider circle of agape without regard for return, which in turn blooms into grace-enabled *caritas*.

> [W]hile charity [*caritas*] consists in a participation in God's love, it does so in a thoroughly human mode—our charity, though it is beyond the resources of nature and is acquired only by the gift of grace, is always "creaturely charity" (caritas creata) (∏-∏.24.2). (Pope 1990, 114–115)

Grace is the accelerant that expands kin/particular loves to love of the stranger and the distant.

> [L]ove of the other—even the nonreciprocating stranger and hostile enemy—builds on and extends the natural entanglements of self-regard and other-regard embedded in kin altruism. God's grace does not suppress kin affections; it builds on and extends these natural affections to include the other, be it nonkin neighbor, stranger, or oppressive and angry opponent. *Extending this natural affection, with the help of God's grace, requires acts of self-sacrifice, but this sacrificial love builds on natural affections. It does not function to extinguish them.* (Browning 2008, 559–560, emphasis added)

Note three critical elements in this description of the expansion of the circle of kin love. First, there is sacrifice involved in widening this circle

of love-responsibility, such as the lack of reciprocity or a hostile reception. Second, grace plays the pivotal role in this enlargement. Third, kin
love is the starting point and the springboard used by grace. An expanded
circle of love-responsibility is not a substitute for the circle of kin love.
Particularistic love and stranger love are not mutually exclusive. In fact,
they need each other and are necessary conditions for each other. Kin
love needs stranger love for its completion and perfection. And as we saw
earlier, stranger love needs kin love as a school and training ground for
learning how to be loved and to love.

Grace Expands the Circle of Love and Responsibility

God is love. It is in the nature of God to love, just as it is in the nature of
God to exist, *ipsum esse subsistens*. God's love is completely gratuitous and
is not given because of an attraction to some quality in the beloved or the
object of love. It is simply given. A good analogy is light – it shines on all
indiscriminately, on the good and the bad. Humans are supposed to love,
and to love in the way God loves – like a light shining on all indiscriminately without exception. However, this is a struggle and is not possible for
humans because we seek the good and therefore tend to love on account of
our attraction to some good in the object of our love. Nevertheless, divine
love and grace transform and suffuse us with God's love. Such transformation enables and empowers humans to love in the way God loves (Burch
1950, 414–26). To summarize, note the formal defining characteristics of
this infused love (*caritas*):

- It is diffusive and given gratuitously without exception, not because
  of some attractive quality in the object of one's love. This is a love
  given not for the benefit of the lover, but for the benefit alone of the
  object/recipient of the love. It is a pure gift.
- It is the result of infused grace and is re-creative.
- While love's immediate object is fellowship (*koinonia*), the formation
  of community, its ultimate end (*telos*) is union/friendship with God.

Expanding beyond kin-particularistic love means extending friendship
to those outside our circle.

> [F]riendship, following Aristotle, exists wherever there is community, that
> is, a grouping of persons around a common good. There is familial friend-
> ship, friendship of citizenship, and so on. The character of friendship then,
> is not merely intersubjective (me and God), but social. *What is opposed to
> friendship is not the enemy, not the unloved or not chosen, but the stranger, the
> one outside the common good which binds us together.* Every friendship comes

into existence and develops around and through a common working for an authentic good. *One realizes here the depth which Aquinas's analysis gives to Saint Paul's statement in the letter to the Ephesians that we are no longer strangers but fellow citizens and members of God's household.* (Mongeau 2013, 293–94, emphasis added)

Thus, expanding the circle of our love-responsibility has for its end the proleptic living of the eschatological One Body in Christ, one family in God (1 Cor 12; Gal 3:28). It is the extension of friendship, and all that it entails (regard for well-being, actual exchange), to the stranger, the distant, and even the shunned. This is along the lines of the table fellowship of Jesus Christ in which he accepted everyone as a child of God, including those rejected by the religious leadership of his time as unclean and sinners. It is a de facto expansion of our circle of friendship.

As we can see, St. Thomas' order of love, which prioritizes kin love, and Outka's agape (love as equal regard) are not mutually exclusive. In fact, both St. Thomas' order of love and Outka's agape bloom and blossom into *caritas* (union with God) in accord with 1 Corinthians 12. Note the trajectory of these three loves.

Natural/kin loves →   agape (equal regard) →   *caritas*

(Circle of →   Circle of →   One Body in
nearest/dearest)   strangers, distant   Christ (1 Cor 12)

We see a movement from the natural → to the supernatural.

The clash between the demands of natural loves (justice) and the demands of agape is more apparent than real. We should not be afraid of living up to the demands of our natural loves. Grace brings such natural loves to bloom in agape and then to their completion and perfection in *caritas*.

Agape is love for persons at its truest, and it must be in control over *philia*, *storge* and *eros*, ... For they are meant to be three God-given channels through which agape will find expression in specific relationships of life. *Only in Christ does this now become a real possibility for man.* (Baker 1984, 127, emphasis added)

Love of God and love of neighbor are distinct but inseparable. We can love, including our neighbors, because we feel loved by God. And as we love our neighbor, we grow stronger in our love of God. Love of neighbor is instrumental to love of God. "[O]ne reaches the heights of charity-friendship with God *only through friendships with persons* who, thanks to God's grace and mercy, need not be perfect" (Wadell 2008, 301, emphasis added). Thus, we cannot stay only within the tight circle of our natural loves. *Caritas* will not permit us to confine ourselves in such a manner but will draw us out. *Conflicts regarding priorities may in fact be grace at work in nature – of grace moving us from natural excellence to transformation and supernatural excellence.*

This growth in *caritas* will necessarily be reflected in the exterior/material manifestation of such love (II-II, 27–30), such as the tangible sharing of material goods. After all, there is a constitutive economic dimension to human life and community. Love, by its nature, does not remain purely affective in inactivity. It must be expressed in action (II-II, 27). This includes corporal works of mercy (II-II, 27, 31–33). "Thomas recognizes that affective responses are nothing but sham sentiment, unless they are expressed in action. The primary act of charity is of course to love (2a2ae 27)" (Porter 1989, 205). Thus, *caritas* brings along significant attendant positive obligations (e.g., John 13:34).

The letter of James and its link between faith and good works says as much. We cannot claim to love God even as we are indifferent to the plight of our distressed neighbors (James 2:14–17). Love of God enlivens and enriches our other loves, including love of neighbors. Note how God provides the means for heroic love, agape, by teaching us through each other in kin-particularistic love. This is an instance of grace working through nature, grace teaching us selfless love through our love for family and friends. This is yet another instance of God providing for us through one another.

Scriptural Insights

Sacred Scripture also shows a similar phenomenon of a circle of natural loves that keeps growing and expanding. In both the Hebrew Scriptures and the New Testament, we see a two-step process whereby one takes care of one's own, after which one moves farther afield.

The Hebrew Scriptures chronicles the building of a nation like no other nation by the Chosen People of God. It was to be a nation held up as a model for emulation by its neighbors. In the blueprint of the ideal society handed to them by the God of Abraham, Isaac, and Jacob, the Mosaic laws were solicitous of strangers and aliens. Nevertheless, these laws also treated Hebrews and strangers differently. For example, Hebrews were not to charge each other interest (Dt 23:19–20), nor were they supposed to enslave one another (Lev 25:39–43). In fact, they were to redeem their kin who end up having to sell themselves in slavery. They were to redeem family ancestral land whenever their kin were forced to sell these. We do not find similar stipulations for the alien or the stranger.

Nevertheless, despite this initial focus on taking care of their own and building the nation, Biblical Israel was keenly aware that the God of Abraham, Isaac, and Jacob was also reaching out to other nations through them. In fact, in the eschatological peace, other nations will follow Biblical Israel in climbing up the mountain of the Lord (Is 2:2–4).

We witness a similar dynamic in the New Testament. Jesus initially limits his ministry among his fellow Jews. In sending his twelve disciples in a ministry of healing and preaching, he was specific in his instructions "Go nowhere among the Gentiles, and enter no town of the Samaritans, but go rather to the lost sheep of the house of Israel" (Mt 10:5–6). Recall the Canaanite woman who begged Jesus to heal her daughter. Tested by Jesus with a dismissive response that it is not right to give the children's food to dogs, the woman of great faith responded, "even the dogs eat the crumbs that fall from their masters' table" (Mt 15:21–28; Mk 7:24–30).

Nevertheless, despite this initial focus on his fellow Jews, Jesus expands his own ministry of preaching and healing to include even the Gentiles. Recall the Samaritan woman at the well (Jn 4:4–26) and the Roman centurion's servant boy who was healed (Mt 8:5–13). Note his call for unconditional love for all, even for one's enemies (Mt 5:46–47). Despite being raised in a religion that adamantly separates the clean from the unclean, Jesus nevertheless breaks ranks to reach out to the sinners, publicans, lepers, and all others who were deemed unclean, and therefore, supposed to be outside one's circle. Note the table fellowship distinctive to Jesus. To break bread with someone is to treat that person as an equal. In the Greco-Roman world, one moves around only within one's own kind, not demeaning oneself to fraternize with those from a lower class nor being presumptuous to associate with those above one's socioeconomic class. Not so for Jesus. Everyone is a child of God. By the end of his ministry, Jesus commissions his disciples to preach the Gospel to the ends of the earth (Mk 16:15). As mentioned earlier, St. Paul captures this dynamic and its terminal point well when he declares in Galatians 3:28 that all are one in Christ regardless of whether one is Greek or Jew, slave or free, male or female. It is a universal *koinōnia*.

The parable of the Good Samaritan (Lk 10:25–37) is an even more direct, explicit affirmation that our duty to love extends beyond our circle of natural loves. Jesus challenges his contemporaries' understanding of their circle of responsibility.

> Until that time, the concept of "neighbour" was understood as referring essentially to one's countrymen and to foreigners who had settled in the land of Israel; in other words, to the closely-knit community of a single country or people. This limit is now abolished. *Anyone who needs me, and whom I can help, is my neighbour.* (Benedict XVI 2005, #15, emphasis added)

Earlier, we had seen the argument that there must be limits to the scope of our moral duties because to be responsible for everything or everyone is to end up being responsible for nothing or no one. Common sense tells us that there are practical limits to our beneficence. Nevertheless, Benedict XVI is adamant in preventing people from taking this duty lightly. He quickly adds to his commentary on the Good Samaritan parable:

> The concept of "neighbour" is now universalized, *yet it remains concrete.* Despite being extended to all mankind, *it is not reduced to a generic, abstract and undemanding expression of love, but calls for my own practical commitment here and now.* (Benedict XVI 2005, #15, emphasis added)

In other words, helping the stranger or the distant is not merely an aspirational goal or ideal but is a real moral duty that calls for concrete action. In effect, Benedict XVI puts a limit to the wide latitude that people have in discharging this imperfect duty as their circumstances permit. It may be an imperfect duty, but it calls for a forward-leaning response.

In both the Hebrew Scriptures and the New Testament, we see the need to respect priorities, and hence, the importance of satisfying the demands of special relationships. Nevertheless, we cannot limit ourselves exclusively to these special relationships. We eventually reach out to those outside our circle of kin-particularistic loves. Indeed, we see a similar two-stage process in Sacred Scripture.

Balancing the Clashing Claims of Agape and Justice

Thus far, we have seen that kin-particularistic loves have strong claims and do enjoy priority in the event of competing claims. Justice demands this. However, since love is diffusive by its nature, agape precludes people from being confined to their circle of natural loves. How then, do we reconcile or balance these two competing claims?

Recall the dilemma that Cambridge philosopher A. C. Ewing posed: spending to provide a university education for one's child or sending these funds instead to save many who are dying of hunger overseas. Most would find the father blameworthy rather than praiseworthy if he had sacrificed his son's education to send the funds to relieve famine elsewhere in the world (Hallett 1998, 1–2). A. C. Ewing's case (that becomes the starting point of Hallett's book) poses the issue as binary (0,1) in which the choices become mutually exclusive. For A. C. Ewing, the decision is an all-or-nothing choice. As we have seen, kin-particularistic love and agape's outreach to the distant and the stranger are not mutually exclusive. Far from it. Both are necessary conditions for each other's good. The question and its resolution cannot in fact be binary. Neither pole is sustainable on its own. *The matter is not about choosing between agape and justice, but about how much of agape and justice's claims to mix. The main issue is not one of priorities (because this is not contested), but one of superfluity – what is enough for one's nearest and dearest.* The task is in identifying the threshold that allows one to start satisfying the claims of agape after having fulfilled the claims of justice to one's own. The father's sending the son to university for education does not preclude the father from also sending whatever is superfluous for his son's education to relieve famine elsewhere.

Cicero

Martha Nussbaum (2000) notes the "problematic legacy" that Cicero left us. On the one hand, he submits that justice as a cardinal virtue calls for beneficence. Moreover, recall that he embeds a strong positive duty to prevent harm as part of justice proper (*iustitia*). On the other hand, Cicero restricts the resulting duty of beneficence in two important ways. First, priority is to accorded to our kin, fellow citizens, or close associates. Relationships, closeness, and shared history determine the strength of our mutual duties of beneficence to each other. Second, the duty of beneficence to those outside our natural circle is premised on its costing the giver nothing.

After describing peoples' strong bonds stemming from their common rational nature and from sharing the bounty of nature, Cicero is nevertheless quick to identify the limits of such universal solicitude. We are to extend assistance to those outside our circle of natural love, but only if it imposes no burdens on the giver. He cites Ennius's example of how lighting a stranger's lamp from one's own lamp does not dim our own lamp.[12] Thus, Cicero distills from Ennius the principle of bestowing even on strangers what costs us nothing. Cicero reinforces this principle even

[12] "Who kindly sets a wand'rer on his way
Does e'en as if he lit another's lamp by his:
No less shines his, when he his friend's hath lit." (I, vxi [51]).

further with his own maxims: "Deny no one the water that flows by"; "Let anyone who will take fire from our fire"; "Honest counsel give to one who is in doubt" (I, vxi [52]). In other words, give freely that which costs nothing.

Despite his acknowledgement that mutual sharing promotes the commonweal, Cicero nevertheless justifies Ennius's principle with hard realism – our means are insufficient.

> [S]ince the resources of individuals are limited and the number of the needy is infinite, this spirit of universal liberality must be regulated according to that test of Ennius-"No less shines his" – in order that we may continue to have the means for being generous to our friends. (I, vxi [52])

Nussbaum (2000) observes that Cicero writes strongly about people's shared humanity and how there should be no difference in the respect and solicitude that we confer on strangers as we give to our kin, fellow citizens, or close associates. We simply treat people as fellow humans (III, vi, [27–28]). Thus, Nussbaum (2000, 185) notes that Cicero is a cosmopolitan. Unfortunately, such cosmopolitanism runs up against Cicero's insistence on Ennius's principle – that we are bound to give aid to the distant or the stranger, but only if it costs us nothing. This, in effect, shuts down most beneficence to those outside our circle of kin, associates, and fellow citizens because beneficence and preventing harm are generally time- and resource-intensive. Cicero's examples of lighting someone's lamp, providing counsel, or providing direction are a far cry from the actual needs and harms that ought to be prevented in the real world. Thus, his exposition on the duty of beneficence and his strong disapprobation of those who fail to prevent harm seem to be for naught because they have very little application in the real world. I propose that this is not so. There is a solution to what Nussbaum calls Cicero's "problematic legacy." It lies with the whole notion of superfluity.

First, juxtaposed against Ennius's principle that it should cost the giver nothing, we have Cicero's earlier guideline that beneficence should not go beyond one's means. His reason for this is that going beyond one's means entails giving to others what we should be giving or bequeathing to our dependents, kin, or close associates (I, xiv [44]). In other words, beneficence is not limited only to that which costs the giver nothing, as per Ennius's principle. Rather, it can cost us, but not beyond our means. This is measured in terms of what we owe as a matter of *iustitia* (justice proper) to our natural loves. Ennius's principle of costless beneficence is too restrictive.

Second, note Cicero's rationale in subscribing to Ennius's principle – so that the giver's means are protected in order to enable the continued generosity to his/her friends (I, vxi [52]). Observe that his critical benchmark is not depleting the means of the giver. Again, in this case, Ennius's principle is too restrictive because the cost of giving can still be well within the means of the giver, thereby not impeding generosity to his/her natural loves.

Third, and most important of all, despite his clear and detailed guidelines on the order of priority in bestowing beneficence, Cicero nevertheless affirms that all these are not hard and fast rules. In the end, one must deliberate on the circumstances and the needs of every individual case confronting us. Despite the strong case he makes on the priority of kin, fellow citizens, and close associates, Cicero nevertheless acknowledges that the "claims of social relationship" may in fact be trumped by the "dictates of circumstances." Thus, he provides the example of how one might have to help a neighbor before assisting one's own brother or a friend depending on the particulars of the case. The key is "to consider what is most needful in each individual case and what each individual person can or cannot procure without our help" (I, xviii [59]). This is consistent with one of his earlier points. At the end of his discussion of the nuances in rank ordering our generosity, Cicero provides a final admonition that, *ceteris paribus*, the "first rule of duty" is to help according to the needs of the recipient (I, xv [49]). In both final caveats of these two sections on the rank ordering of generosity, Cicero acknowledges the need of the recipient as an important criterion in one's beneficence. Need ultimately matters. The claims on us by our kin, fellow citizens, or close associates are not absolute after all. Circumstances can override these claims.

Given all these significant qualifications in Cicero's exposition on beneficence, we should not take Ennius's principle literally – that the duty of beneficence to the stranger and the distant is conditioned on costing the giver nothing. Rather, it is reasonable to say that such beneficence to the stranger and the distant should not impose unreasonable or excessive burdens on the giver; it should be within the means of the giver.

If this is an acceptable interpretation, then we open the door to using superfluity as a measure in implementing Cicero's ideas. Priority is accorded to one's circle of natural relationships. When their needs are satisfied, it is then that we move on to assist the distant and the stranger who would have otherwise not been able to procure their needs or who would have been harmed without our aid. This is a beneficence that costs the giver, but not to the point of depriving the giver or the giver's kin. Thus, the giver lives up to the duties owed to rest of society by virtue of our common humanity, that is, the duty of beneficence and the duty to prevent harm. The key, of course, is in identifying what is the threshold of basic needs satisfaction that permits us to move beyond our kin to help others who need our assistance or who are below this particular threshold. *Ceteris paribus*, we ensure the basic needs satisfaction of our natural loves before moving on to the distant and the stranger. In effect, one could satisfy all the duties in Cicero's exposition on justice and beneficence.

St. Augustine

Even as St. Augustine says that those who are closest to us by accident of time, place, or circumstance should have priority to our beneficence, he is nevertheless clear that besides relationship to us, need is an equally important factor to consider.

> [S]uppose that you had a great deal of some commodity, and felt bound to give it away to somebody who had none, and that it could not be given to more than one person; if two persons presented themselves, *neither of whom had either from need or relationship a greater claim upon you than the other*, you could do nothing fairer than choose by lot to which you would give what could not be given to both. (Augustine, *De Doctrina*, I. 28, emphasis added)

St. Ambrose

St. Ambrose also acknowledges the priority of our natural loves. However, the claims of our kin-particularistic loves are neither absolute nor open-ended.

> True liberality also must be tested in this way: that we despise not our nearest relatives, if we know they are in want. For it is better for thee to help thy kindred who feel the shame of asking help from others, or of going to another to beg assistance in their need. *Not, however, that they should become rich on what thou couldst otherwise give to the poor. It is the facts of the case we must consider, and not personal feeling.* (Ambrose, *De Officiis*, I 30, #150, emphasis added)

Observe that relative unmet need is the operative criterion in how we ought to disburse our beneficence. This standard applies just as well to those who are nearest and dearest to us and not only to those who are strangers or distant to us. While blood ties are clearly an important consideration for St. Ambrose, it is not the decisive criterion. Considerations that are more important are relative need and the use of such benefactions.

For example, he is adamant that benefactions are used for good and do not inflict harm or enable wrongdoing or extravagant living (#144). Furthermore, beneficence should be judicious: "Perfect liberality is proved by its good faith, the case it helps, the time and place when and where it is shown" (#148).

For Ambrose, relative need is the decisive criterion in deciding who has better claims on our beneficence.

> In giving we must also take into consideration age and weakness; some-times, also, that natural feeling of shame, which indicates good birth. One ought to give more to the old who can no longer supply themselves with food by labour. So, too, weakness of body must be assisted, and that read-ily. Again, if any one after being rich has fallen into want, we must assist, especially if he has lost what he had from no sin of his own, but owing to robbery or banishment or false accusation. (Ambrose, *De Officiis*, I 30, #158)

Blood ties and relationships are undoubtedly important. Nevertheless, relative unmet need and people's circumstances turn out to be factors that are even more decisive. In-extremis needs are not the only ones that can trump the claims of our natural loves. For St. Ambrose, the threshold is much lower than that – relative unmet needs.

St. Thomas

Even St. Thomas, a staunch proponent of the priority of natural loves in the order of charity, acknowledges that the claims of kin-particularistic love are not boundless. Relative unmet need determines these limits. In responding to the question on whether we should give alms to those who are closer to us, St. Thomas notes:

> As Augustine says (De Doctr. Christ. i, 28), "it falls to us by lot, as it were, to have to look to the welfare of those who are more closely united to us." Nevertheless in this matter we must employ discretion, according to the various degrees of connection, holiness and utility. *For we ought to give alms to one who is much holier and in greater want,* and to one who is more useful to the common weal, *rather than to one who is more closely united to us, especially if the latter* be not very closely united, and has no special claim on our care then and there, and who *is not in very urgent need.* (II-II 32.9, emphasis added)

Both St. Ambrose and St. Thomas converge in their teachings on the claims of our natural loves: Kin-particularistic loves merit special consideration in our beneficence, but their claims are nevertheless limited by, indeed, even overridden by the relative unmet needs of others who are non-kin and perhaps even strangers or distant to us. Note that these relative unmet needs do not even have to be in extremis.

Neither St. Ambrose nor St. Thomas provides any further guidance on how to implement these teachings in practice. The key is to recognize that the priority that our natural loves enjoy over our beneficence ends as soon as we reach the threshold of superfluity, that is, when we have given enough so that we can move on to address the needs of others. No guideline is explicitly given on how to determine the threshold that allows us to move from providing for our circle of natural loves to an even bigger circle that includes the distant and the stranger. Nevertheless, we can infer such a threshold from St. Thomas' other teachings.

In his exposition on whether almsgiving is a precept or a counsel, St. Thomas notes that almsgiving must take the condition not only of the recipient but also of the giver. Alms cannot be given to the point of harming the giver and those under his/her charge. Both responsibilities (to self and to one's dependents) take precedence. Beyond this is the surplus from which alms can be given.

> Because each one *must first of all look after himself and then after those over whom he has charge, and afterwards with what remains relieve the needs of others.* Thus nature first, by its nutritive power, *takes what it requires for the upkeep of one's own body, and afterwards yields the residue for the formation of another by the power of generation.* (II-II, 32.5, response, emphasis added)

Superfluity is measured in terms of what the people do not need for their station in life and those of their family (II-II, 32.6, reply). If this standard of superfluity applies to one's own person and those of one's immediate dependents, we could surely use the same standard for our other kin-particularistic loves. An alternative measure is the Patristic standard that is also used by John XXIII: superfluity is measured by the relative unmet needs of one's neighbor (Vatican II 1965, *Gaudium et Spes* Part II, Ch 3 #69, fn 10).

Kant

Superfluity is also implicit in Kant's duty of beneficence. In the first place, he is emphatic that even as we are bound by such a strong duty of beneficence, we should nevertheless not give beyond our capabilities and resources, lest we find ourselves in need of others' beneficence as well.

Second, need is an important consideration in Kant's understanding of his duty of beneficence.

> To be beneficent, that is, to promote according to one's means [*Vermögen*] the happiness of others *in need*, without hoping for something in return, is every man's duty …. the maxim of common interest, of beneficence *toward those in need*, is a universal duty of men, just because they are to be considered fellow men, that is, rational beings *with needs*. (Kant 1991, *Metaphysics, Doctrine of Virtue*, Part II, Ch I, Sect I, #30, emphasis added)

Note that Kant is not referring merely to in-extremis needs but also to others' relative unmet needs.

> Finally, for Kant, beneficence out of our surplus is not meritorious because it is something that is expected. The reward for such beneficence is the personal satisfaction and the moral uplift that one feels from such generosity. A rich man (one who has abundant means [*Mitteln*] for the happiness of others, i.e., means in excess of his own needs), should hardly even regard beneficence as a meritorious duty on his part, even though he also puts others under obligation by it. The satisfaction he derives from his beneficence, which costs him no sacrifice, is a way of reveling in moral feelings. (Kant 1991, *Metaphysics, Doctrine of Virtue*, Part II, Ch I, Sect I, #31)

Scope of Moral Obligation and the Ethics of Care

Barbara Herman (2001, 227–228) observes that in the duty of beneficence, there are two obligations that are widely accepted – the duty of easy rescues and its "companion duty of consideration or helpfulness" whereby we "lend a hand" and assist someone who would otherwise not be able to complete a worthwhile project. The difficulty arises beyond these two obligations: what other needs deserve our assistance, how much should we provide, and whom should we aid?

We must work out these questions within two parameters set by our moral intuitions. On the one hand, we cannot run ourselves to do the ground in looking after others to the point of making our lives "unlivable or too severe" in having to interrupt or perhaps even forego our own worthwhile goals (p. 228). On the other hand, we know that we must respond to others' needs and that we cannot simply be indifferent or walk away from these. Meeting these needs can be demanding, indeed, even intrusive in our pursuit of our own projects, but unfortunately, moral theory is silent on the precise threshold when these two moral intuitions switch over in their precedence to the other. How much and how far we ought to sacrifice our own and our nearest-dearest's interests for the sake of the strangers' need at-a distance is unclear.

After grappling with these questions and after making critical conceptual distinctions, Herman (2001) eventually concludes that there are "no tidy answers." The duty of beneficence is not determinable in advance without information on its context, such as, the relationship between the parties involved, the social institutions with the primary obligations, and the needs of the benefactor at that particular juncture. The most that could be done is to come up with "a wide-ranging deliberative resource ... if moral theory is to cohere with real-world moral complexity" (p. 255). Among the deliberative resources she puts forward is the following:

> If, however, our duties to others at-a-distance fall under beneficence as an inheritance of defaulted social obligations, the inherited obligations must fit with the structure of relational duties we already have, and also with our morally required concern for ourselves. For this reason, not only will the general duty to others be limited, in order to meet our primary duties of beneficence, *we may also be required to expend resources on higher-function needs close to us rather than on more basic needs at a distance.* (Herman 2001, 253, emphasis added)

Herman's moral triage[13] presents the following obligations in descending strength of obligatoriness:

- Our moral duty to our own well-being and perfection
- Our primary obligations (circle of kin, friends, and associates)
- Our secondary (inherited) obligations to others (duty of beneficence)

The disparity in the strength of claims of primary and secondary obligations is such that higher-function needs of our kin and associates trump even the basic needs (non-in-extremis) of the stranger and the distant. Of course, the next question is how far one should go in satisfying the higher-function needs of our primary obligees (kin and associates). Herman notes that common sense or our moral intuition will readily flag superfluity for one's nearest and dearest that should be used to satisfy need at-a-distance.[14]

Proponents of an ethics of care also arrive at a similar balancing act between competing obligations. The ethics of care acknowledges strong duties owed to those who are related or near to us. Unlike moral

---

[13] She defines triage as sorting through needs "according to values other than urgency" (p. 254).
[14] The example she gives is that of the nth year of recreational dance lessons for one's child or a summer hiking in the mountains (p. 241).

cosmopolitanism, which calls for strict impartiality and the uniform treatment of all individuals, near or far, the ethics of care stresses the importance of people's immediate context and relationships. It is not as if humans are born as atomistic individuals. Rather, they are born into and raised within a particular family and within a close circle of friends, fellow citizens, and associates. Humans have a social ontology that is comprised of webs of relationships. In fact, the moral self can even be described as a "self-in-connection" (Miller 2011, 396). Furthermore, caring for another begins with awareness of and attentiveness to the particular needs of that person, rather than what we think the person needs. This requirement is most likely satisfied in the case of those who are near and dear to us, rather than the stranger and the distant. Thus, the ethics of care affirms the priority of kin and particularistic loves. These are deemed our primary obligations, using Herman's terminology.

Nevertheless, the ethics of care is also cognizant that its duty to care is a global duty. This stems from the keen awareness that humans share a most significant set of characteristics – they are vulnerable to the vicissitudes of life, they are dependent on each other in getting over these challenges and hurdles, and they have needs that they cannot fill on their own. Vulnerability, interdependence, and the needy state of humans are among the strong common bonds that bind humans to one another, regardless of whether they are kin, near, strangers, or distant. Thus, the duty to care is a global duty and not something that is localized to a limited circle of natural loves.

Advocates of the ethics of care are comfortable in combining and living up to the competing demands of caring for their close relations and for distant persons at the same time. In fact, some claim that people who take to heart the global duty to care "will rarely tend exclusively to relations in their own households and communities" (Miller 2011, 401). The key to achieving such balance is to distinguish primary beneficence (those closest and related to us, etc.) from secondary beneficence (the distant others), and how the former takes precedence over the latter. However, we cannot devote all our care exclusively to primary beneficence. We must attend to the duties of our secondary beneficence because of our acknowledgement of the importance of addressing such needs, no matter how distant. Nevertheless, there is a limit to how far we can pour out ourselves for others, whether for our primary or secondary duty – that we do not go beyond the point of hurting our own agency or putting at risk our ability to pursue our own ends and happiness.

Kant himself is aware that the duty of beneficence, the obligatory end of promoting others' happiness, is necessarily a wide duty (an imperfect duty).

It cannot be made a universal law because it would otherwise clash with our other obligatory end of working toward our own perfection. Promoting others' happiness often requires a diminution of our own welfare. Thus, Kant concludes that people have wide discretion in how they combine both obligatory ends, considering their own true needs and others' requirements (Kant 1991, *Metaphysics, Elements of Ethics*, VIII, 2, a. 393).

In the end, it is prudential judgment that effects this balance, taking into account the circumstances of time and place (II-II, 31.2). Both justice and agape are needed in providing guidance for this prudential judgment. Justice has a critical role in defining the moral floor beneath which no one will be allowed to sink. Nevertheless, justice is limited in the insights it can provide. It has much less leeway since it is precise and measured. Agape is much better suited for this difficult task of constantly balancing the demands of justice and agape.

Agape, by its nature, must consider justice as part of the regard that it accords to everyone. In contrast, justice need not take agape into account. Even as it may present competing claims to those of justice, agape will not want egregious violations of justice either. Hence, agape can be said to have a "natural" guardrail in that out of regard for its object, it will not do so at great expense to justice because it goes against agape's nature to inflict grievous harm on anyone, much less the object of its love. There may be some trade-off with justice's claims, but not to the extent of a severe violation of justice.

As we have seen earlier, agape is internalized in its enforcement. It seeks that which is both good and right. At the very least, agape has human well-being as its proximate end, whether for the nearest/dearest or the distant and the stranger. Agape will not go below a certain moral floor in its self-sacrifice because it is founded on a requisite *philautia* and *storge*. Agape is familial, rather than contractual, in its interpersonal relations. While the imprecise nature of agape might be deemed a disadvantage relative to the precision of justice, such indeterminacy can be turned into an advantage in the flexibility it accords to agape. This allows for responsiveness to the context of the case for adjudication. It is a better fit for the needs of prudential judgment.

Universal love is accorded to all, but it does not mean that it must be given equally. Hence, it is selective in the sense that not all are equal in the way they are loved. However, such selective love does not mean that one can exclude anyone from this love (Irwin 2006, 47). The nub of this issue is that love comes in different types and degrees, as in the case of kin-particularistic love vis-à-vis love for the distant, the stranger, or the undeserving. These differences give rise to conflicting claims. Each relationship holds the seeds of different types of love to be actualized. That is the challenge for prudential judgment in balancing the claims of natural loves (inner circle) and agape's expansive outer circle.

In sum, our most significant finding in this chapter is that in settling many real-life agape-justice conflicts, the issue is not about priorities – on whether the claims of our kin-particularistic loves take precedence over the claims of our impartial, universal loves. Rather, the issue is ultimately about superfluity – how much of our beneficence suffices for our nearest and dearest (the claims of justice) so that we can move on to extend the same kindness to our non-kin and the distant (the claims of agape). Note how the expansion of our circle of kin-particularistic loves toward universal love corresponds to moving from columns 1 and 2 to columns 3 and 4 in Table 1.2. We move toward our general moral obligations after satisfying our particular legal and moral obligations.

Sample Applications

Lifesaving Equipment and Vaccines

Going back to the case at the start of this chapter, how should the United States, the EU, and India have allocated their scarce supplies of lifesaving medical equipment and vaccines during the deadly, early phase of the Covid pandemic? Were they morally blameworthy in prioritizing their citizens first and only later giving their surplus to other countries? This case highlights the time- and place-utility of the claims of justice and agape. The right parties must satisfy them at the right time and place, in the right manner, in the right amounts, and for the right beneficiaries.

Using Table 6.1, the fault line in this particular case during the early days of the Covid pandemic is the clash of claims between a legal and moral due to their own citizens and the moral debt of quasi-obligatory beneficence to poor countries. It may even be a supererogatory act, had the United States, EU, or India shared with other countries out of their substance despite their own needs during the deadly days of the pandemic, rather than share only from their surplus after the danger was past.

The moral dilemma over the distribution of vaccines and PPE during the deadly period of the pandemic illustrates that even the most difficult and seemingly intractable cases of agape-justice conflicts are manageable. What makes this case difficult is that all nations were in-extremis conditions at the start of the pandemic, including advanced countries. The

Table 6.1 *Vaccine and personal protective equipment (PPE) allocation*

Justice		Agape	
Legal due	**Particular Moral Debt**	**General Moral Debt**	**Supererogatory**
Codified in law	Community expectation	Divine expectation; virtuous act	
X-- X*			
X--------Sharing at the expense of one's own citizens dying--------------------X*			

*During deadly early phase of the pandemic

United States, EU, and India were suffering high death rates at that time, as were other nations. How should the United States, EU, and India have allocated PPE and vaccines at that time?

Based on the literature we have just reviewed, this chapter finds that the United States, EU, and India should not have completely shut down their exports of vaccines and PPEs at a critical juncture of the pandemic. Not with Kant's acknowledgement of needs as an important consideration in his moral theory and not with his universalizability rule. Not with the ethics of care's acceptance of its global duty to care despite its firm stance that primary obligations (kin love) take precedence over secondary, inherited obligations (the stranger and the distant). Not even with a Thomistic order of charity that prioritizes kin love but that is nonetheless attentive to relative unmet need as a limiting criterion.

Even as all nations were in extremis during the deadly phase of the pandemic, poor countries had far greater relative unmet needs vis-à-vis Covid-19 compared to the United States and the EU. Low-income developing nations have poor healthcare infrastructure and a dearth of medical personnel. The health and nutritional status of large segments of their populations is marginal at best given their destitution thereby making them even more vulnerable to the consequences of getting infected. Moreover, poor people live in cramped and crowded households, conditions that are conducive to the rapid spread of the virus. Compared to advanced nations, poor countries faced far greater dangers from the pandemic because of their limited means to pursue risk-mitigation measures. The United States and the EU had at least the medical and economic resources to moderate the impact of the virus or even hold it at bay. Thus, even as all nations were in-extremis conditions early in the pandemic, poor nations were in relatively greater need and peril. There was a moral duty for the United

States and the EU to share at least some of their lifesaving PPE and vaccines based on our common humanity during this early deadly stage of the pandemic. In the case of India, it could have shared some of its vaccines with countries that were in worse shape or in greater poverty than it was. The deadly phase of the pandemic presented the United States, EU, and India an opportunity to truly live out agape by expanding their circle of love and responsibility beyond their natural loves, even at great sacrifice to their own citizens.

The case of PPE and vaccine allocation during a deadly pandemic is neither an issue of priorities nor an issue of superfluity. The in-extremis conditions for all parties concerned turn it into an issue of our shared humanity. The real difficult, unresolved question is how much the United States, EU, and India should have shared.[15] Their national leaders would have had to make the key prudential judgment call in determining the threshold of the burdens that they can ask their own citizens to bear as they extend humanitarian assistance overseas in sharing vital lifesaving equipment and vaccines. This would have been a hard decision as it involves the question of how many deaths among their own citizens the leaders would have been willing to accept in order to prevent deaths overseas. This is an unpalatable political and moral decision to make. Depending on the cost (hospitalizations and deaths) that the United States, EU, and India were willing to incur, their sharing might have even been supererogatory, perhaps even heroic. The next two chapters present further insights on how to deal with this challenging question of how much to share.

International Trade as Foreign Aid

Consider another agape-justice conflict that pits our natural loves vis-à-vis the non-kin: the case of international trade and foreign aid. Economists rarely arrive at a near-consensus on any topic. The overwhelming benefit of international trade is one of these. Most economists agree that economic history and empirical evidence have repeatedly shown that trade has been, for the most part, beneficial in improving human well-being. Adam Smith's (1776) exposition on specialization and the division of labor provides an intuitive explanation for how and why economic exchange between individuals and between nations produce a synergy – the resulting

---

[15] India's Serum Institute negotiated a 50-50 split between India and the rest of the world, with the Indian government having priority in accessing their production. In the case of 3M, it negotiated a 90-10 split for its N95 masks. www.nytimes.com/2020/08/01/world/asia/coronavirus-vaccine-india .html last accessed May 27, 2022.

whole being larger than the mere sum of its individual parts. Ricardian trade theory predicts that smaller economies reap relatively greater benefits compared to their larger trading partners (Appleyard and Fields 2017, 26–39). Thus, trade is ideal for poor countries.

The Stolper-Samuelson theorem of international trade theory finds that countries that engage in international trade will see an unambiguous increase in the real income of their most abundant factor of production (Appleyard and Fields 2017, 135–36). For poor developing countries, this is labor. Economic theorems do not always stand the test of time and empirical studies. However, in the case of the Stolper-Samuelson theorem, we have ample historical evidence since the end of World War II that supports this theory.

Consider the economic history of the East Asian miracles – Japan in the immediate post–World War II era; the Asian Tigers (Taiwan, Hong Kong, Singapore, and South Korea) in the 1970s–1980s; and now China since the 1990s. These countries lifted their populations out of poverty successfully, and they are now global economic powerhouses. The common denominator behind these singular accomplishments is the central role of their export industries. These export industries generated the necessary foreign exchange with which to import the technology, equipment, and raw materials to build their countries' industrial base. Given extremely competitive global markets, these export industries quickly learned to be cost-efficient. They were driven to emulate the best practices and the latest advances of their foreign competitors and then innovate even further.

The governments of these Asian miracles were forced early on to be fiscally responsible and adopt good policies to attract much-needed foreign investments. These governments also had the incentive to invest in and improve their ports, utilities, roads, bridges, telecommunications, and other infrastructure that were vital to keep their export industries competitive. Such vigorous engagement in international trade opened new markets, new sources of credit and capital, and new partnerships for these poor countries. These export industries spawned a web of domestic suppliers within the local economy, thereby creating even more jobs and other beneficial ripple effects. The technical and managerial skills learned within these export industries spilled over to the rest of the economy.

Indeed, international trade is a vital pathway for alleviating poverty. No modern country has been able to rise above poverty without the help of international trade. Thus, it is not a surprise that free trade has been used as a vehicle of foreign aid. Note, for example, the preferential trade for African banana and sugar from their foreign colonizers. Similarly, preferential trade is common practice among advanced nations as a way of helping poor countries (Appleyard and Fields 2017, 259–60, 263–64). Agape would call on wealthier nations to open their economies to trade with developing countries as a way of assisting the poor to help themselves out of poverty.

Unfortunately, this is only half the story. While trade indeed improves the overall welfare of the trading countries, trade is also a de facto redistribution of wealth and income within the countries themselves. In other words, there are both "winners and losers" among the local citizens and residents of the trading countries. To be sure, these countries benefit overall. However, the same cannot be said of individual citizens or sectors within these countries. Some will lose, while others will gain much.

Consider the well-known distress of labor unions, manufacturing workers, and small domestic businesses in advanced countries. Cheap imports of manufactures from overseas destroy good-paying domestic manufacturing jobs. Note the demise of the steel industry, shipbuilding, textile mills, and many more in the advanced economies including the United States. The once dominant Big Three US automakers are now much reduced in their role in the global automotive industry relative to their heyday. Mom-and-pop stores on Main Street have been driven out of business because of their inability to match the much wider variety and cheaper imports offered by Walmart. We need not rehearse all these deleterious side effects, as they are well known by now from the backlash from anti-globalizers. It is sufficient to note that for all its much-touted economic benefits, the cost and adjustment burdens of international trade are not always borne by the people who reap the benefits. People who could ill afford them often have to bear these costs. This explains why nations restrict trade via tariffs, quotas, and other protectionist policies despite its well-known overall gains.

One important explanation for the disconnect between the sanguine view of economic theory regarding trade versus what happens on the ground is that economic theory assumes a frictionless marketplace in which factors of production and resources can easily move across economic sectors and geographic regions. The laid-off manufacturing worker in his/her early 50s may not necessarily have the interest nor the aptitude to take the new jobs created in computer programming. In other words, distributive, social, and general-legal justice may demand that governments restrict international trade to protect vulnerable workers and small businesses within their domestic economies from being displaced by foreign competition.

Cases in point: NAFTA and offshore outsourcing. Both are in line with agape's call for compassionate assistance to poor developing countries.

NAFTA has benefited many Mexican manufacturing workers (even as it has also hurt Mexican farmers). Overall, however, NAFTA's benefits have been positive in contributing to the alleviation of Mexican poverty (Kose et al. 2004). Outsourcing has been a boon for India, the Philippines, and other emerging nations. However, for both NAFTA and offshore outsourcing, there is fierce domestic opposition in advanced nations because of the adverse impact on their local economies and workers.

Herein lies the clash of competing legitimate moral claims. On the one hand, agape would call for international trade as a form of assistance to poor developing countries. This is particularly so because of overwhelming empirical evidence and economic history that attest to the central role of international trade in emerging nations' escape from poverty. On the other hand, justice would call for restrictions to international trade to protect the rightful claims of local residents and workers to a livelihood and to preserve their way of life (in the case of agriculture) despite the benefits that domestic consumers and many firms reap from international trade.

OECD Agricultural Subsidies

Another trade-related issue that gives rise to agape-justice conflicts is the problem of OECD[16] agricultural subsidies. The EU, United States, Japan, and other wealthy countries have restricted access to their agricultural markets to support their struggling and much-diminished agricultural sectors. France justifies its farm subsidies as a necessary step in preserving the culture of the nation. Indeed, many farms in the OECD would not survive if their governments allowed free trade in agricultural goods.

Such agricultural protectionism and subsidies have adverse ripple effects on farmers in poor developing countries. In particular, prices for their crops drop in the global or even in their own domestic markets because of the glut of supplies. (The OECD subsidies lead to a much greater output from their farms than is warranted by allocative efficiency.) These competing claims between OECD farms, on the one hand, and farmers in poor developing countries, on the other hand, could be cast as an intra-justice conflict. OECD farmers could appeal to demands of distributive justice within the OECD, while farmers from poor countries could also appeal to the demands of global distributive justice. Nevertheless, the fallback position is to argue the case for poor farmers based on agape – an equal regard for all farmers, whether from the OECD or from a developing country.

---

[16] Organisation for Economic Co-operation and Development.

Export Controls

Other trade-related issues that give rise to agape-justice conflicts are export controls. China and Russia are among the world's top exporters of fertilizers. These are vital for global food production and many poor nations' agricultural sector. To ensure domestic supplies and combat rising domestic prices for fertilizers, both China and Russia imposed export controls on this commodity, thereby exacerbating the price increases for the rest of the world, especially poor countries (Bloomberg News 2021; Gro Intelligence 2021). To ensure their domestic supplies, India and Vietnam imposed export controls on rice, an important staple for many countries (Economic Times 2008; Reuters 2020).

Because of the Russian invasion of Ukraine in February 2022, commodity prices for cooking oil, grains, and fertilizers rose dramatically worldwide. Prior to the invasion, both Ukraine and Russia were among the top three exporters of sunflower oil, wheat, and fertilizers (Food and Agriculture Organization 2022). To protect its own citizens, Indonesia banned all exports of its palm oil (Jadhav 2022). It is the world's largest producer of palm oil, and the brunt of such export ban will be borne most acutely by poor countries in Asia and Africa who are already reeling from price hikes across all the vital commodities they need but could now no longer afford – oil, grain, and cooking oil. India, the world's second biggest producer of wheat, followed suit not long thereafter, banning all exports of wheat to ensure supplies for its own people in light of the Russia-Ukraine war (Good 2022).

Solution

How much should advanced nations open up their economies to trade with poor countries as a form of foreign assistance? Should OECD countries continue protecting their own farmers and preserve their culture and way of life, or should they cease their agricultural subsidies and protectionist policies altogether for the sake of poor farmers overseas? The fault line in these cases is similar to those of PPE and vaccine allocation during the deadly early phase of the pandemic. They are a clash between legal and moral dues to one's own citizens (justice) versus the duties of humanity (agape).[17]

In all these cases, we have the clashing claims of a country's obligations to its own citizens (legal and moral dues) versus its humanitarian, moral obligations to other nations (agape). Unlike the case of vaccines and PPE

---

[17] Many will disagree with my characterization of this fault line and argue that this is a case of justice, rather than of compassion (e.g., Pogge 2008). However, as mentioned earlier in the Preface, the fallback position is to argue from compassion. I am bypassing arguments based on justice and going directly to the fallback argument.

during the deadly phase of the pandemic, these other cases provide much more leeway because they are generally not in-extremis cases. Hence, we can readily apply this chapter's findings that the issue is not one of priorities but one of superfluity, that is, sharing with others as soon as there are supplies that can be made available.

International trade as a form of foreign aid, OECD agricultural subsidies, and export controls on key commodities are agape-justice conflicts that are much more amenable to this chapter's finding on the importance of superfluity as a criterion for resolving competing claims from agape and justice. While OECD countries and exporting nations have reason to protect their culture, their agriculture, and the welfare of their own citizens, they must nevertheless still be mindful of the hardships they inflict on farmers and citizens from poor countries.

These cases are not issues of priorities, but of superfluity. National leaders will have to make the judgment call in identifying the threshold of superfluity that would allow them to extend some concessions or relief to poor nations. The greater their compassion, the lower the threshold for superfluity, and the sooner they can provide assistance and relief to others besides their own citizens. The key to settling these agape-justice conflicts is to set at the lowest possible level the all-important threshold that identifies what is sufficient for one's own citizens that permits extending humanitarian help to others, out of one's sense and duty of humanity. *Setting that threshold is ultimately a question of how much these nations are willing to share in the suffering of others.* That is the topic of the next chapter.

Summary and Conclusions

Human life is characterized by a multiplicity of relationships. We must live in community, even with people who are strangers or may even be enemies. There are as many types of love as there are relationships. Thus, we are exposed to different types of love corresponding to the wide variety of relationships we have. In other words, love is not homogeneous. From human experience, self-love is foundational. Thus, Sacred Scripture says to love others as you love yourself (Lev 19:18). Similarly, the Golden Rule is a reminder to do unto others, as you would want them to do unto you. Natural love – self-preservation is instinctive and second nature to humans. It is part of natural law.

In the Hebrew Scriptures, *tzedeq* (righteousness) is about the fulfillment of all the demands of our relationships. We are righteous only after we have fulfilled them. This includes both the nearest and dearest as well as the distant and the stranger. For example, note the inclusion of aliens in their listing of the four most vulnerable groups deserving special protection and assistance: widows, orphans, aliens, and the poor, including servants and the enslaved.

Many agape-justice conflicts entail the claims of our natural loves (kin-particularistic love), on the one hand, versus universal love (agape), on the other hand. Recall the moral dilemma A. C. Ewing presents on whether to send one's child to college or to use the funds instead to relieve the desperate needs of the poor dying from famine in East Bengal. Justice demands the satisfaction of the claims of those nearest and dearest to us (*philautia, storge, philia*), while agape calls for an equal regard for all.

Natural love is a necessary condition for moral cosmopolitanism. Partial (kin-particularistic) love is a stepping-stone to impartial (universal) love. We are better able to live up to our general moral obligations because we have lived up to our relational moral obligations. Benevolence (for all) does not simply arise from nowhere nor is it handed down on a silver platter in its perfected form. Natural love is its incubator. This is literally a case of going from the local to the global. Natural loves must bloom to their fullness in universal benevolence, *caritas* – the One Body in Christ (1 Cor 12). Natural loves and agape (compassion for others) are necessary conditions for each other. Just like the socioeconomic homeostasis required by a functioning economy (Chapter 4), we need a delicate balance of natural and universal love if agape is to truly grow and take hold. The conflicting claims of agape and justice may in fact be the growing pangs of the human community as grace moves it from natural excellence to supernatural excellence. Ultimately, how far we widen our circle of love and responsibility depends on us. There are no hard and fast rules, except for the certainty that such love grows in completion and perfection only as it expands over time.

In sum, agape-justice conflicts may in fact be:

- An indication that people need to expand their circle of love and responsibility to catch up with their growing capabilities and circle of interpersonal relationships. (Think of globalization and its new attendant obligations.)
- A unique opportunity to perfect and complete our natural loves by reaching out to the distant and the stranger.
- An instance of grace building on nature as our natural loves (particularistic love) bloom into agape (universal love) and eventually into *caritas* (supernatural love).

CHAPTER 7

Adjudication of Last Resort
To Love as Christ Loves

Introduction

Maintaining balance in socioeconomic homeostasis is ultimately reliant on the prudential judgment of the public and its leaders (Chapter 4). Identifying what serves general-legal justice best often entails dealing with many gray areas in which right or wrong, good or bad is not always clear. It is a similar dilemma when it comes to mitigating the consequences of unattended past wrongs as a way of resolving current agape-justice conflicts (Chapter 5). This, too, is a terrain fraught with its own share of uncertainties. Expanding people's circle of love and responsibility beyond their natural loves to include the distant and the stranger requires not only goodwill but also courage and openness that are often in short supply (Chapter 6). One pattern that has come out strongly in our study thus far is that there is no single universal solution to deciding agape-justice conflicts given their multiple causes and, even worse, given a complex and ever-changing socioeconomic landscape. Moreover, these multiple causes often mutually reinforce each other to produce even more severe and intractable agape-justice conflicts, as in the case of migration-related issues. Indeed, Herman (2001) is correct in concluding that there are "no tidy answers" in sorting through competing duties of justice and agape.

The presumption in the literature for most policymakers, philosophers, and theologians is to defer to justice over agape in such conflicts given the foundational role of justice and given its perfect duties (Chapter 2). After all, no functional community can exist without at least a minimum set of rules that members are expected to follow. Justice is needed if there is to be a social contract at all that prevents people from descending into a Hobbesian state of nature. Rule of law is necessary if there is to be a community. People willingly give up some of their freedoms to Leviathan in exchange for just protection. Thus, in this chapter, we consider, for the sake of argument, the extreme scenario in which justice presents the strongest possible claims while agape is unable to present any legal claim at all, except for a plea for compassion. In such a lopsided situation, is there anything else that can or should be done with agape's claims? If so, why? What is agape's best "last resort" justification for its claims?

Parties to the Clashing Claims

We need to make important distinctions regarding the parties involved when we speak of agape-justice conflicts, namely:

Justice: Obligor – Obligee (right holder/claimant)
Agape: Philanthropist/Benefactor – Beneficiary

The obligor is the party bound by the duties of justice. The obligee is the claimant or the right holder who awaits what is due to him/her from the obligor. The philanthropist/benefactor is the donor of the benefaction, while the beneficiary is the recipient of such gift. Kant notes, "Someone who finds satisfaction in the well-being (*salus*) of men considered simply as men, for whom it is well when things go well for every other, is called a friend of man in general (a philanthropist)" (Kant 1991, *Metaphysics, Doctrine of Virtue*, Part II, Ch I, Sect I, #26).

In agape-justice conflicts, the benefactor and the obligor are the same party. The obligor-benefactor faces the competing claims of the obligee (based on law and rights; justice) and the claims of the beneficiary (based on the duty of humanity or by divine command; agape). In effect, justice's obligees and agape's beneficiaries are competing for the same resources. The clashing claims of agape and justice are about the claims of justice's obligees versus agape's beneficiaries.[1] Most people settle agape-justice conflicts based on which party has the stronger claim and not on which party has the greater need. After all, the crux of the matter for most people is the satisfaction of rightful claims and not the question of deservingness. Deservingness is already a settled matter for them – based on rightful claims.

---

[1] From a secular viewpoint, the former has much stronger claims than the latter because as we have seen in Chapter 1, obligees' claims stem from strict legal and moral debts' perfect duties while agape's beneficiaries rely on imperfect duties whose main strength comes from either our shared humanity or the divine precept to love one's neighbor. Moreover, recall Cicero's rule of costless beneficence that can diminish even further the strength of the claims of these imperfect duties.

Adjudication of Last Resort

Incoherence of Agape as Universal Love

Given the phenomenon of rival consumption,[2] agape-justice conflicts mean that there will always be an unmet claim(s). Splitting the limited resources between agape and justice to satisfy at least part of each side's claims does not solve this moral dilemma. After all, justice is about giving people their due. It is precise in its requirements. In fact, even if such a Solomonic solution mitigates the resulting moral injuries on some, it will inflict new harms on those who must bear the resulting opportunity cost.

Nicholas Wolterstorff (2011, 50–61) notes the impossibility of ever satisfying agape's aims. Agape is supposed to be universal – a love for all. However, like most other human choices, it spawns unintended consequences that disadvantage others whose well-being is diminished as a result. However, this goes against what agape is supposed to be – active concern for the well-being of all. The universality-impartiality requirement of agapic love is incompatible with the unaddressed, unmitigated adverse externalities of love. It is agapic love for some but not for those who are hurt as a result. The latter's well-being is reduced. Thus, there is conflict and a violation of agape's universal love because it comes only at the cost of diminishing others' welfare. Note the actual cases we have examined thus far in which the gains of agape's beneficiaries come at the expense of justice's obligees, or vice versa.

Recall the case of the parable of the vineyard owner in Matthew 20:1–16. The vineyard owner wanted to make sure that even the last hires who had worked only an hour had enough for their basic needs for the day. He paid them a full day's wage. Earlier hires who had toiled the whole day felt aggrieved because of the resulting wage compression. For them, it was a violation of distributive justice's due proportion – equal pay for equal work.[3] This is an example of a disexternality of agape.

---

[2] Rival consumption means that consumption of a good by one person leaves that much less for others. These are goods or services that cannot be enjoyed simultaneously by more than one person. An example of a good or service not subject to rival consumption is the beacon from a lighthouse.

[3] Commenting on Aristotle's *Nichomachean Ethics*, St. Thomas (1964, V 4.935) observes "[Q]uarrels and complaints arise as if justice had been neglected because, either persons who are equal do not receive equal shares, for example, if laborers are paid wages for doing an unequal amount of work, or are paid unequal wages for doing an equal amount of work. So then it is evident that the mean of distributive justice is taken according to a certain relationship of proportions."

These disexternalities should not preclude the practice of agape. Two considerations present themselves. First, we can make sure that those affected by agape's disexternalities are the people who can bear the cost. In effect, agape redistributes burdens and benefits across the community. This is unavoidable whenever we deal with socioeconomic life. Anything that leads to opportunity costs necessarily produces disexternalities. Agape's quest for impartiality and universality simply runs up against the need to allocate as part of human nature.

Second, there is a solution to this seeming incoherence of universal-impartial agape. The key to resolving this conundrum lies in the hands of those who bear the cost of agape's disexternalities – justice's obligees. Those who hold strong legal and moral claims can voluntarily and generously choose to forego their claim-rights in favor of those who have none – agape's beneficiaries. Such munificence dissolves the competing claims of agape and justice.

Attending to Agape's Disexternalities

Stage #1 and Gift #1: The Foregone Claims

A possible solution to intractable agape-justice conflicts is for *the obligees themselves to forego their strong rightful claims in favor of beneficiaries of agape who have no legal claims at all, except for an appeal to a shared humanity.* Obligees do so out of benevolence for their fellow humans or out of a desire to promote the good of the community. Agape is about giving that which is not owed (Schlag 2012, 96). Had the United States, the EU, and India shared scarce lifesaving PPE and vaccines during the deadly early phase of the Covid pandemic despite their own needs and the perils they faced, they would have been excellent examples of obligees forgoing their rightful legal claims for the sake of others who have far weaker claims or perhaps even none at all. They would have been models of what supererogation is all about. Such an act is what this chapter examines.

In generously foregoing their rightful claims, obligees disentangle the Gordian knot of many agape-justice conflicts. In doing so, no claims of justice are violated. The erstwhile rights holders, former obligees now turned donors-benefactors themselves, grow in virtue and move a step closer to natural excellence. At the very least, their generous act moves them toward the acquired virtues of justice and charity – justice because liberality is a potential part of justice and charity because benevolence and beneficence are exterior acts of charity.

There is a gradation to obligees' foregoing their rightful claims. The following sliding scale shows the varying degrees of self-emptying (*kenosis*) or beneficence in increasing order of cost to self:

- Risk – putting oneself at risk for the well-being of others
- Self-limitation – foregoing/giving up prerogatives due to self in favor of others
- Self-giving – some measure of self-determination is given up as well (in addition to self-limitation) for the sake of others or some good
- Self-sacrifice – the self is actually lost for some good or for the sake of others
- Self-annihilation – the loss incurred is for no *telos* or end at all (Coakley 2001, 203; Lippit 2009, 130–131)

Obviously, what is called for is not self-annihilation. The goal is the well-being of the beneficiaries of one's *kenosis*, from simple risk-sharing, to foregoing prerogatives (self-limitation), to giving up substance or diminishing self-determination (self-giving), to the loss of one's own vital interest (self-sacrifice).

Transcending Oneself   Skeptics may see such generosity as far-fetched or unrealistic and unlikely given human woundedness. However, we should remember that people transcend themselves all the time in their daily interactions with one another. Even satisfying the demands of justice itself entails having to transcend oneself – to give to others what is their due over and above one's own preference and benefit.[4]

> ... the ability to adjust or adapt oneself to the universe and to society by making claims and discharging duties to others. This is a question of discerning and choosing what is proportionately due to the other, a question of *being disposed to valuing the other over my own particular pleasure. In this sense, the virtue of justice helps Aquinas articulate the shift from self to other in human moral and spiritual development.* (Mongeau 2013, 294, emphasis added)

In other words, people are used to having to transcend themselves in satisfying the demands of justice and in dealing with others. They can do so once again, but this time to satisfy the claims of agape. Obligees transcend themselves in foregoing what is rightfully due to them in favor of those

---

[4] Thus, transcending oneself is needed for the entirety of our continuum of obligatoriness in Table 1.2, from legal debt to moral debt to the complete gift of supererogation.

who have no rightful claims at all or who have much weaker claims.[5] This is in the realm of the possible despite critics' skepticism. Of course, transcending oneself in justice and transcending oneself in agape entail differing degrees of sacrifice. Supererogation involves loss or hardship for the self because of the shift in focus from oneself to others. Despite the losses and hardships it imposes, supererogation is nevertheless much more common than most people think.

Viewed within the continuum of claims in Table 1.2, these generous obligees move from the left-hand end (legal due) all the way to the right-hand end of the spectrum, the realm of supererogation. In foregoing their strong legal claims in favor of those who have none, they advance the good of the whole community, thus, also satisfying the demands of general-legal justice. The strength of the rightful claims they forego highlights the degree of their supererogation.

Justice argues. In fact, justice is argumentative by nature. In contrast, "love does not argue" (1 Cor 13:5). Love is accommodating and walks the extra mile (Mt 5:38–47). Justice operates by the logic of equivalence and reciprocity. In contrast, love operates by the logic of superabundant gift. It is given not because it is deserved by the object-recipient but out of the sheer goodness of the lover. Love is given for the benefit of the object and not the lover, as we see in Luke 6:32–34 (Ricoeur 1995, 29). Love underwrites "the costs of justice and benevolence" (McClure 2003, 24). Obligees enter the realm of agape from the realm of justice as they forego their rightful claims as a way of resolving agape-justice conflicts.

Stage #2 and Gift #2: Taking Responsibility for Strangers' Well-being
Generally, to provide assistance is to take on new responsibilities beyond the initial help provided. There is often need to ensure that the help really gets through or that the intended recipient does indeed receive the assistance or is able to maximize it to the fullest. These follow-on responsibilities that we undertake are common in life (Herman 2001, 231).

Similarly, obligees can do more than just forego their rightful claims. They can go further in taking responsibility for their beneficiaries' well-being. But why? Kant's categorical imperative invites us to act in such a way that the principle of our action can be generalized for everyone else.

---

[5] For example, using Herman's (2001) distinctions, the claims of agape are merely secondary, inherited obligations compared to the primary obligations of the claims of justice. These secondary obligations are less stringent. This only goes to underscore and widen even further the disparity in the strength of the claims of agape and justice. In foregoing their rights-claims, obligees are thus much more sacrificial and heroic in their action.

Humans naturally desire that others come to their aid in their moment of need. If I were, for example, to refuse to aid someone in need, and if my action can indeed be generalized as a universal permissive law for everyone else to follow, then I should not expect others or anyone to come to my help in my own moment of need. Thus, there is a universal "maxim of common interest, of beneficence toward those in need … just because they are to be considered fellow … rational beings with needs, united by nature in one dwelling place so that they can help one another" (Kant 1991, *Metaphysics, Doctrine of Virtue*, Part II, Ch I, Sect I, #25). In other words, for Kant, obligees can heed this universal maxim of mutual beneficence. Obligees forego their rightful claims by acknowledging their duty to respect and aid others (#25).

In contrast, Harry Frankfurt (1998) argues that there is no duty or moral obligation in love because love acts with spontaneity and alacrity for the good of the beloved for his/her/its own sake. Love's action is not mediated by any exercise in inferring requirements or duties. Such spontaneous acts of love are constitutive of what it is to be a person. Consider the difference between duty and love for the one who gives to the poor.

The one who gives out of duty is motivated by a moral obligation. In contrast, one who gives out of love desires to improve the well-being of the needy person, for the sake of the needy person alone. The reason for giving is the needy person herself/himself, plain and simple. Thus, when obligees forego their rightful claims, they merely manifest an even more profound act – moral commitment to the well-being of their erstwhile competition – agape's beneficiaries. (Recall that justice's obligees and agape's beneficiaries compete for the same resources in agape-justice conflicts.)

However, there is more. Obligees will often find that they are invited to forego their rightful claims, not once, but repeatedly. Their self-limitation or self-giving, or even self-sacrifice may in fact not be a one-time act of generosity, but an ongoing or repeated exercise by the nature of the social problem, which is what we find in many of the actual cases we bring up in this study. Agape asks for more than just a one-time concession or for forgoing one's rightful claims only on a single occasion. Such agapic acts would most likely call for follow-up benefactions or even become a regular "obligation" that one voluntarily embraces. (Consider, for example, the need for ongoing work to help women in Afghanistan.)

> [B]oth Kierkegaard and Levinas link one's giving in love to one's indebtedness and *one's obligation to give again*, no matter if one receives anything in return or not. Thus, the very gift of love requires sacrifice – sacrifice in the

sense *of giving-up* one's expectation of reciprocity (though not necessarily one's hope for it) and *one's freedom from obligation*. Without this renunciation, love would be selfish. (Welz 2008, 257, emphasis added)

Locating this in the abovementioned sliding scale, obligees move from self-limitation (foregoing their rightful claims) to self-giving (giving up some of their self-determination in being bound voluntarily by new follow-on obligations). Note how the initial act of foregoing rightful claims becomes even more sacrificial because that initial act of sacrifice brings up the expectation of further similar acts going forward. Indeed, both Kierkegaard and Levinas have a point in their observation that people give up part of their self-determination (e.g., freedom from obligation) in taking on additional responsibility for the well-being of beneficiaries. They become encumbrances on obligees' freedom of action.

As obligees keep giving and living up to their new obligations without thought of return but only the good of the recipients, they grow ever more profoundly in agape. Such chronic giving may turn out to be a boon rather than a loss. Thus, there is something to be said about continually expanding people's circle of love and responsibility and making habitual their willingness to forego their rightful claims in favor of promoting the well-being of the distant and the stranger who are in need (Chapter 6).

Stage #3 and Gift #3: Growth in Interpersonal Relationship
The obligees' foregoing their rightful claims turns out to be three gifts altogether. The third gift entails the gift of an ongoing relationship as equals. Jeffrey Tillman (2008, 548–49) citing Outka (1996, 35) differentiates altruism from agape. On the one hand, altruism is exclusively concerned with the well-being of others and not one's own. It is prioritizing and giving greater weight to other's well-being than oneself. On the other hand, agape balances concern for the well-being of both others and oneself. The self expects reciprocity, but even if it is not given, the action for others' well-being will still be pursued. In other words, reciprocity is expected but it is not a necessary condition for one to give agape.

What is essential to point out from Tillman's distinction is the expected reciprocity in agape. *The expectation of reciprocity implies an expectation of a relationship as equals. Reciprocity implies a desire for an ongoing relationship.* There would be no expectation of reciprocity at all if the donor-benefactor did not seek or was not interested in a relationship. It would have been a straightforward philanthropy – unidirectional in the giving. It would have been an act of almsgiving and nothing more than that. However, this is not so when there is an expectation of reciprocity.

This mutuality in giving implies a much more profound relationship as an equal, as an I-Thou, compared to altruism's benefactor-beneficiary relationship.[6]

Obligees' act of foregoing their rightful claims is not altruism but agape. Taking responsibility for others' well-being, especially if they have no rightful claims or are strangers, bespeaks of an openness to a more profound relationship between benefactors and beneficiaries. Owens (2012) observes how obligations and relationships are obverse images. We can infer one from the other. Love and justice as obligations imply underlying relationships. By their demands, we can infer the characteristic features of their constitutive relationships. For example, commutative justice in the marketplace reflects an underlying contractual relationship. Christianity's love of neighbor reflects an underlying relationship as a fellow child of God in God's one family. Josef Pieper (1990, 58) notes that, "every moral obligation has a personal character, the character of the commitment to the person to whom I am under an obligation."

There is a difference in the depth and profundity of the moral commitment to the object depending on whether it stems from a duty of justice or of love. As we have seen earlier, agape is animated by a moral commitment to the well-being of the beloved, the object of one's love. In contrast, justice is undergirded by duty – to give to the obligee what I as obligor owe him or her.

Kant underscores another reason for why beneficence must bloom into an interpersonal relationship as equals between the benefactor and the beneficiary. He is keenly aware that beneficence can paradoxically put their recipients in an awkward position of feeling shamed and humiliated in having to be on the receiving end of a benefaction.

> [W]e are under obligation to help a poor man; but since the favor we do implies that his well-being depends on our generosity, and this humbles him, it is our duty to behave as if our help is either merely what is due him or but a slight service of love, and to spare him humiliation and maintain his respect for himself. (Kant 1991, *Metaphysics, Doctrine of Virtue*, Part II, Ch I, Sect I, #23)

Later, Kant suggests once again that benefactors should make light of their benefaction as a duty that they were merely exercising. He goes even further to suggest that the benefaction could be done in secret (#31). All this is to mitigate the shame of recipients. Indeed, most people derive their

---

[6] Recall also the Greco-Roman patron-client relationships in which benefactions were given to promote the benefactor's interests and not the beneficiaries.

self-respect from being able to provide for themselves and their dependents. During the Covid-19 lockdown, people were apologetic and in fact were ashamed to have to go to food banks to request for assistance. Not surprisingly, Kant proposes that donors minimize their benefaction by citing it as their collective duty, as an integral part of their ongoing relationship. It softens the pain and the shame of the beneficiaries.

In sum, a "last resort" adjudication of agape-justice conflicts is for justice's obligees to forego their rightful claims in favor of those who have none, agape's beneficiaries. In practical terms, this proposed "last resort" adjudication entails three stages, each representing a gift.

Gift #1: Obligees foregoing their rightful claims in favor of beneficiaries who have no legal claim(s) at all.

Gift #2: Obligees take responsibility for the well-being of their beneficiaries by foregoing their rightful claims repeatedly or on an ongoing basis.

Gift #3: Obligees accept beneficiaries as equals in the resulting relationship they forge with them.

Real-World Applications

Besides what could have been self-sacrificial giving had the United States, the EU, and India shared their scarce lifesaving vaccines and N95 masks with other countries during the deadly early phase of the pandemic, there are many other occasions for varying degrees of self-giving. Consider the following cases.

Tied-In Aid

Foreign aid is an important venue for poverty alleviation for poor developing countries. Such aid brings in much-needed foreign exchange, technical know-how, capital, managerial talent, concessional loans, grants, and economic expertise and advice, among many other benefits. It can also come in the form of in-kind aid. It is a vital link for poor developing countries to the larger global economy.

Foreign economic assistance often comes in the form of tied-in aid in which the grants, concessional loans, or gifts must be spent in the donor country. Tied-in aid has many advantages for the donor country. It creates a demand for its own goods and services. Government money eventually finds its way to benefit the donor economy. More importantly, it translates to domestic jobs. Legislators are much more likely to approve such aid because of its benefits to their domestic economy and perhaps even their local constituents. Donors can better monitor and ensure that such assistance is used properly and not merely stolen or dissipated in kickbacks or other forms of bribery if left in the hands of bureaucrats in the receiving countries. Indeed, tied-in aid has many practical and economic advantages.

Unfortunately, tied-in aid also comes with significant problems, more so for the recipient countries. The goods and services and their underlying technology may not be appropriate for the local conditions of the receiving country.[7] Moreover, these goods and services may cost much more than if these had been bought from other countries. Similarly, the servicing, maintenance, and spare parts to keep the equipment working eventually cost more when purchased from the donor countries compared to alternative sources, thereby exacerbating the chronic balance of payments deficits of the recipient country in future years. Many tied-in aid also require the use of labor from the donor country. Consequently, workers in the recipient countries miss the chance to develop their skills through the jobs that these projects could have provided.

In the United States, there have been long-standing campaigns to switch out of tied-in aid. Take the case of PL 480 and food aid. This is ideal for the country because surplus grain is purchased by the Federal government as a way of mopping up surplus, preventing volatility in farm prices, and stabilizing the income of its domestic farmers. The nation then uses such surplus grain as aid in many parts of the world. It is a win-win proposition in that US farmers gain from foreign aid funds, even as poor developing countries also benefit.

Many have observed that PL 480 is not the ideal aid from the point of view of the recipient country for many reasons. Giving such aid in cash is much better because the food could have been bought locally or from nearby poor countries, thereby pumping much needed income into the local economy or the surrounding region. Furthermore, the cost of transporting the in-kind aid could have been used instead to augment the assistance provided to the poor country. Moreover, in not having to transport the in-kind aid from the United States, assistance could reach the poor countries much faster. From the point of view of compassion and agape, it makes more sense to provide cash rather than in-kind aid. However, from

---

[7] For example, we have farm tractors with heated cabs sent to tropical poor countries.

the viewpoint of US farmers, taxpayers, and businesses, they would appeal to distributive justice in arguing that US-taxpayer funds should be used in such a way as to benefit the local US economy and its citizens as well.

In this case, when domestic constituents, local communities, and companies (the obligees) forgo their right to benefit from the aid sent overseas, they advance the well-being of many other additional beneficiaries in the poor developing regions who receive such aid. By freeing such tied-in aid, they get "a much bigger bang for the buck," so to speak. It is a de facto increase in the size and perhaps even the quality of the assistance provided. In the end, this is a sensitive political decision since change will have to be effected through legislation or through the implementing protocols of the agencies in charge, such as the US State Department. It all depends on the degree to which agape animates these decision makers and their constituents.

Gravity Payment

The conflict between the vineyard owner and the early hires in the parable of Matthew 20:1–16 turns out to be more than just a pedagogical tool. It happens in real life. Take the case of Gravity Payments.

In 2015, Dan Price, founder and CEO of Gravity Payments, sacrificed his own take-home pay in order raise the minimum annual pay of the lowest paid workers in his firm to $70,000 out of concern for their well-being. A quarter of the employees saw their salaries double. To fund this, he cut his million-dollar annual salary to $70,000 and used part of the company's profits. By any reasonable measure, Dan Price's action was supererogatory because even if the living wage were truly at $70,000 a year, he could not be expected to solve this societal problem singlehandedly. His action was clearly in line with the duty of compassion.

Two senior staff resigned over what they thought was an injustice. One observed, "[Dan Price] gave raises to people who have the least skills and are the least equipped to do the job, and the ones who were taking on the most didn't get much of a bump." Another complained, "Now the people who were just clocking in and out were making the same as me .... It shackles high performers to less motivated team members" (Cohen 2015).

The two senior staff who resigned had a point. Since the pay raise was not proportionate across all the wage levels, Dan Price caused a wage compression. Staff who had served for more years in the company and who have far more experience, better skills, and much more significant contributions to the firm's operations were now worth less relative to the new or entry-level hires with less skills, experience, and contribution. Mid-level staff took years of effort and hard work to reach the pay level of those benefiting from Mr. Price's largesse. This goes against distributive justice (pay according to contribution or merit), and it also goes against commutative justice (equal exchange in compensation for the services rendered). Long-time employees had reason to feel aggrieved in what they perceived was an injustice inflicted on them by Dan Price's generous action. There is an opportunity here for senior staff to forego their claims for the sake of agape.

Remuneration Based on Need or Contribution

Gravity Payments reminds us of a long-standing question when it comes to workers' compensation. There is conflict in the choice of criterion for worker compensation between need, on the one hand, and merit/contribution, on the other hand. One reason given for why women have historically been paid less than men doing the same work dates back to the days when the latter were deemed to be the primary breadwinners for their families. The male-breadwinner norm was about providing the male worker sufficient wages as to be able to provide for his family without the wife and children having to work (Seccombe 1986). Working women were often seen merely as "second incomes" for the family. This was a case in which need trumped contribution or merit. The attentiveness to need is very much along the lines of the duty of humanity, even as it is merely one of the many possible criteria for distributive justice. Need as a criterion of distributive justice is affirmed, reinforced, and consistent with agape's own claims. Today, such gender pay disparity is being addressed. Besides, with a proliferation of single-headed households, people can no longer assume that women are merely second-income earners in the family. In many cases, they are the primary breadwinners.

Nevertheless, the tension between compensation according to need versus pay according to merit/contribution is still very much with us. Take the case of healthcare insurance as part of a compensation package. Many companies include workers' families in the health insurance premium that companies bear. In addition, we have a second-order effect in that the premium rises because of the much heavier use of the health insurance by workers' family members. In effect, these companies are paying more benefits per hour of similar work to married workers than to those who are single. The rationale for this, of course, is compensation according to need. Again, this is the compassionate route to take. It is consistent with the duty of humanity. Nevertheless, it goes against commutative justice or even distributive justice if the basis were merit/contribution. It violates the principle of equal pay for equal work, which most people use as a standard for what is fair and just.

Such differential compensation according to need is not limited to health insurance. Take the case of tuition remission as a long-standing benefit from many colleges and universities. Children of their faculty and staff may matriculate for free at the colleges or universities where their parents work. In some cases, there is an equivalent sum provided or an exchange arrangement with other colleges/universities. In effect, married faculty and staff with children get more benefits compared to their single co-workers or co-workers who are childless. In this case, we once again have a disparity in compensation.[8] This, too, is an opportunity for people to forego their grievances and claims for the sake of agape.

Family Reunification or Skill-Based Immigration?

Canada is much more open to receiving immigrants compared to other nations when measured as a proportion of its population. However, migrants with special skills that will benefit the country are given preference in its skill-based immigration. Australia also uses skills as a criterion in selecting migrants into the country. In contrast, migration to the United States is largely based on family reunification. Earlier migrants petition to have members of their immediate families reunite with them in the country. There have been debates and attempts to change US immigration policy to favor a more skill-based criterion, but people who argue that family reunification is a much more humane approach have opposed these (Hesse 2018).

From a purely transactional and economic approach, a skill-based migration, in theory, provides more economic benefits for the host country. The receiving country gets all the benefits of a well-developed pool of skills without having to incur investments and spending to develop these. This is not even to mention the training time saved. It is essentially a windfall for the receiving country.[9] In contrast, critics have complained that a

[8] Some will see this as an agape-justice conflict, while others will view it as an intra-justice conflict (need vs contribution/merit as criterion of distributive justice).
[9] Such brain drain is not a complete loss for the sending country because global remittances are a major source of income for them. There are also spillover effects of capital, ideas, and best practices eventually making their way back to the sending countries.

family-reunification approach does not necessarily guarantee that the new migrants will have the skills most appropriate for the host countries. Some would even go so far as to claim that they are a drain on the receiving country's social safety net.

Agape would look more favorably on a family-reunification approach while distributive and commutative justice would side with a skill-based criterion because of the clear and immediate economic benefits it confers on the local economy and its citizens. Mixing the two will most probably be presented by most as a happy compromise in being humane while being just at the same time. Nevertheless, it will still redound to the question of whether the host country will be more humane or more just in the way it receives new migrants. There will still be an opportunity cost. This may yet be an occasion to forego the claims of justice in favor of agape by adopting a family reunification approach.

Public Charge Rule

In the United States, Canada, Australia, and New Zealand, a requirement of permanent residency or citizenship is that the migrant not end up as a burden to the state. General-legal and distributive justice require that a new migrant not impose an additional cost on everyone else but provide for his/her own upkeep. Most people consider this to be fair. The threshold for maximum allowable state support before being considered an undue public charge is important because it most likely will disqualify families with a disabled child or those who are disabled. Canada rejected 361 cases annually on average from 2013 to 2016 because of the excessive burdens put on the state as a public charge. In 2018, the threshold was raised threefold (Leary 2018).

Australia and New Zealand routinely reject long-term immigrant visa applicants who pose significant healthcare cost to the taxpayer because of their pre-existing medical condition, including autism, intellectual disability, obesity, multiple sclerosis, and until October 2021, those who tested positive for H.I.V. As of 2022, Australia sets this cost limit at $32,000 and New Zealand at $45,000 over five years. Around 1,600 people are affected by these policies every year (Frost 2022). In contrast, countries in the European Union are legally required to provide health care to migrants with disabilities.

Where to set the threshold for what constitutes an undue public charge falls within the tension between agape and justice. Such threshold could be made as generous or as restrictive as legislators make them to be. To raise the threshold for such cost containment in public-charge cases is to forego the rightful claims of justice for fiscal discipline in the use of taxpayer funds in favor of agape.

Job-Sharing Schemes

During the 2008 Great Recession and the 2020 pandemic lockdown, job-sharing schemes were devised to spread the few remaining jobs to as many people as possible. Instead of laying off people according to a last in-first out rule, some workers opted to have their hours trimmed instead of the firm laying off their peers (Leonard 2018). During the pandemic when many lost their employment, new jobs were suddenly available from PPE manufacturers. Workers shared their hours with their neighbors, friends, and relatives so that they, too, could have some income to bring home for their expenses during the lockdown. The US Census estimates that between 11 to 13 million Americans gave or planned to give their stimulus check in 2020 to charity or to someone in greater need. An estimated 6 to 7.5 percent of stimulus check recipients donated their money to others (Albrecht 2021). All these are examples of people foregoing their rightful claims in the name of agape and their concern for the well-being of their needier neighbors.

Living Wage versus Employment Generation

There is no consensus regarding the empirical evidence on whether minimum wages lead to job losses. Since a living wage (also called a just wage) is multiple times more than a minimum wage, the trade-off between high pay and job creation is even more pronounced. Should society or the business sector prioritize a living wage for a select few or job creation for more people but at a pay less than a living wage? This may present an opportunity in some cases for people to forego a living wage in favor of more job creation for the sake of more people getting employed.

Labor-Saving or Labor-Intensive Technology

In setting up a new plant in a poor developing country, it is possible to employ technology more appropriate for advanced countries in which equipment is labor-saving and highly technical. The few workers hired earn more than a living wage, in addition to the skills, training, and experience they get. An alternative model, however, is to use the most basic technology that employs more labor, but at a much lower skill level and at a much lower pay. The question becomes which is a better approach, especially in a poor developing country in dire need of jobs. The easier route for management is to use labor-saving technology. Personnel management becomes much simpler. It also often maximizes shareholders' returns. In contrast, agape would support the job-creation route, even if it generates many more labor-management headaches, quality-control problems, and higher cost for the firm.

Special Drawing Rights (SDRs)

The International Monetary Fund (IMF) increased Special Drawing Rights (SDRs)[10] by $650 billion effective August 23, 2021 in order to assist nations with their expenditures on Covid-19 mitigation. However, because these are allocated according to countries' subscription to the bank, most of the new SDRs went to wealthy nations. In fact, low-income countries received only 3 percent, while middle-income nations collected only 30 percent (Zafar et al. 2021). Nevertheless, the expectation in issuing such new SDRs was that wealthy countries would forego their share in favor of poor developing nations with greater needs and uses for these funds. As of April 2022, the IMF was still in the process of establishing a Resilience and Sustainability Trust that will facilitate wealthy countries' use of their new SDRs in assisting poor nations recover from the Covid pandemic (International Monetary Fund 2022).

Note the common feature in all these cases. First, they are instances of agape-justice conflicts. Second, there are ways of balancing the competing claims in a graduated way, that is, in a non-binary fashion of all or nothing (0,1). Third, one possible solution is the "last resort" proposal of this chapter. When all else fails, obligees might be willing to forego voluntarily their rightful claims in favor of those with weaker or no claims at all. This is always a possible solution. It is a "last resort" solution that has varying degrees of commitment, from simple risk-sharing, all the way to a self-sacrificial giving. Undoubtedly, we need mutual goodwill if this proposed solution is to be heeded at all. Let us now examine the consequences of this proposed "last resort" adjudication.

---

[10] Special Drawing Rights (SDRs) are additional international reserve assets created in 1969 by the IMF to supplement its member nations' foreign exchange reserves.

Profound Growth in Virtue and Natural Excellence

Personal Impact: Growth in Virtue

Aristotle highlights the importance and role of virtues in human life in his *Nicomachean Ethics*. Virtues make for balance in the character of people. After all, virtues are the mean between the extremes of deficiency and excess. For example, the virtue of fortitude is the mean between cowardice and foolhardiness. Besides being constitutive of people's character, virtues are instrumental in helping people reach their *telos* (end).

Virtues and their antithesis (vices) are formed over time through people's habitual choices. People are not born with fully formed personalities. Instead, they have a lifetime of growth ahead of them. Their moral choices and actions come back and define their character and personality. Repeated moral choices and actions are formative of these virtues or vices. People who are in the habit of being selfish will eventually suddenly find that it is second nature to them to be self-centered in what they do. Being selfish becomes deeply ingrained in their character, personality, and self-identity because of their repeated selfish acts and maltreatment of others in the past and present. Of course, it is the same dynamic for virtues. Consequently, these are called acquired virtues. People develop them largely through their own efforts.

Most people strive to be the best of who they can be. This means putting their skills, talents, and all their other personal and material assets to their best uses. If they succeed in this lofty goal, they become a credit to their community. They become a model for emulation. People recognize and acknowledge excellence in their midst. Natural excellence is about being the best that one can be as a human person. Acquired virtues are the tangible manifestation of such natural excellence. More than that, however, these acquired virtues are in fact also the building blocks in reaching such natural excellence. Acquired virtue is both a cause and an effect of natural excellence.

Adversity and self-sacrifice are important catalysts to a much more profound growth in these acquired virtues. The sustained effort and the deep commitment needed in the face of great hardship or challenge lead to an even more intense advancement in virtue than any ordinary action could generate. What is gained at great cost is not only appreciated better, but it also leaves an even more profound impact on people's character and personality. That which is attained at great personal cost or sacrifice leaves a much more significant reflexive effect on the agent. So it is with self-sacrificial agape. It costs much, but it also leaves the agent with much.

Love's self-emptying paradoxically leads to self-enrichment. The profundity of sacrificial giving is that it is a gift of oneself. The greater the
opportunity cost, the greater is the gift of the self. Claudia Welz (2008, 241)
describes this phenomenon well by reflecting on the insights of Emmanuel
Levinas in *Otherwise Than Being or Beyond Essence:*

> To give means to be for another "despite oneself," interrupting one's being
> for oneself, "to take the bread out of one's own mouth, to nourish the hun-
> ger of another with one's own fasting" (OB 56) [Levinas 1981, 56]. This form
> of giving is an unselfish dis-interestedness that "has the form of a corporeal
> life devoted to expression and to giving" including the possibility of "offer-
> ing, suffering and trauma" (OB 50). *It is giving that is sacrificial – not only
> in the sense that one gives of oneself, lets another participate in one's life and
> liveliness, in one's passions and projects, but also in the sense that one gives away
> from oneself what sustains one's existence. Is it correct to conclude that giving up
> and giving away out of love comes down to giving up and giving away oneself?*
> (Welz 2008, 241, emphasis added)

The opportunity cost of forgoing one's rightful claims is real, and it can
be sizeable. Nevertheless, this giving of oneself should not be viewed as a
diminution of oneself. In fact, far from it, this self-emptying turns out to
be paradoxically an augmentation of oneself.

> The idea of love as self-sacrifice suggests that giving is a self-diminishment
> or even self-destruction, while the idea of love as gift suggests that giving is
> a self-fulfillment that edifies the self: *it receives in giving. Through the abun-
> dance of the gift, it receives new energy to give of itself and to give up something
> else.* Moreover, *giving out of love does not involve purposeful giving-for-the-
> sake-of, but rather the gratuity of a free gift given for nothing.* (Welz 2008, 251,
> emphasis added)

Instead of obligees depleting themselves – whether of their substance or
surplus – in foregoing their claims, they enrich themselves unintentionally
because they receive far more than they have given. This is the pleasantly
surprising outcome of the reflexive dynamic of self-giving.

Justice pertains to right action at this particular place and time. It is
also dependent on rational appetite. Because its task is merely to give
people their due, justice is limited in its scope and in its object. In contrast, love induces the intellectual, rational appetite to seek and promote
that which is good in ourselves and in others, and in the process of such
pursuit, to be transformed in *being morally good* ourselves. Love transforms the subject even more than it changes the object. Supererogation
in the natural realm has a profound reflexive impact in enriching the
subject (in our case, the obligees turned benefactors), in addition to the

object, the beneficiaries. There is a much stronger reflexive impact and dynamic in love than in justice by the nature of the exacting nature of love and the object of its appetitive action. Love has a much broader scope than justice.

Besides, in addition to growing in the virtue of charity, love itself is a gift. "The point is that loving is valuable inherently, and for its own sake. To love is valuable in itself, and not only in virtue of the value of what is loved. Other things being equal, our lives would be worse without it" (Frankfurt 1998, 6). Furthermore, love opens the door to self-knowledge and self-understanding. Love is an enabler. It allows us to accomplish that which is difficult and impossible. It provides motivation, and more importantly, perseverance (cf. 1 Cor 13), which is especially critical in difficult environments and taxing cases that can be discouraging.

Ameliorating Wrongs

Whether they deliberately intend to do so or not, in foregoing their rightful claims, obligees contribute to mitigating the consequences of wrongdoing or other social ills, past and present.

> Christian love as equal-regard and mutuality *requires the Christian to sacrifice, go the extra mile, and reach out in an attempt to bring the relationship back to a place of equal-regard, mutuality, and genuine community.* Janssens writes, "After the model of God's love in Christ who loved us and gave himself up for us, our love is to include self-giving and self-sacrifice as long as we live in a world of conflict and sin. We should love our enemies and persecutors, take the initiative in forgiving, overcome evil with good, and even lay down our life for our friends" (1977, 228). Christians should do this not as an end in itself … but *as an effort to restore and maintain true equal-regard and mutuality.* (Browning 2008, 560–61, emphasis added)

Love entails self-sacrifice. Self-sacrifice is needed to mitigate or counteract a world of sin and violence. In an ideal world, we hope our love will be reciprocated, but not so in a world of sin and violence. In such a case, we sacrifice and continue to love despite the absence of reciprocity. (Recall Tillman's distinction between altruism and agape.) In effect, self-sacrifice tries to heal a wounded world. The preceding chapters vividly illustrate this ameliorative role:

- Self-sacrifice in restoring socioeconomic homeostasis (Chapter 4)
- Self-sacrifice in correcting past wrongs (Chapter 5)

- Self-sacrifice in expanding our circle of kin love to a much wider circle of love that includes the distant, the stranger, and even the undeserving (Chapter 6)
- Self-sacrifice in foregoing our rightful claims for the sake of the needy (this chapter)

Paying Back Social Mortgage

Strictly speaking, obligees relinquishing their rightful claims in favor of the needy is not entirely gratuitous. In terms of strict accounting, these obligees are merely returning to society some of the benefits that they themselves had drawn from the community. Unlike the heuristic perfectly competitive markets of perfect knowledge and perfect mobility, markets in practice are fraught with incomplete and inaccurate pricing. Ownership externalities are the phenomena whereby markets are unable to provide an accurate account of true costs and contributions. Consequently, market participants are either paying or receiving too much or too little in their transactions. Underpayment implies a social mortgage that beneficiaries owe to the community. For example, market participants do not pay the full cost, if they even pay at all, of what it takes to put up a functional marketplace. After all, there are no entry fees to be able to participate in the marketplace.

Take the case of Milton Friedman's illustration of the power of markets in a pencil. One could purchase a pencil for mere pennies despite the enormous amount of work and coordination that goes into making a pencil.[11] The costs associated with setting up a marketplace for pencils randomly fall on people or preceding generations who had already paid for them (e.g., existing institutions, infrastructure). The same is true for all the goods and services that are conveniently at our fingertips with the click of a mouse. Market participants do not have to pay Adam Smith's "invisible hand" for this amazing service. They simply inherit a functional system that had been built over multiple generations which kept refining and adopting best marketplace practices. We are literally standing on the shoulders of these earlier market participants. This bequest is aptly called a social mortgage. Thus, obligees are simply "paying forward" what they themselves had received free from society from such social mortgage. After all, the community had nurtured and educated these obligees and provided them

---

[11] "Milton Friedman – Lesson of the Pencil." www.youtube.com/watch?v=4ERbC7JyCfU last accessed February 2, 2022.

with all that they need for survival, growth, and development. Obligees should not begrudge having to forego their rightful claims for the sake of agape. They themselves have reaped gratuitous benefits from society and earlier generations.

Theological Foundations

Obligees' generosity in foregoing their strong legal and moral claims in favor of those who have much weaker claims – agape's beneficiaries – finds much resonance and support in Judeo-Christian thought and praxis. A secular public square can nonetheless still benefit from Sacred Scriptures by reading them as literature rather than as Revelation. Read and viewed as literature, they provide useful insights and ideals, just as people still draw inspiration today from the heroes and gods of the Greek classics. After all, both the Hebrew Scriptures and the New Testament are said to be an account of human hopes, dreams, successes, brokenness, and failures. They are the story of human life.

Hebrew Scriptures

Hebrew Scriptures explain why there is reason for self-limitation and self-giving. Biblical Israel provides many instances of benevolent acts of foregoing one's rightful claims. Consider the following stipulations from the Mosaic laws. Given an ancient economy of scarcity, it is not surprising that high interest rates were charged for loans of grain (33 1/3 percent) or money (20 percent). These are average rates. They may not seem high by modern standards, but not so for the ancient economy of subsistence living. There are even records from that era that show interest rates going as high as 200 percent. In Biblical Israel, they were not to charge each other any interest at all (Ex 22:24–25; Dt 23:19–20). Moreover, they were to write off debt after six years. Furthermore, lenders were restricted in the collateral that they may take from debtors (Dt 24:6, 10–13). In addition to all these, the Chosen People had the moral obligation to lend to those who ask them, even as the year of debt forgiveness approached or even as they would much rather not lend at all to avoid all these restrictions.

It is a similar dynamic when it comes to the enslavement of people. Masters were to release the enslaved after six years of service. Moreover, masters were supposed to weight them down with provisions at the time of their emancipation. They were not to be released empty-handed (Dt 15:12–18). We see these generous practices during the time of harvest as well. The poor were allowed to glean on the land. In fact, the law instructed land-owners not to be thorough in harvesting their vines, orchards, and fields and to leave some for the benefit of those who will be gleaning so that they too could have their fill (Lev 19:9–10). Moreover, the law permitted people to "scrump" (Dt 23:24–25). For the sabbatical years, any yield from the land went to the poor, not the landowners. At the Jubilee Year, landown-ers were to return land to their original ancestral owners, in addition to releasing all the enslaved and forgiving debt (Lev 25).

In all these cases, observe that the laws were in effect requiring lenders, masters, and landowners to forego their legal claims in favor of those who would have little to no claim at all to the benefactions that they receive. The Mosaic laws acknowledged the exacting nature of these laws. Nevertheless, these laws explain why God could ask them to forego their own claims as a matter of reciprocity from earlier divine favors.

> 39 If any who are dependent on you become so impoverished that they sell themselves to you, you shall not make them serve as slaves. 40 They shall remain with you as hired or bound laborers. They shall serve with you until the year of the jubilee. 41 Then they and their children with them shall be free from your authority; they shall go back to their own family and return to their ancestral property. 42 *For they are my servants, whom I brought out of the land of Egypt; they shall not be sold as slaves are sold. 43 You shall not rule over them with harshness, but shall fear your God.* (Lev 25:12–15, emphasis added)

The law reminds the Israelites that God was merely asking them to extend to each other the same favors that they themselves had received in their own moment of need. Viewed in terms of the relationship between God and the Chosen People, this may in fact be a demand of commuta-tive justice – God's act of kindness requited in an act of kindness to fellow humans. However, viewed at the level of human-to-human relationships, the Chosen People did not have any legal claims for such benefactions from each other, except for the Golden Rule.

In addition, there is another justification for such self-limitation and self-giving in the Hebrew Scriptures. H. Eberhard von Waldow (1970) observes that many of the Mosaic laws on releasing the enslaved, debt forgiveness, and others were in fact nomadic practices that were codified into law when the Chosen People finally transitioned into settled agricul-ture from their itinerant pastoral life. Given the harsh conditions of the ancient world, mutual assistance was a rational strategy for mutual sur-vival. Thus, in lending generously to a distressed neighbor today without any interest at all, the lender may also expect to receive the same favor in the future from neighbors. In other words, the Chosen People were each other's safety net. Thus, there is an obligatory element to such acts of self-limitation and even of self-giving.[12] Recall from Table 1.2 how these acts fall under the category of relational moral debts – obligations from our bonds and ties and the community's expectations and praxis.

We find yet another rationale for self-limitation and self-giving from the entirety of the Old Testament. The Chosen People were said to view the God of Abraham, Isaac, and Jacob as a "God of radical freedom and fidelity" (Birch 1991). A "God of freedom" – because God could do anything God pleased, even going so far as to take land from many nations to give it to God's Chosen People. A "God of Radical Fidelity" – because despite Biblical Israel's repeated egregious violations of the Covenant, God never walked away from the Covenant, but was always there for the Chosen People – the child of God's womb (Is 49:14–15). Biblical Israel keenly felt and experienced how God was always there for them to lavish further kindness on them despite God having every right to walk away from the Covenant on so many occasions. We find this in the prophetic books, particularly in Hosea, Amos, and Micah. God never invoked God's rights from the Covenant in response to Biblical Israel's wanton infidelities, but nurtured and healed her instead (e.g., Jer 30). Having been a beneficiary of such kindness, it was now their turn to be generous to others.

These motivations from the Old Testament extend to our own day and age, especially for people of the Abrahamic faiths. At the level of Divine-human relationships, acts of self-limitation and self-giving (such as foregoing one's rightful claims in favor of those who have none) can be inspired by the thought that we are merely extending to others God's graces that we ourselves had received. Thus, God could command humans to love their neighbors. After all, were it not for the grace of God, we would be naught. At the level of human-to-human relationships, however, such acts carry a lesser degree of obligatoriness (general moral debt in Table 1.2).

New Testament

The New Testament also gives similar reasons for acts of mutual self-limitation and self-giving. Matthew 18:21–35 is the famous parable of the unforgiving servant who was punished for not having extended to his fellow servant the same forgiveness that he had received. In sending off his apostles to preach and to heal, Jesus reminds them that freely they had

---

[12] The Golden Rule and Kant's universalizability rule reach the same conclusion.

received, freely they were now to give (Mt 10:5–8). In teaching his disciples
to pray, Jesus asks them to pray to God for forgiveness just as they themselves had forgiven others (Mt 6:12). Reciprocity is a constant theme in the
New Testament:

> 37 Do not judge, and you will not be judged; do not condemn, and you will
> not be condemned. Forgive, and you will be forgiven; 38 give, and it will
> be given to you. A good measure, pressed down, shaken together, running
> over, will be put into your lap; for the measure you give will be the measure
> you get back. (Luke 6:37–38)

In his second letter to the Corinthians, St. Paul urges them to be generous
in the collection he was taking for the poor of Jerusalem so that they in
their own turn might also receive assistance in their own moment of need
(2 Cor 8:13–14). Indeed, we find many reminders in the New Testament
that beneficence is an obligation because we ourselves have been beneficiaries of others' generosity.

Observe that such giving is not merely one of self-limitation (foregoing/
giving up prerogatives due to self in favor of others) but is also of self-
giving (some measure of self-determination is given up as well for the sake
of others or some good).

> 27 But I say to you that listen, Love your enemies, do good to those who
> hate you, 28 bless those who curse you, pray for those who abuse you. 29 If
> anyone strikes you on the cheek, offer the other also; and from anyone who
> takes away your coat do not withhold even your shirt. 30 Give to everyone
> who begs from you; and if anyone takes away your goods, do not ask for
> them again. 31 Do to others as you would have them do to you. (Lk 6:27–31)

In all these cases, we find Jesus asking people to forgo their rightful claims –
retribution after having been slapped; holding on to their property; getting back what others had taken from them. Clearly, this is an invitation
to self-limitation and self-giving. This is in sharp contrast to the Levitical
lex talionis (Lev 24:19–20): "Anyone who maims another shall suffer the
same injury in return: fracture for fracture, eye for eye, tooth for tooth; the
injury inflicted is the injury to be suffered."

However, there is more. Christians are asked to go beyond even self-
giving to self-sacrifice itself (the self is actually lost for some good or for
the sake of others). This is not merely a matter of being the servant of
all, of being the last of all, it is also about laying down one's life so that
others might live. Jesus Christ, whether viewed as a literary hero-ideal by
nonbelievers, or as a great prophet by Islam, or as the Messiah-God by
Christians, presents the paradigm for such self-sacrifice.

⁴ Let each of you look not to your own interests, but to the interests of others.
⁵ Let the same mind be in you that was in Christ Jesus,

> ⁶ who, though he was in the form of God,
>   did not regard equality with God
>   as something to be exploited,
> ⁷ but emptied himself,
>   taking the form of a slave,
>   being born in human likeness.
> And being found in human form,
> ⁸   he humbled himself
>   and became obedient to the point of death—
>   even death on a cross. (Philippians 2:4–8)

Benedict XVI's (2005) *Deus caritas est* succinctly captures the significance of this sacrificial event. Far from demanding just accountability from humans for their repeated infidelities, God's loving forgiveness "turns God against himself, his love against his justice … [S]o great is God's love for man that by becoming man he follows him even into death, and *so reconciles justice and love*" (#10, emphasis added). This is the exemplary instance of foregoing one's strong, rightful claims in favor of those who have no claims at all. Indeed, Jesus had every right to be respected and even be adored in his divinity. Instead, he foregoes such divine prerogative, becomes incarnate, and goes even further to die on the cross. The New Testament goes beyond the Hebrew Scriptures in calling not only for self-limitation or even self-giving but also for self-sacrifice itself. This is Christified agape. "This is my commandment, that you love one another as I have loved you" (John 15:12). "I give you a new commandment, that you love one another. Just as I have loved you, you also should love one another" (John 13:34).

As we have seen earlier, obligees turned benefactors often have to go beyond a one-time act of generosity and to keep repeating such benefactions. Obligees in such cases end up taking responsibility for the well-being of their beneficiaries. Jesus Christ's taking on the sins of humanity on his shoulders – blameless and sinless as he was – typify a voluntarily embraced liability for the sake of others. This is a self-sacrificial gift for the sake of the beloved. Jesus Christ takes responsibility for humanity's sins by shouldering the liability of paying for the damages of such sins and preventing future harms. (This is particularly true for past wrongs and for rectifying sinful social structures.) Jesus' action takes on additional heroism since he did not contribute to bringing about such liability through moral failure.

Love is about exceeding the demands of justice: "The teaching of Jesus and of the Gospels is rather to call people *to participate now in a new order in which love both excludes and exceeds the demands of justice*" (Mealand 1980, 98, emphasis added). St. Paul is also an example of an obligee turned benefactor. By apostolic right, he could have asked material support from the faith communities he was serving. Instead, he worked as a tentmaker to support himself in order not to burden the various church communities (1 Cor 9:1–19; Acts 18:3).

Divine agape is the model for human agape (*imitatio Dei* and *imitatio Christi*) (Mt 5:48). Jesus asks that we love one another as he has loved us (John 15:12). It is an invitation to a sacrificial agape in imitation of Christ. Nevertheless, this call for self-sacrifice is a counsel and not a precept. Christians are not obligated to self-sacrifice. Sacrificial agape is supererogatory. This poses an immediate challenge because such emulation of divine agape, to the extent possible, calls for radical self-donation and even radical divestment – acts that are out of the ordinary and beyond the capacity of most people.

Nevertheless, God's agape empowers and enables humans to live up to such divine agape. God never asks humans to do things without providing more than sufficient means to accomplish the task. Thus, the apostles were able to leave everything, even their families, to follow Christ because of the power and the grace that Jesus radiated. Through the grace poured forth from the Holy Spirit, the early Church community members held everything in common, giving all they had to the common pot and then taking only what they needed (Acts 2:42–47; 4:32–35). God always provides the means to whatever it is God asks of humans.

Christ invites us to love as he loved us. We can love because God loved us first (1 John 4:19). God's love is a gift. As we have seen earlier, it is given not on account of the merits of the beloved but because God simply loves. In the new dispensation, humans have been re-created as new creatures in Christ. Thus, St. Paul could say that it is no longer he who lived, but Christ lived in him (Gal 2:20).

Christians have been empowered by Christ's love, and nothing can separate them from this love (Rom 8:35–39). Moreover, it is Christ himself who promises the provision of all the means that will be needed to accomplish what God asks, especially in the moments of greatest need and peril (Lk 21:12–19). These means and empowerment from Christ will permit them to accomplish that which is difficult and perhaps even impossible (Mk 16:15–17). In sum, the New Testament provides a vivid example of self-sacrifice. It also provides the assurance that the means will be provided for whatever self-sacrifice God may ask. Infused agape is one such means provided by God to enable humans to love as Christ loves.

Infused Agape: Caritas

Outka's agape as equal regard, Cicero's duty of beneficence, Hume's duty of humanity, and Kant's duty of benevolence are acquired agape. They are called "acquired" because humans, by their own efforts, develop and practice such virtuous solicitude for each other (I-II, 65.2; 23.7). In contrast, it is God who imbues humans with infused virtues. These are neither acquired nor earned; they are not the result of human effort. They do not reflect human accomplishments. Instead, they reveal God at work in human lives. Infused virtues are pure gifts from God (I-II, 63.3; 109.2 and 4). The most well-known of these infused virtues are the three theological virtues of faith, hope, and charity.

Infused Agape Gives Direction to the Rightful Final End

Acquired and infused charity are similar in their normative content (II-II, 23.8) but differ as to their end (I-II, 63.4) (Porter 1989, 211). Acquired virtues are those that can be achieved in the natural realm by living according to what human nature requires. The end of acquired virtues is natural excellence, that is, to be all that we are and can be as beings with a human nature (I-II, 62.1). Infused virtues are different in that they are geared toward moving the subject to its Final End in God. The end here is supernatural excellence (friendship with God). Indeed, the formal defining characteristic of infused love (in contrast to acquired love) is the end to which it is oriented – God. Thus, infused charity is the imperium of moral virtues. As imperium, charity can be likened to the architect giving instructions to the masons, thus, giving direction to the exercise of the moral virtues, and pointing them to God (Mongeau 2013, 296; II-II, 23.8). It is through infused charity that all moral virtues find their perfection.

According to St. Augustine, even the cardinal virtues of temperance, fortitude, justice, and prudence, which have been so highly valued by the Greek philosophers, run the danger of turning into "prideful vices" if they are not animated by the virtues of faith, hope, and love. These latter three ensure that these cardinal virtues are oriented to God as their end (Albert et al. 1984, 95–97). Justice finds its perfection in charity as it contributes to achieving the Final End in God.

Love imbues mundane economic life and agency with transcendence. Love turns economic agency into a participation in the divine providence and governance of the world. *Caritas* turns ordinary economic agency into something extraordinary – the building of the Kingdom of God.

Infused charity as the imperium of moral virtues is important for resolving agape-justice conflicts. For the sake of union with God, charity as imperium may ask justice to forego its rightful claims. In elevating justice to the supernatural realm and aiming for supernatural and not merely natural excellence, justice may be required by infused justice itself to forgo its rightful claims in self-sacrifice. After all, the pursuit and satisfaction of justice is motivated with God as end in mind. Foregoing such rightful claims and embracing self-sacrifice may seem to be illogical for the *homo oeconomicus* of mainstream economic thought and perhaps even foolish according to common praxis.[13] With God as the person's Final End, foregoing rightful claims in self-sacrifice may in fact not only be possible but also be the optimum choice to make even by the standards of mainstream economics. Indeed, infused agape with its *telos* in God upends traditional ways of thinking and acting.

Infused Agape Transforms and Empowers: Infused *caritas* transforms its recipients, although this does not generally happen overnight. In most cases, it unfolds over time. Infused agape enlivens all the other loves of our lives – *philautia, storge, philia, eros, pragma,* (acquired) agape – and imbues them with a new purpose. Natural excellence moves toward supernatural excellence. After all, as mentioned earlier, grace does not destroy nature. Rather, grace empowers nature and builds on it.

Infused virtue, charity in particular, radically re-orients the person to God as its Final End. This is necessarily a complete metamorphosis. Welz describes the process of such re-orientation and makeover well:

> [F]or Kierkegaard and Levinas, love as gift and love as sacrifice are bound together. True love cannot be without a sacrifice, and sacrifice cannot remain without a hidden gift … '[S]elf-sacrifice' and 'self-giving' is in most cases not to be taken literally as a loss of self or giving-up of oneself. *Rather, the self that is capable of giving and renouncing is a self that remains and becomes itself in this process.* (Welz 2008, 257–58, emphasis added)

The self becoming itself in the process of self-emptying is, in fact, being Christ-like – *imitatio Christi*. To love as Christ loves us. It is to internalize our *imago Dei*. Paradoxically, the self-forgetfulness and self-emptying in *kenosis* leads to a self-discovery of an even more profound self like we have never seen before. St. Paul says it well in the midst of his self-emptying in

---

[13]   Mary Hirschfeld (2018) shows the shortcomings of traditional economic thinking and its rational choice model in its inability to deal with "infinite goods."

his missionary journeys: "[I]t is no longer I who live, but it is Christ who lives in me. And the life I now live in the flesh I live by faith in the Son of God, who loved me and gave himself for me" (Gal 2:20). Paul internalized Christ's love for him, and in the process, found himself transformed and empowered.

Jean Porter (1989, 200) arrives at the same conclusion: "[C]harity is ordered both with reference to its end – God himself – *and with refer-ence to the individual that is its subject*" (emphasis added). Indeed, love has a potent reflexive impact. *Love, by its nature, transforms the subject, the lover*. All moral choices are reflexive by nature. However, some are more potent than others in their reflexive impact. The greater the nature of the moral choice (e.g., love, self-sacrifice), the more profound and the more life-transforming the impact. In transcending himself/herself, the love extended to others (beyond his/her circle of natural loves) is effica-cious and potent in returning to the subject, only to transform and grow that love even further. This is particularly so if our common end in God is the rationale and motivation for love of neighbor. Thus, we have growth in *caritas* (friendship with God). Indeed, besides the Final End, charity is also ordered in reference to the subject.

> God creates friendship with the justified by so transforming the human soul that it becomes, in some sense, connatural to God (2a2ae 23.2), and united to him without any intermediary (2a2ae 23.6. 27.4; 1a2ae 66.6) .... Through the theological virtues (faith, hope, and charity), we become partakers in the divine nature (1a1ae 62.1). Through charity, we enjoy "a certain familiar colloquy" ... with God (1a1ae 65.5). Still more strongly, the grace of God, by which faith, hope and charity are bestowed, can be said to deify (deificet) us (1a.2ae 112.1) .... [C]*harity itself transforms its subjects into participants in the very mind and will of God.* (Porter 1989, 204, emphasis added)

What does it mean to be "in the very mind and will of God"? It is "to grasp intuitively what God's will for that individual is in any given situation (2a2ae 45.1,2)" (Porter 1989, 204).

In his *Deus caritas est*, Benedict XVI (2005, #17) describes the transfor-mative nature of the human's encounter with God. The human person's love, mind, and will are ever more conformed to that of God.

> [T]his process is always open-ended; love is never "finished" and complete; throughout life, it changes and matures ... [T]o want the same thing, and to reject the same thing—was recognized by antiquity as the authentic con-tent of love: the one becomes similar to the other, and this leads to a com-munity of will and thought. The love-story between God and man consists in the very fact that this communion of will increases in a communion of

thought and sentiment, and thus our will and God's will increasingly coincide: ... Then self-abandonment to God increases and God becomes our joy. (cf. Ps 73 [72]:23–28)

Love is not a decision or an idea but an encounter with God, a revelation (Bernstein 2008, 340). To encounter God is to be changed. The resulting alteration is a function of the degree to which grace is internalized and not impeded.

Søren Kierkegaard in his *Works of Love* (#281) notes that "the one who loves *'receives what he gives'* and *'becomes what he does'* when he understands God as middle term of the interhuman relation" (Welz 2008, 253, emphasis added). Indeed, the one who loves is transformed. Welz (2008, 253) elaborates on Kierkegaard's position: "[A]s long as one loves, one remains in love and remains in God who has given his love to us before we could begin to love. Thus, *the one who relies on being loved by God and gives himself in love without waiting for gifts in return becomes what he does: a loving person*" (emphasis added). Further, he notes the reflexive transformative power of love:

> Love's blessedness lies not only in the good it achieves for the other, but already in itself, in its meaning for the lover. *The loving one is transfigured through love and becomes what (s)he could not be by him- or herself. In love, one is oneself in relation to another.* Whether it is reciprocal or not, *the very relating enriches the self that would otherwise relate to itself through the world of things alone.* (Welz 2008, 257, emphasis added)

This explains how it is that we end up being far richer than when we started out as we give of ourselves.

The transformation is well on its way when we no longer love because we are commanded to do so, but because we want to. Unlike justice (which is purely deontic), love is not limited to being deontological. In fact, love is largely teleological. For example, in infused agape, people love not because it is their duty to do so, not because they are commanded by God, but because of their love of God and neighbor. What started out and what is objectively a command is internalized in genuine acts of love. *Infused agape's claims arise no longer because of our neighbor's needs but because of our need to empathize with them.* This has enormous implications in resolving agape-justice clashes because there is more leeway, more daring, more heroism, and more creativity that people aflame with love can give. This is the compelling dynamic of infused agape. The prophet Jeremiah and St. Paul exemplified this phenomenon (Jer 20:9; Phil 1:18b–26).

Supererogation: Grace Builds on Nature This chapter's suggested adjudication of last resort – to love as Christ loves – is not far-fetched after all. It is within the realm of human possibilities because of infused agape – *caritas*. Justice grows and finds its perfection and completion in charity when obligees forego their rightful claims instead of demanding them. True power lies in the restraint or the magnanimity in not exercising that power. This is infused agape at work.

Agape-justice conflicts may be divinely initiated occasions for humans to be transformed by infused charity, that is, *caritas* or friendship with God (II-II, 23.1). Agape-justice conflicts and the sacrificial choices they entail give vent to such infused *caritas* welling up in the human heart. Supererogatory acts may in fact be instances of grace building on nature via the diffusive nature of love. As we have seen in the preceding chapter, there is an expansive dynamism to charity. Love is about "being for the other" (Wolterstorff 2011, 23 citing Barth). *Caritas*, by its nature, is inexorably diffusive.

> The typically Thomistic sense of moderation and balance should not obscure the essentially expansive spirit of charity that pushes beyond mere "legal debt" to spontaneous generosity and beyond acts consistent with the requirements of justice into the area of the "supererogatory." *The grace-inspired love for God moves the person toward the fullness of charity (II-II.27.6), toward an ever-deepening love for God which overflows in self-forgetful devotion to the good of others, returning good for evil and transforming enemies into friends (II-II.27.7). This [is the] expansive dynamism of charity*[.] (Pope 1990, 123, emphasis added)

The clashing claims between agape and justice may in fact be instances of grace already at work and building on nature – using our ordinary circumstances to bring us from natural excellence to supernatural excellence. It entails self-sacrifice: Christ-like agape. Benedict XVI (2005) captures the essence of such love well when he observes, "My deep personal sharing in the needs and sufferings of others becomes a sharing of my very self with them: ... *I must give to others not only something that is my own, but my very self; I must be personally present in my gift*" (#34, emphasis added). Indeed, *Deus caritas est*, God is love.

Value of Difficulty of Sacrifice
The greater the degree of sacrifice and supererogation, the greater is the growth in virtue. St. Thomas uses love of one's enemy as an example.

> [O]ur love for God is proved to be all the stronger through carrying a man's affections to things which are furthest from him, namely, to the love of his enemies, even as the power of a furnace is proved to be the stronger,

according as it throws its heat to more distant objects. Hence *our love for God is proved to be so much the stronger, as the more difficult are the things we accomplish for its sake, just as the power of fire is so much the stronger, as it is able to set fire to a less inflammable matter.* (II-II, 27.7, response, emphasis added)

Of course, we find this also vividly taught in the Gospels:

32 "If you love those who love you, what credit is that to you? For even sinners love those who love them. 33 If you do good to those who do good to you, what credit is that to you? For even sinners do the same. 34 If you lend to those from whom you hope to receive, what credit is that to you? Even sinners lend to sinners, to receive as much again. 35 But love your enemies, do good, and lend, expecting nothing in return. Your reward will be great, and you will be children of the Most High; for he is kind to the ungrateful and the wicked. 36 *Be merciful, just as your Father is merciful.* (Lk 6:32–36, emphasis added)

Commenting on St. Thomas' exposition on the object of charity (II-II, 25.9), Mongeau (2013, 293) notes that the greater the effort required or the greater the abhorrence overcome, the greater is the self-transcendence involved:

Love of enemy is in this sense more perfect than love of a friend. The love of enemy is a more perfect act of dilectio, since the movement of the will here demands greater self-transcendence: one loves the enemy as a potential friend, which manifests a deeper and wider ranging charity. (emphasis added)

St. Thomas notes that the value of a sacrifice is not the worth of the thing sacrificed but the profundity of the gift of the self that is behind such a gift (II-II, 85.2, ad 2) (Mongeau 2013, 295). Love of an enemy takes a lot more out of us and requires that much more effort of the will. The profundity of love is directly proportional to the degree of sacrifice.

Kant lauds heroic self-sacrificial giving. He notes that the virtue is so much greater the more limited the means of the benefactor. Moreover, he extols as particularly "morally rich" those who quietly take on upon themselves the hardships that others would have otherwise had to bear. In effect, they endure these hardships to spare others of these (Kant 1991, *Metaphysics, Doctrine of Virtue*, Part II, Ch I, Sect I, #31). Clearly, such burden-shifting is what obligees do in foregoing their rightful claims in favor of those who have no claims at all.

A word of caution: The above-mentioned close connection between the degree of sacrifice involved and the resulting reflexive impact on the lover cannot be misused to claim that humans can earn their way to salvation.

The preceding dynamic should not be taken as Pelagian because it is God's grace (infused charity, *caritas*) that empowers humans to do that which is difficult or even impossible to begin with.

Conclusion

We can circle back to the topic of the preceding chapter on the importance of expanding one's circle of natural loves to a much larger sphere that includes the distant and the strangers, even one's enemies. The above point on how it is more perfect to love one's enemies than one's friends dovetails the preceding chapter well. Justice requires that we love those who are closest to us by virtue of kinship or our established relationships. Satisfying the demands of these obligations is important. Nevertheless, we cannot be content or stay put with satisfying only these obligations. We must go further in pushing the envelope to love God or to grow deeper in the love of God by loving those for whom we owe no natural obligations. We love those on the fringes or outside our circle simply for love of God. Both St. Thomas' and the New Testament's passages on enemies affirm the importance of going beyond our natural loves to reach out and love those at the edges as well.

This chapter does not argue that agape should always carry the day in agape-justice conflicts. As we have seen in the preceding chapters, both justice and agape have their unique roles to play in human flourishing. Justice and agape cannot substitute for one another. All this chapter claims is that if we are able to give of ourselves with alacrity, then even the most intractable agape-justice conflicts can be resolved with the adjudication of last resort – to love as Christ loves.

Justice's obligees can always forego their rightful claims in favor of agape's beneficiaries. We have a fallback solution even with the most complex competing claims between agape and justice. One insight that even non-Christians can draw from Jesus Christ, as a human hero-ideal, is the value of self-sacrifice. They do not have to believe that Jesus is the Messiah or the Son of God to appreciate the value of the self-sacrifice, love, and forgiveness that he exemplifies. That is a lesson for all humanity and not only for believers. When the right and the good path going forward in agape-justice conflicts is unclear or is difficult to embark on, agape invites all parties concerned to love as Christ loves.

CHAPTER 8

Growth in Collective Virtue

Introduction

Thus far, we have been talking of progress in acquired and infused charity toward natural and supernatural excellence at the personal level of individuals. However, as we have seen in most of the cases we have examined, agape-justice conflicts generally require collective decisions and action. Many agape-justice clashes, especially the more intractable and complicated ones, are at the community level. Nevertheless, this is fortuitous because imperfect obligations, such as beneficence, are best performed as a group.

Recall that imperfect duties allow us to fulfill these obligations as our situation permits. People are subject to different circumstances, and as a result, if I am unable to be beneficent today to this particular person in need, someone else in the group might be in a position to be beneficent at this time. Hence, there is a better probability of being able to satisfy imperfect duties as a group rather than if I were to go it alone. A particularly good example of how imperfect duties are best met as a group is crowd-funding.[1] We see this in the cases presented in this study – conflicts best addressed as a group. These are occasions to grow in collective virtue. In what follows, we examine the nature of collective virtues, including how they are formed and why they matter.

What Is Collective Virtue?

The notion of collective virtue has not received the kind of scrutiny in scholarship that individual virtues have. Ryan Byerly and Meghan Byerly (2016, 43) describe collective virtues as those qualities that people exemplify *qua members of a group*. These actions and predispositions are central

---

[1] Schroeder (2014, 582–584) provides another account for why imperfect duties are better met as a group.

248

to their collective self-identity and, by extension, to their individual, personal self-understanding. Despite not receiving much attention in the literature, collective virtues are readily seen in both history and contemporary practice.

For example, the Chosen People were called to an election of responsibility in their Covenant with the God of Abraham, Isaac, and Jacob. They were to be a nation different from all the other nations of the world. The Israelites were keenly conscious that God could have chosen many other nations far mightier and more numerous to be God's own (Dt 7:1, 7–8). Nevertheless, God chose them and gave them the blueprint – the Mosaic laws – on how to build the ideal nation worthy of emulation by their neighboring empires. Thus, Israelites, qua members of the Chosen People of God, were to lend to each other without interest (Dt 23:19–20). They were to welcome into their households those who had fallen on hard times, not enslave one another, and return land to their original ancestral owners (Lev 25). They were to tithe for the poor, give alms, and take responsibility for the most vulnerable in their midst – the widows, aliens, and orphans.

Such genuine mutual solicitude was to be the hallmark of the Chosen People. There was to be no poor among them, and they were to live in prosperity. In other words, the land flowing with milk honey will come about only if they live up to their election of responsibility as a nation (Dt 15:4–6; Dt 27–28). As mentioned earlier, the laws' motive clauses repeatedly point out that God was asking them qua the Chosen People to do all these because they had received the same favors from God. Indeed, the righteous economic conduct called for under the Mosaic laws is a prime example of collective virtue. Individual Israelites live up to them, not because of their personal virtue, but because they are numbered among the Chosen People of God entrusted with the Covenant. This is the economic conduct expected of them qua members of the Chosen People.

The early Christian communities of Acts 2:42–47 and 4:32–35 also exemplify collective virtues. They put their properties in the community pot, gave according to what they had, and took only according to what they needed. Such generosity was precipitated not by their individual virtues, but by their incorporation into the One Body of Christ. Their apparent simplicity of life, generosity, solidarity, and concern for the community of believers are collective virtues. And no one among them was said to be in want. Similarly, the various Mediterranean Christian communities gave to St. Paul's collection for the poor of Jerusalem because of their newfound collective identity as followers of Jesus Christ. Such sharing reflected their collective virtues of solidarity and generosity.

Collective virtues abound in history and down to our own day and age. Religious orders have emerged with their distinctive charisms and service, whether it is providing hospitality, preaching, teaching, ministering to street kids or caring for the sick and the poor, among many other unstinting acts. These are all done by individuals qua members of a religious order charged with a specific mission. Similarly, *sevā* ("selfless service") and *langar* ("free community kitchen") are characteristic of what it is to be a Sikh community (Singh 2024). Islam has its unique practices that are performed by its adherents precisely because of their collective self-identity qua Muslims. Thus, they give *zakat*, not charge interest in lending, and pray five times a day at the designated hours (Hassan and Muneeza 2024). These are all examples of collective virtues because people do them on account of their membership in a group for which such actions are constitutive and expected. Observe how collective virtues are both the causes and effects of successful communal action. They are the building blocks of Augustine's much-desired City of God.

Dynamics of Collective Virtue Formation

Having to resolve agape-justice conflicts at the collective level adds multiple hurdles, including difficulties posed by collective-action problems and the reality of sinful social structures. Nevertheless, even these added challenges turn out to be welcome opportunities to accomplish one of the more difficult feats in social ethics and praxis – growth in collective virtue.

Collective-Action Problems

Resolving agape-justice conflicts becomes much more difficult when it requires overcoming collective-action problems. Getting a community to act in unison is difficult as it is. One can only imagine how much more challenging it will be when it comes to getting the community to embrace self-limiting, self-giving, or even self-sacrificial agape (recall the differing degrees of beneficence), especially if the target beneficiaries are strangers halfway across the globe, as in many of our actual cases.

As we have seen earlier, the inability of the global community to address climate change or to beat the Covid-19 pandemic are just two of the most recent examples of collective-action problems. Collective-action problems are such that effective solutions are dependent on the cooperation of the vast majority, if not all, of the constituents. Major developed nations with highly educated populations and with excellent health infrastructure could not achieve herd immunity from the Covid-19 virus because many of their citizens and residents refused to be vaccinated or to wear a mask. This deficiency in public cooperation and national leadership had gotten so bad to the point where many nations had to legislate mandatory vaccination, masking, or weekly testing. These illustrate how collective-action problems arise because of people who are indifferent to the good of others or who put their private interests ahead of the community's welfare. It is a similar problem for climate change, overfishing, recycling, and the plastic pollution of the oceans, only much worse, because there is no mechanism for global legislation that can get around collective-action problems via coercive fiat.

To be sure, we have successful examples of overcoming collective-action problems, such as the formation of the United Nations, the worldwide effort to eradicate polio, the mitigation of the ozone depletion and hole, and the international trade infrastructure provided by the General Agreement on Trade and Tariffs (GATT) which has since then been replaced by the World Trade Organization (WTO). Note, too, the multilateral institutions, such as the World Bank, the International Monetary Fund (IMF), and the various regional development banks. Other examples include the successful global Nestlé infant formula and Cesar Chavez table grape boycotts, the US college students' anti-sweatshop movement, the global South African anti-apartheid campaign, and the G-8's debt forgiveness for the highly indebted poor countries on the occasion of the new millennium in 2005. Nevertheless, all these entailed enormous effort that had to be sustained over time. This is particularly so for the grassroots campaigns. Moreover, note the many instances of failed collective action, such as the trade embargoes imposed on rogue regimes, because of cheating and half-hearted cooperation.

In other words, collective-action problems require an enormous expenditure of time, effort, and resources. This is not even to mention goodwill and honesty. Nevertheless, these demands also provide opportunities when it comes to settling agape-justice conflicts at the collective level.

Sinful Social Structures and Accumulative Harms

There is little on collective virtue in the academic literature. Nonetheless, we can understand what it is and how it comes about by looking at the literature on sinful social structures and accumulative harms. Much has been written on these two phenomena. Both collective and personal virtues are formed in the same manner as sinful social structures and accumulative harms: via repetition and internalization until they become deeply embedded or second nature to the moral agent(s) and via mutual reinforcement.

The literature on sinful social structures shows how damaging they can be and how they can take a life of their own in further strengthening and adding momentum to sinful or problematic actions. Problems can beget even more difficulties, often much more challenging.[2] Venal governments are good examples. These are both causes and effects of endemic graft in societies.

Accumulative harms occur when an act at the individual level is not detrimental at all but become terribly injurious when replicated across millions of other individuals who act in a similar fashion. The best example of this is driving a car that runs on fossil fuel. Person A driving such a vehicle does not damage the ecology beyond the latter's ability to heal itself. However, hundreds of millions driving such vehicles over time precipitate a global climate crisis. Another example is the case of saving. A family putting away its income into savings rather than spending it in consumption is indeed laudable and even considered virtuous. However, if every other household were to be similarly frugal, the entire economy will descend into a recession for lack of aggregate demand and find itself in deep trouble. This savings conundrum is an example of the fallacy of composition in which what is good for the part is not necessarily good for the whole.[3]

This accumulative dynamic cuts both ways. In the same way that moral choices can cause harm, they could also produce enormous good. This accumulative dynamic also applies to virtue formation. Virtues at the personal level benefit not only the subject individual but also the entire community. (Think of St. Thomas' general-legal justice.) If this is so, how much more goodness is produced if personal virtues were widespread or even universal. Virtue at the personal level is even more effective with virtue at the collective level.

One can only imagine the potency that emerges when we overlay the virtue of acquired or infused charity on this accumulative dynamic. The accumulative nature of love follows the dynamic of accumulative harms or benefits. Think of what happens when members of that One Body in Christ (1 Cor 12) are aflame with the characteristic features of love (1 Cor

---

[2] Daniel Finn (2016) employs insights from critical realism and sociology to account for how sinful social structures emerge from multiple unrelated individual actions or events.

[3] For the mathematically inclined, the accumulative phenomenon is multiplicative rather than merely additive as more elements are incorporated.

13). That is the paradigmatic accumulative phenomenon. That is the paradigmatic synergy – the resulting whole being greater than the mere sum of its parts. This is collective agape. Collective virtue reflects the character of the community. Even more, collective virtue bolsters the community's capacity to undertake tasks that are difficult or even impossible because it transforms its members' ability to work together as a group. The early Church community that held everything in common is another good example of collectively achieving what would normally be unthinkable (Acts 2:42–47; 4:32–35).

Challenge and Opportunity for Collective Virtue

Despite the accumulative dynamic forming both sinful social structures and collective virtue, there is nonetheless an asymmetry in that it is far easier to create and maintain sinful social structures than it is to attain and hold on to collective virtues. Sinful social structures arise spontaneously in the wake of wrong moral choices. They come about regardless of whether the subject moral agents intended them or not. In addition, sinful social structures are usually self-reinforcing and spiral into a vicious cycle of decline because of bounded rationality and the phenomenon of network externalities.[4] Furthermore, they are often deeply entrenched. The inertia and the inability of the community to act together result in just leaving these sinful social structures in place. It is the path of least resistance. It is the default condition – leaving the status quo as it is and as a result, further reinforcing it as the common praxis and expectation.

In contrast, virtuous social structures are difficult to establish and maintain because:

- They require redressing or at least mitigating deeply rooted sinful social structures that are ingrained in the people's ethos or praxis. Besides, special interests and community members who have reaped great personal gains from the status quo will fiercely defend such sinful structures.
- They require substantial deliberate effort and demand self-sacrifice, unlike sinful social structures that arise spontaneously in the wake of wrong moral choices, personal or collective, or both.
- They need to be practiced and sustained over time (like any virtue).

---

[4] Recall the discussion of these in Chapter 3. In bounded rationality, people simply follow established rules of thumb in making decisions. Network externalities are standards that become *the* norm as more people follow them.

- They are dependent on purposeful collective action and are therefore vulnerable to collective-action problems.
- They are prone to a free-ridership problem whereby some community members do not sacrifice at all or as much as they could but simply let others bear the cost (e.g., 2 Thess 3:10–12).

Nevertheless, even as the additional hurdles from sinful social structures, accumulative harms, and collective-action problems pose great challenges, they also provide welcome opportunities. The enormous effort and the process of getting over these impediments are in fact occasions for acquiring collective virtue and for building virtuous social structures, the opposite of the more common sinful social structures to which we have become accustomed. As we have seen earlier, adversity and great sacrifice are springboards to a more profound growth in virtue. The sustained group effort needed over time turns out to be already the practice of the collective virtue itself.

Note the double accumulative feature involved in collective virtue formation: (1) It is accumulative over time, and (2) it is accumulative across people. Similarly, as we have seen earlier, agape-justice conflicts can only be resolved in a diachronic manner (that is, taking the history of the conflict into account). Moreover, such conflicts require resolution over time and across people. In other words, both collective virtue formation and resolving agape-justice conflicts are operating on the same axes: across time and across people.

The reflexive dynamic becomes even more potent when talking of a community. The reflexive impact strengthens and improves the quality of the interpersonal love within that collective. Agape strengthens collective *storge* given the people's shared project in jointly reaching out to others with empathy and compassion. The shared self-sacrifice imbues their common endeavor with even more depth and a more profound reflexive impact. It is a collective self-forgetfulness and self-giving. It is a collective foregoing of entitlements and rightful claims for the sake of the neediest. This collective supererogation leads to mutual and collective growth in charity. Indeed, the reflexive impact of self-sacrificial giving improves both the collective as a whole and the interpersonal relationships of its constituent members.

In Actual Practice

As mentioned earlier, obligees can resolve agape-justice conflicts by foregoing their collective rightful claims. However, they cannot do so as individuals or even forego their own personal share of the collective rightful claims. Obligees need to work as a group. It is akin to the collective decision that is needed when workers engage in collective bargaining or in class-action suits that are resolved in out-of-court settlements. Thus, agape-justice conflicts contribute to forming collective virtue in two ways. First, they provide the occasion for all affected parties (obligees, obligors, donors, and beneficiaries) to talk with each other and to work together as a group to come to a decision. In effect, agape-justice conflicts provide the opportunity for them to become a community by confronting a common problem and pursuing a common goal.

Second, as mentioned earlier, the high cost and the sacrifice that resolving agape-justice conflicts often entail can be used to advantage. The greater the adversity and the shared sacrifice, the more profound is the potential growth in collective virtue and the stronger are the resulting bonds and ties among group members. Community members gain depth in their collective self-identity through their shared sacrifice. Their self-sacrifice gives them a real sense of ownership and responsibility for their life together as a community. Obligees' sacrifice in foregoing their collective rightful claims at great personal cost deepens their ties and commitment to each other and to their community, including the strangers and the distant beneficiaries of their benefaction.

Viewed in another way, self-sacrifice may be easier at a collective level in that one has company, and people can mutually encourage each other. People realize that they are not alone in their self-sacrifice and that others are bearing their share as well. Thus, collective self-sacrifice produces a windfall not available to personal virtue formation – it is an exceptional group exercise and a stepping-stone to forming community because of the common experience of self-deprivation and the shared experience of adversity.[5] Recall the national bond among the British people who had to endure the blitz during World War II. More recently, note the newfound national solidarity and forbearance among Ukrainians as they share the dangers, deprivations, and displacement from their country's invasion. Individuals are more inclined to be self-giving or even to be self-sacrificing if they feel that they are part of something or a cause much larger than themselves. Such challenges and added difficulties are rewarded by the even greater intensity and profundity of the results. Collective virtue is greater than personal virtue in terms of overall impact because of its accumulative nature (synergy) and its networking effect.

---

[5] Note the deep lifetime bonds that bind soldiers who fought together in war. Observe, too, how the collective fasting during Ramadan and the celebrations at the breaking of the fast (Eid al-Fitr) are effective in building community and in strengthening Muslims' collective self-identity qua Muslims.

Impact: The Difference that Collective Virtues Make

Collective virtues make a substantial contribution to the community in at least four major areas:

- They rectify sinful social structures.
- They build up civil society.
- They shape the public ethos.
- They are constitutive elements of the common good.

We discuss each of these in what follows.

Rectifying Sinful Social Structures

As we have seen earlier, Don Browning (2008) observes that simple acts of self-limitation, self-giving, or self-sacrifice even at the personal level restore or bolster mutual trust and harmony that have been lost or are at risk in the community. If such a dynamic occurs with personal virtues, how much more for collective virtues with their accumulative synergy. In collective virtues, individual virtues are not merely additive but multiplicative, whereby peoples' virtues reinforce each other's virtues and impact. How much more potent are collective virtues in ameliorating wrongdoing when virtue is widespread and deeply ingrained in the self-identity of the people as a community. For example, in their mutual empathy and solicitude, the Chosen People were to have no poor among them (Dt 15:4), and they were to bring about the land flowing with milk and honey (Dt 27–28). Similarly, there was said to be no poor in the early Church community that held everything in common, gave according to their means, and only took according to their needs (Acts 2:42–47; 4:32–35). Note how religions, in general, have been at the forefront in addressing the root causes of poverty among the very poor through communal action.

Collective Virtue and Civil Society

As we have seen in Chapters 3 and 4 on socioeconomic homeostasis, civil society is a pillar in the triad of institutions that are foundational for the modern political economy (markets and government being the other two). Recall the role of civil society in mitigating market and government failures, even as it shapes the all-important public ethos that determines customs, law, and usage within the community.

The character and quality of civil society are a function of the character and the quality of its constituent members. Thus, virtues or vices at the personal level affect the whole. Recall that St. Thomas refers to legal justice as general justice because virtues and human actions at the individual level ultimately redound to the benefit and promotion of the good of the whole community (II-II, 58.5).

Widespread personal virtues plus their accumulative dynamic that produce collective virtues promote and advance the good of the community even more given their resulting synergy and the widespread possession of individual virtues within the community. In other words, collective virtue is an important and effective building block of civil society.

For example, the widely held value of "ubuntu" (solidarity, mutual respect, shared humanity) sustained South African society as it endured and survived the trauma and the violence of decades-long apartheid inflicted by its own government. In World War II, Denmark had the highest Jewish survival rate of any Nazi-occupied country during the war (120 Jews died during the Holocaust from a population of over 7,000) because Danish society stepped in to circumvent Nazi orders for the arrest and deportation of Danish Jews.[6] Or, consider the list of countries in Transparency International's ranking of countries marred by corruption. Note the instability of the countries with the most graft and the weakness of their civil societies. Indeed, one could aptly describe collective virtues and vices as the warp and weft of civil society.

Collective Virtue and Public Ethos

Collective virtue (or vice) is both a cause and effect of the public's ethos. The public ethos fosters collective virtue/vice, even as the collective virtue/vice feeds back to further strengthen or change the public ethos and its customs, law, and usage (CLU). Recall that in economic theory and analysis, *homo oeconomicus* maximizes and optimizes the utility or profit function for every economic decision. In actual practice, people do not conduct such a maximization exercise for every economic choice they face. Otherwise, they would have no time for anything else. Instead, they use rules of thumb based on their experience of what had worked in the past. As we have seen in Chapter 3, bounded rationality is the phenomenon whereby people use such formal and informal rules of thumb

---

[6] "Denmark," United States Holocaust Museum. https://encyclopedia.ushmm.org/content/en/article/denmark last accessed February 4, 2022.

in "satisficing" rather than optimizing in their economic decisions, both at the individual and collective level (Simon 1957). People aim for what is satisfactory rather than for what is optimum. These rules of thumb eventually form the public ethos. These become the distinctive group virtue or vice.

For example, the EU is known for being a welfare economy versus the United States, which is deemed to be more market-oriented. The former is far more protective of the well-being of its citizens and residents compared to the latter. Japanese businesses tend toward consensus in decision-making, even as economic transactions in Confucian cultures rely on *guanxi*. Unlike the West, individualism is not extolled in these cultures. Family, group, and harmony take precedence over individual interests. Graft is said to be endemic in many developing nations. Populism is also said to be prevalent and deeply rooted in some countries despite its repeated failed economic policies. These are collective virtues or vices – behavior that becomes second nature or are practiced qua members of a group with spontaneity and alacrity without much more thought or effort. It is part of the national or community psyche. We see a similar dynamic in longstanding cultural practices in some regions of the world, such as, female genital mutilation (FGM) and the view that women are inferior to men.

Public ethos and its customs, law, and usage constantly shift the boundaries between the various categories and degrees of obligatoriness in Table 1.2. These borders are never static. The line between duty and supererogation shifts over time or in response to major community trauma. For example, note the post–World War II Universal Declaration of Human rights in the wake of the Holocaust. Recall the various shifts cited in Chapter 1, such as the provision of US healthcare and the changing expectations on corporate good citizenship. Civil society plays a leading role in these shifts. Agape and collective virtues contribute to these shifts through civil society.

H.L.A. Hart (1961, 84–85, 167) provides a good account of how the public ethos, customs, law, and usage are in a constant state of flux. He notes that rules, obligations, and moral ideals are constitutive elements of morality. Moral and legal rules are needed if people are to live with each other and survive as a society. Not all rules impose obligations, such as the prudential rules of etiquette. He contends that rules become obligations when:

- There is great social insistence on compliance with these rules.
- There is extensive and serious communication and great social pressure on community members to conform to these rules.

- They ask great sacrifice from individuals.
- Heavy sanctions and consequences are applied for noncompliance.
- Compliance with these rules becomes critical for the survival or viability of the community.

Some examples of elementary rules that impose obligations are nonviolence with one another, truthfulness, honesty, and mutual respect of properties, among others. Note how similar these are to the moral debt 1 under St. Thomas' potential parts of justice (II-II, 80.1; O'Brien 1971). These obligations are essential if there is to be virtue and if there is to be a viable community at all.

Besides these basic virtues, legislation has also been used to pro-actively shape public virtue. Recall Prohibition in the United States in the 1920s with its Eighteenth Amendment that banned the manufacture, transport, and sale of alcohol. Blue laws, which restrict certain activities on Sundays, were once prevalent in some Western nations and local communities. Modern-day Israeli regulations curtailing Shabbat activities are still officially on the books but increasingly ignored by the public. Nations and local communities have campaigned for greater public environmental consciousness by banning single-use plastic bags, straws, utensils, and water bottles. Laws have been enacted that regulate how people are to dispose of batteries, appliances, tires, etc. for mandatory recycling. Some communities charge households garbage fees based on weight in an effort to save landfill space and prevent further damage to the environment. And, of course, there is the longstanding and widespread practice of imposing sin taxes on alcohol and tobacco products and lately on sugary drinks in an effort to promote healthier life choices. These are some examples of how customs, law, and usage are used to form individual and collective virtue.

Hart (1961, 176ff) also notes that duty and obligation are merely starting points – the bedrock foundation of morality. However, there is more to morality than duties and obligations. There are also the moral ideals, such as fraternity, liberty, and equality. The attainment of these moral ideals is deemed praiseworthy. These moral ideals become the occasions and the catalysts for social criticism because they set the standards and the expectation of what constitutes a good society to which the community aspires. These ideals become an "invitation to reform" (Hart 1961, 179). Moreover, they also inspire and lead to changes at the individual level when people embrace these moral ideals for themselves.

These rules, obligations, and moral ideals are constitutive of the public's ethos. Such public morality is not fixed but evolves over time and responds accordingly to shifts in social life. Civil society, along with its constitutive elements of agape and collective virtues, is an integral part of this process.

Even the obligations and claims of justice change in response to shifts in public thinking on moral ideals initiated by actors from within civil society. Take the case of Peter Singer's arguments for an obligation of easy rescues. His seminal 1972 article "Famine, Affluence, and Morality" in *Philosophy & Public Affairs* spawned a rethinking of the obligations we owe one another to the point of alarming his critics who defend the status quo.

> Singer's proposals have struck many as overly demanding, impracticable, and a significant departure from the demands of ordinary morality .... Critics continue today to argue that *a principle of beneficence that requires persons, governments, and corporations to seriously disrupt their projects and plans in order to benefit the poor and underprivileged exceeds the limits of ordinary moral obligations and have no plausible grounding in moral theory.* They argue that the line between the obligatory and the supererogatory has been unjustifiably erased by such a principle. In effect, the claim is that *an aspirational moral ideal has redrawn the lines of real moral obligation* (Beauchamp 2013, #4, emphasis added).

Singer spawned discussion and a rethinking of the public's ethos. His duty of easy rescues or the duty of beneficence ratchets up what he believes ought to be the minimum in our ordinary moral obligations as part of our moral ideals. The debates surrounding Singer's duty of beneficence underscore the importance of public morality and who or what gets to shape it. It gives us a glimpse into the dynamics underlying collective virtue formation, which begins at the individual level (Peter Singer's queries in this case).

The shifting line between what is obligatory and what is supererogatory is a function of community standards and expectations, prevailing practices, and the sway of thought leaders and other influencers especially in the age of social media. All these change over time. This is where and how agape and collective virtue can be effective. It is important to be pro-active in shaping these lest the market ethos fill the void by default. Recall the earlier account in Chapter 3 of market-generated values displacing long-standing Confucian values in South Korea, China, and Singapore. Recall, too, the many examples of practices that were supererogatory in the past but which have since then become increasingly part of community expectation and in some cases codified in law: social security as a matter of legal entitlement, healthcare, conditional cash transfers, subsidized childcare, and many others.

The clashing claims of agape and justice may in fact expose the gap between the status quo and the "moral ideals" that Hart (1961, 176ff) speaks of.[7] Widespread dissatisfaction with this gap leads to social criticism and possibly reform.[8] It could then also seep down to the level of individuals. Agape-justice conflicts may augur forthcoming changes in ordinary public morality. Such clashes between agape and justice may in fact be the catalysts for such adjustments in ordinary public morality. The public's ethos is important. It determines what is expected as a duty and what is supererogatory. The more disruptive and the more sacrificial is the final adjudication, the more likely it is to be a case of agape overriding justice, and the more likely it is to contribute toward collective virtue formation.

For example, social enterprises go against traditional shareholder business models of profit-maximization and are animated instead by a genuine concern for the well-being of others (agape). This is agape in production. Similarly, people go through the added expense and the trouble of recycling or doing carbon offsets. They voluntarily buck prevailing praxis and values through the simplicity of their lives. This is agape in consumption. Others pay more in fair trade for coffee, chocolate, and apparel for the sake of the well-being of the workers who provide these. This is agape in exchange. These are all examples of agape at work in shaping the public ethos and in forming nascent collective virtues. And, of course, think of the agape that could been achieved had the United States, the EU, and India chosen to be self-sacrificial in sharing lifesaving vaccines and PPE during the deadly early days of Covid-19 when they themselves had great need. "No one has greater love than this, to lay down one's life for one's friends" (John 15:13).

This is a full circle completed. In Chapter 3 we saw the importance and role of civil society and how agape plays a major role in animating and forming civil society. In this penultimate chapter, civil society also plays a major role in leading and nourishing collective virtue formation. It has been said that a useful measure in gauging the character of a community

---

[7] Unlike justice whose claims are mandatory, moral ideals are easily foregone because they may not be as immediate in ensuring the survival of the community. These moral ideals correspond to St. Thomas' moral debt 2 rather than the strict legal debts of justice proper (II-II, 80.1; O'Brien 1971).

[8] For example, note the push for universal Pre-K (pre-kindergarten programs) and childcare in the aftermath of Covid-19 in the United States. Or, recall the Occupy Wall Street protests and the anti-globalization campaigns that have pushed for reforms in redressing some of globalization's ills.

is to look at how it cares for the most vulnerable members in its ranks. We can generalize this by noting that the character of a community is on full display in its collective virtues or vices, as the case may be.

Collective virtue requires collective self-limitation, collective self-giving, or even collective self-sacrifice. The preceding chapters show three occasions for such collective beneficence:

- Foregoing one's legitimate rightful claims in order to correct past wrongs (Chapter 5).
- Foregoing one's legitimate rightful claims in order to expand one's circle of natural loves (nearest and dearest) to include the distant and the stranger (Chapter 6).
- Foregoing one's legitimate rightful claims in order to resolve intractable agape-justice conflicts (Chapter 7).

In sum, collective virtue and its formation are essentially coincident with and indistinguishable from the formation of the public's ethos. In effect, collective virtue has a dual function because it forms part of the public ethos itself, even as it normatively shapes civil society, markets, and government.

Common Good

Formation and growth in collective virtue will eventually lead to St. Augustine's City of God rather than the city of man. We have glimpses of such a City of God in Deuteronomy 27–28's account of the blessings that Biblical Israel will bring upon herself if she lives up to her election to responsibility as the Chosen People of God. We also see a glimpse of this in the early Church community of Acts 2:42–47 and 4:32–35.

Collective virtue is a necessary condition for the common good. This is a minimum condition that must be present in any reasonable account of the common good. A community is only as good as the character and virtue of its constituent members. After all, the common good requires collective action and a shared orientation toward the good. These are what collective virtues are all about. Moreover, collective virtues are in fact the building blocks of the common good. We become a just society, a caring society, a community in which there is no one poor, but only if we have widespread justice, compassion, and care for the poor at the individual level, and only if we have a shared commitment to be so qua members of a caring and just community. In effect, competing claims between agape and justice turn out to be a godsend in that they occasion collective virtue formation that in turn contributes toward the attainment of the common good.

Agape-Justice Conflicts as Diagnostic Tool for the Common Good

Agape-justice conflicts can also be helpful in our understanding of the common good. The common good is extremely difficult to define because of the fluidity and complexity of social life. Thus, the most that can be done is to specify its minimum conditions in any reasonable account of the common good. One possible minimum condition is setting the ideal threshold for the degree to which we attain different elements or parts of justice and agape.

The fullness of justice is attained only as the different dimensions of justice are satisfied (e.g., commutative, social, distributive, and general-legal). This is so because (1) each of these deals with a facet of justice, and (2) they mutually reinforce one another. The same can be said of love. The fullness of love (love of God and neighbor) can only be achieved as the foundational loves are thriving (*philautia, storge, philia*). Biblical *tzedeq* (righteousness) is defined as the condition whereby all the demands of one's relationships are fully met. It is reasonable to believe that the satisfaction of most, if not all, of the elements of justice and love is a minimum condition in any acceptable account of the common good.

Thus, the mutual interaction between the various components of justice and love are among the building blocks of the common good. *The degree to which a community satisfies the various elements of justice and love is a measure of the extent to which it is able to approximate the common good. Agape-justice conflicts inadvertently identify the specific deficiencies in our collective virtue.* Such conflicts lend themselves well as diagnostic tools in showing what the community ought to work on in moving closer toward its common good. For example, the conflicts that arise because of disequilibria in socioeconomic homeostasis (Chapter 4) alert the community to how it ought to tweak its customs, law, and usage. Similarly, the conflicts that arise from unattended past wrongs expose the impediments to the community's progress toward the common good (Chapter 5). The tensions between our natural loves and agape for the stranger and the distant (Chapter 6) flag the relationships that demand immediate collective accommodation for the sake of the common good.

Summary and Conclusions

Virtue is usually discussed at the level of the individual. Resolving clashing claims between agape and justice provides an occasion for growth not only in personal virtue, but also for advancement in collective virtue. After all, most of these conflicts can be solved only at the communal level. Personal and collective virtues enhance the character of civil society and shape the public ethos. Such changes in public morality, in turn, are instrumental in shifting the dividing line between duty and supererogation. Recall Table 1.2 and its continuum of obligatoriness, legal and moral, that range from strict duties to purely supererogatory acts.

The challenges and the dynamics of virtue formation at the personal level are replicated at a collective level with even greater reflexive impact. Conflicts between agape and justice can be resolved with the obligees jointly foregoing their rightful claims in favor of those who are needier but who do not have strict legal claims. These are unique opportunities for the entire community to experience varying degrees of self-emptying (*kenosis*), from self-limitation, to self-giving, and perhaps, even all the way to self-sacrifice. These occasion profound growth in collective agape and virtue. The intensity and profundity in growth in virtue are proportional to the degree of *kenosis* and sacrifice required. Such growth in turn builds and strengthens communities. Paradoxically, agape-justice conflicts turn out to be surprising building blocks of the common good given the deliberate effort and intense collaboration they require. Indeed, acquiring collective virtue is no small accomplishment. Successfully grappling with agape-justice conflicts together as a community brings about advancement in such virtues.

CHAPTER 9

Summary and Conclusions
Epistemological or Ontological?

Findings

Agape and justice surprisingly clash in many of their claims. What do we do when we face contradictory duties from agape and justice? Chief executives, judges, legislators, bureaucrats, and even ordinary citizens make such hard choices all the time. This happens across a wide range of social issues.

How much should advanced countries open their markets to international trade and outsourcing to help poor nations, but at the expense of their domestic manufacturing and service workers? How much vital lifesaving vaccines and medical equipment ought the United States, the EU, and India share during the deadly phase of a pandemic, knowing that such overseas humanitarian assistance will lead to illness and death for many of their own citizens? How much inflation should food-producing nations inflict on their own people as they loosen their export controls to alleviate hunger and rising food prices in other nations, especially poor countries? Should one break the law to aid distressed migrants fleeing to the EU or the United States? In deciding how generous to make their country's social safety net, should legislators stress mutual compassion or personal responsibility?

Even Cicero himself acknowledges that settling agape-justice conflicts is not a straightforward process. For Cicero, justice as a cardinal virtue comprises *iustitia* – justice proper itself[1] and (2) *beneficentia* – beneficence (*De Officiis*, I, vii [20]). In other words, for him:

Justice as a cardinal virtue = *iustitia* (justice proper) + *beneficentia* (beneficence)

Both *iustitia* and *beneficentia* present their own set of claims, and Cicero himself acknowledges that they can and do present competing claims that need to be resolved.

---

[1] Readers are cautioned that the same English term is used for justice as a cardinal virtue and *iustitia* – justice proper itself.

Such questions as these must, therefore, be taken into consideration in every act of moral duty [and we must acquire the habit and keep it up], *in order to become good calculators of duty*, able *by adding and subtracting to strike a balance correctly and find out just how much is due to each individual.* (I, xviii, [59], emphasis added)

Agape-justice conflicts lie along three fault lines, namely:

- Legal debt versus moral debt
  (e.g., breaking the law to aid distressed migrants, Chapter 5)
- Stringent moral debt versus less stringent moral debt
  (e.g., trade as foreign aid but at the expense of domestic workers, Chapter 6)
- Legal and moral debt versus supererogatory acts
  (e.g., foregoing tied-in aid, Chapter 7)

These competing debts vary in the strength of their claims. As a result, they give the impression that agape-justice conflicts can be easily resolved by merely following the degree of their obligatoriness as presented in Table 1.2 (Chapter 1). Social philosophers, theologians, and policymakers defer to justice in deciding agape-justice conflicts based on three rules, namely:

- The subsistence test: The strictness of an obligation is a function of its importance for the existence of society.
- Perfect duties (justice) take precedence over imperfect duties (agape).
- The rank order in the strength of claims is as follows:

  Legal debt > relational moral debts > general moral debts > supererogation

Fault Line #1

Adam Smith, Hugo Grotius, Samuel von Pufendorf, Lord Kames, and John Stuart Mill argue that justice takes priority because legal institutions are foundational if there is to be any society at all. In fact, justice is deemed the only prerequisite for the socio-economy. Everything else is merely ornamental, including agape (Chapter 2). Thus, they defer to the claims of justice and subscribe to this rule of thumb:

Fault line #1: Legal dues vs. moral dues Rule: Legal dues > moral dues

Of course, in-extremis cases trump this rule altogether. Even the strongest demands of justice bound by the strictest of obligations give way to satisfying claims that are essential in life-and-death cases. For example, private property rights are trumped by the exigencies of war. It is morally permissible for starving citizens of a besieged city to scavenge for food from abandoned homes or locked commercial warehouses. In-extremis claims take priority.

We should observe caution before conferring such deference to justice in non-in-extremis cases of agape-justice conflicts. First, context is extremely important. In dealing with obligations, we can only arrive at general principles for adjudication, but when applied to specific cases, we must consider the circumstances that gave rise to these clashing claims (O'Brien 1971). Thus, unlike Adam Smith et al., we cannot prioritize the claims of justice over those of agape without examining how these competing claims arose to begin with and what is at stake. These conflicts are much more complicated in the considerations they present, many of which are compelling from both contending sides.

Second, while many leading social philosophers prioritize legal claims[2] over moral claims, as in the case of Adam Smith et al., why should enforceability or strictness of obligations be the overriding criterion? This is a heavily and exclusively deontological adjudication of the conflict in which conformity to law is the ethical standard. Deontology suffers from a major flaw – it is oblivious to consequences that may in fact threaten and bring down the very structures, institutions, or state that these laws/rules are shoring up. Moreover, depending on the context, other standards, such as wisdom or common sense, may be superior to strict legal due. Besides rule of law, individuals and communities value other goals that are better served by prioritizing moral over legal claims. Take the case of Angela Merkel's generosity in unilaterally accepting a million Syrian war refugees at the height of the migrant crisis in 2015, bypassing EU protocols on migration altogether. Similarly, recall the ordinary citizens who chose to assist distressed migrants or give food to the homeless despite the threat of prosecution, fines, or even jail time.

Third, Chapter 3 shows that agape plays a vital role in the real economy. Socioeconomic life cannot run on justice alone, *pace* Adam Smith et al. While justice is indeed foundational for the existence of any community, it is nevertheless unable to meet the key requirements of a functional community. Agape fills many of the gaps that justice is unable to satisfy. Recall

---

[2] The assumption here, of course, is that the laws undergirding these legal claims are just.

the necessary institutional preconditions of the marketplace that agape alone can fill, such as mutual trust and goodwill. Or note the vital role of agape in lowering the frictional and transaction costs of the marketplace. These critical contributions ensure not only the much-sought allocative efficiency of the marketplace but also its sustainability. Agape is a necessary complement to justice in socioeconomic life. Community life cannot be conducted purely on a transactional or contractual basis. No community can long survive without mutual compassion and empathy. Agape passes the Enlightenment philosophers' subsistence test, just like justice.

Fourth, contrary to Adam Smith et al.'s deference to justice, there is no blanket, universal rule for dealing with agape-justice conflicts. Cicero himself does not contend that there is a single general rule for settling these clashing claims. Rather, it ultimately requires the use of prudential judgment. Moreover, for Cicero, resolving these clashing claims well is a process of learning by doing. We get better at doing it with practice over time.

> But as neither physicians nor generals nor orators can achieve any signal success without experience and practice, no matter how well they may understand the theory of their profession, so the rules for the discharge of duty are formulated, it is true, as I am doing now, but *a matter of such importance requires experience also and practice.* (I, xviii, [60], emphasis added)

We should find great encouragement from these insights from Cicero, considering the problematic nature of the agape-justice conflicts that we examined in this study. We ought to get better at balancing these competing claims as we gain more experience grappling with them.

In sum, we cannot immediately claim that legal debt always takes priority over moral debt because moral debt is foundational for legal debt. One must also be attentive to the satisfaction of moral debt and not only legal debt. One cannot employ a universal rule that prioritizes legal over moral debt. Thus, we conclude:

$$\text{Legal dues} = f \text{ (moral dues)}$$

In other words, legal dues are a function of moral dues. David Hume is right all along when he observes that the duty of humanity forms the very foundation of justice. The duty of humanity is the first experience of people growing up in a family, and it serves as the school for them to learn the importance of being just. One must satisfy moral dues, as a necessary condition, if one is to be able to enact and to live up to just customs, law, and usage. Hume has a point when he notes that the duty of humanity provides the very people who will act justly.

In addition, our exposition shows that agape-justice conflicts arise from unattended past wrongs or unmitigated past disequilibria in socio-economic homeostasis. Thus, satisfying legal and moral dues today is a function of how well we had satisfied both legal and moral dues in the preceding periods (Chapter 5). We find that

$$\text{Legal/moral dues}_I = f(\text{Moral dues}_{-1}; \text{Legal dues}_{-1}; \text{Moral dues}_{-2};$$
$$\text{Legal dues}_{-2}; \ldots)$$
$$\text{Time periods} = 1, 2, \ldots, n$$

Both legal and moral dues have a time- and place-utility to them. Both need to be satisfied at the right time and place, among the right parties, and in the right manner. It is an exacting homeostasis. Agape-justice conflicts cannot be settled with a general rule that says legal dues always take priority over moral dues.

Fault Line #2

A frequent source of agape-justice conflicts is when the just demands of our natural loves clash with the demands of agape that push us to include the distant, the stranger, and the undeserving in our circle of love. Another rule of thumb is what St. Thomas calls the order of charity, whereby our nearest and dearest take priority over those who are distant or strangers to us.

Fault line #2: Relational moral dues vs. General moral dues
Rule: Our nearest/dearest > distant/stranger

Chapter 6 shows that love by its nature is diffusive, and as a result, the strength, growth, and quality of our natural loves are a function of our love for the distant, the stranger, and even the undeserving. We find that:

Perfection of our natural loves = f (love for strangers and the distant)

Fault Line #3

Many assume that people with claims from legal and moral dues take priority over those with no claims at all.

```
Fault line #3: Legal & moral dues vs. Supererogation
         Rule: Legal or moral debts > no claims
```

Chapters 7 and 8 show that this is not necessarily always the case. In fact, agape-justice conflicts may be unique opportunities not only to grow in virtue but also to build community through supererogation. We find that in terms of impact on all the parties concerned:

```
Supererogation > Legal-moral claims
```

Supererogation may in fact have a much more profound and lasting reflexive impact on relationships, especially when they are sacrificial. Heroic or even saintly supererogation is particularly life-transforming and life-affirming in its impact, as Raoul Gustaf Wallenberg and St. Maximilian Kolbe have demonstrated.

Conclusion: Epistemological or Ontological?

Clearly, many agape-justice conflicts pose difficult questions and unpalatable trade-offs. But it is well worth spending the time and effort to weigh them and to talk with each other as we grapple with them. How we resolve these trade-offs will ultimately shape our personal and collective self-respect and self-understanding of who we are as individuals and as a human community. Equally important, how we decide agape-justice conflicts today will leave future generations either with even bigger problems or with examples of how to choose wisely and well.

Nevertheless, settling the clashing claims of agape and justice is one of the more vexing problems in public policy, social philosophy, and moral theology. This study set out to address the following questions, namely:

- How and why do these agape-justice clashes arise in a world that is supposed to be governed by a perfect divine providence and a coherent divine will?

- How do we decide such clashing claims? Whose demands take priority, agape or justice? Why?
- Are such conflicts due to human limitations in knowing (epistemological) or are they part of the cosmic order itself (ontological), or both?

Epistemological in Nature

The question of how to settle agape-justice conflicts and the question of whether such clashing claims are epistemological or ontological both turn out to be dependent on the even more fundamental question of how and why these conflicts arise in the first place. Edmund Santurri (1987) proposes that such moral dilemmas arise because of limitations in humans' ability to know what they ought to do or because of consequences from past wrongs or bad decisions, or both.

This study finds that agape-justice conflicts are indeed epistemological in nature and the result of past wrongdoing or mistakes. We find this epistemological dimension on display in the first three of our four proximate causes of agape-justice conflicts. First, society requires a delicate balancing of the claims of justice and agape. Both are indispensable for the existence and smooth functioning of the community. Both justice and agape complement each other. Chapter 4 borrows from biology to describe this critical balance as socioeconomic homeostasis. Agape-justice conflicts are telltale signs that this requisite balance is out of kilter and requires adjustment. They may in fact be symptomatic of the need to change the customs, law, and usage (CLU) that are the bases for justice's claims. Just as a fever calls attention to an infection somewhere in the body, agape-justice conflicts may in fact point to something awry in the body politic that needs to be addressed.

Take access to healthcare in the United States as an example. During World War II, some US employers gave healthcare benefits to their workers as an enticement to prevent them from working elsewhere. (There was a nationwide wage freeze as part of the war effort.) Employer-provided healthcare was supererogatory then or an act of liberality (columns 4 and 3, Table 1.2). Over time, however, employer-provided healthcare became common practice and the industry norm (column 2: relational moral debt). Three generations later, the Affordable Healthcare Act mandated that employers with at least fifty full-time workers had to provide such healthcare for their workers (column 1: legal due).

Take the case of neglected elderly parents. Public ethos, natural law, and longstanding, deeply-rooted Confucian family values underscore the need to care for one's parents in the twilight of their years (relational moral debt). This was, in fact, the case in China and Singapore until the economic globalization of the last forty years. Since then, children have routinely neglected their elderly parents as they prioritize their careers. The problem has gotten so bad to the point that the Chinese and Singaporean governments have had to formalize in legislation the duty of children to support their elderly parents, going so far as to specify the number of visits and to allow parents to sue their children (Serrano et al. 2017). This is a case of moral debts being codified and made into legal debts in response to exigencies.

These are examples of what used to be supererogatory or merely a moral debt ultimately becoming a legal due. Of course, along with this is the change from being merely an imperfect duty to being a perfect duty. Universal basic income today is considered supererogatory. In the future, as more communities experiment with this practice, it may yet become an entitlement by law. The living wage is deemed supererogatory in some local jurisdictions but is now law in others. It was the same trajectory for how modern social safety nets came about, from Bismarck's social security in Prussia in the nineteenth century, to Franklin Delano Roosevelt's US social security in the 1930s, to Lyndon Johnson's Medicare, Medicaid, and war on poverty in the 1960s.

New scientific and technological breakthroughs alter how humans work, live, consume, and collaborate with one another. Some of these changes are so revolutionary as to transform human society thoroughly. We have seen this twice – in the Industrial Revolution of the eighteenth and nineteenth centuries that inaugurated the modern industrial era of great wealth and mass consumption and then in the Microelectronics Revolution of the late twentieth century and its resulting globalized knowledge economy. Shifts in the socioeconomic landscape require corresponding requisite adjustments in its homeostasis. Agape-justice conflicts alert humans to the needed alterations – where, when, how, and the extent of the needed adjustments (e.g., Chapter 6 on expanding circle of kin love). These conflicts are epistemological indeed.

A second finding on the epistemological nature of agape-justice conflicts comes from numerous examples of how these clashing claims arise from the unattended consequences of past wrongs or from unresolved past disequilibria in agape and justice's homeostasis. For example, Chapter 5 finds this to be indeed at the root of the contemporary problems of cross-border migration. On the one hand, chronic economic mismanagement and corruption in many poor countries have spawned gang violence and profound destitution that have driven their populations to flee. On the other hand, wealthier nations have been indifferent and have failed to help in the development of their lagging neighbors. The consequence has been the current massive exodus from failed, failing, or destitute countries in the South to the more prosperous and safer countries in the North. Unattended past disequilibria in the socioeconomic homeostasis and uncorrected past wrongs lead to even more and bigger problems down the road, including clashing claims between agape and justice. Agape-justice conflicts may serve a diagnostic function by informing us of past wrongs and nudging us to mitigate or correct them before they get worse. Agape-justice conflicts may provide the occasion to correct unaddressed past wrongs or disequilibria.

Third, this study finds that many agape-justice conflicts are about the tension between the claims of our natural, kin-particularistic loves, on the one hand, and the claims of universal love for all, including the distant and the stranger, on the other hand. Chapter 6 notes that love is diffusive, and our circle of love and responsibility ought to expand over time as part of our moral development. Agape-justice conflicts are part of such growth and provide the opportunity to deepen our natural loves.

Thus, agape-justice conflicts present humans with learning opportunities on how to maintain balance in the socioeconomic homeostasis; which past wrongs and disequilibria they ought to address; and when and how far they ought to expand their circle of love and responsibility beyond their kin love. Agape-justice conflicts do reveal our limitations in human knowing. This study presents concrete cases for how and why it is that agape-justice conflicts are in fact epistemological in nature, as Santurri (1987) observes.

Ontological in Nature

Agape-justice conflicts present unique and powerful occasions for the infused virtue of *caritas* to do its transformative work. Salvation is a pure gift. Humans can never earn it through their own merits. Nevertheless, God works through nature to accomplish divine ends and plans. God builds on nature. The ongoing divine work of Creation-Providence unfolds through nature. The most vivid proof and instance of this is the incarnation of the Second Person of the Blessed Trinity – Jesus Christ.

God does not force grace on humans. God is ever respectful of human free will to do that, as we have seen repeatedly in salvation history. Rather, grace is given and is ever-present. However, humans for their part must voluntarily open their hearts and minds to these graces producing an abundant harvest for them and for others. Agape-justice conflicts provide the occasion for such human response to grace at work in the here and now. In particular, these conflicts provide the chance to cooperate with God's infusion of *caritas* in our world. Agape-justice conflicts are especially fertile ground for such growth because of the difficulties generated and the sacrifices demanded. Indeed, a *caritas*-animated resolution of agape-justice conflicts provides a glimpse into God at work in human lives.

Given God's track record of working through nature, is it inconceivable that God's purposes are also at work through agape-justice conflicts? This study finds that agape-justice conflicts turn out to perform significant, indeed, indispensable functions for both personal and community life besides their aforesaid epistemological contributions. We have identified at least three of these additional functions.

First, agape-justice conflicts may in fact be the venue by which *philautia, storge*, and *philia* find their completion and perfection in agape. The expansion in our circle of love and responsibility is not merely an episte-mological matter. Rather, it is about growth in virtue and love. Agape-justice conflicts prevent these natural loves from shriveling into narcissism or into a cocoon that goes no further than our own self-interest and our kin love. Agape-justice conflicts may in fact be the catalysts for giving full vent to love's diffusiveness and thereby soar to the upper reaches of agape and beyond (Chapter 6). Such agape-justice conflicts may in fact be the venue for deepening our natural loves.

Second, as we have seen across all these chapters, agape-justice conflicts are extremely difficult to resolve because of their complexity, multiple causes, and the disexternalities they spawn, whereby even more injustice or disequilibria inadvertently arise no matter how we resolve them. Despite their seeming intractable hurdles, agape-justice conflicts can ultimately be resolved by loving as Christ loves (Chapter 7). However, loving as Christ has loved us is easier said than done.

Growth in agape is possible only in a process of learning by doing. It is never merely theoretical. Agape is never merely possessed in theory but can only be lived and experienced in actuality. That is the opportunity that supererogation provides. Thus, it is plausible that the Divine Creator has embedded agape-justice conflicts in the order of creation itself – as opportunities and building blocks for growth in virtue and love. This is especially so considering the sacrificial self-giving that they often demand. These conflicts may in fact be occasions whereby grace builds on nature, and infused agape is given as a gift. The heroic supererogation called for by agape-justice conflicts is infused agape at work – turning acquired agape into Christified agape, culminating in *caritas*, friendship with God. Indeed, it is entirely plausible that Divine Providence uses these agape-justice conflicts as stepping-stones for humans in their grace-empowered journey toward their *telos* of union with God. Agape-justice conflicts are part of the growth pangs of the human journey toward divine love.

Caritas reorients every aspect of the recipient's life. This includes the loves of that person. *Caritas* reorients the loves of that person and lets them grow to their supernatural fullness, and this includes transcending oneself and one's circle of natural loves to expand into a wider circle that includes the distant, the strangers, and even the enemy. It is to move toward the One Body of Christ (1 Cor 12).

Third, resolving agape-justice conflicts becomes much more difficult and complex because they mostly require collective action. The human community is fraught with daunting collective-action problems. Contemporary society is witness to this in their collective helplessness and inaction even amid an imminent climate-change crisis, the international depletion of fish stocks, and the plastic pollution of the oceans, just to name a few examples. This is not even to mention the inability of nations and the global community to combat pandemics due to the sore lack of cooperation and mutual assistance.

Chapter 8 shows that problematic agape-justice conflicts turn out to be excellent occasions for working with one another and building community. Moreover, they provide unique opportunities for growth not only in personal virtue but also in collective virtue, an even more significant accomplishment. Many of the cases we have seen in the study require collective self-sacrifice. These are occasions for forming collective virtue and a shared self-understanding qua members of a community. After all, infused virtue is also imparted at a collective level, as in the case of Pentecost Sunday and the early Church (Acts 2).

These three cases are examples of grace building on nature. Agape-justice conflicts are conduits for infused agape (*caritas*) to bring about human flourishing as:

- Our circle of kin-particularistic love expands to include the distant, the stranger, and perhaps even the undeserving (Chapter 6).
- Obligees voluntarily forego their rightful claims in favor of those without claims and, consequently, experience how it is to love as Christ loves in such supererogatory self-sacrifice (Chapter 7).
- The community grows in collective virtue (Chapter 8).

All these are important venues for growth in supernatural excellence so much so that it is reasonable to think that there are divine reasons for sowing agape-justice conflicts in the order of divine creation. It is plausible to believe that some agape-justice conflicts are part of divine governance and providence by design. In other words, some agape-justice conflicts may in fact be ontological in nature as openings to give vent to love's diffusiveness, to develop the moral faculties of reason and freedom, to acquire personal and collective virtue, to build community, and, most of all, to grow in Christified agape (*caritas*). In fact, the earlier epistemological limitations may, by divine design, also be meant to be channels for growth in these critical areas. Even the epistemological limitations turn out to be ultimately ontological in nature.

Possibilities Going Forward

Paul Tillich (1954) concludes his study of the ontology of justice and love by suggesting that we could avoid conflicts and alienating people altogether by simply freezing economic life to a set formula that satisfies justice and everyone else's claims. However, he observes that the absence of such struggles would also impoverish life of its dynamism and creativity. It will also severely restrict freedom. I agree. We should not be afraid of sorting through the moral dilemmas posed by agape and justice with their competing claims because humans are more than up to rising above them because of grace. After all, God is the source of love and justice.

Unlike Santurri (1987), Ruth Marcus (1980, 1996) observes that there are genuine moral dilemmas, and that the foregone duty is nevertheless still a live obligation, an unfulfilled duty. This is what she calls a moral residue. We have a duty to minimize such moral residues in the future by rearranging our practices or taking preemptive measures to the extent that we can do so. Patricia Marino (2001, 204–206) notes that such moral residue may in fact be the catalyst for a collective effort that leads to moral progress when we collectively and individually put in the effort to head off such moral dilemmas going forward. She notes that "the occurrence of dilemmas forces us to see where we are failing" (p. 219).

Indeed, agape-justice conflicts may in fact be instrumental for humans' eventual union with God, their *telos*. Far from intimidating us, agape-justice moral quandaries should be welcomed for the opportunities they bring. They are occasions for grace to build on our human frailties and brokenness – grace building on nature in the ongoing divine creation of a world that is both loving and just.

References

3M. 2021. "3M Response to Defense Production Act Order," https://news.3m.com/2020-04-03-3M-Response-to-Defense-Production-Act-Order last accessed July 5, 2021.

Akerlof, George A. 1970. "The Market for 'Lemons': Quality Uncertainty and the Market Mechanism," *Quarterly Journal of Economics* 84 (3): 488–500.

Albert, Ethel, Theodore Denise, and Sheldon Peterfreund (Eds.). 1984. *Great Traditions in Ethics*, Fifth edition. Belmont, CA: Wadsworth.

Albrecht, Leslie. 2021. "This Is How Many Americans Gave Away Their Stimulus Check Money," MarketWatch (Apr 2). www.marketwatch.com/story/americans-increased-their-charitable-giving-in-2020-helped-by-stimulus-checks-and-a-stock-market-recovery-11617372478 last accessed May 13, 2022.

Allbee, Richard. 2006. "Asymmetrical Continuity of Love and Law between the Old and New Testaments: Explicating the Implicit Side of a Hermeneutical Bridge, Leviticus 19.11–18," *Journal for the Study of the Old Testament* 31 (2): 147–166.

Ambrose. 1952. "*De Officiis Ministrorum Libri Tres* (On the Duties of the Clergy)," in *Nicene and Post-Nicene Fathers of the Christian Church: Second Series*, Philip Schaff and Henry Wace (Eds.). Grand Rapids, MI: W.B. Eerdmans. www.ccel.org/ccel/schaff/npnf210.html last accessed March 18, 2022; www.documentacatholicaomnia.eu/03d/0339-0397,_Ambrosius,_De_Officiis_Ministrorum_Libri_Tres_[Schaff],_EN.pdf last accessed March 18, 2022

Appleyard, Dennis and Alfred Field. 2017. *International Economics*. New York: McGraw-Hill.

Aquinas, Thomas. 1920. *Summa Theologiæ*. Translated by Fathers of the English Dominican Province. www.newadvent.org/summa/ last accessed April 16, 2022.

Aquinas, Thomas. 1964. *Commentary on the Nichomachean Ethics*. Translated by C. I. Litzinger, O.P., Chicago: Henry Regnery Company. https://isidore.co/aquinas/english/Ethics5.htm#4 last accessed April 16, 2022.

Aronson, Ronald. 1990. "Responsibility and Complicity," *Philosophical Papers* 19: 53–73.

Associated Press. 2007. "Malden Mills Bankrupt Again," *Berkshire Eagle* (Jan 11). www.berkshireeagle.com/archives/malden-mills-bankrupt-again/article_0cf345f7-bb84-5928-a77c-6c664c96ecod.html

Associated Press. 2019. "Alabama City Backs Off Jail Time for Helping Panhandlers," *Tuscaloosa News* (Nov 6). www.tuscaloosanews.com/story/news/state/2019/11/06/alabama-city-backs-off-jail-time-for-helping-panhandlers/2352887007/ last accessed May 14, 2022.

Augustine. 1998. *De Doctrina Christiana* (On Christian Doctrine). eBook. Grand Rapids, MI: Christian Classics Ethereal Library. https://faculty.georgetown.edu/jod/augustine/ddc1.html last accessed February 19, 2022.

Azmi, Hadi and Ushar Daniele. 2021. "As Malaysia's Bumiputra Policy Turns 50, Citizens Debate Impact of Affirmative Action," *This Week In Asia* (Nov 6). www.scmp.com/week-asia/people/article/3154980/malaysias-bumiputra-policy-turns-50-citizens-debate-impact last accessed April 19, 2022.

Baker, John. 1984. "Biblical Attitudes to Romantic Love," *Tyndale Bulletin* 34: 91–128. The Tyndale Biblical Theology Lecture 1983.

Barber, Harriet and Mason Boycott-Owen. 2022. "UK the Only G7 Country to Cut Aid during Covid Pandemic," *The Telegraph* (Apr 12). www.telegraph.co.uk/global-health/climate-and-people/uk-g7-country-cut-aid-covid-pandemic/ last accessed June 1, 2022.

Beauchamp, Tom. 2013. "The Principle of Beneficence in Applied Ethics," *Stanford Encyclopedia of Philosophy*. https://plato.stanford.edu/entries/principle-beneficence/ last accessed June 28, 2021.

Becker, Gary. 1981. "Altruism in the Family and Selfishness in the Market Place," *Economica* 48 (189): 1–15.

Behsudi, Adam. 2022. *Denmark's Social Trust in Action*. IMF Country Focus. Washington, DC: IMF. www.imf.org/en/News/Articles/2022/02/01/cf-denmark-social-trust-in-action#:~:text=Whether%20it's%20based%20in%20enlightened,will%20maintain%20the%20social%20fabric last accessed April 23, 2022.

Benedict XVI. 2005. *Deus Caritas est*. Rome: Vatican.

Benedict XVI. 2009. *Caritatis in veritate*. Rome: Vatican.

Beran, Harry. 1972. "Ought, Obligation, and Duty," *Australasian Journal of Philosophy*, 50 (3): 207–221.

Bernstein, Jeffrey. 2008. "Righteousness and Divine Love: Maimonides and Thomas on Charity," in *Questions on Love and Charity: Summa Theologiae, Secunda Secundae*, Questions 2 3–46: Thomas Aquinas. Edited by Robert Miner. New Haven, CT: Yale.

Birch, Bruce. 1991. *Let Justice Roll Down: The Old Testament, Ethics, and Christian Life*. Louisville, KY: Westminster/John Knox Press.

Bishop, Harold. 2015. "Individual Compassionate Use: Concerns for Drug Manufacturers Considering Participation," Wolters Kluwer Law and Business White Paper (Apr). www.ebglaw.com/wp-content/uploads/2015/04/Dow-Individual-Compassionate-Use-Concerns-for-Drug-Manufacturers-Considering-Participation.pdf last accessed May 15, 2022.

Bloomberg News. 2021. "China's Curbs on Fertilizer Exports to Worsen Global Price Shock," (Oct 19). www.bloomberg.com/news/articles/2021-10-19/china-s-curbs-on-fertilizer-exports-to-worsen-global-price-shock last accessed April 30, 2022.

Boseley, Sarah. 2017. "Threats, Bullying, Lawsuits: Tobacco Industry's Dirty War for the African Market," *The Guardian* (July 12). www.theguardian.com/world/2017/jul/12/big-tobacco-dirty-war-africa-market last accessed January 6, 2022.

Bramer, Marilea. 2010. "The Importance of Personal Relationships in Kantian Moral Theory: A Reply to Care Ethics," *Hypatia* 25 (1): 121–139.

Breuninger, Kevin and Christina Wilkie. 2020. "Trump Bans Export of Coronavirus Protection Gear, says he's 'not happy with 3M'," www.cnbc.com/2020/04/03/coronavirus-trump-to-ban-export-of-protective-gear-after-slamming-3m.html last accessed July 5, 2021.

Browning, Don S. 2008. "Love as Sacrifice, Love as Mutuality: Response to Jeffrey Tillman," *Zygon* 43 (3): 557–562.

Bruni, Luigino and Stefano Zamagni. 2007. *Civil Economy: Efficiency, Equity, Public Happiness (Frontiers of Business Ethics)*. Oxford & Bern: Peter Lang.

Buchanan, Allen. 1987. "Justice and Charity," *Ethics* 97 (3): 558–575.

Burch, George Bosworth. 1950. "The Christian Philosophy of Love," *The Review of Metaphysics* 3 (4): 411–426.

Busby, Joshua William. 2007. "Bono Made Jesse Helms Cry: Jubilee 2000, Debt Relief, and Moral Action in International Politics," *International Studies Quarterly* 51 (2): 247–275.

Byerly, T. Ryan and Meghan Byerly. 2016. "Collective Virtue," *Journal of Value Inquiry* 50: 33–50.

Campbell, T. D. 1965. "Perfect and Imperfect Obligations," *Modern Schoolman* 52: 285–294.

Carmichael, E. D. H. 2004. *Friendship: Interpreting Christian Love*. New York: T&T Clark.

Chalifoux, Mark. 2020. "Teacher Creates a Community Library in Her Garage [a]mid COVID," The Dad (Sept 19). www.thedad.com/garage-library/ last accessed April 16, 2022.

Chisolm, Paul. 2018. "The Food Insecurity of North Korea," National Public Radio (NPR) (June 19). www.npr.org/sections/goatsandsoda/2018/06/19/620484758/the-food-insecurity-of-north-korea last accessed May 30, 2022.

Cicero. 1913. *De Officiis*. English translation by Walter Miller. New York: MacMillan. https://ryanfb.github.io/loebolus-data/L030.pdf last accessed March 29, 2022.

CNN Money. 2001. "Malden Mills in Chapter 11," (Nov 30). https://money.cnn.com/2001/11/30/companies/malden_mills/ last accessed May 17, 2022.

Coakley, S. 2001. "Kenosis: Theological Meanings and Gender Connotations," in *The Work of Love: Creation as Kenosis*, J. Polkinghorne (Ed.), pp. 192–210. Grand Rapids: Eerdmans.

Cohen, Patricia. 2015. "A Company Copes with Backlash Against the Raise That Roared," *New York Times* (July 31). www.nytimes.com/2015/08/02/business/a-company-copes-with-backlash-against-the-raise-that-roared.html last accessed May 13, 2022.

Congressional Research Service. 2018. "Overview of the ACA Medicaid Expansion," https://sgp.fas.org/crs/misc/IF10399.pdf last accessed May 28, 2022.

Crawford, A. Berry. 1969. "On the Concept of Obligations," *Ethics* 79 (4): 316–319.

Dewan, Lawrence. 1992. "St. Thomas, God's Goodness, and God's Morality," *The Modern Schoolman* 70: 45–51.

Dijsselbloem, Jeroen. n.d. "Enter the Troika: The European Commission, the IMF, the ECB," European Stability Mechanism. www.esm.europa.eu/publications/safeguarding-euro/enter-troika-european-commission-imf-ecb last accessed May 20, 2022.

Duckett, Stephen John. 2023. *Healthcare Funding and Christian Ethics*. UK: Cambridge.

Economic Times. 2008. "India Rice Export Ban Hits UAE Badly," (Apr 3). https://economictimes.indiatimes.com/markets/commodities/india-rice-export-ban-hits-uae-badly/articleshow/2923173.cms?from=mdr last accessed April 30, 2022.

Economist. 2022a. "Meanness to Migrants: Educating the Undocumented," (May 14).

Economist. 2022b. "Human Capital in the 21st Century: How Modern Executives Are Different from Their Forebears," (June 16).

Eisner, Peter. 2009. "Saving the Jews of Nazi France," *Smithsonian Magazine*. (Mar). www.smithsonianmag.com/history/saving-the-jews-of-nazi-france-52554953/ last accessed January 16, 2023.

Elster, Jon. 1983. *Sour Grapes: Studies in the Subversion of Rationality*. Cambridge: Cambridge University Press.

Erickson, Britt. 2017. "Activists Sue over Revamped U.S. Chemical Law," Chemical and Engineering News 95 39 (Oct 2). https://cen.acs.org/articles/95/i39/Activists-sue-over-revamped-US.html last accessed May 7, 2022.

Ferry, Michael. 2013. "Does Morality Demand Our Very Best? On Moral Prescriptions and the Line of Duty," *Philosophical Studies* 165: 573–589.

Finn, Daniel. 2016. "What Is a Sinful Social Structure?" *Theological Studies* 77 (1): 136–164.

Fisher, Max. 2022. "How Domestic Politics Unravel the World's Pledge to Refugees," *New York Times* (Apr 18).

Flanagan, Owen and Kathryn Jackson. 1987. "Justice, Care, and Gender: The Kohlberg-Gilligan Debate Revisited," *Ethics* 97 (3): 622–637.

Floyd, Shawn. 2009. "Aquinas and the Obligations of Mercy," *Journal of Religious Ethics* 37 (3): 449–471.

Food and Agriculture Organization (FAO). 2022. *The Importance of Ukraine and the Russian Federation for Global Agricultural Markets and the Risks Associated with the Current Conflict*. Rome: FAO. www.fao.org/3/cb9013en/cb9013en.pdf last accessed April 30, 2022.

Fox, F. Earle. 1959. "Defining 'Oughtness' and 'Love'," *Journal of Religion* 39 (3): 170–182.

Frank, Robert H., Thomas Gilovich, and Dennis T. Regan. 1993. "Does Studying Economics Inhibit Cooperation?" *Journal of Economic Perspectives* 7 (2): 159–171. https://doi.org/10.1257/jep.7.2.159

Frankfurt, Harry. 1998. "Duty and Love," *Philosophical Explorations* 1 (1): 4–9.

Friedman, Milton. 1970. "A Friedman Doctrine: The Social Responsibility of Business Is to Increase Its Profits," *New York Times* (Sept 13).

Frost, Natasha. 2022. "If Migrants Are Disabled, 2 Nations May Bar Them Based on Costs of Care," *New York Times* (Oct 31).

Fukuyama, Francis. 1995. *Trust: The Social Virtues and the Creation of Prosperity.* New York: Free Press Paperbacks.

Fukuyama, Francis. 1999. *Social Capital and Civil Society.* IMF Conference on Second Generation Reforms. Washington, DC: IMF. www.imf.org/external/pubs/ft/seminar/1999/reforms/fukuyama.htm last accessed May 23, 2022.

Gardner, E. Clinton. 1957. "Justice and Love," *Theology Today* 14 (2): 212–222.

George, David. 2004. *Preference Pollution: How Markets Create the Desires We Dislike.* Ann Arbor: University of Michigan Press.

George W. Bush Institute. 2018. "President George W. Bush on Compassionate Conservatism," Fall Issue 12. www.bushcenter.org/catalyst/opportunity-road/george-w-bush-on-compassionate-conservatism.html last accessed April 19, 2022.

Gert, Bernard. 2005. *Morality.* New York: Oxford University Press.

Geest, Paul van. 2021. *Morality in the Marketplace: Reconciling Theology and Economics.* Leiden & Boston: Brill.

Gilmore, Anna B., Gary Fooks, Jeffrey Drope, Stella Aguinaga Bialous, and Rachel Rose Jackson. 2015. "Exposing and Addressing Tobacco Industry Conduct in Low and Middle Income Countries," *Lancet* (Mar 14) 385 (9972): 1029–1043. www.ncbi.nlm.nih.gov/pmc/articles/PMC4382920/ last accessed May 7, 2022.

Good, Keith. 2022. "India Bans Wheat Exports," *Farm Policy News* (May 14). https://farmpolicynews.illinois.edu/2022/05/india-bans-wheat-exports/ last accessed May 27, 2022.

Gregory, James. 1975. "Image of Limited Good, or Expectation of Reciprocity?" *Current Anthropology* 16: 73–92.

Gro Intelligence. 2021. "Russia Imposes Fertilizer Export Quotas to Control Inflation," (Nov 5). https://gro-intelligence.com/insights/russia-fertilizer-export-quotas-to-control-inflation last accessed April 30, 2022.

The Guardian. 2017. "French Farmer on Trial for Helping Migrants across Italian Border," Agence France-Presse in Nice (Jan 4). www.theguardian.com/world/2017/jan/04/french-farmer-cedric-herrou-trial-helping-migrants-italian-border last accessed May 3, 2022.

The Guardian. 2020. "French Court Scraps Farmer's Conviction for Helping Migrants Cross Border," Agence France-Presse in Lyon (May 13). www.theguardian.com/world/2020/may/13/french-court-scraps-olive-farmers-conviction-for-helping-migrants-cross-border last accessed May 3, 2022.

Guarnieri, Grace. 2018. "Why It's Illegal to Feed the Homeless in Cities Across America," *Newsweek* (Jan 16). www.newsweek.com/illegal-feed-criminalizing-homeless-america-782861 last accessed May 5, 2022.

Hallett, Garth. 1998. *Priorities and Christian Ethics.* UK: Cambridge.

Hardin, Garrett. 1968. "The Tragedy of the Commons." *Science* 162: 1243–1248.

Harrelson, Walter. 1951. "The Idea of Agape in the New Testament," *Journal of Religion* 31 (3): 169–182.

Harris, Ron. 2020. "A New Understanding of the History of Limited Liability: An Invitation for Theoretical Reframing," *Journal of Institutional Economics* 16 (5): 643–664.

Hart, H. L. A. 1961. *The Concept of Law*. Oxford: Clarendon.

Hassan, M. Kabir and Muneeza, Aishath. 2024. "Islamic Economics," in *Oxford Handbook of Religion and Economic Ethics*, Albino Barrera and Roy Amore (Eds.). UK: Oxford.

Hays, Constance. 2000. "Ben & Jerry's To Unilever, With Attitude," *New York Times* (Apr 13).

Held, Virginia. 2006. *The Ethics of Care: Personal, Political, and Global*. New York: Oxford University Press.

Herman, Barbara. 2001. "The Scope of Moral Requirement," *Philosophy & Public Affairs* 30 (3): 227–256.

Hernandez, Samantha. 2021. "When Teachers Brought Free Lunch to Kids Amid COVID-19, They Saw Poverty Up Close," *USA Today* (Jan 3).

Hesse, Mary Margaret. 2018. "U.S. Legal Immigration: Family Reunification vs Skills-Based Points Systems," International Preparedness Associates. www.theipagroup.com/global-strategy-group/forum/14-immigration/12-u-s-legal-immigration-family-reunification-vs-skills-based-points-systems?layout=edit last accessed May 4, 2022.

Himmelfarb, Gertrude. 1996. "The Illusions of Cosmopolitanism," in *For Love of Country?* by Martha Nussbaum (Author), Joshua Cohen (Ed.), pp. 72–77. Boston: Beacon.

Hirschfeld, Mary. 2018. *Aquinas and the Market: Toward a Humane Economy*. Cambridge, MA: Harvard University Press.

Homan, Maya. 2020. "Changemaker: Teacher Designs Traveling Library to Lend Books to Students during COVID-19," *The Boston Scope* (Sept 29).

Hume, David. 1896. *A Treatise of Human Nature*. UK: Oxford-Clarendon. http://files.libertyfund.org/files/342/0213_Bk.pdf last accessed March 19, 2022.

Hume, David. 1902. *Enquiries Concerning the Human Understanding and Concerning the Principles of Morals*. Second edition. UK: Oxford-Clarendon. https://oll-resources.s3.us-east-2.amazonaws.com/oll3/store/titles/341/0222_Bk.pdf last accessed March 19, 2022.

Igneski, Violetta. 2007. "Equality, Sufficiency and the State," *Dialogue* (Canadian Philosophical Association) 46: 311–334.

Ingram, Paul. 2019. "No More Deaths Volunteers Fined $250, Sentenced to 15 mos. Probation," *Tucson Sentinel* (Mar 1). www.tucsonsentinel.com/local/report/030119_no_more_deaths/no-more-deaths-volunteers-fined-250-sentenced-15-mos-probation/ last accessed May 4, 2022.

International Monetary Fund (IMF). 2017. "Multilateral Debt Relief Initiative – Questions and Answers," www.imf.org/external/np/exr/mdri/eng/index.htm last accessed July 18, 2022.

International Monetary Fund (IMF). 2022. "Proposal to Establish a Resilience and Sustainability Trust," IMF Policy Paper No. 2022/013 (Apr 18). www.imf.org/en/Publications/Policy-Papers/Issues/2022/04/15/Proposal-To-Establish-A-Resilience-and-Sustainability-Trust-516692 last accessed May 13, 2022.

Irwin, Terence. 2016. "Conceptions of Love, Greek and Christian," in *Love and Christian Ethics*, Frederick Simmons and Brian Sorrells (Eds.). Washington, DC: Georgetown University Press.

Jackson, Timothy P. 1992. "Christian Love and Political Violence," in *The Love Commandments*, Edmund Santurri and William Werpehowski (Eds.), pp. 182–220. Washington, DC: Georgetown University Press.

Jadhav, Rajendra. 2022. "Indonesia's Palm Oil Export Ban Leaves Global Buyers with No Plan B," Reuters (Apr 25). www.reuters.com/business/indonesias-palm-oil-export-ban-leaves-global-buyers-with-no-plan-b-2022-04-25/ last accessed April 30, 2022.

Janssens, Louis. 1977. "Norms and Priorities of a Love Ethics," *Louvain Studies* 6: 207–238.

Jayanetti, Chaminda. 2018. "NHS Denied Treatment for Migrants Who Can't Afford Upfront Charges," *The Guardian* (Nov 13). www.theguardian.com/society/2018/nov/13/nhs-denied-treatment-for-migrants-who-cant-afford-upfront-charges last accessed May 17, 2022.

Kamm, F. M. 2000. "Does Distance Matter Morally to the Duty to Rescue?" *Law and Philosophy* 9:6:655–681.

Kant, Immanuel. 1991. *The Metaphysics of Morals*. Translated by Mary Gregor. UK: Cambridge. https://ld.circuitdebater.org/w/archive_files/%5BImmanuel_Kant%5D_Kant_The_Metaphysics_of_Morals.pdf/507955836/%5BImmanuel_Kant%5D_Kant_The_Metaphysics_of_Morals.pdf last accessed March 19, 2022

Kant, Immanuel. 1993. *Grounding for the Metaphysics of Morals*. Third edition. Translated by James W. Ellington. Indianapolis: Hackett Publishing.

Kavi, Aishvarya. 2022. "They Grew Up Legally in the U.S., but Can't Stay After They Turn 21," *New York Times* (Apr 30). www.nytimes.com/2022/04/30/us/politics/documented-dreamers.html last accessed May 23, 2022.

Kitsantonis, Niki. 2021. "Greece to Put Aid Workers Who Helped Migrants on Trial on Espionage Charges," *New York Times* (Nov 17). www.nytimes.com/2021/11/17/world/europe/greece-migrants-aid-workers-espionage.html last accessed May 4, 2022.

Kolodny, Niko. 2003. "Love as Valuing a Relationship," *Philosophical Review* 112 (2): 135–189.

Kose, M. Ayhan, Guy Meredith, and Christopher Towe. 2004. "How Has NAFTA Affected the Mexican Economy? Review and Evidence," IMF Working Paper 04/59.

Koutsouvilis, A. 1976. "On Benevolence," *Mind, New Series* 85 (339): 428–431.

Kwai, Isabella. 2021. "Australia to Shift All Offshore Processing of Migrants to Island Nation of Nauru," *New York Times* (Oct 6). www.nytimes.com/2021/10/06/world/australia/australia-migrants-nauru-papua-new-guinea.html#:~:text=the%20main%20story-,Australia%20to%20Shift%20All%20Offshore%20Processing%20of%20Migrants%20to%20Island,on%20the%20island%20of%20Nauru last accessed May 20, 2022.

Labonte, Marc and Lida Weinstock. 2022. "Inflation in the U.S. Economy: Causes and Policy Options," Congressional Research Service. R47273 (Oct 6). https://crsreports.congress.gov last accessed January 6, 2023.

Lawder, David. 2021. "Taliban Rule Presents Aid Agencies with Moral, Fiscal Dilemma," Reuters (Aug 24). www.reuters.com/world/taliban-rule-presents-aid-agencies-with-moral-fiscal-dilemma-2021-08-24/ last accessed May 30, 2022.

Leary, Alaina. 2018. "How Proposed Changes to Public Charge Will Make It Hard to Immigrate with a Disability," Rooted in Rights.org. https://rootedinrights.org/how-proposed-changes-to-public-charge-will-make-it-hard-to-immigrate-with-a-disability/ last accessed May 3, 2022.

Leonard, Mary Delach. 2018. "How a Clayton manufacturer shared sacrifice to avoid layoffs during the Great Recession," St. Louis Public Radio (July 16). https://news.stlpublicradio.org/government-politics-issues/2018-07-16/how-a-clayton-manufacturer-shared-sacrifice-to-avoid-layoffs-during-the-great-recession last accessed May 13, 2022.

Levinas, Emmanuel. 1981. *Otherwise Than Being or Beyond Essence*. Translated by Alphonso Lingis. The Hague: Ni jhoff.

Lippitt, John. 2009. "True Self-love and True Self-sacrifice," *International Journal for Philosophy of Religion* 66 (3): 125–138.

Loewenstein, Mark. 2013. "Benefit Corporations: A Challenge in Corporate Governance," *The Business Lawyer* 68 (4): 1007–1038. American Bar Association (Aug 3). www.americanbar.org/groups/business_law/publications/the_business_lawyer/find_by_subject/buslaw_tbl_mci_benefitcorp/ last accessed July 18, 2022.

Lupkin, Sygney. 2019. "A Decade Marked By Outrage Over Drug Prices," (Dec 31). www.npr.org/sections/health-shots/2019/12/31/792617538/a-decade-marked-by-outrage-over-drug-prices last accessed April 16, 2022.

MacNeil, Sara. 2019. "Do You Give to Panhandlers? It Could Be Punishable with Jail Time in Montgomery," *Montgomery Advertiser* (Oct 15). www.montgomeryadvertiser.com/story/news/2019/10/15/giving-to-panhandlers-could-be-illegal-jail-time-soon-montgomery/3986214002/ last accessed May 3, 2022.

Makujina, John. 1991. "The Second Greatest Commandment and Self-Esteem," *The Master's Seminary Journal* 8 (2): 211–225.

Marcus, Ruth Barcan. 1980. "Moral Dilemmas and Consistency," *Journal of Philosophy* 77: 121–136.

Marcus, Ruth Barcan. 1996. "More about Moral Dilemmas," in *Moral Dilemmas and Moral Theory*, H. E. Mason (Ed.). New York: Oxford University Press.

Marino, Patricia. 2001. "Moral Dilemmas, Collective Responsibility, and Moral Progress," *Philosophical Studies* 104 (2): 203–225.

Maritain, Jacques. 1947. *The Person and the Common Good*. Translated by John J. Fitzgerald. New York: Charles Scribner's sons.

Marshall, Alfred. 1890. *Principles of Economics*. London: Macmillan.

Martell, Allison and Euan Rocha. 2021. "How the U.S. Locked up Vaccine Materials Other Nations Urgently Need," Reuters (May 7). www.reuters.com/business/healthcare-pharmaceuticals/how-us-locked-up-vaccine-materials-other-nations-urgently-need-2021-05-07/ last accessed May 4, 2022.

Martin, Drew. 2022. "Council Takes Action on Panhandling, Animal Ordinance," *The Montgomery Independent* (Apr 22). www.montgomeryindependent.com/news/council-takes-action-on-panhandling-animal-ordinance/article_ab178efa-c267-11ec-92ac-e79e56e37dc9.html last accessed May 20, 2022.

Mason, Rowena. 2021. "Outrage Aimed at No 10 as MPs Back £4bn Cut to Foreign Aid Budget," *The Guardian* (July 13). www.theguardian.com/politics/2021/jul/13/tory-rebels-unsure-if-they-have-numbers-to-block-foreign-aid-cut last accessed July 13, 2021.

McCloskey, Deirdre Nansen. 2007. *The Bourgeois Virtues: Ethics for an Age of Commerce*. Chicago: University of Chicago Press.

McClure, Joyce Kloc. 2003. "Seeing Through the Fog: Love and Injustice in Bleak House," *Journal of Religious Ethics* 31 (1): 23–44.

McDonnell, Patrick and Jorge Poblete. 2021. "Haitians in Chile: Rough Going for Many Prompts Large-scale Migration toward U.S.," *Los Angeles Times* (Oct 1). www.latimes.com/world-nation/story/2021-10-01/chile-haitians-migration last accessed May 20, 2022.

Mealand, David L. 1980. *Poverty and Expectation in the Gospels*. London: SPCK.

Milne, Sandy. 2021. "How Water Shortages Are Brewing Wars," BBC (Aug 16). www.bbc.com/future/article/20210816-how-water-shortages-are-brewing-wars last accessed May 4, 2022.

Mish'alani, James. 1969. "'Duty', 'Obligation' and 'Ought'," *Analysis* 30 (2): 33–40.

Miller, Sarah Clark. 2011. "A Feminist Account of Global Responsibility," *Social Theory and Practice* 37 (3): 391–412.

Mongeau, Gilles. 2013. "A More Cosmopolitan Salvation: Aquinas, Formation for Beatitude, and the Cross," *Lonergan Workshop* 24: 287–301.

Mulhere, Kaitlin. 2021. "Should Biden Cancel Student Debt? The Loan Forgiveness Debate, Explained," *Money* (May 21). https://money.com/student-loan-forgiveness-pros-cons/ last accessed May 16, 2022.

Mushaben, Joyce Marie. 2017. "Angela Merkel's Leadership in the Refugee Crisis," *Current History* 116 (788): 95–100.

Nagesh, Ashitha. 2021. "Afghanistan's Economy in Crisis after Taliban Take-over," *BBC News* (Aug 25). www.bbc.com/news/world-asia-58328246 last accessed May 30, 2022.

Naraya, Deepa, Raj Patel, Kai Schafft, Anne Rademacher, and Sarah Koch-Schulte. 2000. *Voices of the Poor: Can Anyone Hear Us?* Vol. 1. New York: Oxford University Press.

National Law Center on Homelessness and Poverty. 2019. *Housing Not Handcuffs 2019: Ending the Criminalization of Homelessness in U.S. Cities*. Washington, DC: National Homelessness Law Center. https://homelesslaw.org/wp-content/uploads/2019/12/HOUSING-NOT-HANDCUFFS-2019-FINAL.pdf last accessed May 16, 2022.

National Law Review. 2022. "Administrative Law Takeaways from the Federal Travel Mask Mandate Decision," *National Law Review* XII:112. www .natlawreview.com/article/administrative-law-takeaways-federal-travel-mask-mandate-decision last accessed May 6, 2022.

New York Times. 1964. "37 Who Saw Murder Didn't Call the Police; Apathy at Stabbing of Queens Woman Shocks Inspector," (Mar 27).

New York Times. 1987. "Merck Offers Free Distribution of New River Blindness Drug," (Oct 22). See also "Over 30 Years: The Mectizan® Donation Program." www.merck.com/stories/mectizan/ last accessed April 16, 2022.

Niazi, A. and H. Hassan. 2016. "Trust and Economic Performance: Evidence from Cross-country Panel Data Analysis," *Review of International Business and Strategy* 26 (3): 371–391. https://doi.org/10.1108/RIBS-02-2016-0010

Nicas, Jack. 2020. "The Man with 17,700 Bottles of Hand Sanitizer Just Donated Them," *New York Times* (Mar 15).

Niebuhr, Reinhold. 1953. "The Christian Faith and the Economic Life," in *Goals of Economic Life*, A. Dudley Ward (Ed.). New York: Harper

Niebuhr, Reinhold. 1957. *Love and Justice*. Edited by D. B. Robinson. Louisville: Westminster.

Nieto del Rio, Giulia McDonnell, and Miriam Jordan. 2021. "What Is DACA? And Where Does It Stand Now?," *New York Times* (July 16). www.nytimes .com/article/what-is-daca.html last accessed May 16, 2022.

Nussbaum, Martha. 2000. "Symposium on Cosmopolitanism: Duties of Justice, Duties of Material Aid: Cicero's Problematic Legacy," *Journal of Political Philosophy* 8 (2): 176–206.

Nussbaum, Martha. 2002. "Patriotism and Cosmopolitanism," in *For Love of Country?*, Joshua Cohen (Ed.), pp. 3–18. Boston: Beacon Press.

Nygren, Anders. 1953. *Agape and Eros*. Translated by Philip S. Watson. Philadelphia: Westminster Press.

O'Brien, T. C. (Ed.). 1971. "Appendix 1: Legal Debt, Moral Debt," in *Summa Theologiae* (Thomas Aquinas), vol. 41 (Virtues of Justice in the Human Community), pp. 316–320. New York: McGraw-Hill.

Oesterle, John. 1970. "Morally Good and Morally Right," *Monist* 54:1: 31–39; Gilby, Thomas (editor) 1964–1981. "Appendix 1: Legal Debt, Moral Debt," in *Summa Theologiae* (Thomas Aquinas), vol. 41, pp. 316–320. New York: McGraw-Hill.

Olthuis, James. 1983. "Book Review of Testaments of Love. A Study of Love in the Bible, by Leon Morris," *Calvin Theological Journal* 18 (1): 109–112.

Otis, Ginger Adams. 2022. "People Are Booking Airbnbs in Ukraine as a Way to Send Aid," Wall Street Journal (Mar 5).

Outka, Gene. 1972. *Agape: An Ethical Analysis*. New Haven: Yale University Press.

Outka, Gene. 1996. "Theocentric Agape and the Self: An Asymmetrical Affirmation in Response to Colin Grant's Either/Or," *Journal of Religious Ethics* 24 (1): 35–42.

Owens, David. 2012. "The Value of Duty, Part II of Relationships and Obligations," *Proceedings of the Aristotelian Society Supplementary* 86: 199–215.

Parlapiano, Alicia, Deborah B. Solomon, Madeleine Ngo, and Stacy Cowley. 2022. "Where $5 Trillion in Pandemic Stimulus Money Went," *New York Times* (Mar 11). www.nytimes.com/interactive/2022/03/11/us/how-covid-stimulus-money-was-spent.html last accessed April 19, 2022.

Perricone, John A. 2012. "The Relation between Justice and Love in the Natural Order," *Journal of Catholic Legal Studies* 51 (1): 55–75.

Phillips, Kristine. 2019. "They Left Food and Water for Migrants in the Desert. Now they Might Go to Prison," *Washington Post* (Jan 20). www.washingtonpost.com/ nation/2019/01/20/they-left-food-water-migrants-desert-now-they-might-go-prison/ last accessed May 4, 2022.

Pieper, Josef. 1990. *Four Cardinal Virtues, The: Human Agency, Intellectual Traditions, and Responsible Knowledge.* Notre Dame: University of Notre Dame Press.

Pink, Thomas. 2004. "Moral Obligation," in *Modern Moral Philosophy*, Anthony O'Hear (Ed.), pp. 159–186. UK: Cambridge.

Pius XI. 1931. *Quadragesimo Anno.* Vatican.

Plé, Albert. 1986. "The Morality of Duty and Obsessional Neurosis," *Cross Currents* 36 (3): 343–358.

Pogge, Thomas. 1992. "Cosmopolitanism and Sovereignty," *Ethics* 103 (1): 48–75.

Pogge, Thomas. 2008. *World Poverty and Human Rights.* Second edition. New York: Polity.

Pope, Stephen. 1990. "The Moral Centrality of Natural Priorities: A Thomistic Alternative to 'Equal Regard'," *The Annual of the Society of Christian Ethics* 10: 109–129.

Pope, Stephen. 1991. "Aquinas on Almsgiving, Justice and Charity: An Interpretation and Reassessment," *Heythrop Journal* 32: 167–191.

Pope, Stephen J. 1993. "The "Preferential Option for the Poor": An Ethic for "Saints and Heroes"?," *Irish Theological Quarterly* 59 (3): 161–176.

Pope, Stephen. 1995. "Love in Contemporary Christian Ethics," *Journal of Religious Ethics* 23 (1): 167–197.

Pope, Stephen. 1997. "'Equal Regard' versus 'Special Relations'? Reaffirming the Inclusiveness of Agape," *Journal of Religion* 77 (3): 353–379.

Popovich, Nadja, Livia Albeck-Ripka, and Kendra Pierre-Louis. 2021. "The Trump Administration Rolled Back More Than 100 Environmental Rules," *New York Times* (Jan 20). www.nytimes.com/interactive/2020/climate/trump-environment-rollbacks-list.html last accessed May 7, 2022.

Porter, Jean. 1989. "De Ordine Caritatis: Charity, Friendship, and Justice in Thomas Aquinas' Summa Theologiae," *Thomist* 53 (2): 197–213.

Porter, Jean. 2002. "The Virtue of Justice (IIa IIae, qq. 58–122)," in *The Ethics of Aquinas*, Stephen J. Pope (Ed.), pp. 272–286. Washington, DC: Georgetown University Press.

Post, Stephen. 1994. *Spheres of Love: Toward a New Ethics of the Family.* Dallas, TX: Southern Methodist University Press.

Quell, Molly. 2021. "Environmentalists Score Dual Wins at EU High Court," Courthouse News Service (Feb 25). www.courthousenews.com/environmentalists-score-dual-wins-at-eu-high-court/ last accessed May 7, 2022.

Rainbolt, George. 2000. "Perfect and Imperfect Obligations," *Philosophical Studies* 98: 233–256.

Rawls, John. 1971. *A Theory of Justice.* Cambridge, MA: Belknap Press.

Reid, Thomas. 1967. "Essays on the Active Powers of the Human Mind," in *Philosophical Works*, vol. 2. Hildesheim: Georg Olms Verlag.

Reuters. 2020, "Vietnam PM Says to Fully Resume Rice Exports from May," (Apr 28).

Rhonheimer, Martin. 2002. "Sins against Justice (IIa IIae, qq. 59–78)," in *The Ethics of Aquinas*, Frederick Lawrence (Trans.), S. Pope (Ed.), pp. 287–303. Washington, DC: Georgetown.

Ricoeur, Paul. 1995. "Love and Justice," *Philosophy and Social Criticism* 21 (5–6): 23–39.

Riley, Stephen. 1999. "Petty Corruption and Development," *Development in Practice* 9 (1/2): 189–193.

Roy, Rajesh and Vibhuti Agarwal. 2021. "India Suspends Covid-19 Vaccine Exports to Focus on Domestic Immunization," *Wall Street Journal* (Mar 25). www.wsj.com/articles/india-suspends-covid-19-vaccine-exports-to-focus-on-domestic-immunization-11616690859 last accessed May 4, 2022.

Samuels, Alec. 2019. "The NHS Refuses Treatment," *Medico-Legal Journal* 87 (1): 23–26.

Sandel, Michael. 2012. *What Money Can't Buy: The Moral Limits of Markets*. New York: Farrar, Straus and Giroux.

Santurri, Edmund. 1987. *Perplexity in the Moral Life: Philosophical and Theological Considerations*. Charlottesville: University Press of Virginia.

Schlag, Martin. 2012. "Justitia est amor: Love as Principle of Social and Economic Life?" *Acta Philosophica* 21 (1): 77–98.

Schneewind, J. B. 1987. "Pufendorf's Place in the History of Ethics," *Synthese* 72 (1): 123–155.

Schroeder, S. Andrew. 2014. "Imperfect Duties, Group Obligations, and Beneficence," *Journal of Moral Philosophy* 11: 557–584.

Schwartz, Daniel. 2007. *Aquinas on Friendship*. New York: Oxford University Press.

Scott, Emilee Mooney. 2010. "Unfunded Liabilities of Social Security and Medicare," Connecticut General Assembly. 2010-R-0197. www.cga.ct.gov/2010/rpt/2010-R-0197.htm last accessed April 19, 2022.

Seccombe, Wally. 1986. "Patriarchy Stabilized: The Construction of the Male Breadwinner Wage Norm in Nineteenth-Century Britain," *Social History* 11 (1): 53–76.

Serrano, Ray, Richard Saltman, and Ming-Jui Yeha. 2017. "Laws on Filial Support in Four Asian Countries," *Bulletin World Health Organization* (Nov)95 (11): 788–790. https://doi.org/10.2471/BLT.17.200428

Shaver, Robert. 1992. "Hume on the Duties of Humanity," *Journal of the History of Philosophy* 30 (4): 545–556.

Shih, Gerry. 2017. "China Ponders Public Morality after Video of Gruesome Death," *The Mercury News* (June 10). Associated Press.

Sigerist, Henry. 1999. "From Bismarck to Beveridge: Developments and Trends in Social Security Legislation," *Journal of Public Health Policy* 20 (4): 474–496.

Singer, Peter. 1972. "Famine, Affluence, and Morality," *Philosophy & Public Affairs* 1 (3): 229–243.

Singh, Pashaura. 2024 "Sikh Economic Ethics," in *Oxford Handbook of Religion and Economic Ethics,* Albino Barrera and Roy Amore (Eds.). UK: Oxford.

Sinnott-Armstrong, Walter. 2005. "You Ought to be Ashamed of Yourself: (When You Violate an Imperfect Moral Obligation)," *Philosophical Issues* 15: 193–208.

Simon, Herbert. 1957. "A Behavioral Model of Rational Choice," in *Models of Man, Social and Rational: Mathematical Essays on Rational Human Behavior in a Social Setting*. New York: Wiley.

Smith, Adam. 1790. *The Theory of Moral Sentiments*. Sixth edition. EconLibBooks. www.econlib.org/library/Smith/smMS.html?chapter_num=3#book-reader last accessed March 9, 2022.

Socrates. 1941. *The Republic of Plato*. Translated by Francis MacDonald Cornford. London: Oxford. http://faculty.smcm.edu/jwschroeder/Web/ETHR1002/Global_Jutice_Readings_files/3.PlatoRepblic.pdf last accessed April 19, 2022.

Solomon, Dan. 2014. "San Antonio's Plan to Criminalize Giving to Panhandlers Is Drawing Fire," *Texas Monthly* (Sept 9). www.texasmonthly.com/the-daily-post/san-antonios-plan-to-criminalize-giving-to-panhandlers-is-drawing-fire/ last accessed May 3, 2022.

Stevis-Gridneff, Matina. 2021. "E.U. Will Curb Covid Vaccine Exports for 6 Weeks," *New York Times* (Mar 23).

Stohr, Karen. 2011. "Kantian Beneficence and the Problem of Obligatory Aid," *Journal of Moral Philosophy* 8: 45–67.

Swanson, Ana, Zolan Kanno-Youngs, and Maggie Haberman. 2020. "Trump Seeks to Block 3M Mask Exports and Grab Masks from Its Overseas Customers," www.nytimes.com/2020/04/03/us/politics/coronavirus-trump-3m-masks.html last accessed July 5, 2021.

Tillich, Paul. 1954. *Love, Power, and Justice: Ontological Analyses and Ethical Applications*. UK: Oxford.

Tillman, J. Jeffrey. 2008. "Sacrificial Agape and Group Selection in Contemporary American Christianity," *Zygon* 43 (3): 541–556.

Toombs, Lawrence. 1965. "Love and Justice in Deuteronomy: A Third Approach to the Law," *Interpretation* 19: 399–411.

Traub, James. 2021. "Even Sweden Doesn't Want Migrants Anymore," *Foreign Policy* (Nov 27). https://foreignpolicy.com/2021/11/17/even-sweden-doesnt-want-migrants-anymore-syria-iraq-belarus/ last accessed May 30, 2022.

Trilling, Daniel. 2020. "How Rescuing Drowning Migrants became a Crime," *The Guardian* (Sept 22). www.theguardian.com/news/2020/sep/22/how-rescuing-drowning-migrants-became-a-crime-iuventa-salvini-italy last accessed May 3, 2022.

Tsang, Linda and Alexandra Wyatt. 2017. 'Key Historical Court Decisions Shaping EPA's Program Under the Clean Air Act," *Congressional Research Service* (Feb 16). https://sgp.fas.org/crs/misc/R43699.pdf last accessed May 7, 2022.

Tuchman, Barbara. 1962. *The Guns of August*. New York: Macmillan.

UK Home Office. 2022. "Memorandum of Understanding between the Government of the United Kingdom of Great Britain and Northern Ireland and the Government of the Republic of Rwanda for the Provision of an Asylum Partnership Arrangement," (Apr 14) www.gov.uk/government/publications/memorandum-of-understanding-mou-between-the-uk-and-rwanda/memorandum-of-understanding-between-the-government-of-the-united-kingdom-of-great-britain-and-northern-ireland-and-the-government-of-the-republic-of-r last accessed May 20, 2022.

Vatican II. 1965a. *Decree on the Apostolate of the Laity (Apostolicam Actuositatem)*. Rome: The Vatican.

Vatican II. 1965b. *Gaudium et spes*. Rome: The Vatican.

Văduva, Dumitru. 2008. "Justice, the Law of Contracts, and the Economics of Law," *Linguistic and Philosophical Investigations* 7: 357–360.

Vernon, Mark. 2009. "Book Review of Liz Carmichael. 2004. Friendship: Interpreting ChristianLove," *Theology and Sexuality* 15 (1): 128–130.

Vincent de Paul. 1997. *Correspondence Vol 7 (Correspondence, Conferences, Documents)*. New York: New City Press.

Volcovici, Valerie. 2019. "Trump EPA Allows Use of Controversial Pesticide," Reuters (July 18). www.reuters.com/article/us-usa-epa-pesticide/trump-epa-allows-use-of-controversial-pesticide-idUSKCN1UD35D last accessed May 7, 2022.

Wadell, Paul. 2008. "Review of Aquinas on Friendship by Daniel Schwartz," *Modern Theology* 24 (2): 299–301.

Waldow, H. Eberhard von. 1970. "Social Responsibility and Social Structure in Early Israel," *Catholic Biblical Quarterly* 32 (1970): 182–204.

Wallace, R. Jay. 2012. "Duties of Love, Part I of Relationships and Obligations," *Proceedings of the Aristotelian Society Supplementary* 86: 175–198.

Wang, Vivian and Joy Dong. 2021. "In China, Bragging About Your Wealth Can Get You Censored," *New York Times* (Dec 25).

Weinrib, Ernest. 1980. "The Case for a Duty to Rescue," *The Yale Law Journal* 90 (2): 247–293.

Welz, Claudia. 2008. "Love as Gift and Self-sacrifice," *Neue Zeitschrift für systematische Theologie und Religionsphilosophie* 50 (3–4): 238–266.

White House. 2021. "Executive Order on Protecting Public Health and the Environment and Restoring Science to Tackle the Climate Crisis," www.whitehouse.gov/briefing-room/presidential-actions/2021/01/20/executive-order-protecting-public-health-and-environment-and-restoring-science-to-tackle-climate-crisis/ last accessed May 7, 2022.

Whittaker, Matt. 2016. "Polartec: A New Chapter for the Storied Company that Has Survived a Fire, Bankruptcies, and Manufacturing's Flight Overseas," *Outside Business Journal* (Nov 1). www.outsidebusinessjournal.com/brands/polartec-factory-closing/ last accessed April 19, 2022.

Williston, Byron. 2006. "Blaming Agents in Moral Dilemmas," *Ethical Theory Moral Practice* 9: 563–576.

Wingrove, Josh. 2021. "Biden Uses Trump's 'America First' Vaccine Plan to Corner the Market," *Bloomberg News* (Mar 24). https://financialpost.com/news/economy/biden-uses-trumps-america-first-vaccine-plan-to-corner-market last accessed May 4, 2022.

Wiseman, Michael. 1986. "Workfare and Welfare Policy," *Focus* 9 (3): 1–8. University of Wisconsin-Madison, Institute for Research on Poverty.

Wolterstorff, Nicholas. 2011. *Justice in Love*. Grand Rapids, MI: Eerdmans.

World Bank. 2019. *Leveraging Economic Migration for Development: A Briefing to the World Bank Board*. Washington DC: World Bank. www.knomad.org/

publication/leveraging-economic-migration-development-briefing-world-bank-board last accessed May 4, 2022.

Wright, John. 1957. *The Order of the Universe in the Theology of St. Thomas Aquinas*. Analecta Gregoriana 89. Rome: Apud Aedes Universitatis Gregorianae.

Young, Elizabeth Drummond. 2013. "God's Moral Goodness and Supererogation," *International Journal of Philosophical Religion* 73: 83–95.

Zafar, Ali, Jan Muench, and Aloysius Uche Ordu. 2021. "SDRs for COVID-19 Relief: The Good, the Challenging, and the Uncertain," Brookings (Oct 21). www.brookings.edu/blog/africa-in-focus/2021/10/21/sdrs-for-covid-19-relief-the-good-the-challenging-and-the-uncertain/ last accessed May 13, 2022.

Zamagni, Stefano. 2021. "The Quest for an Axiological Reorientation of Economic Science," *Structural Change and Economic Dynamics* 58: 391–401.

Zamagni, Stefano. 2022. "The Family and Policy Making in the Post-Modern Society," Plenary Session on "The Family as a Relational Good: the Challenge of Love." The Pontifical Academy of Social Sciences, Casina Pio IV, April 27–29, 2022.

Index